MODERN HUMANITIES RESEARCH ASSOCIATION
TUDOR AND STUART TRANSLATIONS
VOLUME 2/2

GENERAL EDITORS
ANDREW HADFIELD
NEIL RHODES

PLUTARCH IN ENGLISH, 1528–1603
VOLUME TWO: *LIVES*

MODERN HUMANITIES RESEARCH ASSOCIATION
TUDOR AND STUART TRANSLATIONS

General Editors
Andrew Hadfield (University of Sussex)
Neil Rhodes (University of St Andrews)

Associate Editors
Guyda Armstrong (University of Manchester)
Fred Schurink (University of Manchester)
Louise Wilson (Liverpool Hope University)

Advisory Board
Warren Boutcher (Queen Mary, University of London)
Colin Burrow (All Souls College, Oxford)
A. E. B. Coldiron (Florida State University)
José María Pérez Fernández (University of Granada)
Robert S. Miola (Loyola College, Maryland)
Alessandra Petrina (University of Padua)
Anne Lake Prescott (Barnard College, Columbia University)
Quentin Skinner (Queen Mary, University of London)
Alan Stewart (Columbia University)

texts.mhra.org.uk

Plutarch in English, 1528–1603

Volume Two: *Lives*

Edited by Fred Schurink

Modern Humanities Research Association
Tudor and Stuart Translations 2/2
2020

Published by

The Modern Humanities Research Association
Salisbury House
Station Road
Cambridge CB1 2LA
United Kingdom

© *Modern Humanities Research Association 2020*

Fred Schurink has asserted his right under the Copyright, Designs and Patents Act 1988 to be identified as the author of this work. Parts of this work may be reproduced as permitted under legal provisions for fair dealing (or fair use) for the purposes of research, private study, criticism, or review, or when a relevant collective licensing agreement is in place. All other reproduction requires the written permission of the copyright holder who may be contacted at rights@mhra.org.uk.

First published 2020

ISBN 978-1-90732-242-6 (PB)
ISBN 978-1-78188-755-4 (HB)

CONTENTS

Henry Parker, Lord Morley, *The Story of Paullus Aemilius* (1542–1546/7) 1

Thomas North, *The Life of Demosthenes,*
The Life of Marcus Tullius Cicero, and
The Comparison of Cicero with Demosthenes, from *The Lives* (1579) 45

Thomas North, *The Life of Julius Caesar,* from *The Lives* (1579) 155

Textual Notes 241

Glossary 272

Neologisms 290

Bibliography 294

Index 317

For Boe, Annie, and Sam

GENERAL EDITORS' FOREWORD

The aim of the *MHRA Tudor & Stuart Translations* is to create a representative library of works translated into English during the early modern period for the use of scholars, students and the wider public. The series will include both substantial single works and selections of texts from major authors, with the emphasis being on the works that were most familiar to early modern readers. The texts themselves will be newly edited with substantial introductions, notes, and glossaries, and will be published both in print and online.

The series aims to restore to view a major part of English Renaissance literature which has become relatively inaccessible and to present these texts as literary works in their own right. For that reason it will follow the same principle of modernisation adopted by other scholarly editions of canonical literature from the period. The series will have a similar scope to that of the original *Tudor Translations* published early in the last century, and while the great majority of the works presented will be from the sixteenth century, like the original series it will not be rigidly bound by the end-date of 1603. There will, however, be a very different range of texts with new and substantial scholarly apparatus.

The *MHRA Tudor & Stuart Translations* will extend our understanding of the English Renaissance through its representation of the process of cultural transmission from the classical to the early modern world and the process of cultural exchange within the early modern world.

Andrew Hadfield
Neil Rhodes

ACKNOWLEDGEMENTS

These volumes have been a long time in the making, and I have incurred many debts along the way. I am grateful, first and foremost, to the General Editors of the series, Andrew Hadfield and Neil Rhodes, for originally inviting me to submit a proposal for these volumes and for keeping faith with the project despite its numerous delays. I am also thankful to the anonymous reader for the series for their detailed and astute comments and suggestions, and to the copy-editor, Simon Davies, and the MHRA's Senior Publishing Manager, Gerard Lowe, for their help with getting the volumes into shape. Numerous people generously answered queries, made comments and suggestions, or provided support for my research, in particular Hal Gladfelder, Jill Kraye, David Matthews, John North, Jason Powell, and Cathy Shrank. My wonderful research assistants, Lucy Nicholas, Katherine Goodson Walker, and Juan Acevedo, saved me from countless inaccuracies and offered much helpful advice. Any remaining errors are, of course, my own.

I am grateful for a research grant from the British Academy in collaboration with the Newberry Library in Chicago and the Huntington Library in San Marino, which allowed me to establish the texts of the translations in 2010. I would also like to thank the librarians at both institutions, as well as at the Bodleian Library, the British Library, and especially the John Rylands Library in Manchester. Two periods of research leave, one each from Northumbria University and the University of Manchester, facilitated the writing of the commentary and introductions.

I am grateful to the Institute of Classical Studies for permission to reprint my essay '"Scholemaister and Counsailour vnto Traianus": Plutarch, the Institutio Traiani, and Humanist Political Advice in Renaissance England', in *The Afterlife of Plutarch*, ed. by John North and Peter Mack (London: Institute of Classical Studies, 2018), pp. 85–98, which appears in a lightly revised version as the second section of the General Introduction ('Scholemaister and Counsailour unto Trajanus': Plutarch and Power). The cover image is André Thevet, *Les vrais pourtraits et vies des hommes illustres grecz, latins et payens* (Paris: widow of Jacques Kerver and Guillaume Chaudière, 1584), sig. P6r, copyright of the University of Manchester: John Rylands Library, Richard C. Christie Printed Collection 25 b 8.

My greatest debt, as ever, is to my wife and my two children, who grew up with these volumes and put up with them cheerfully, if not without bafflement. This book is dedicated to them with love.

ABBREVIATIONS AND REFERENCES

Quotations from ancient Greek and Latin texts are from the editions and translations in the Loeb Classical Library unless indicated otherwise, on account of consistency and ease of reference, their relatively literal translations of Greek and Latin, and their wide availability in print and online. Occasionally, I have preferred a more up-to-date translation (noted in parentheses following the quotation) or adapted the phrasing (where the Loeb version is less clear or precise or in order to bring out a specific point about the Greek). The English titles of the works in the *Moralia* are taken from the appendix of D. A. Russell, *Plutarch* (London: Duckworth, 1973). I have used the subdivisions of the chapters of Plutarch's *Lives* in the Loeb editions. All quotations from Shakespeare's works are from *The Oxford Shakespeare: The Complete Works*, ed. by Stanley Wells, Gary Taylor, John Jowett, and William Montgomery, 2nd edn (Oxford: Oxford University Press, 2005). I have normally used sigla in references to early modern books (as they are more reliable than page numbers) but have given the page and folio numbers of the source editions in the notes to the translations for ease of reference.

Allen	*Opus epistolarum Des. Erasmi Roterodami*, ed. by P. S. Allen, 12 vols (Oxford: Clarendon Press, 1906–1958)
ASD	*Opera omnia Desiderii Erasmi Roterodami*, ed. by F. Akkerman and others (Amsterdam: North-Holland, 1969–)
Bergk	*Poetae lyrici graeci*, ed. by Theodor Bergk, 5th edn, 3 vols (Leipzig: Teubner, 1914–1923)
BL	The British Library, London
CWE	*Collected Works of Erasmus*, ed. by Peter G. Bietenholz and others (Toronto: University of Toronto Press, 1974–)
Diehl	*Anthologia lyrica Graeca*, ed. by Ernst Diehl, 3 vols (Leipzig: Teubner, 1949–1952)
D–K	*Die Fragmente der Vorsokratiker*, ed. by Hermann Diels and W. Kranz, 3 vols (Berlin: Weidmannsche Verlagsbuchhandlung, 1960)
EEBO	Early English Books Online <http://eebo.chadwyck.com/>
ESTC	The English Short Title Catalogue <http://estc.bl.uk/>
Huntington	Henry E. Huntington Library, San Marino, California
ISTC	Incunabula Short Title Catalogue <http://www.bl.uk/catalogues/istc/>
Kock	*Comicorum atticorum fragmenta*, ed. by Theodor Kock, 3 vols (Leipzig: Teubner, 1880–1888)
Lewis-Short	*A Latin Dictionary*, ed. by Charlton T. Lewis and Charles Short (Oxford: Clarendon Press, 1879)

LCL	Loeb Classical Library
LSJ	*A Greek-English Lexicon*, ed. by Henry George Liddell and Robert Scott, rev. edn (Oxford: Clarendon Press, 1940)
Nauck	*Tragicorum Graecorum Fragmenta*, ed. by August Nauck, 2nd edn (Leipzig: Teubner, 1889)
ODNB	*Oxford Dictionary of National Biography* <https://www.oxforddnb.com>
OED	*Oxford English Dictionary* <https://www.oed.com>
RCC	Brenda Hosington and others, The Renaissance Cultural Crossroads Catalogue <https://www.dhi.ac.uk/rcc/>
Rylands	John Rylands Library, University of Manchester
STC	*A Short-Title Catalogue of Books Printed in England, Scotland, & Ireland and of English Books Printed Abroad, 1475–1640*, ed. by A. W. Pollard and G. R. Redgrave, 2nd edn, rev. by Katharine F. Pantzer, 3 vols (London: Bibliographical Society, 1976–1991)
Teubner	Bibliotheca scriptorum Graecorum et Romanorum Teubneriana
Tilley	Morris Palmer Tilley, *A Dictionary of the Proverbs in England in the Sixteenth and Seventeenth Centuries* (Ann Arbor: University of Michigan Press, 1950)
USTC	Universal Short Title Catalogue <https://www.ustc.ac.uk>
Wing	*Short-Title Catalogue of Books Printed in England, Scotland, Ireland, Wales, and British America, and of English Books Printed in Other Countries, 1641–1700*, ed. by Donald Wing, rev. edn, 4 vols (New York: Modern Language Association of America, 1982–1998)

HENRY PARKER, LORD MORLEY
THE STORY OF PAULLUS AEMILIUS (1542–1546/7)

Introduction

Aemilius Paullus

Aemilius Paullus is no longer a household name, but his victory over the Macedonian army led by King Perseus at the battle of Pydna in 168 BCE has been considered a turning point in the history of the ancient Mediterranean from an early date. His contemporary Polybius (c. 200–118 BCE) presented it as the apex of Rome's rise to power in the introduction to his history:

> is there anyone on earth who is so narrow-minded or uninquisitive that he could fail to want to know how and thanks to what kind of political system almost the entire known world was conquered and brought under a single empire, the empire of the Romans, in less than fifty-three years [from 220 BCE, the beginning of the Second Punic War, to 168 BCE] — an unprecedented event?[1]

Aemilius's victory finally brought to an end two hundred years of Macedonian rule in Greece — Perseus was the last descendant of the dynasty that came to power in the wake of Alexander the Great's conquests — and established Rome as the dominant power in the Eastern Mediterranean for centuries to come. Given that Polybius was one of Plutarch's main sources, it is perhaps unsurprising that Aemilius's victory at Pydna takes centre stage in the Life. *Aemilius Paullus* is unusual, however, in its concentration on a single event, which took place when Aemilius was around sixty years old. Plutarch briefly touches upon Aemilius's background and personal life, his public offices, and his exploits in Spain and against the Ligurians in the first half dozen paragraphs of the Life, but nearly all of the remaining thirty-odd paragraphs are taken up with the conflict with Macedon and its immediate aftermath.

The focus on a single conflict is accompanied by a sharp, almost caricatured, contrast between the two main protagonists. On the one side, Aemilius is not only a brilliant general but also a moral exemplar. On the other side, Perseus is portrayed as avaricious, base, and ignoble in almost every respect. In contrast to most Lives, Plutarch includes little material that might reflect less well on the character of his protagonist. As Timothy Duff has noted, 'the *Aemilius-Timoleon* pair [...] is one of the most encomiastic; its subjects are explicitly "the best of examples" (*ta kallista tōn paradeigmatōn*)'.[2] In drawing a sharp contrast between the vice and extravagance of the Eastern monarch Perseus and the

---

[1] Polybius, *The Histories*, trans. by Robin Waterfield, ed. by Brian McGing (Oxford: Oxford University Press, 2010), p. 3 (I. 1).

[2] Duff, p. 31. See also Alan Wardman, *Plutarch's 'Lives'* (London: Paul Elek, 1974), p. 132, and Pelling, *Plutarch and History*, p. 248, who draws a distinction between the 'protreptic' moralism of *Aemilius Paullus* and similar Lives and the 'descriptive' moralism of Lives such as *Caesar*.

virtue and moderation of the Roman general Aemilius, Plutarch's narrative also reinforces the ideology of the Roman Empire, which justified its conquest of foreign lands on the basis of the supposed moral and cultural superiority of the Romans, often cast in terms of the opposition between East and West, and familiar to modern readers from Virgil's *Aeneid*. Aemilius's exemplarity is likely to have been a major attraction of the Life for Morley. As we shall see, Morley produced his translations of the Lives both as models for and likenesses of King Henry VIII, to whom he presented them. The final sentence sums up the implications of Morley's translation, unusually adding two laudatory adjectives to describe the protagonist: 'Such *honest* conditions and such a *honourable* life led Aemilius, as it is said'.[3]

If the victory in the battle of Pydna is the chief subject of the Life, its thematic core is the concept of fortune. Fortune (*Tychē*) is introduced as the main concern of the Life in the preface, which is omitted by Morley but reworked in his dedication to Henry VIII (as we shall see), and it is taken up at crucial points in the narrative. Fortune is also integral to the design of the Life, which is structured around the opposition between Aemilius's good fortune in his campaign against the Macedonians and his bad fortune in losing his two young sons at nearly the same time as his triumph in Rome. The theme is highlighted in two set-piece speeches by Aemilius, which are among the most memorable parts of the Life.[4] Fortune was, of course, a major concern of late medieval and early modern English literature and culture, and was identified in particular with the genre of the fall of princes, from Boccaccio's *De casibus virorum illustrium* ('On the Falls of Famous Men') and Lydgate's adaptation *The Fall of Princes* to the Tudor best-seller *A Mirror for Magistrates*.[5] Morley's translation echoes the language of the literature of the fall of princes, for instance in its description of Perseus's defeat: 'Aemilius considering the high and great estate that he [Perseus] was fallen down from, he went to meet him with his friends, and in manner weeping for the compassion he had of his overthrow' (557–59).[6] The Christian moral, that life is fragile and changeable and we should put our faith in God rather than ourselves, is once again reflected in Morley's additions to his source: 'At the last he began to speak in this manner of the *frail miserable*

---

[3] *Aemilius Paullus*, 39. 5 (my italics); Bruni has simply: 'Tales mores vitaque Pauli Aemilii fuisse dicuntur' (Such, we are told, were the character and life of Paullus Aemilius): Plutarch, *Vitae* (Paris: Josse Bade and Jean Petit, 1514), fol. 139r.
[4] *Aemilius Paullus*, 27, 36.
[5] See H. R. Patch, *The Goddess Fortuna in Medieval Literature* (Cambridge, MA: Harvard University Press, 1927); Paul Budra, *'A Mirror for Magistrates' and the De casibus Tradition* (Toronto: University of Toronto Press, 2000).
[6] Boethius refers to this episode in similar terms in *The Consolation of Philosophy*, a major source of the *de casibus* tradition: 'Have you forgotten how Aemilius Paulus, good man that he was, shed tears over the fate of King Perses, whom he had captured?' (II. 2; see Budra, p. 44).

state of mankind ...' (573–74; my italics).⁷

Aemilius is also located in the context of the related tradition of the 'remedies of both kinds of fortune' in medieval and early modern literature, epitomised by Petrarch's extended dialogue *De remediis utriusque fortunae*.⁸ Although Petrarch's work was not translated into English until 1579, it was widely influential in medieval and early modern England.⁹ Petrarch counselled not only a Stoical acceptance of fate and suppression of the passions in the face of adverse fortune but also moderation in response to good fortune. Time and again, Plutarch's narrative highlights that Aemilius expects fortune to turn after his victory and has thereby armed himself against disaster when it eventually strikes. Morley underscores this point in the dedication: 'there [was] none nother Grecian nor Roman that more could moderate himself in both fortunes, that is to say the good and the ill fortune, than he of whom we write' (Prologue, 13–15). It is also echoed in his translation, where he departs from his source to show up the appropriate response to both kinds of fortune in two key instances: 'those stand in best estate that have of neither of the twain, that is to say nother of too much felicity nor of too much adversity' (714–15) and 'nother for good fortune nor for ill fortune was he moved therefore anything at all whereby might be thought that he had a unconstant mind' (726–28).¹⁰ Fortune, both good and bad, becomes the opportunity for Aemilius to prove his virtue.

Translation

Translator

Henry Parker, Lord Morley (1480/81–1556), was an early translator of ancient Greek and Roman literature in Renaissance England and a minor figure at the court of Henry VIII.¹¹ Educated in the household of Lady Margaret Beaufort, Morley was conservative in religion, but he had close ties with Cromwell and

---

⁷ Plutarch, *Vitae* (1514), fol. 137v: 'exorsus deinde sermonem de humanarum rerum conditione'.

⁸ See *Petrarch's Remedies for Fortune Fair and Foul: A Modern English Translation of 'De remediis utriusque fortune', with a Commentary*, ed. by Conrad H. Rawski, 5 vols (Bloomington: Indiana University Press, 1991); Nicholas Mann, *Petrarch* (Oxford: Oxford University Press, 1984), pp. 76–82.

⁹ *Physicke against fortune, aswell prosperous, as adverse*, trans. by Thomas Twyne (1579). See Robert Coogan, 'Petrarch's Latin Prose and the English Renaissance', *Studies in Philology*, 68 (1971), 270–91; Nicholas Mann, 'Dal moralista al poeta: appunti per la fortuna del Petrarca in Inghilterra', *Atti dei convegni lincei 10: convegno internazionale Francesco Petrarca* (Rome: Accademia Nazionale dei Lincei, 1976), pp. 59–69.

¹⁰ Plutarch, *Vitae* (1514), fol. 138v. See nn. ad loc.

¹¹ On Morley's life, see David Starkey, 'An Attendant Lord? Henry Parker, Lord Morley', in *'Triumphs of English'*, ed. by Axton and Carley, pp. 1–25; James P. Carley, 'Parker, Henry, tenth Baron Morley', *ODNB*.

the Boleyns in the 1530s and was a reliable servant to King Henry in a variety of roles. Sometime in the 1520s or early 1530s, he began to present gift manuscripts to Henry VIII (as well as his daughter Mary) for New Year, a practice he would continue until the end of the king's reign (and beyond). Morley's presentations to Henry consisted largely of translations of secular works in Italian and Latin, including Petrarch's *Trionfi* ('Triumphs'), Paolo Giovio's *Commentario de le cose de' Turchi* ('Commentary on the Affairs of the Turks'), and a number of Plutarch's *Lives*, translated from the Latin.[12] At some point before 1535, Morley presented his king with *The Lives of Scipio and Hannibal* (included in Morley's Latin edition of the *Lives* but in fact written by the fifteenth-century Italian humanist Donato Acciaiuoli), followed *c.* 1538 by the pseudo-Plutarchan *Life of Agesilaus*, dedicated to Cromwell but including an extended comparison with Henry VIII in the dedication. Between 1542 and 1546/7 he presented two genuine *Lives* by Plutarch to Henry VIII: *Theseus* and *Aemilius Paullus*.[13] In some instances, Morley's presentations offered a direct response to events at the court of Henry VIII, for example when he used his exposition of a psalm in 1539 to proclaim his anti-Catholicism, or his translation of Boccaccio's *De claris mulieribus* ('On Famous Women') in 1543 to distance himself from his daughter, who had been executed for her role in Katherine Howard's alleged adultery.[14] In many cases, however, the works served to reinforce the relationship between author and dedicatee in a more general sense, in a similar fashion to other kinds of New Year's gifts. Whether as a result of his manuscript presentations or not, Morley managed to survive an especially tumultuous period of English history relatively unharmed, despite his deep personal involvement in the events of the time.

Historical Context

The only firm evidence for the date of Morley's translation of *Aemilius Paullus* comes from the address, which designates Henry VIII king of Ireland, a title he assumed in 1541; the *terminus ad quem* is the king's death in January 1547. As James Carley notes, in the prologue to *Theseus*, which has the same terminal dates, Morley unusually labels Henry 'moste victorius' — twice in fact — and

---

[12] Morley's *Trionfi* is included (in part) in one of the other volumes in this series: *Petrarch's 'Triumphi' in the British Isles*, ed. by Alessandra Petrina (London: Modern Humanities Research Association, forthcoming).

[13] For an overview of Morley's works, see James P. Carley, 'The Writings of Henry Parker, Lord Morley: A Bibliographical Survey', in *'Triumphs of English'*, ed. by Axton and Carley, pp. 27–68; on his versions of Plutarch's *Lives*, see Maule.

[14] See Richard Rex, 'Morley and the Papacy: Rome, Regime, and Religion', in *'Triumphs of English'*, ed. by Axton and Carley, pp. 87–105; James Simpson, 'The Sacrifice of Lady Rochford: Henry Parker, Lord Morley's Translation of *De claris mulieribus*', in *'Triumphs of English'*, ed. by Axton and Carley, pp. 153–69.

also alludes to his 'worthi conquestes', which points to a date after Henry's capture of Boulogne in September 1544, most likely New Year's Day 1545.[15] It is probable that Morley's translation of *Aemilius Paullus*, which includes no reference to Henry's martial feats, was written before his version of *Theseus* and presented to the king for New Year in 1542, 1543, or (less likely) 1544.

In the dedication of his translation of *Aemilius Paullus* to Henry VIII, Morley gives an account of the function of Plutarch's Life: 'Who then he be that doth not know what the mean is in such a case, let him look upon the life of this noble Roman, Paullus Aemilius, and there shall he see, as in a glass or mirror, the perfect sure way how to govern him with reason in all kind of prosperity or adversity' (lines 19–23). The life of Aemilius Paullus, in other words, offers an exemplary model for readers to follow. The image of the mirror derives from Plutarch's programmatic preface to the *Aemilius-Timoleon* pair, in which he presents himself as a model reader who improves his character by studying the outstanding achievements and characteristics of figures from history.[16] By the sixteenth century, however, the image was inextricably linked with the genre of the mirror for princes, which taught rulers how to conduct their lives either through direct instruction or example. It is likely, therefore, that Plutarch's preface was one of the key features of the Life that caught Morley's eye, even though he omitted it from his translation, or, more precisely, replaced it with his own dedicatory preface.[17]

While Morley thus aligns the Life with the literature of advice for princes, he also uses the life to praise his dedicatee, Henry VIII, by comparison with Aemilius: 'ye may well be compared not only to this Paullus but to Trajan, Titus, and Antonius Pius or to any other Grecian or Roman of what state or dignity so ever they have been before this day'. In extolling Henry VIII by comparison with Aemilius and other ancient statesmen and generals, Morley exploits the principles of parallelism and comparison (*synkrisis*) central to Plutarch's *Lives*. To modern readers, however, his praise of Henry may seem in contradiction to the instructive role he claims for the Life. If Henry already possessed Aemilius's virtues, what could he (as its dedicatee and sole reader) learn from the Life? It was, however, a commonplace of Renaissance humanist literature that praise could act as counsel to princes, from Erasmus, who claimed that his panegyric

---

[15] Carley, 'Writings of Morley', p. 43; *Forty-Six Lives: Translated from Boccaccio's 'De claris mulieribus' by Henry Parker, Lord Morley*, ed. by Herbert G. Wright, Early English Text Society, Original Series no. 214 (London: Published for the Early English Text Society by Oxford University Press, 1943), p. 164.

[16] *Aemilius Paullus*, 1. See General Introduction, p. 53.

[17] In the *Aemilius-Timoleon* pair, the Roman life unusually precedes the Greek life, and many editions, including some of the Latin translation that Morley used as his source (and the Loeb), invert the order and include the preface before *Timoleon*. Morley's use of the image of the mirror in his dedication, however, demonstrates that he connected the preface with *Aemilius*, whether it was printed with it in the edition he used or not.

of archduke Philip the Handsome was 'not so much praise as precept', to Bacon, who wrote in his essay 'Of praise': '*Laudando praecipere* [to instruct by praising]; When by telling Men, what they are, they represent to them, what they should be'.[18]

Several other features of Plutarch's biography of Aemilius Paullus might have presented themselves to Morley as relevant to Henry VIII's life and situation. Aemilius, for example, re-establishes proper observation of 'the divine ceremonies' (36) in Rome in his role as augur; he divorces his first wife, and when his friends rebuke him, the narrator blames 'the manifest and great errors of women' (66) and 'the variable changes of manners of women secretly begun' (67–68); Aemilius is a fond parent and takes special care over the education of his children (106–15 and passim). Presented to the king during the years of war of the mid-1540s, whether immediately before, during, or straight after Henry's campaigns in France and the conflict with Scotland, however, the aspect of the life that would have immediately stood out was Aemilius's success in the war against Perseus and the Macedons. It is all the more notable for that reason that in the dedication Morley contrasts the greater military achievements of other ancient generals with Aemilius's superior inner virtue. What matters most (he argues) is not victory or defeat, but the proper moral response to either:

> And surely, most noble prince, there hath been and is divers that can and hath done great conquests, but there be very few that when such good prosperous fortunes happen unto them, but that they either be too much proud thereof or when ill fortune comes to them too much abashed thereof, so that the best part, which is the mean, is quite set apart. (Prologue, 15–19)

Given that Henry was fervently determined to invade France to increase his personal glory, this is a powerful message. Despite its origins as a gift from a courtier to the king and its apparent flattery of the dedicatee, Morley's translation did far more than simply provide entertainment or oil the social relations between patron and client.

Sources

Aemilius Paullus was one of the first Plutarchan Lives to be turned into Latin in quattrocento Italy. The translation was produced by the well-known Florentine humanist Leonardo Bruni, who dedicated it to the Venetian patrician Pietro Miani in 1408/09.[19] By that date, Bruni had already produced two other Plutarchan *Lives* (*Antonius* and *Cato Minor*) and he would go on to translate several more. Bruni was one of the first proponents of the new *ad sententiam* (following the sense) method of translation advocated by Renaissance humanists

---

[18] Bacon, *Essayes*, ed. by Kiernan, p. 160; Rundle, pp. 148–69.
[19] Pade, *Reception*, I, 141–43.

in place of medieval *ad verbum* (word for word) translation. Bruni's translations have been termed *traduzioni oratorie fideli* (faithful rhetorical translations); they attempt to follow the Greek text as literally as possible while preserving the meaning of the original and using correct and eloquent classical Latin. However, Bruni did use some freedom in his translations of Plutarch's *Lives*, and his contemporary Pier Candido Decembrio noted some omissions in the margin of a manuscript of his *Aemilius Paullus*.[20] As it is uncertain which manuscript formed the basis for his translation, it is often difficult to determine whether apparent changes from the Greek are due to Bruni's interventions as a translator or to the state of his source text.[21] However this may be, Bruni's translation of *Aemilius Paullus* was evidently popular and circulated widely in manuscript in the fifteenth century. It was further included in the complete collection of Plutarch's *Lives* in Latin published by Giovanni Antonio Campano in Rome in 1470, which was frequently reprinted over the course of the following century.[22]

Due to his paraphrastic method of translation, it is difficult to establish with certainty which edition Morley used. It is evident that he did not base his translation on the Greek scholar Simon Grynaeus's Latin version, first published by Johannes Bebel in Basel in 1531, with several subsequent reprints, which includes a revised translation of the epigram on the height of Mount Olympus that deviates significantly from Morley's translation; it also includes a comparison between Agesilaus and Pompey, whereas Morley specifically notes that the *Agesilaus* has no *synkrisis*.[23] Equally, there are indications that Morley did not use one of the fifteenth-century editions, including his correct identification of Xenagoras as the son of Eumelus in the same epigram, obscured by a misprint in early editions of 'filii' for 'filius' (genitive for nominative case, agreeing with Eumelus instead of Xenagoras).[24] The editions closest to Morley's text overall are those published by the Parisian scholar and printer Jodocus Badius Ascensius (Josse Bade) from 1514 (used in the commentary to this

[20] James Hankins, 'Translation Practice in the Renaissance: The Case of Leonardo Bruni', in *Méthodologie de la traduction: de l'antiquité à la Renaissance: théorie et praxis*, ed. by C. M. Ternes and M. Mund-Dopchie (Luxembourg: Actes des 3es rencontres scientifiques de Luxembourg, 1994), pp. 154–75, repr. in *Humanism and Platonism in the Italian Renaissance*, 2 vols (Rome: Edizioni di storia e letteratura, 2003–04), I, 177–92; Pade, *Reception*, I, 129, 147.
[21] Pade, *Reception*, I, 142. The manuscript used by Bruni does not correspond closely with any of those cited in Teubner.
[22] Pade, *Reception*, I, 385–90, II, 97.
[23] *Aemilius Paullus*, 15. 6; Plutarch, *Vitae graecorum romanorumque illustrium* (Basel: Johannes Bebel, 1531), sigs u3v, O6r-v; Axton and Carley, p. 227. See Frank Hieronymus, *Griechischer Geist aus Basler Pressen: Katalog der frühen griechischen Drucke aus Basel in Text und Bild*, ed. by Christoph Schneider und Benedikt Vögeli (Universitätsbibliothek Basel, 2003) <http://www.ub.unibas.ch/cmsdata/spezialkataloge/gg/>, GG 102 [accessed 7 March 2017].
[24] E.g. Plutarch, *Vitae illustrium virorum* (Venice: Nicolaus Jenson, 1478), sig. r6v; cf. Plutarch, *Vitae* (1514), fol. 135v.

edition), even if they too have a couple of discrepancies with Morley's version.[25]

Translation Method

Morley acknowledges that his translation is based on Bruni's version in the dedication: 'Which said life I have translated out of the Latin tongue into our maternal tongue rudely but truly, I trust, according to the sense' (lines 23–25). His reliance on Bruni's Latin version is, in fact, everywhere evident in the translation. He follows both the structure and the phrasing of the Latin closely and where Bruni adds, leaves out, or changes something, Morley does likewise. Morley has a tendency to use cognates in his translation ('apt' (21 and passim) for *aptus*, 'duke' (40 and passim) for *dux*, etc.) and he often translates the Latin word for word.[26] Because English is not an inflected language like Latin, however, retaining the order frequently causes anacoluthon (changes in grammatical construction halfway through sentences) and other grammatical defects.

Morley's assessment of his own achievement as a translator, 'rudely but truly, I trust, according to the sense', while evidently a modesty topos, also rings true. Although he generally conveys the overall sense of the Latin, his translation is far from precise. This is partly a result of his limited knowledge of Latin. Frequently, Morley leaves out small details that either help to clarify the meaning and structure of the text or give colour to it. When Aemilius rebukes one of his captains for wanting to take on the well-prepared army of the enemy immediately following a march, Morley renders the crucial phrase 'ex via' (straight after a march) with the generic 'in haste': 'it seemeth not good unto me in haste to set on such a army in good order of battle and ready for to fight' (351–52).[27] Similarly, Morley misses out the evocative comparison of the protagonist in charge of his army with the pilot of a boat who foretells a storm from the turmoil of the water in the following passage: 'Thus Aemilius even now, like a pilot, foreseeing from the present storm and commotion of the military camps the greatness of the coming battle' ('Aemilius igitur veluti gubernator praesenti tempestate ac motu castrorum, magnitudinem futuri certaminis iam inde prospiciens'), translating 'Aemilius then as a governor well perceiving by the moving of the two armies that the battle began' (382–83), presumably because he overlooks the meaning of the Latin 'gubernator' as pilot and selects a cognate ('governor') instead.[28] Morley's insecure grasp of Latin commonly leads him to leave out or summarise passages where he is unsure of the exact meaning

---

[25] See notes on lines 588–90 ('And [...] pleasures') and 680–84 ('And after that sort [...] Thericles').
[26] Plutarch, *Vitae* (1514), fols 133v ('non ineptus'), 134r.
[27] Plutarch, *Vitae* (1514), fol. 136r.
[28] Plutarch, *Vitae* (1514), fol. 136r.

of his source text. On other occasions, however, Morley's omissions are clearly deliberate. He leaves out several substantial sections, for example in paragraphs 14 (detailed debate about the existence of sources of water under mountains), 20 (facts of battle), 30 (particulars of the discontent of Aemilius's soldiers and the faction that gathers around his enemy Galba), and 38 (Aemilius's political reputation in the time of his son Scipio). Many references to the specifics of ancient society — offices and officers, locations in Rome, foreign places and tribes, and so on — are likewise omitted, while others are domesticated, as in the case of horse races ('spectaculo equestrium ludorum') becoming 'plays' (i.e. spectacles, line 506).[29] In general, Morley tends to condense the text so that it conveys basic information, but leaves out details, to the point that his version often resembles paraphrase more closely than exact translation.

A further feature of his source text that Morley's translation makes little attempt to reproduce is eloquence. As we have seen, Bruni's ideal as a translator was to recreate an eloquent Latin version that matched the original Greek. Morley repeatedly declines the opportunity to follow the rhetorical structure of the Latin, even when a straightforward equivalent is available in English. Where Bruni is careful to use a parallel construction, for example, in 'deeming things to be bought with money, not money with things' ('res pecuniis, non rebus pecunias emi existimantes'), Morley simply translates 'that more weighed the great things than the money' (241–42).[30] If a similar construction is not available in English, Morley, unlike his contemporary Elyot for instance, makes few efforts to find an equivalent rhetorical structure, nor does he commonly add the doublets, for example, that are the hallmark of humanist prose.[31] Morley has a tendency to use co-ordination or parataxis where the Latin uses subordination, which goes well with the fast-paced narrative passages of Plutarch's Life, but is less suited to conveying more complex philosophical ideas.

A previous editor of Morley's prose concluded: 'Learning Morley certainly had, but none of the qualities of a great writer, and his relations to contemporary personages and problems are a far more interesting object of study than his translations. Consequently, any importance that he may have is purely historical.'[32] Certainly, Morley's translation in many respects looks back to the medieval period rather than forwards to the ideals of Renaissance humanist translators, which have been influential in shaping our own expectations of what constitutes a good translation. Morley conveys the basic content of his source, but with little consideration either for textual and historical accuracy or for expression, although in contrast to many medieval translators he added little padding to the text. His translation then may not accord with modern

---

[29] Plutarch, *Vitae* (1514), fol. 137r; *OED*, play, *n.*, 16. a.
[30] Plutarch, *Vitae* (1514), fol. 135r.
[31] See Morley's comments in other translations, cited in Morley, *Forty-Six Lives*, ed. by Wright, p. cii.
[32] Morley, *Forty-Six Lives*, ed. by Wright, p. civ.

norms of translation, and it is limited by his knowledge of Latin and skill as a writer of English prose. However, it deserves our attention precisely because it reflects a different theory and practice of translation from the one that became dominant over the course of the sixteenth century in the translation of Plutarch as well as other authors.[33]

Reception

Aemilius Paullus was not as familiar a figure as many other Plutarchan protagonists were in early modern England. It is, moreover, not always possible to determine whether references to his life derive from Plutarch's biography or other classical sources. Livy's *History of Rome* covers the events of his life, and even before Plutarch, Aemilius had become an example of how to respond to adversity, for instance in Cicero, who refers to him in several of his works, and in Valerius Maximus, who includes him under the heading 'Parents who have borne the death of their children with strength of mind'.[34]

There is a rare extended account of the life of Aemilius Paullus towards the end of Sir Walter Ralegh's unfinished *The History of the World* (1614), based on Plutarch and Livy.[35] Far more common are the many brief references to episodes from Aemilius's life in the historical and moral compendia so popular in early modern England. Different episodes from the life could yield different, and sometimes contradictory, meanings. On the one hand, Aemilius was the model of the triumphant general and therefore an example for later rulers and magnates. Piers Gaveston, in Michael Drayton's poem, for instance, pictures himself in the image of the great Roman general:

> As when Paulus Aemilius entred Roome,
> And like great Jove, in starlike triumph came,
> Honored in Purple by the Senats doome,
> Laden with gold, and crowned with his fame.
> Such seems our glory now in all mens eyes,
> Our friendship honored with applaudities.[36]

The triumphs of Aemilius were also invoked to glorify real-life early modern English monarchs. In the wake of the defeat of the Spanish Armada, Elizabeth

---

[33] On changes in the theory and practice of translation during this period, see Massimiliano Morini, *Tudor Translation in Theory and Practice* (Aldershot: Ashgate, 2006), especially pp. 3–34.
[34] Livy, *Ab urbe condita libri*, 44–46; Valerius Maximus, *Factorum ac dictorum memorabilium libri IX*, v. 10. 2; *Plutarchus' Biographie van Aemilius Paulus: Historische Commentaar*, ed. by Christiana Liedmeier (Utrecht: Dekker & Van de Vegt, 1935), p. 266. Polybius's history also covers the war between Rome and Macedon, but the relevant part is lost, although a few scattered references to Aemilius Paullus survive (XVIII. 35, XXXII. 8).
[35] Sir Walter Ralegh, *The history of the world* (1614), sigs 6R5r–6S2v (Bk 5, Ch. 6, Para. 8).
[36] Michael Drayton, *Peirs Gaveston Earle of Cornwall. His life, death, and fortune.* (1594?), sig. H1v.

is described as sailing up the Thames in triumph as Aemilius Paullus has sailed up the Tiber after his victory over Perseus, although the immediate source here is Livy rather than Plutarch.[37] A book titled *The Triumphs of King James the First* likewise enjoins: 'Let us prepare the hauty Trophees of his heroick actions, farre more surpassing in noise, sound, and glorie, then all the pompous Triumphes of Pompey, Aemilius, Scipio, or Vespasian.'[38] James's successor Charles I was compared to the triumphant Aemilius Paullus on his accession in 1625 by the Dutch humanist and polymath Barlaeus (Caspar van Baerle).[39]

On the other hand, Aemilius could signify the transitory nature of fortune, as in Cadwaladr's complaint in Thomas Blenerhasset's addition to *The Mirror for Magistrates*:

> For that which seemeth best, is soonest brought to naught,
> Which plainely doth appeare by that which I have taught.
> The worthiest in the worlde, princes, philosophers,
> Will teach that I have taught, and prove it passing plaine.
> Paulus Aemilius did die but wretchedly.[40]

But episodes from Aemilius's life could teach other lessons too. He is regularly invoked in pleas to suffer death patiently, for instance.[41] For Thomas Elyot, Aemilius's restraint in presenting the spoils of the conquest of Macedon to the common treasury while remaining relatively poor himself made him an example of 'abstinence and Continence'.[42] Like other figures from ancient history, Aemilius Paullus could serve a range of purposes for early modern readers, depending on the episode from his life that was chosen and the context in which it was invoked. What set him apart was that he was consistently portrayed as an exemplary figure.

Further Reading

Aemilius Paullus: Duff; Liedmeier; Simon Swain, 'Plutarch's Aemilius and Timoleon', *Historia: Zeitschrift für Alte Geschichte*, 38 (1989), 314–34.

Sources: Paul Botley, *Latin Translation in the Renaissance: The Theory and*

---

[37] Anthony Miller, *Roman Triumphs and Early Modern English Culture* (Basingstoke: Palgrave, 2001), p. 74.

[38] George Marcelline, *The triumphs of King James the First, of Great Brittaine, France, and Ireland, King; Defender of the Faith* (1610), sig. C3v.

[39] Miller, p. 119.

[40] Thomas Blenerhasset, *The seconde part of the mirrour for magistrates, conteining the falles of the infortunate princes of this lande. From the conquest of Caesar, unto the comming of Duke William the Conquerour* (1578), sig. K3v.

[41] There is an ironic example in Fernando de Rojas, *The Spanish bawd*, trans. by James Mabbe (1631), sig. 2C3v.

[42] Elyot, *Governour*, sigs d3v, d6v–7r. See also Thomas Wilson, *A discourse uppon usurie* (1572), sig. E2v.

Practice of Leonardo Bruni, Giannozzo Manetti and Desiderius Erasmus (Cambridge: Cambridge University Press, 2004); Hankins; Pade, *Reception*.

Translation: Axton and Carley; Morley, *Forty-Six Lives*, ed. by Wright.

Reception: Miller.

Abbreviations and References

M. Morley.

P. Plutarch. Quoted from LCL, 98 (*Plutarch's 'Lives'*, vi).

B. Bruni. Quoted from Plutarch, *Vitae* (Paris: Jodocus Badius and Jean Petit, 1514). Available online at <http://mdz-nbn-resolving.de/urn:nbn:de:bvb:12-bsb10195599-4>.

To the most high, most mighty, and most puissant prince, Henry the Eight, by the grace of God of England, France, and Ireland King, Defender of the Faith and supreme Head of the Church of England and Ireland, your humble subject Henry Parker Knight, Lord Morley, desireth to your highness honour, health, and victory.

The prologue

Amongst all the lives of the noble Romans and Grecians which Plutarch doth write of in his book intituled *Plutarchi Vitae*, most gracious and most victorious sovereign lord, there is none in my simple opinion that more ought to be noted than the life of Paullus Aemilius, which° subdued Perseus and his kingdom of Macedony.¹ And my reason is such, that although that Scipio, Caesar, and Hannibal and Pompey and divers other did more victorious acts than this Paullus did, yet was there none nother° Grecian nor Roman that more could moderate himself in both fortunes, that is to say the good and the ill fortune, than he of whom we write.² And surely, most noble prince, there hath been and is divers that can and hath done great conquests, but there be very few that when such good prosperous fortunes happen unto them, but that they either be too much proud thereof or when ill fortune comes to them too much abashed thereof, so that the best part, which is the mean, is quite set apart. Who then he be that doth not know what the mean is in such a case, let him look upon the life of this noble Roman, Paullus Aemilius, and there shall he see, as in a glass° or mirror, the perfect sure way how to govern him with reason in all kind of prosperity or adversity.³ Which said life I have translated out of the Latin tongue into our maternal tongue rudely but truly, I trust, according to the sense, and do present the same this New Year to your highness, most noble and most christen° king and my most dear sovereign lord, as to a prince honourable amongst all other princes in the world that hath showed in the ruling of your mighty empires such moderation, clemence,° pity, and merciful justice that ye may well be compared not only to this Paullus but to Trajan, Titus, and Antonius Pius or to any other Grecian or Roman of what state or dignity so ever they have been before this day.⁴ God preserve your highness long so to continue

---

¹ *Plutarchi Vitae*] *The Lives of Plutarch*. On M.'s use of the Latin translation of the *Lives*, see Introduction, p. 9.
² Scipio, Caesar, Hannibal, and Pompey are all subjects of Lives included in the Latin translation of Plutarch used by Morley; the pseudo-Plutarchan Scipio and Hannibal pair had been translated by Morley and presented to Henry VIII some time before 1535. On the concept of the two kinds of fortune, see Introduction, p. 4.
³ The vital image of the mirror is from Plutarch's preface to the life, which M. omits. See Introduction, p. 6.
⁴ M. appropriates the structure of the comparison, central to P.'s *Lives*, to praise Henry VIII by comparing him to the great statesmen and generals of antiquity. Titus, Trajan, and

and the fair flower of the world, your dear son and our comfort to come, Prince Edward, in perpetual health and victory. Amen.

Antoninus (rather than Antonius, as M. has) Pius were considered to be beneficent Roman emperors.

The story° of Paullus Aemilius

[2] The family of Paullus Aemilius in the city of Rome divers do affirm that it had continued there a long time.¹ And he that was the first that gave this surname of Aemilius to his family was named Marcus Aemilius for the fair elegant speech that he had, for *haemulia* is to say in the Greek tongue elegant speech, and he was also called the child of Pythagoras, as Numa Pompilius was.² Now of this noble family descended many excellent and honourable persons that gave themselves to all virtues. And among other Lucius Paullus was one, which by misfortune at the Battle of Cannae showed not only his wisdom but also his valiantness. For, after that he could by no means persuade his fellow from giving battle to Hannibal, albeit that against his will he was partner of the same, yet of fleeing from the battle he was no partner as his fellow was, but being author and causer of the battle fled from him, where Paullus, abiding the peril and manfully fighting, was there slain.³ This Paullus had a son and a daughter. The daughter was married to the great Scipio; the son was this Paullus of whom we write, which, coming to full and flourishing age in glory and virtue, showed himself noble among the most noblest of his city, not in following such light fashions as young men did, nor going nothing that way;⁴ for he nother° gave himself to pleading of causes nor to flattering of them that were of great authority, by which many get themselves much favour of the people, although by his high wit he was apt to either of these twain, but seeking more higher things and showing thereby what courage and heart was in him.⁵

[3] Among all the magistrates of the city of Rome he demanded the office of aedile, twelve other asking the same, of which one after the other were consuls by suffrage of the people.⁶ This Aemilius was elect to that office afore them all, and shortly after that promoted to the office named augur, which he so used and after his father's conditions so knew he how to order himself about the

---

¹   M. omits that Aemilius's family were patricians.
²   Marcus] Mamercus.   as Numa Pompilius was] P. (followed by B.) in fact states that some attributed the education of King Numa to Pythagoras.
³   L. Aemilius Paullus was compelled by his fellow commander to fight Hannibal at Cannae in 216 BCE, which resulted in a catastrophic defeat. The subject of 'being author and causer of the battle fled from him' (M.'s attempt to render B.'s ablative absolute construction) is his fellow commander.   manfully] M.'s addition.
⁴   coming [...] virtue] In P. (followed by B.) it is the era that is full of men of glory and virtue rather than Aemilius's age.   light] M.'s addition.
⁵   flattering of them that were of great authority] B. has 'salutando ac prensando homines' (greeting men and soliciting them for an office, fol. 133v). M.'s emphasis on flattery of those 'of great authority' may reflect his own experience at the court of Henry VIII. See Introduction, pp. 4–5.
⁶   In 193 BCE. Aediles supervised various areas of municipal government.   magistrates] B. 'magistratibus' (civil offices, fol. 133v); M. selects the alternative meaning of the word.

divine observances that he brought that name in such honour and reverence that it was taken among the first offices of all the magistrates in Rome,[7] proving by the sentences° of the philosophers that the science° and knowledge of the divine things and the religion° thereof was most worthy to be had in most supreme dignity.[8] Thus whatsoever that he did in that office, he did it with great industry and study, and he, given to that one thing, setting other business apart, lest not to do the least thing that pertained thereunto, and nother in adding nor detracting, towards his fellows so wittily he instructed and taught them that he showed how it was not to be suffered in a city the divine ceremonies to be negligently ministered.[9] In like wise in observing the feats of war, he showed by his wit such observances to be had therein, not in flattering of the soldiers as divers other did, but as he could well use himself about the divine ceremonies, so could he show himself a prudent duke° and leader of a army in the camp, first to overcome and next to rule with wisdom such as were men of war under him.[10]

[4] Now in those days the Romans having great war with the great Antiochus, and the elect men of war intending° thereunto, it so chanced that in Hesperia, in a province named Iberia, there rose a great commotion against the Romans.[11] To appease those rebels was Aemilius sent, not with six praetors, but with twelve of those that commonly bore afore the consuls certain weapons to do justice to such as did offend the laws, that it might appear in him to have the dignity of a consul.[12] And twice with banners displayed he overcame them and slew of them about a 30,000,[13] so that it might well appear that by his witty° fashions he

---

[7] Probably in 192 BCE. his father's conditions] i.e. his ancestors' customs (B. 'patriis moribus', fol. 134r).

[8] proving [...] dignity] P. (closely followed by B.) 'testified in favour of those philosophers who define religion as the science of the worship of the gods'.

[9] M. omits 'for no man begins at once with a great deed of lawlessness to disturb the civil polity, but those who remit their strictness in small matters break down also the guard that has been set over greater matters'.

[10] In like wise in observing the feats of war] The specific point of comparison with his religious practice is that he preserved the ancient customs in military matters as well. not in flattering of the soldiers as divers other did] P. adds that he did not seek a second military appointment by doing so. first to overcome and next to rule with wisdom such as were men of war under him] B. (following P. but using different phrasing): 'he considered it a secondary responsibility to conquer enemies, but a primary one to guide the citizens' ('ut secundarum partium existimaret, hostes vincere: primarum vero, cives dirigere', fol. 134r).

[11] Hesperia] The west.

[12] In 191 BCE. Paullus was a praetor, but he was given proconsular authority. As a consequence, he was accompanied by twelve lictors, attendants carrying axes to signify authority (B. metonymically refers to them as 'securibus', executioner's axes, fol. 134r), as consuls were, instead of the six lictors that usually accompanied praetors.

[13] with banners displayed] in pitched battle: a literal translation of B. 'signis collatis' (fol. 134r).

obtained the victory by spying the place and the passage of the fords where most surely° he and his army might pass, and by that policy took about fifty towns.¹⁴ And so setting the country in peaceable obeisance, he reverted home again, not the richer of a farthing for all that he had gotten; for among other virtues that was in him, he was not covetous to hoard up money, but liberal and sumptuous, in so much that uneath° his patrimony sufficed him to weigh his charge.¹⁵

[5] His wife was named Papiria, daughter to Maso, a man of consular dignity, which after many a day that he was married to her he forsook her, albeit that he had had of her many fair children, for this woman had brought forth most noble and victorious Scipio.¹⁶ But the cause of the divorce, what it was, it is not very well known, but that there was some evident reason why he forsook her. But this is very plain, that when some of his familiar friends and acquaintance reproved him for so doing, in saying 'Is she not fair?', 'Is not your wife fruitful?', he answered in putting forth his foot: 'Is not this', said he, 'a fair shoe and a new, but yet none of you know where it pincheth or grieveth me.'¹⁷ But thus it chanceth oftentimes that the manifest and great errors of women hath been the cause of divorcing from their husbands, and sometime° also the variable changes of manners of women secretly begun hath in like wise been the cause of such divorce.¹⁸ But thus it was after he was departed from Papiria, he married another wife, of whom he begat two children, which he kept with him at home in his house. And the tother° twain, that he had by his first wife, he joined them with the most noblest families of the city: the elder to Fabius Maximus, five times consul; and the youngest, by adoption he joined to Scipio, surnamed African. His daughter, to the son of Marcus Cato; the tother he married to Aelius Tubero. This Tubero was a passing good man and of great authority in the commonwealth, but he and his family had so small a patrimony that ten of

---

¹⁴ and by that policy] In fact, this tactic applied to his victories in pitched battle.　fifty] P. and B. 250.

¹⁵ weigh his charge] 'To measure (a sum of money) by weight, in order to pay it to (a person)' (*OED*, weigh, *v.*¹, 8. b). P. and B. specifically relate this comment to the repayment of his wife's dowry on his death.

¹⁶ P. further mentions Fabius Maximus, but B.'s 'gloriosissimum Scipionem et maximum' (fol. 134r) makes the uncapitalised 'maximum' look like an adjective qualifying 'Scipionem' instead of a further name.

¹⁷ P. ascribes this quotation to an unidentified Roman, but B. gives it to Aemilius. The same anecdote is told in P.'s 'Advice on Marriage', 22 (141A).

¹⁸ Modern editions tend to follow Ziegler in adding 'not' to 'the manifest and great errors of women hath been the cause of divorcing from their husbands', i.e. it is often *not* great flaws that cause married couples to break up. Instead, P. and B. state, frequent small disagreements deriving from differences in character sometimes result in the estrangement of married couples. M.'s mistranslation of B.'s phrase 'ex quadam diversitate morum' (from the incompatibility of manners, fol. 134r) as 'the variable changes of manners of women' puts greater emphasis on the responsibility of women for divorce.

them dwelt together in one little house, with their wives and their children.[19] In that little house, the daughter of Paullus Aemilius, twice consul and twice triumphing, was brought up and nourished, nor she was nothing ashamed of her poor husband, but marvelling how it might be that so virtuous a man as he was should be poor.[20] But now in our days, the brothers and kinsmen of that family cannot be contented unless that with great walls and rivers the one separate himself from the other, and to this cease not to strive and to chide one family with another. This story giveth monition what a man may within himself consider of this so diverse a change.

[6] But to revert to the story, Paullus, elect to be consul, went to give battle to the Genoways,° a nation, because they were nigh neighbours to the Romans, very warlike men.[21] They dwelt in the very extreme confines° of Italy, of that part whereas° the high mountains of the Alps be, as much as it is compassed with the Sea of Tyrrhenum extending towards Libya, mixed with the sea borders of the Gauls and of the Iberians, and in that time they robbed with their pirate ships all those parts to Hercules' Pillars.[22] Against these people then went Aemilius, being made consul, with 8000 men, and with so few a number gave the onset against 30,000 and put them to flight into their city, and yet notwithstanding that they were closed within their walls, he gave them good hope of pardon, for the Romans would in nowise utterly destroy them, but rather use them as a hope against the rebelling Gauls that continually infested and troubled the confines of Italy.[23] The Genoways then putting their confidence and trust in Aemilius gave to him their ships and their towns, and he, possessing them, oppressed them no more but that only he beat down their walls of their towns and, that done, restored them to rule as they would, but their ships he took all into his use, and of so great a navy as they had he left them no more but three galleys,[24] and the men which the Genoways had taken prisoners, as well citizens[25] as other, he set at liberty and freedom. This did Paullus Aemilius in

---

[19] ten] P. and B. 'sixteen'.
[20] marvelling [...] poor] P. 'admired the virtue that kept him poor'. M. appears to have been confused by B.'s use of the verb *admiror* (fol. 134r), which can mean wonder as well as admire.
[21] In 182 BCE.
[22] the Sea of Tyrrhenum] Mare Tyrrhenum, or the Tyrrhenian Sea.   Hercules' Pillars] Two promontories on either side of the Strait of Gibraltar.
[23] 30,000] Modern editions have 40,000, but M. follows B.   a hope against the rebelling Gauls] M. apparently misread 'sepem' (i.e. 'saepem' (fence), fol. 134r) as 'spem' (hope).
[24] left them no more but three galleys] P. 'left them no boat that carried more than three oars'. M. appears to have been confused by B.'s unusual Greek-derived 'triscalmum' (with three oar pegs, fol. 134r).
[25] citizens] i.e. Romans.

105 his first election of consul worthy to be remembered.²⁶

And after that, when he had often required° and asked to be chosen consul and could not obtain the favour of the senate,²⁷ therein esteeming himself in manner despised and abjected,° he determined to live in quiet, giving himself only to the divine knowledges and to bring up in learning his children. And he taught them the Roman science, wherein he was very wise, and the Greeks' arts also, and he not only had about his children grammarians, sophisters,° and rhetoricians, but also painters and carvers° and riders of horses and hunters and such other,²⁸ and when no nother cause was occurrent, he himself would be among them in this exercise.²⁹ Thus with a great love was he affectionate towards his children.

[7] In those days, the people of Rome had wars with Perseus, the king of Macedony, and the dukes that were sent against him were put to great shame, forasmuch as by their unprudent governance foolishly and scornfully they were repulsed of Perseus, so that it seemed rather that they suffered invasion than for to invade. And yet it was not long after that or° the Romans had expulsed Antiochus beyond the mount Taurus and constrained him to render up all Syria and to pay to tribute 15,000 talents, and in Thessaly they had put to flight King Philip and delivered the Grecians from their servitude of the Macedons, and had to° this overcome Hannibal, whom they esteemed much more than to vanquish any other king.³⁰ Whereof the Romans were half ashamed that he should match them.³¹ But they remembered not that, after they had put to flight Philip, that Macedony began to wax more puissant than ever it was, as in declaring somewhat of their beginning ye shall more plainly understand.³²

[8] Antigonus, that among all the successors of the great Alexander was esteemed most mighty and was also next akin unto Alexander — this said

---

²⁶ election of consul] period in office as consul (meaning not recorded in *OED*).
²⁷ the favour of the senate] B. 'suffragia civium' (the votes of the citizens, fol. 134r).
²⁸ P.'s point is that these are all Greek. Sophisters are 'teachers of wisedome and eloquence' (*OED*, sophist, *n*., 1, citing Nicholas Udall).
²⁹ when no nother cause was occurrent] when no other business presented itself.
³⁰ P. refers to the Roman defeats of Antiochus the Great at Thermopylae in 191 BCE (as a result of which he was confined to Syria instead of having to surrender it, as M. translates), of Philip V of Macedon at Cynoscephalae in 197 BCE, and of the Carthaginian Hannibal at Zama in 204 BCE.
³¹ M. considerably shortens this sentence and obscures its meaning: 'this people thought it unendurable that they should be compelled to contend with Perseus as though he were an even match for Rome, when for a long time already he had carried on his war against them with the poor remains of his father's routed army'.
³² remembered not] Rather, they were unaware (B. 'Ignorabant', fol. 134v).

Antigonus usurped the crown of Macedony and had a son named Demetrius, that had to his son one called Antigonus, surnamed Gonatas, and he begat Demetrius, which reigned but a little while, and left behind him Philip but very young of age.³³ The Macedons then, fearing lest that being without a king discord might fall among them and their commonweal thereby be subverted, chose to their king Antigonus, the nephew to Antigonus that was dead, and gave him also to that the rule of the young child Philip as a tutor and governor, and seeing his humanity and nobleness, as said is, took him as king.³⁴ And this Antigonus was named Doson, which is to mean as he that promised much and pays very little. And after him reigned Philip, which from his tender youth marvellously flourished and in such wise that the Macedons hoped by him to obtain their ancient high glory.³⁵ But this Philip, overcome in battle at a place called Scotussa of Titus Quintus Flaminus, withdrew his pride and, suffering the Romans in manner to do what they would, was well contented to live off little.³⁶ But afterward, seeing that those that ruled the Romans at their pleasure to be men rather given to delices° than men of courage and heart, repented him to do as he had done and set his mind secretly and craftily to make war.³⁷ And all those towns and cities which stood nigh the sea coasts that were out of order and reparation, he suffered them still to fall to ruin, to the intent to avoid all suspicion and to make his enemies the more to contemn him.³⁸ But the higher parts of Macedony, he not only restored as well towns as castles, but farther stuffed them privily° with men of war, to the number of 30,000,³⁹ and within every town put an incredible quantity of wheat, and gathered as much money as might pay 10,000 knights for ten years their wages. But this notwithstanding, ere he could bring that to pass which he minded to do, for the sorrow that he had

---

³³   and was also next akin unto Alexander, this said Antigonus usurped the crown of Macedony] P. and B. 'and acquired for himself and his line the title of king'.
³⁴   and their commonweal thereby be subverted] M.'s addition.   chose [...] king] P. 'called in Antigonus, a cousin of the dead king, and married him to Philip's mother, calling him first regent [B. 'tutorem', fol. 134v] and general, and then, finding his rule moderate and conducive to the general good, giving him the title of King'.
³⁵   M. omits 'and that he [...] would check the power of Rome, which already extended over all the world'.
³⁶   The Battle of Cynoscephalae in 197 BCE.   Titus Quintus Flaminus] Titus Quinctius Flamininus.
³⁷   rather given to delices than men of courage and heart] This description applies to Philip rather than to the rulers of Rome in P.: 'thinking that to reign by favour of the Romans was more the part of a captive satisfied with meat and drink than of a man possessed of courage and spirit'.
³⁸   nigh the sea coasts] M. omits 'and on roads'.
³⁹   M. (in contrast to B., who closely tracks P.) significantly condenses this passage: 'while in the interior he was collecting a large force; he also filled the fortresses, strongholds, and cities of the interior with an abundance of arms, money, and men fit for service, in this way preparing himself for the war, and yet keeping it hidden away, as it were, and concealed. Thus, he had arms to equip thirty thousand men laid up in reserve ...'.

for killing of Demetrius his son, moved to that deed by the unjust slandering of his brother, he miserably ended his life.⁴⁰ But Perseus, that succeeded him, he no sooner obtained the kingdom but forthwith he showed what malice he bore in mind against the Romans, albeit he was nothing meet to do so great a feat for the faintness of his heart and for the manifold vices that were in him, specially the exceeding covetousness that was rooted in him, and in such manner that it is plainly believed that he was not the legitimate son of Philip but a bastard, and for that cause conspired the death of Demetrius, lest the realm knowing him to have been not legitime should deprive him from the crown.⁴¹

[9] And albeit that he was nothing honourable nor noble, yet by the occasion of the great riches he had, he a long time resisted the Romans, and their dukes and consuls he often vanquished as well by land as by sea. For Publius Lucinius, the which first entered into Macedony, he overcame him in a skirmish and slew 2000 and 500 of the Romans and took 600 alive.⁴² And at a place called Oreum suddenly, ere the Romans were aware, he took of theirs twenty great ships and a great number of small galleys.⁴³ And Hostilius, that thought to invade him by the country of Thessalia, provoking Perseus to battle, he vanquished him also.⁴⁴ And in the same season, as though he had little regarded the power of the Romans, he went against the Dardans and slew 10,000 of them and made rich his whole army with the great exceeding rich prey° that he got.⁴⁵ And he stirred to take his part the nation of the Galatians, dwelling about Istria;⁴⁶ in those days they were named Bastarnae, a people much valiant and specially good horsemen. And he assayed to join with him in amity the Illyrians by the friendship of Genthius their king. And the fame° went that he had hired for

---

⁴⁰ In 179 BCE.

⁴¹ he was not the legitime son of Philip but a bastard] B. (and consequently M.) omits the alleged circumstances of Perseus's birth reported by P.: 'Philip's wife took him at his birth from his mother, a certain sempstress, an Argive woman named Gnathaenion, and passed him off as her own.'

⁴² In 171 BCE.   Lucinius] Licinius.

⁴³ Oreum] Oreus (M. retains the Latin accusative).   and a great number of small galleys] Modern editions read 'and sank the rest together with the grain that filled them; he also made himself master of four quinqueremes'. There is a lacuna in the text here, and B. (followed by M.) follows a different tradition from modern editions (see Teubner).

⁴⁴ provoking [...] also] In fact, Perseus frightened Hostilius by offering him battle (B. 'ad pugnam provocando conterruit', fol. 134v). In 170 BCE.

⁴⁵ Dardans] Dardanians, a people who lived in Illyria in the western part of the Balkan peninsula.

⁴⁶ And he stirred to take his part the nation of the Galatians] And he stirred up the country of the Galatians to take his part. P. writes of the Gauls (Γαλάται) who dwell along the Danube (Ἴστρος), but M. follows B., who translates 'Galatas circa Histrum incolentes' (fol. 134v). The Galatians lived in modern-day Turkey, while Istria or Histria is a peninsula on the far North East of the Adriatic (spanning parts of modern Italy, Slovenia, and Croatia). The same geographical confusion occurs two sentences down.

money the barbarous nations thereabout to have passed by the low places of Galatia to the Sea Adriaticum and by that ways to go into Italy.

[10] And these things declared to the Romans made them to set apart the request of them that sued for dignities and to seek out a man meet and apt to withstand so fearful a power. And thus was Paullus Aemilius, at that time in great age, at the least sixty years, but healthful and strong, having about him as well children as friends, a great number which exhorted him to follow the will of the Romans that would elect him to be consul. But at the beginning he would in nowise consent thereunto, but rather blaming their covetousness and making himself as it were unsufficient for such a great matter, he refused to be consul.[47] But at the last, by the great continual multitude of the people that day by day resorted unto his house, he was provoked to descend into the marketplace. And it seemed at the first unto the Romans, when they saw him among them, that the matter should well succeed to them and that by him they should obtain the victory.[48] Thus, not without a great hope and will of the Romans, he was elected consul, nor they tarried not to cast lots to what province he should be lotted unto but forthwith the province of Macedony was committed unto him to make war against them.[49] And it is told that when he went with a great multitude of people and in entering of his house found his youngest daughter, a little girl, weeping, he took her in his arms and asked her the cause why she wept, and that she should answer and say 'because my Perseus is dead'.[50] The child had a little kitling° that was so named, and this said Paullus took it for a good token and sign and said the gods turn it to good. Thus the orator Cicero writes in his books of divination.[51]

[11] And forasmuch as the guise° was then that he which was elect to be consul should give thanks unto the people, Aemilius calling to him the multitude said that he took that office specially to give thanks to himself and next to the people

---

[47] but [...] matter] B. (following P. but expressing the content slightly differently): 'censuring their eagerness and desire as if it was not convenient for him to bear the office of consul' ('eorum studium et cupiditatem arguens: quasi sibi non expediret consulatum gerere', fol. 134v).

[48] that the matter should well succeed to them and that by him they should obtain the victory] B. (following P. but again using different phrasing): 'that by putting himself forward as a candidate he did not so much strive to obtain the consulate as promise victory to his fellow citizens again' ('nec in eius petitione tam affectare consulatum, quam civibus suis victoriam repromittere', fol. 135r).

[49] In 168 BCE.

[50] youngest] Apparently M.'s translation of 'Tertiam' (fol. 135r), which can mean 'third' but in fact refers to her name, Tertia.

[51] Cicero, *De Divinatione*, I. 103.

of Rome;[52] that at their petitions he took such a charge upon him, saying that if they thought any other more expedient for that office than he, that with a glad mind he would be dismissed of it; and if that they would needs put their trust in him, that they should say nother this nor that, but with silence make ready and minister such things as should be meet for the wars.[53] With these and such other words, he got himself in great estimation among the Romans and gave them great comfort to do well, as it followeth after indeed. And thus the Romans, rejoicing that they had set apart flatterers and chosen a wise witty captain,[54] [12] preparing all things necessary for his voyage, Paullus sailed forward with so prosperous and happy and ready sailing that it is marvel to tell. But that may very well be imputed to his good fortune, but that which he did in battle may well be imputed to his boldness, his readiness, and wit and wise counsel that he gave, and finally the constant reason of his mind, with the true love and service of his friends.[55] And I cannot see which ways this may be said, that it was by the favour of fortune, for where wise wit and good forecast and boldness hath place, fortune is little to be praised,[56] unless a man might say that the exceeding misorder and covetousness of Perseus helped Aemilius well in his affairs, that° where the realm of Macedony was in great prosperity and force, by his avarice he made it feeble and weak, and finally thereby subverted it.[57]

For there came unto him of the country of Basternis 10,000 horsemen and as many footmen, accustomed to nothing else but to live by the wars, and were used nother to plough nor to sow, nor to sail, nor to feed and bring up cattle, but to fight and overcome their enemies.[58] Which said men, after they were joined with his army nigh to a place called Maedica, men of great stature and

[52] specially [...] Rome] B. (following P. but changing the phrasing) 'primum quidem consulatum, gratia sui ipsius: secundum vero, gratia populi Romani' (the first consulship for his own sake, the second for the sake of the Roman people, fol. 135r). M. appears to have taken 'gratia' to mean 'thanks to' rather than 'for the sake of'. At the end of the sentence, M. (perhaps confused by the further use of 'gratias') omits B. (following P.) 'Itaque se nullas eis habere gratias: quinimmo ...' (And that therefore he was under no obligation to them. Nay rather ...', fol. 135r).
[53] that they should say [...] wars] M. omits the following explanation in P. and B. 'since, if they sought to command their commander, their campaigns would be still more ridiculous than they were already'.
[54] M. omits B. (using slightly different phrasing from P.) 'Ita in vincendo et aliis dominando populus Romanus ipse virtutis et honestatis servus erat' (Thus in conquering and ruling others was the Roman people itself the servant of virtue and honesty, fol. 135r).
[55] the constant reason of his mind] M.'s addition.
[56] P. 'I cannot assign his remarkable and brilliant success to his celebrated good fortune, as I can in the case of other generals.' M. follows B., who appears to rely on a different textual tradition here.
[57] The recurring doublets in this sentence ('misorder and covetousness', 'prosperity and force', 'feeble and weak') are all additions by M.
[58] Basternis] The Basternae. M. uses the inflected form of the Latin.

of a fierce regard, they gave so great comfort to the army of Perseus that they thought the Romans durst never abide them but at the first terrible aspect of them to flee away. This great fellowship and help so full of hope, this Perseus by his imprudence and covetousness cast it clean aside. When for every captain of them they demanded a 1000 pieces of gold in reward over and besides their common stipends, by great oversight he refused to pay them, as though he warred not against the Romans, but as that he meant to spare his treasure for the Romans, and as though he should make his accounts to the Romans of the money he spent against them in the wars.[59] And he did not that as Lydius nor yet as Phoenix,[60] but as he, although he boasted to be of consanguinity and affinity to Alexander and to King Philip, that more weighed the great things than the money, and so, when he all madly and contrariways weighed the money afore the things, he thereby lost all.[61] For it is a ancient proverb, not King Philip, but King Philip's gold overcame Greece. And Alexander going against the Indians, when he saw his host rich with the spoils of the Persians, first he caused in the sight of his army his own golden chariots to be burnt, and after commanded other to do the same, that so light and jolly and without cumbrance they might invade their enemies. But Perseus, more loving his gold than himself and his children and his kingdom, would not for his own wealth spend a small portion of money, but rather as captive with much abundance of gold and treasure be led therewith into extreme misery.

[13] And with these other afore rehearsed, he refused the aid of the Galatians and of Genthius, king of the Illyrians, who hoped to have had for his stipend of Perseus 300 talents, which he caused to be numbered afore his ambassadors, and after thinking that he needed no foreign soldiers, he not only paid not the money, but by fraud took the king and his children and expulsed him contrary to his promise as well from his money as from his realm.[62] Against such a

---

[59] B. (followed by M.) omits two sentences here, which have various lacunae in the extant manuscripts, but are not left out altogether from any of the manuscripts recorded in Teubner: 'and yet he had his foes to give him lessons, for, apart from their other preparations, they had a hundred thousand men assembled and ready for their needs. But he, though contending against so large a force, and in a war where such large reserves were maintained, measured out his gold and sealed it up in bags, as afraid to touch it as if it had belonged to others.'

[60] i.e. he did that neither as a Lydian nor as a Phoenician (B. 'hoc fecit non Lydus quidam, nec Phoenix', fol. 135r, following P. but with different phrasing). M. has taken the nationalities as proper names.

[61] contrariways] a variant of *contrariwise*, evidently in the meaning 'perversely, contrarily' (*OED* contrariwise, *adv.*, 5), although *OED* records no example before 1629.

[62] Genthius [...] realm] M. significantly condenses and misrepresents P.'s account of Genthius (followed by B. with minor variations): 'Apart from the fact that he dismissed the Gauls [B. and M. 'Galatians'] after misleading them, there was also his treatment of Genthius the Illyrian, whose support in the war he won with an offer of three hundred

dishonest prince Aemilius set forward. Albeit that he despised his dishonest manners, yet he marvelled much at his great puissance, for he had about 4000 spears° furnished° and of other men of war about the number of forty thousand. With this number, nigh the borders of Olympus Perseus tarried° the places by the very nature thereof strong and without any right way, and where was any way likely whereby the Romans might pass, he had so fortified it that it seemed in manner impossible his enemies should pass that way, supposing thereby that Aemilius at length for lack of victual to be brought to extreme necessity.[63] But Aemilius was such a wise captain that he left nothing untempted° to invade him. And his captains and soldiers, little esteeming Perseus, doubted° nothing his puissance, but rather for penury of water they should be compelled to go away.[64] And when his soldiers would counsel together of that matter, Aemilius would charge them not to meddle with such fancies but rather look to arm and trim° themselves ready to the battle, that when time came, they might declare what the Romans could do against them with the sword. And Aemilius in the nights suffered them to rest unarmed, that they might the better refresh their bodies and be more strong to wake when they should wake.[65]

[14] And now, forasmuch as that the army began to lack water, for it was very scant about the place where his army lay, Aemilius perceiving that all about the hill there were great trees and bushes, which covered a great part thereof, the

talents — money which he showed all counted out to Genthius' agents, and even allowed them to store in their own sealed caskets. Genthius, secure in the conviction that his requirements had been met, then committed a sacrilegious and terrible deed: he seized the members of a delegation which had come to him from Rome and threw them into prison. At this point Perseus thought that the money was no longer needed to make Genthius an enemy of Rome, since with this awful crime Genthius had already given absolute guarantees of his hostility and committed himself to the war, so he robbed the poor man of his three hundred talents, and then a little later sat by and watched as Lucius Anicius, the Roman commander who had been sent at the head of an army to deal with Genthius, flung Genthius out of his kingdom, along with his children and his wife, like birds ousted from their nest' (Plutarch, *Roman Lives*, trans. by Waterfield).

[63] nigh the borders of Olympus] B. (following P.) 'by the sea-shore at the foot of Mount Olympus' ('iuxta litus sub ipso Olympo monte', fol. 135r).

[64] M.'s translation here is perplexing. The first part of the sentence follows B. 'Et milites quidem (nam hostem non metuebat)' (But the soldiers (for they did not fear the enemy), fol. 135r), which renders P.'s somewhat eliptical reference to the soldiers' 'former freedom from fear' (ὑπ' ἀδείας δὲ τῆς πρόσθεν), but the second half appears to be M.'s invention, for his next sentence translates what follows in B. (again not quite the same as P.): 'et qui se consiliis admiscentes rem perturbabant increpuit: eisque edixit, ne se supervacuis onerarent curis' (and rebuked [the soldiers] who, meddling with counsels, threw matters into disarray and ordained them not to burden themselves with needless trouble, fol. 135r).

[65] P. and B. 'Furthermore, he ordered the night watchmen to keep watch without their spears, with the idea that they would be more on the alert and would struggle more successfully against sleep, if they were unable to defend themselves against their enemies when they approached.'

hill being of a great height, and seeing the leaves fair and green, he conjectured that under the sides thereof that there should be water. He caused to be digged there certain pits, and suddenly, even as he supposed, sprang fair water which refreshed him and his whole army. And yet there be many that denies any springs to be there, but that by the moisture that descended from the hill, that thereby the water hath his course, and the more that it is digged, the more the water discendeth to it, even as the order of breasts of beasts, the more the breasts be pressed, the more they flow and give milk.[66] But of this we have enough spoken.

[15] Aemilius certain days lay in quiet with his army, and it is told that twain so great armies being so nigh joined together, that there was never a more quietness than betwixt Perseus' army and his. But in conclusion, when all the ways possible was sought how best to invade Perseus, there was but one only way to go against him, that was by Pythium and a place called Peram,[67] left by Perseus without guard or keeping, wherein there was more hope because it was unkept° than possible to go onto it by the hard and difficult way of it, for which cause Aemilius called to him his council what was to be done in it. The first of them all was Scipio Nasica, which took the matter in hand that by that way he would invade Perseus' camp. The second was the eldest of Aemilius' sons, being then very young of age, which offered to go with Nasica.[68] Wherefore Aemilius, praising their much great valiantness, gave to them certain soldiers, and so dismissed them, not with as many as Polybius doth write they had but as many as Nasica in a certain pistle° that he wrote to a certain king, that he had in the extreme of his company about three thousand of the Latins and about five thousand of the left wing of him, and about two hundred and thirty horsemen of them of Crete, mingled with the other of Thracia.[69] With this company, Nasica took his way towards the borders of the sea-side and by a place called Heracleum pitched his camp, as though by sea he should with his ships bring his men about to invade Perseus. And when his camp had supped and that the dark night was, he then opened to his captains his intention, and by contrary way far from the sea he returned, labouring all the night with his army, and somewhat afore day pitched his camp nigh to the place called Pithium, which

---

[66] M. very significantly reduces P.'s long and technical account of the question of where the water derived from (leaving out about a page in the Loeb translation) and muddles his account of liquefaction and condensation (which prompt P.'s comparison with women's breasts, which 'are not, like vessels, full of ready milk which flows out').
[67] Peram] Petra, near Mount Olympus.
[68] the eldest of Aemilius' sons] Named as Fabius Maximus in P. and B.
[69] two hundred and thirty horsemen] The most authoritative manuscripts of P. have 120, plus 200 of the mixed Thracian and Cretan contingent; B. has 220.

is a place higher in height than the hill of Olympus is by ten furlongs.⁷⁰ And that is marked with a certain epigram in this wise: 'The part of Olympus where Apollo's temple is in height truly measured ten furlongs. Xenagoras the son of Emilii Celeuti made this to be measured.⁷¹ Farewell, Apollo, and we pray thee to give us good.' This was the epigram. But the geometricians contrary to this say that neither the height of the hill to the depth of the sea of neither part passeth not ten furlongs. But Xenagoras not unwittily° but with sure certain reason seemeth to have measured so the mountain.

[16] But to revert to the matter, Nasica lay there that night, Perseus nothing mistrusting° him so to do, forasmuch as that afore his eyes he might see Aemilius quietly in his camp. But one of Crete had run away from the Romans and declared to Perseus how the case stood. At which news Perseus being somewhat troubled did not remove° but sent 10,000 of soldiers which he had hired and 2000 Macedons, Milo being their captain, that should prevent ° Nasica and occupy the straits and where Nasica should pass. And Polybius writes that as they rested and were asleep for the most part the Romans assaulted them, but Nasica writes that not without great danger they fought on the hill and that he himself slew there with his sword a captain of the Thracians and so overcame his enemies in such wise that Milo the captain shamefully threw his armour from him and fled away, whereby Nasica brought his company to that place that he would in safeguard. In this victory the Macedons were greatly astoned,° in so much that the king Perseus withdrew his army backward, not very well assured, but other° there or else at a place called Pydna he purposed to abide the fortune of battle.⁷² The friends of Perseus exhorted him to give battle, forasmuch as he had with him men enough, the which for their wives and their children would fight surely, specially he being present in person and putting himself in peril with the other. And Perseus, confirmed with these reasons, prepared himself to give the onset, and chose his ground necessarily and wittily, and commanded his captains to be in readiness as sure straightways to fight. The place where he was in was fair and plain, meet for his army, and on every side were little

---

⁷⁰ which [...] furlongs] P. and B. 'From this point Olympus rises to a height of more than ten furlongs'.

⁷¹ P. 'It was the son of Eumelus who measured the distance of the path [μέτρα κελεύθου], Xenagoras.' M. follows B. (fol. 135v), who has mistaken κελεύθου (path) for the second name of Eumelus, Celeutus, due to the correspondence of the case and ending (genitive -ου); as usual, M. has retained the inflected form of the name (genitive -i). See Introduction, p. 8.

⁷² but [...] battle] P. and B. 'But nevertheless he was under the necessity of standing his ground there in front of Pydna and risking a battle, or else of scattering his army about among the cities and so awaiting the issue of the war.' B. omits the subsequent clause, included in the manuscripts cited in Teuber: 'which, now that it had once made its way into his country, could not be driven out without much bloodshed and slaughter.'

hills, that from one place to another the light horsemen might run and succour the footmen and invade their enemies. In the mids° thereof was a little river, Aeson, and albeit that then it was not deep because it was then midsummer, yet it seemed to be some let to the Romans and advantage to Perseus.[73]

[17] But when Aemilius and Nasica were met together and went against Perseus, seeing the great multitude and the wise order of Perseus, he stayed° a little season, thinking within himself what was best to do. But the young men that were present, desirous to give battle, prayed him no longer to dally but to set on, most of all Nasica, which comforted and proud of his fresh victory compelled him in manner so to do. But Aemilius, smiling, said to Nasica: 'If I were', said he, 'as young as thou art; although I had obtained many victories by the oversight of mine adversaries, yet as now it seemeth not good unto me in haste to set on such a army in good order of battle and ready for to fight.' And saying these words, those that were in the front of his army, he distributed them and set them in order, that by his so doing his enemies should hope no nother but he would give them battle. The last of his army he commanded them to cast a trench and to keep them within their camp, and so without any noise he brought them all for that night to quiet. And that self° night, when they had supped and the soldiers had given them to sleep and rest, the moon began to wax dark and to change into many and divers colours, so that by little and little her light vanished, that it seemed she had been gone away. The Romans, seeing that as their old guise was calling her light with the sound and ringing of basins° and lighting of many torches and cressets,° rested not till she shone again. But the Macedons did no such thing at all, but among them was fear and horror on all sides, and privily the one would say unto the other that it was a prognostication of the ruin of the king. But Aemilius, albeit he was not ignorant of the variable mutation of the moon and that because of the shadowing of the earth for a time she is not seen, yet as a worshipper of divine things as soon as he saw her again he sacrified° to her eleven oxen. And in like manner, when the day appeared, he offered to Hercules twenty beasts, and in the opening of the bodies of the beasts in the last appeared to him tokens of victory. And when the sun began to ascend upward, he sat in his tent and looked to that part where he might see and behold his enemies.[74]

---

[73] P. and B. name a second river, Leucus.
[74] M. significantly abbreviates and alters the text here. P. and B. 'Accordingly, having vowed to the god a hecatomb and solemn games, he ordered his officers to put the army in array for battle; but he himself, waiting for the sun to pass to the west and decline, in order that its morning light might not shine in the faces of his men as they fought, passed the time sitting in his tent, which was open towards the plain and the enemy's encampment.'

[18] And about nine of the clock,⁷⁵ Aemilius wittily set his army in array, and willing that Perseus should begin the fight, it so fortuned that a strong-headed horse ran from Aemilius' camp toward Perseus, and anon they of Thracia ran towards the horse and came so fast on that thereby the battle began.⁷⁶ And some say that divers horse which had broken out from Aemilius' camp ran about the fields and that the Thracians ran after them and that when the Genoways perceived that, they were wroth at it and ran towards the Thracians, on either party about a seven hundred men, and so as they did skirmish, the one against the other, little and little the hosts on either side approached, till the whole battle joined together.⁷⁷ Aemilius then as a governor well perceiving by the moving of the two armies that the battle began came out of his tent and coming to his legions with his words and with his ways exhorted them to do well.⁷⁸ And Nasica riding by that place where they fought saw a wondrous multitude approaching towards the forward of the Romans. And they were Thracians, which somewhat astoned him, for they were mighty men of body and had white shining shields and black boots, and black coats also on their backs, and great mighty swords in their hands, which they shook fearfully. And by those of Thrace were foreign soldiers, which had as well diverse coats as they had weapons. And in the rearward were the Macedons, chosen and elect men, well trimmed with wondrous fair bright harness so that their armour shone over all the field, and they made such a horrible cry that the hills and the mountains all about redounded of the noise. To° this, they exhorted the one the other to do well, and they gave the onset with such a fury that they that were first slain fell not from the Romans' camp scant two furlongs.

[19] And as the one assaulted the other fiercely in the beginning, Aemilius saw that the Macedons that were in a plump° together put back the Romans with the force of their encounters, by the means that they approached them so near that they could not occupy° their swords, and perceiving their fashion and strength, he did often say that he never saw a more terrible sight.⁷⁹ But he then like a valiant captain came to the field with a glad and joyous cheer, without either

---

⁷⁵ nine of the clock] P. 'afternoon' (δείλη), translated by B. as 'horam [...] nonam' (fol. 136r), the ninth hour, which equates to about 3pm in Roman time.
⁷⁶ it so fortuned] In fact, B. (following P.) specifically states this was done on purpose, using the idiomatic expression 'dedita [...] opera' (fol. 136r), apparently mistranslated by M. as 'set his army in array'.
⁷⁷ divers horse which had broken out from Aemilius' camp ran about the fields] In P. and B., these beasts of burden were attacked when they were bringing in forage.
⁷⁸ Aemilius [...] began] M.'s translation fails to reproduce P.'s comparison with the pilot of a ship (B. 'gubernator', fol. 136r, translated by M. as 'governor'). See Introduction, p. 9.
⁷⁹ M. significantly condenses P. and B. here. In particular, he does not explain how the Macedonians used their pikes to hold off the Romans.

helmet or shield. But Polybius writes that Perseus, when the battle began, for fear entered unto the town, as though he had gone to do sacrifice to Hercules — unfitting that Hercules should accept of a coward any acceptable sacrifice. For it is none reason that he that shoots not should hit the mark, nor he that stands not with his men to overcome his enemies, nor he that do nothing to do well, nor a naughty° person to be happy. But God accepted well Aemilius' vows, for he prayed that he might obtain the victory with the sword in his hand. But there is one Possidonius, that was in that time, which saith that Perseus for no fear that he had fled from the battle, but by the occasion that a horse had hurt him on the knee he withdrew him for a time and came after to the battle,[80] where as it fortuned among many arrows and darts that were cast on every side, it so chanced that one hit Perseus on the side in such wise that it passed thorough° his harness and entered somewhat into the flesh, so that the mark thereof remained there a long while after. Thus writeth Possidonius of Perseus.

[20] But the Romans fighting against the Macedons could in nowise put them back, till one of the prefects named Savis took the ensign in his hand and ran fiercely against his enemies and threw it among them.[81] And it was not convenient for the Italians that the Macedons should enjoy it, wherefore with a rage as it had been mad men they fought till at the last the Romans, being surely armed and in such wise that their enemies could not hurt them, little and little withdrew themselves and began to turn their backs.[82]

[21] And whiles they fought thus horribly, it chanced that Marcus Cato, the son of Cato and son-in-law to Aemilius, when he had most valiantly fought in the battle and done many a notable deed of arms, that his sword fell out of his hand. And he, as may be very well thought, being a man of great and high heart and courage and descended of a noble father, would show himself noble also, and desired not to live so to leese° his weapon and to have his enemies enjoy the same, wherefore, running here and there in the battle, where that he met any that he knew, he exhorted them to help him. And so gathering together a great multitude of the Romans ran against his enemies, and slaying a great number of them, in the mids° of the dead bodies he found his sword. And being

---

[80] and came after to the battle] M. condenses P. 'in the battle, although he was in a wretched plight [due to the kick he had received from the horse], and although his friends tried to deter him, the king [ordered a pack-horse to be brought to him, mounted it, and] joined his troops in the phalanx without a breastplate' (passage in brackets not in B.). Possidonius is Posidonius.
[81] Savis] Salvius (B. 'Saus', fol. 136r).
[82] This paragraph summarises the much longer and more detailed account in P. and B., omitting many of the more technical descriptions of the weaponry, combat, military tactics, and battle formations. It is the Macedonians who flee the battlefield, not the Romans, as the grammatical structure of the final sentence suggests.

wondrous glad thereof, more fiercely than ever he did, he assaulted them, and in such wise that without any resisting they turned their backs and ran away. And those that abode and kept their array were all slain unto one man.[83] Over and besides those that fled, there were so many slain that the woods and the little brooks all ran of blood.[84] It is said that there was about 25,000 men of Perseus' army that died that day, and of the Romans no more but one hundred, and, as Nasica writes, but fourscore.[85]

[22] This battle was shortly fought, for they began to fight at nine of the clock and by ten the Romans had the victory. The rest of the day they persecuted° their enemies, and the chase endured well near a hundred and forty furlongs.[86] And when the night came, they retired, and the ministers° and servants met them with torches and lights, making great feasts and cheer the one unto the other, having garlands on their heads of ivy and of the laurel tree, with a joyous cry they went into their tents. But in this great gladness that the other had, Aemilius was wondrous heavy and sad, because that of the two sons he had with him, one of them which was in the field no man could tell where he was become.° And this was Nasica,[87] which he most loved, that among the rest he accounted in virtue to be most toward and noble, wherefore he imagined that being most valiant and hardy that he had so advanced himself amongst his enemies that he had been slain. Now at the sorrow of the captain, all the army complained and rose from their supper and sought amongst the dead bodies to have found him, and they cried thereto so loud 'Scipio, Scipio' that all the field redounded by the exceeding noise.[88] But for all their crying and calling he appeared not, till at the last, with three or four of his trusty fellows, as a gentle whelp, when Aemilius despaired of his life, he returned full of the fresh blood of the killing and persecuting of his enemies. This is that noble and valiant Scipio that subverted Cartage and strong Numanse in virtue and power, for his time far above all other princes.[89] But fortune, the malicious, desiring to venge°

---

[83] P. and B. distinguish between the three thousand elite troops, who kept their ground but were all slain, and the remainder of the enemy soldiers, who fled (apparently transposed to the previous sentence by M.).

[84] Over and besides those that fled] In P. and B., it is in fact those that fled that were slain.

[85] M. leaves out a number of details, e.g. the discrepancy between the historical accounts of Posidonius and Nasica and the name of the river that was red with blood (Leucus).

[86] a hundred and forty] P. and B. have 120.

[87] M.'s addition. As the rest of the paragraph makes clear, it was in fact Scipio Aemilianus (Aemilius Paullus's son), not Scipio Nasica.

[88] M. omits B. 'Nam ab ipsa pueritia inter caeteros adolescentes natura longe excellebat: dabatque expectationem futurae tam domi quam militiae probitatis' (For from his very youth he far surpassed other young men through his natural gifts, and raised expectations of future political as well as military greatness, fol. 136v, phrased somewhat differently from P.). The repetition of the name Scipio is an unusually lively dramatic touch by M.

[89] Numanse] Numantia, in Spain.

The Story of Paullus Aemilius 33

herself till another time, gave to Aemilius then the full gladness of his victory.

[23] And to revert to this story, Perseus fled from Pydna to a castle called Pellant, having with him in manner his whole troop of horsemen.⁹⁰ But the footmen and the horsemen brawled together in suchwise that the footmen called the horsemen cowards and traitors and after such words fell together by the ears and in suchwise that the footmen unhorsed some of the horsemen. Wherefore Perseus, seeing their company, declined° another way, and the purple coat which he had on his back, he pulled it off and put it under him, for fear lest he should be known what he was, and took his diadem and bore it in one of his hands. And as he descended from his horse, one of his twain friends that were with him feigned as though he would have amended his shoe, and the other feigned as though he would have put his horse in the stable, and the third as though he would have brought him drink. But when they saw that he made no semblance to them,⁹¹ dreading no less his madness than the Romans which had them in chase, suddenly they ran away, for he began to lay to their charge as though by their oversight he had been overrun.

And when that by the twilight he was arrived at Pelthan and there by chance met with twain of his treasurers, which blamed him rather than comforted him, he being therewith in a rage ran upon them with his sword and slew them both.⁹² For fear whereof, of all his friends there was no more that tarried with him but only Evander of Crete and Archedamus of Aetolia and Memonem of Boeotia, and of the rest of his soldiers but only the soldiers of Crete, not for no love nor faith they bore to him, but only to rob him of his gold, for he promised to them many great gifts in prey, as jewels and plate to the value of fifty talents.⁹³

And so from thence he departed to Amphipolis and after to Alepsum, still in great dread and yet not forgetting the odible° wise of covetous.°⁹⁴ He complained to his friends there that they of Crete had of him certain rich cups which sometime were the great Alexander's and prayed them weeping that they would help him that he might have them again, promising if they so did to give them much money in reward. Nor they were not ignorant that well knew his conditions that against the craft of them of Crete he could use the Cretical craft and deceive them that believed him, as he did indeed, for he received at their

---

⁹⁰ Pellant] Pella, the royal capital of Macedon, *c.* 50 km west of modern Thessaloniki.
⁹¹ i.e. he revealed nothing to them through his outward expressions.
⁹² Pelthan] Pella.
⁹³ Memonem] Neon. B. 'Menonem' (fol. 136v), the accusative form of 'Meno'.
⁹⁴ Alepsum] Galepsus, a port east of Thessaloniki. B., apparently working from a defective manuscript, has 'Alepsum' (fol. 137r); M., as is often the case, reproduces the inflected form of the name.

hands the cups and contrary to his promise gave them not a penny but took from his friends that which shortly his enemies should have.⁹⁵ And thus using such false casts,° he fled by water into Samothrace and took there the temple for his safeguard.

[24] And the Macedons, that evermore afore that time were trusty to their kings, then as a broken stock altogether within two days put them⁹⁶ and their realm in Aemilius' hands. Those that hear these great acts of Aemilius cannot but account them to his great felicity.⁹⁷ And this beareth testimony thereof, that as he did sacrifice, it chanced in the doing a bolt of lightning smote the author and burnt all the sacrifice.⁹⁸ But all the signs which I have afore told, this only sign which we will declare passeth all the other, that the fourth day after Perseus was put to flight the tidings was told at Rome. For as the people were sitting to behold certain plays,⁹⁹ suddenly from the first part of the theatre a rumour began that Aemilius in great conflict had vanquished his enemies and had taken all the kingdom of Macedony. And this spread abroad thorough all the theatre, which filled the same with great joy and gladness and thanksgiving to their gods. The next day following, when it was uncertain who brought the news, the fame thereof ceased. But within few days after when there came certain sure news of the victory, it was taken for a miracle, the news which was thought to be a lie before.

[25] It is said further that at the battle done at Sagra, that same day the fame thereof was told in Peloponnesus, and in the streets of Myle, it was when the Romans chased away the Tarquins.¹⁰⁰ And to this is said that there was seen two men of fair stature that came towards them, and these men, it is thought they were the twain brethren Castor and Pollux, and when they declared it, that the horses they rode upon sweat out of all measure, and when among other

---

⁹⁵ Cretical] Cretan. Not in *OED*, but recorded in Thomas Blount, *Glossographia: or a dictionary interpreting all such hard words, whether Hebrew, Greek, Latin, Italian, Spanish, French, Teutonick, Belgick, British or Saxon, as are now used in our refined English tongue* (1656), sig. L5v. Cretans were proverbially deceiving, as the entry in Blount's dictionary makes clear: 'Cretical (from Creta) belonging to a Cretan or lier'.
⁹⁶ i.e. themselves.
⁹⁷ great felicity] P.'s use of the word εὐτυχία (good fortune) signals his return to this major theme of the two Lives. M. follows B. 'felicitate' (fol. 137r).
⁹⁸ author] altar (B. 'aram', fol. 137r). As the Latin is clear and straightforward, this appears to be a transcription error ('Avtor' for 'Altar').
⁹⁹ Spectacles. See Introduction, p. 10.
¹⁰⁰ M.'s translation conflates three separate historical events: the news of the battle of Sagra in the sixth century BCE reaching Olympia on the Peloponnesus; that of the victories of the Greeks over the Persians at Mycale (B. 'Miele', fol. 137r) in 479 BCE arriving at Plataea; and that of the victory of the Romans over the Tarquins and their allies in 499 BCE getting to Rome. The subsequent sentences relate to the last of the three incidents.

one affirmed it was not so, that then one of these twain took him by the beard and that which was black afore was converted into yellow, and had ever after the surname of Enobarby, which is to mean a changeable beard.¹⁰¹ But all this passeth that which in our days fortuned. When Antonius had rebelled against Domitian, and had reared up° a great discord in Germany, in so much the Romans were afeared thereof, ere any man were ware° the fame of the victory was declared to the Romans, that Antony with all his army was overcome and slain.¹⁰² And divers gave so much credit to this that some sacrificed to the gods therefore. But when he was sought for that should have told these tidings, and no man could tell what he was, but that one alleged another to have told it, at the last the thing declared among the unstable vulgar people and yet no person apparent who should have told the news, suddenly they ceased to talk of it.¹⁰³ But it was not long after, when that Domitian set forward with his army thitherward, there came a sure messenger with letters of the victory had against Antonius, that the same self day that the news were told at Rome the same day the battle was fought. And there is very few now in our days are ignorant of this.

[26] But to return to Perseus, when he was arrived at Samothrace, Octavius, legate of Aemilius, sent thither to take him, albeit he abstained for the reverence of the gods and the temple to lay hands upon him, but yet nevertheless he watched him so that to scape° from him he could not. But Perseus, supposing to beguile Octavius, privily did make covenant with Oroandes of Crete, that had a little ship to receive him therein and his treasure.¹⁰⁴ And so stealing to the sea-bank, Oroandes first received his treasure and, using the craft of Crete, left Perseus and his wife and his children miserably behind him. And more miserably than ever he was, for he might behold from afar Oroandes sailing

---

¹⁰¹ M.'s translation of this whole episode is confusing: P. 'And when the Romans conquered the Tarquins, who had taken the field against them with the Latins, two tall and beautiful men were seen at Rome a little while after, who brought direct tidings from the army. These were conjectured to be the Dioscuri [B. explains: 'Pollucem et Castorem', fol. 137r]. The first man who met them in front of the spring in the forum, where they were cooling their horses, which were reeking with sweat, was amazed at their report of the victory [B. omits reference to a spring and has them drying off the sweat]. Then, we are told, they touched his beard with their hands, quietly smiling the while, and the hair of it was changed at once from black to red [B. 'flavam' (fol. 137r), which can be 'reddish yellow' (Lewis-Short) but is more commonly simply yellow, as M. translates], a circumstance which gave credence to their story, and fixed upon the man the surname of Ahenobarbus [B. 'Aenobarbi', fol. 137r], that is to say, Bronze-beard.'
¹⁰² Probably in 89 CE.
¹⁰³ at the last the thing declared among the unstable vulgar people] The instability of the 'vulgar people' is M.'s invention and he omits the vivid metaphor in his source: P. and B. 'finally disappeared in the limitless throng [B. 'plebem', fol. 137r], as in a yawning sea'.
¹⁰⁴ supposing to beguile Octavius] M.'s addition.

away in the great sea.¹⁰⁵ And thus void from all hope and not knowing what ways to take, he fled back again to the walls of the temple. Nor the Romans were not ignorant of this, but prevented him to obtain their purpose.¹⁰⁶ And Perseus' children, one named Anotasyon, a little afore Perseus' nigh friend but then a false traitor, delivered them to the Romans.¹⁰⁷ Whereby Perseus, in like manner as it had been a wild beast her whelps taken away, and in doubt himself to be taken, when he saw that there was no remedy but needs to yield him to the Romans, he required° to be delivered to Nasica. But when it was so that Nasica was not then present, by pure necessity he yielded himself to Octavius. In so doing, he declared his covetous desire of life, whereby being in such a miserable estate, he deserved no grace, nor could not obtain to have it.¹⁰⁸ For he prayed that he might be presented to Aemilius, and when according to the same he was brought to him, and that Aemilius considering the high and great estate that he was fallen down from, he went to meet him with his friends, and in manner weeping for the compassion he had of his overthrow, Perseus miserably fell down of his knees and clipping° him about the legs, he spoke unfitting words for a king to speak, which Aemilius would not suffer nor hear, but looking on him with a angry countenance said unto him:¹⁰⁹ 'Why dost thou in manner defile and dishonest° my victory and the acts that I have done against thee, in showing thyself not like a noble man nor such a one as hath been so bold to make war against the Romans? Surely I tell thee, Perseus, that although thou be by me vanquished and overcome, yet if thou had had a noble virtuous heart, it should have been worthy to have been honoured of me. And contrary, thy coward heart, albeit that it hath had sometime good fortune, yet it is not without shame and blame.'

[27] Saying these words, Aemilius with his right hand raised up Perseus and took him to Tubero, and calling apart to him his children and his friends stood a long time ere he spake any word, with a wonderful sad cheer and

---

¹⁰⁵ And so [...] sea] M. leaves out a substantial amount of detail about how Perseus escaped and was duped.
¹⁰⁶ prevented him to obtain their purpose] As the remainder of the paragraph makes clear, they did not anticipate or prevent him. M. apparently takes the Romans (plural) as the subject of B.'s singular 'praevenit' (fol. 137r): 'he [Perseus] pre-empted them'.
¹⁰⁷ Anotasyon] Ion. B. 'Antosion' (fol. 137r), a conflation of 'Ion' and the previous word in many manuscripts, αὐτός, with upsilon inverted to nu.
¹⁰⁸ P. (followed closely by B.) 'thus making it most abundantly clear that his avarice was a less ignoble evil than the love of life that was in him, and that led him to deprive himself of the only thing which Fortune cannot take away from the fallen, namely, pity'.
¹⁰⁹ M. leaves out the first sentence of Aemilius's speech in P. and B.: 'Why, wretched man, dost thou free Fortune from thy strongest indictment against her, by conduct which will make men think that thy misfortunes are not undeserved, and that thy former prosperity, rather than thy present lot, was beyond thy deserts?'.   angry] B. 'tristi' (sad, fol. 137r), translating P. ἀλγοῦντι καὶ λελυπημένῳ (pained and distressed)

countenance, in so much that those that stood about him marvelled at it.¹¹⁰ At the last he began to speak in this manner of the frail miserable state of mankind, saying:¹¹¹ 'What time is there given to man to trust unto, in especial when that he is in most high fortune, then is he most likest to fall?¹¹² Which said fortune never doth give to man any sweet thing without to mingle it with bitter gall. As ye may see by Perseus, descended of the high blood of the great Alexander, environed alate° about with so great a army of footmen and horsemen, having so mighty and great a realm, and so much riches withal, compelled for all this high glory miserably not only to fall into his enemies' hands, but thereunto to ask his bread to sustain his life. Shall not this lamentable sight move you to remember what variable fortune may do to you? Surely, if ye do not think that after this good fortune and victory given to us by the gods that fortune show not some great mishap to us, you are unwise.' These words with other the wise Aemilius spoke unto his friends, and after dismissed them, wondersly° abating the bragging and the boast of them, in manner as a horse is refrained to be ruled with a bridle, [28] and after commanded his army to be in quiet. And he himself, to the intent that he would show his humanity to the cities, he ordained divers fair pastimes and pleasures, and relieved the people, and stabled° their commonwealth, in setting that same in a wondrous wise order.¹¹³ And to show his goodness, he distributed the wheat and the oil that were in Perseus' granges where need was.¹¹⁴ Of which there was so great plenty that whoso asked, had it, and yet there was left over and besides that was given a honest quantity thereof. And at Delphi, where Perseus had caused to be reared a great pillar to the intent to have put his image or picture thereon, in that same place he set his own, as reason was that those that were vanquished should give place to the vanquer.°¹¹⁵ Farther he gave freedom to the Macedons and to their towns to live after their

---

¹¹⁰ with a wonderful sad cheer and countenance] M.'s addition.
¹¹¹ frail miserable] M.'s addition: see Introduction, pp. 3–4.
¹¹² M. leaves out the opening of the speech: 'Is it, then, fitting that one who is mortal should be emboldened when success comes to him, and have high thoughts because he has subdued a nation, or a city, or a kingdom? or should his thoughts dwell rather on this reversal of fortune, which sets before the warrior an illustration of the weakness that is common to all men, and teaches him to regard nothing as stable or safe?'.
¹¹³ And [...] pleasures] B. 'he turned himself to the sight of the Greek cities' ('se autem ad spectaculum graecarum civitatum convertit', fol. 137v). M. seems to render 'spectaculum' as 'fair pastimes and pleasures' and 'gratiarum' (a misprint for 'graecarum' in Plutarch, *Vitae* (1478), sig. r8v and other early editions) as 'humanity', both possible meanings of the Latin. B. has omitted P. 'occupying himself in ways alike honourable and humane'. relieved the people] The Greek specifically means that he restored democratic government.
¹¹⁴ Both 'in a wondrous wise order' at the end of the previous sentence and 'And to show his goodness' at the start of this one are additions by M., who in turn omits 'he also gave gifts to the cities'.
¹¹⁵ M. omits 'And at Olympia, as they say, he made that utterance which is now in every mouth, that Phidias had moulded the Zeus of Homer.'

own laws, paying to the people of Rome in tribute a hundred talents, dismissing them of the tone° half of that which they were accustomed to pay to Perseus. And surely he showed to them such spectacles and plays as were not afore seen, and made them suppers and banquets, and handled them in such a gentle sort that the Grecians wondered at it as a thing which had not been afore seen.[116] And Aemilius rejoiced to do such things, and would often say that it came of a witty mind as well to set in order a feast as a field° or a battle: the battle, because when it were well ordered it should give dread to the enemies; the feast well ordered to give comfort to his friends. And his magnanimity and noble heart was well praised. Forasmuch as the treasure which he found in the treasure° of Perseus, he would not once look at it, but gave it to other officers to distribute the same. But the books which were in the hands of those that were masters to Perseus' children, those he took to his own use. And he forgot not to give to his captains and soldiers many great rewards, remembering that by them he had gotten the victory and honour.[117] Among that sort, Tubero, his son-in-law, was one to whom he caused to be given a cup which weighed five talents. This is the same Tubero of whom we have spoken of before, that with sixteen of his family lay in a little house, and this was (as men say) the first gold and silver of any value which their family obtained to have, by his virtue and valiantness at that time gotten.

[29] And thus, when Aemilius had well ordered all thing, tenderly embracing the Greeks and the Macedons, and exhorting them to have in mind the liberty and freedom they had received by the Romans, and willing them with peace and love to conceive the same, he bad them farewell. And by the exhortation of the Romans and the decree of the senate, he went into Epirus, only to give to his soldiers that country in prey and sackage. And to the intent that this should be altogether done,[118] he called unto him of every city ten of the heads of them and commanded that as well the money that was in the temples and in their houses should be presented unto him, and gave to every one of these heads a ruler of the tribunes and the other captains,[119] and that done gave leave to his soldiers to run and to prey° and catch° what they could, in suchwise that at one time there were taken prisoners above a hundred thousand, what one and what other,

---

[116] M. significantly condenses the account of the entertainments and banquets that Paullus put on and how impressed the Macedonians were with him in his source text. He specifically omits 'and sacrifices' after 'such spectacles and plays'.

[117] M. significantly expands P. and B. 'when he was distributing rewards for valour in the battle, he gave Aelius Tubero …'.

[118] And […] done] B. 'To invade all of them at the same time, however' ('Ut autem omnes simul invaderent', fol. 137v). The Greek offers a little more explanation of Aemilius's ruse: 'Wishing to set upon the inhabitants all at once and suddenly, when no one expected it'.

[119] gave […] captains] Ostensibly to ensure that the money was collected, but in fact to loot the cities unexpectedly.

and ten towns sacked.¹²⁰ And of all this spoil it is said that to every one of the soldiers they had no more for their parts but eleven drams° apiece.¹²¹

[30] This did Aemilius contrary to his good and gentle nature, and so went into Oricum, and from thence into Italy.¹²² But the soldiers, being angry because that they had not so much of Perseus' treasure as they looked to have, privily spoke evil of Aemilius, saying that he had behaved himself proudly in the battle. Which thing when Servius Galba, enemy to Aemilius, knew, he did all that he could to put him from his triumph. Thus the soldiers, more and more having indignation at Aemilius, murmured at him, wherefore he demanded a day to answer to such as slandered him.¹²³

[31] And the next morrow, when the heads of the city were gathered together, although the multitude would not that he should triumph, yet the senators and the heads were evil contented that Aemilius should be defrauded from his purpose. And when they had commanded the mean sort to be in silence, which babbled much out of reason,¹²⁴ at the last Marcus Servilius, which had been consul and had threescore times fought in camp hand to hand with his enemies and evermore was victor, stood up and said that he marvelled much that ever Paullus Aemilius, having under him such a unruly sort of soldiers, could do so great an act as to subdue Perseus, one of the successors of the great Alexander, and to put under tribute so royal a realm, and said further that although Servius Galba, a man more disposed to quiet and rest and pleasure than to wars, railed and moved the people against Aemilius, and that his words ought not to be weighed to Aemilius' acts nor his, that day and night in being in the wars' of the Romans business had received so many a grievous wound.¹²⁵

[32] These words took such place that forthwith all the tribunes and the other officers of Rome decreed Aemilius should triumph. Now this was the manner

---

¹²⁰   prisoners above a hundred thousand, what one and what other, and ten towns sacked] Modern editions of P. have 150,000 prisoners and seventy towns; B. has 120,000 prisoners and seventy towns.
¹²¹   B. (followed by M.) omits 'and all men shuddered at the issue of the war, when the division of a whole nation's substance resulted in so slight a gain and profit for each soldier'.
¹²²   M. omits the detail of his triumphant entry into Rome.
¹²³   murmured [...] slandered him] M.'s summary of the remainder of the paragraph, which describes in detail Galba's attempts to continue his invective against Aemilius in the assembly and the occupation of the Capitol by Aemilius's soldiers.
¹²⁴   And the next morrow [...] reason] M. summarises the much more detailed account in his source, which states that the senators and the common people were united in their opposition against the actions of Aemilius's soldiers. The phrase 'which babbled much out of reason' is M.'s addition.
¹²⁵   although Servius Galba [...] wound] M. summarises Marcus Servilius's long speech.

how he triumphed.¹²⁶ The people of Rome were all clothed in white garments, and there was made in the place where Aemilius should pass scaffolds for the people to stand upon, and all the temples of the city were opened and fulfilled° with certain sweet odours and fumes, and a great multitude of officers with staves in their hands to make room and to keep the people in array. The going of the triumph was divided into three days' space. In the first day, uneath° the tables° that were painted in similitudes of the towns and castles which he had won had space to pass, which said tables were carried in manner as it had been in boats to the number of two hundred and forty.¹²⁷ The second day was carried upon chariots the armour and the shields and ensigns of the Macedons, as well swords, maces, bucklers, bows, and arrows, wonderly set in order and in such wise as though at certain places it had seemed they had fallen down to the ground with a terrible noise, so that it might well fear° the vanquers. After these chariots thus decked followed 3000 harnessed men that bore bullion of silver and gold to the weight of three and forty talents, and the least piece weighed above three talents.¹²⁸ It was enough for four men to carry one of them, they were so great. And after them came such as bore cups and pots of silver of diverse sorts and fashions. And all these went in wonders° good order.

[33] The third day the trumpets blew up, not sweetly but terribly, after the sort as they blew towards the battle. And after them ensued° a hundred and fifty oxen with gilt horns and with garlands about their horns of ivy. And young men led them, arrayed ready to do with them sacrifice to the gods, and little children, which had in their hands golden and silver dishes to receive the sacrifice. And after that sort followed such as had coin of gold in vessels weighing three talents, the which vessels Aemilius had decked with rich precious stones. The number of the plate wherein the coin lay was fourscore and three dishes, which sometime were the vessels of Antigonus the noble, of Seleucus, and of Thericles.¹²⁹ And there ensued after that a fair chariot, wherein

---

¹²⁶ In 167 BCE.

¹²⁷ the tables that were painted in similitudes of the towns and castles which he had won] P. 'statues, paintings, and colossal figures', i.e. the art looted during the campaign. M. tries to make sense of the passage by adding that the paintings represent the territories conquered.   boats] B. 'vehiculis' (fol. 138r), which can mean 'ships', but wagons are intended here.

¹²⁸ bullion of silver and gold to the weight of three and forty talents] B. 'silver coins in 350 receptacles' ('numismata [...] argentea vasis trecentis quinquaginta', fol. 138r). The manuscripts now believed to be more reliable have 750.

¹²⁹ And after that sort [...] Thericles] M. recombines the different clauses in this passage to create a rather different meaning: P. 'Next, after these, came the carriers of the coined gold, which, like the silver, was portioned out into vessels containing three talents; and the number of these vessels was eighty lacking three [B. has 'Triades octoginta' (eighty threes, fol. 138r), but M. appears to follow the reading of Plutarch, *Vitae* (1478), sig. r9v: 'tria et octoginta', three and eighty]. After these followed the bearers of the consecrated bowl,

was the armour of Perseus, and upon his armour his diadem or crown of gold, wonderly rich. And within a little space of the same there followed Perseus' little young children, and with them their masters and teachers and rulers, weeping and making great lamentation, and they were taught to hold up their hands unto the citizens, as it were to pray them to have pity of them. They were three in all, two sons and a young maiden, that for their tender years did not perceive in what miserable estate they were in. Which sight moved divers of the Romans to pity and compassion, insomuch that a great number of them wept to see them, so that the sight was both mixed with tears and gladness till the young children passed by.

[34] And Perseus himself followed them, having upon him a sad coloured garment and buskins of his legs after the manner of his country, fearful and pensive to think what should be done with him after the triumph.[130] And some say that he required° of Aemilius that he might not be so led in the face of all the world. But Aemilius, little regarding his cowardly heart, answered him that sometime it lay in his will and power not to have been so led and that it had been much more honourable to him by a certain death to have eschewed such misery than then to desire life with shame. And after that spectacle went those that bore golden crowns, given to him by the cities of Greece in token of a remembrance of his high virtuous acts. The number to him given was four hundred crowns. Ensuing them went Aemilius himself, sitting in a most honourable and most ornate chair, a man that well worthy seemed to have such honour, clad in purple with a guard° or border of pure gold, and bore in his right hand a fair branch of the laurel tree. And those that were about him of his soldiers had in like manner branches of the same, part of them singing his praises and lauds, and some of them with jests and divers other pastimes environed him all about. Insomuch that uneath it can be esteemed the honour that he had, nor himself could wish no more thereof, unless some devil would go about to mingle with human felicity some ungracious° fortune, after the sentence of Homer the poet, that says that those stand in best estate that have of neither of the twain, that is to say nother° of too much felicity nor of too much adversity.[131]

---

which Aemilius had caused to be made of ten talents of gold and adorned with precious stones, and then those who displayed the bowls known as Antigonids and Seleucids and Theracleian, together with all the gold plate of Perseus's table.' The first two types of bowls are named after the rulers of the Macedon and Seleucid empires; the latter, after a famous Corinthian potter.

[130] In P. and B. Perseus is 'fearful and pensive' because of 'the magnitude of his evils'. M. also leaves out a sentence describing Aemilius's attendants.

[131] those [...] adversity] P. 'those may be thought to fare best whose fortunes incline now one way and now another'. As the reference to Achilles' speech to Priam in *Iliad*, XXIV. 525-33, makes clear, P.'s point is that as nobody has good fortune alone, it is better to have a mix of good and bad fortune than evil fortune only. M., likely prompted by B.'s phrasing

[35] As it fortuned to Aemilius, which having four sons, two of them by adoption,[132] that is to say Scipio and Fabius, and two at home in his house, which he had of his second wife as is afore declared, the tone of these children five days before he triumphed suddenly died, being sixteen years of age, and the tother,° that was twelve years of age, the third day after he triumphed deceased in like wise. And there was none of the citizens of Rome but that sorrowed and mourned for that hard chance, so that this great triumph was suddenly converted into sorrow and lamentation.

[36] But Aemilius, that not only against armour and shield but also against the furious assault of fortune could well use a right reason, did so moderate himself for the death of his children that nother for good fortune nor for ill fortune was he moved therefore anything at all whereby might be thought that he had a unconstant mind.[133] He then, according to a wise noble man, was present at the burying of the first that died.[134] And when the last died, he called to his presence the multitude of the people, saying to them in this wise, not as one that needeth consolation but as one could well in sorrow comfort other. He said then that he never doubted° worldly things but always dreaded false fortune as a thing never to be trusted, and specially because he had had so prosperous chance concerning the battle against Perseus that there should shortly ensue some diverse and sudden mutation. 'For', says he, 'in one day's space going from Brundisium I landed in Corsica;[135] the fifth day after I arrived in Delphi; and when I had finished the divine sacrifice, in five days after I arrived in Macedony, where the whole army and I joined together; and setting the army in good order and beginning to set forward, within fifteen days after I gave battle and obtained the victory. For this good hap I had fortune in suspect, and when that as victor with mine army and with the king Perseus and the spoil of mine enemies I reverted homewards, even in sailing I looked for some displeasure. But now that safe and sound I and the army is come to you, and do behold the city fulfilled with joy and gladness, yet I doubted still fortune's unhappy turns, which I knew perfectly that she never rewards no mortal man withal without envy and malice. Nor my mind could never be in quiet for dreading lest she would revenge herself of the commonwealth till she had rewarded me as she

('cum iis optime actum esse videatur: quos fortuna ad utramque partem convertit', fol. 138v: 'those appear to have been treated best, whom fortune turns to both sides'), takes this as a warning against the extremes of good as well as bad fortune.

[132] As other parts of the Life make plain, these two sons had been given up by Aemilius for adoption when he remarried, rather than adopted by him.

[133] nother [...] mind. P. 'the bad was lost sight of in the good, and his private sorrow in the public welfare, thus neither lowering the grandeur nor sullying the dignity of his victory'.

[134] The point of this statement, that Paullus held his triumph immediately after he buried his first son, is lost in M.'s translation; 'according to a wise noble man' is his addition.

[135] In fact, Corcyra (Corfu).

hath done. For my sweet and best beloved children which only I had ordained to be mine heirs even suddenly the tone after the tother departed. And now I think I am out of peril, and take a good heart unto me and trust surely that the people of Rome shall be without spot of hurt or misfortune, forasmuch as by her malice she hath recompensed my triumph in this fashion and guise. Nor there is no less wonderful example of the frailty and misery of man than is to be noted of Perseus and me, for Perseus, though he be overcome, hath his children alive, and I, the victor of him, have lost both mine.'

[37] Such a wise oration it is said that Aemilius should make to the people. But albeit he did what he could to have had Perseus to have been put at some liberty, he could not obtain the same. Wherefore, as some men write, the said Perseus for pure sorrow shortly after died.[136] And some write again that he died after another manner, that those that kept him, being weary with watching and keeping him, agreed the one with the other that they should by course never suffer him to rest till that by that manner they had caused him die.[137] And two of his children also shortly after him deceased, that is to say, one of his sons and his daughter. The third, that was named Alexander, learned the craft to work in copper and brass and to make many diverse things of the same and was much excellent therein, and further he was also well learned in the Latin tongue, insomuch that he became a scribe.

[38] Now for the things done by Aemilius against the Macedons, the people of Rome gave him great thanks therefore, for he brought in so much gold and silver into the common treasure of Rome that the citizens needed not to pay no more tribute till the days of Hirtius and Pansa, which were consuls when Antonius and Caesar reigned.[138]

---

[136] M. significantly condenses the account in B., who in turn makes some changes to P.: 'With such noble and lofty words, we are told, did Aemilius, from an unfeigned and sincere spirit, address the people. But for Perseus, although he pitied him for his changed lot and was very eager to help him [clause omitted by B.], he could obtain no other favour than a removal from the prison which the Romans called 'carcer' [B. naturally has simply 'carcere', fol. 138v] to a clean place and kindlier treatment; and there, being closely watched, according to most writers the king starved himself to death [B. 'moerore animi confectus est' (fol. 138v): he died from sadness in his mind].'

[137] weary with watching and keeping him] B. 'disgusted and furious at him' ('pertaesos, et adversus eum infensos', fol. 138v). 'Pertaesos' can mean 'wearied' (in the sense of 'fed up'), but as the juxtaposition with 'infensos' indicates, P.'s meaning is that the soldiers were angry.

[138] In 43 BCE, when Mark Antony and Octavian (Caesar) were waging war against each other, as P. points out. M. omits the remainder of the paragraph, which tells how a rival accused his son Scipio Aemilianus of siding with the people, when his father had always been on the side of the aristocracy, but notes that he enjoyed the support of the people, who elected him as censor, and gives an account of his period in office.

[39] But for conclusion, when he had long occupied the office of censor, he fell in a sickness, which at the beginning seemed to be parlous but by process of time without danger, but nevertheless a disease not suddenly to be cured but rather to seem long and grievous.[139] Using therefore the counsel of physicians, he went unto a place called Vellam, and there was conversant° and quiet a good season.[140] The people of Rome wonderfully desired his presence and often in the theatre murmured for his absence. Wherefore when it seemed that he was very well amended and that there was certain sacrifices to do to the gods, he reverted to Rome, and he did the sacrifice with his fellows right honourably. And the next day following in like wise he sacrificed to the gods for his own health, which done he returned home to his own house. And suddenly as he rested, ere any man were ware, his reason was taken from him, and within three days after he died, lacking nothing of that felicity which men do call worldly felicity, for his burial was done as to a most best man appertained, that was nother with gold, nor with silver, nor with other riches, nor with magnificence, but with charity, with love, not only of his citizens but also of his enemies.[141] For look, as many as there was by chance either of Iberia or of the Genoways° or of the Macedons or of the Romans, the most youngest and most noblest of them sustained the bier whereon he lay. And the elders of the Romans followed him, naming him the conserver and the benefactor of their commonwealth, for not only when he had the victory of his enemies but also to all men he was gentle, treatable,° and honest, in such fashion that it seemed to all men as though they had been of his proper household. He left scant behind him in value 37,000 pound of all the patrimony he had, and that left he to both his sons which he had by his first wife. But Scipio that was the youngest of the twain released all to his elder brother, forasmuch as he was taken or adopted into a much more richer family. Such honest conditions and such a honourable life led Aemilius, as it is said.[142]

---

[139] In 164 BCE.
[140] Vellam] Velia (Elea), a coastal town in southern Italy. As usual, M. reproduces the inflected form in B. ('Veliam', fol. 139r); the second 'l' may be a transcription error for 'i'.
[141] In 160 BCE.
[142] The laudatory adjectives 'honest' and 'honourable' are M.'s additions: see Introduction, p. 3.

THOMAS NORTH

THE LIFE OF DEMOSTHENES

THE LIFE OF MARCUS TULLIUS CICERO

THE COMPARISON OF CICERO WITH DEMOSTHENES

FROM THE LIVES (1579)

Introduction

Demosthenes and Cicero

Uniquely in Plutarch's *Parallel Lives*, the protagonists of *The Lives of Demosthenes and Cicero* are orators rather than soldiers. In contrast to the other Greek and Roman statesmen, their political influence derives from their skill as public speakers instead of military successes. While Plutarch makes it plain from the outset that the rhetorical qualities of their speeches will not be the focus of his comparison (although he is not always faithful to his declared intention, especially in *Demosthenes*), the power of oratory and its role in public life is a central concern of both Lives. At the height of his influence,

> not only the captains of Athens obeyed Demosthenes, doing all that he commanded them, but the governors also of Thebes and of all the country of Boeotia besides. And the assemblies also of the council of Thebes were as well governed by him as the assemblies of Athens, being alike beloved both of the one and the other and having alike authority to command both. (*Demosthenes*, 508–13)

The most powerful ruler of the time, Philip of Macedon, is forced by Demosthenes' speeches to sue the Greeks for peace, and after his victory in the Battle of Chaeroneia is said to have 'consider[ed] the force and power of such an orator that in a piece of a day had enforced him to hazard his realm and life at a battle' (*Demosthenes*, 564–65). Demosthenes himself compares the orators of Athens to mastiffs that protect their flock (the citizens) against the wolf Alexander the Great (*Demosthenes*, 662–67). The most striking example of oratory's 'great force to persuade' (*Cicero*, 143) comes in the graphic description of Caesar's response to Cicero's speech in defence of a professed enemy of the de facto ruler of Rome:

> But when Cicero had begun his oration, he moved Caesar marvellously: he had so sweet a grace and such force in his words that it is reported Caesar changed colour often and showed plainly by his countenance that there was a marvellous alteration in all the parts of him. For, in the end when the orator came to touch the battle of Pharsalia, then was Caesar so troubled that his body shook withal and besides certain books he had fell out of his hands and he was driven against his will to set Ligarius at liberty. (*Cicero*, 1223–30)

The power of Cicero's speech to direct Caesar's feelings is physically witnessed in his facial expressions and even in a kind of seizure. The orator gains full control over Caesar's will, with the result that the most powerful man in Rome is compelled to release the accused despite having already judged him guilty. It is this ability of eloquence to 'move' (*kinein* or *movere*) its auditors that was celebrated by Cicero himself in his writings on rhetoric, and of which he presented Demosthenes as the outstanding exemplar.[1] The power of eloquence to control the audience's mind also underpinned the phenomenal popularity of rhetoric in the English Renaissance and was central to literary and political writings of the period.[2]

If the idea of the power of oratory is central to *Demosthenes* and *Cicero*, however, both Lives end in the defeat of the orators by the military men against whom they set themselves up. What is more, the deaths of Demosthenes and Cicero are accompanied by the loss of the participatory forms of government that guaranteed the place of oratory in society in the first place, Athenian democracy and the Roman republic. The opposition between oratory and warfare is emphasised by the identification of fearfulness in war as one of the shared characteristics of the two rhetors in the introduction to the pair, and summed up in a verse attributed to Cicero in the Comparison, 'Let spear and shield give place to gown | And give the tongue the laurel crown' (*Comparison of Demosthenes and Cicero*, 45–46). *Cicero* can be read as an extended series of encounters of the orator with the strongmen of the late republic. In the first major political battle of Cicero's life, he sharply contrasts his own use of oratory and Catiline's reliance on force: 'at length Cicero rose and commanded him [Catiline] to avoid out of Rome, saying that there must needs be a separation of walls between them two, considering that the one used but words and the other force of arms' (*Cicero*, 477–80). While he manages to overcome Catiline, Cicero is eventually defeated by the military might of Mark Antony and Octavian, who became the first emperor of Rome. The implications of the transition from republic to principate for the role of oratory in ancient Rome is sharply illustrated by Mark Antony's command that '[Cicero's] head and his hands should straight be set up over the pulpit for orations in the place called Rostra' (*Cicero*, 1518–20), echoing Caesar's earlier attempt to prevent Cicero from addressing the people by 'set[ting] their benches upon the pulpit for orations which they call at Rome Rostra, and [not suffering] him to set foot in it' (*Cicero*, 681–82). By physically denying access to the Rostra, the platform in the Forum Romanum from where orators addressed the Roman people on political questions, and then displaying Cicero's body parts as a warning there, the triumvirs, with their aspirations to absolute rule, mount a direct assault on the participatory political system in which oratory thrived. In *Demosthenes*, Plutarch similarly reports the rumour that the Macedonian captain Archias cut off the tongue of the orator Hyperides, whose murder foreshadows Demosthenes' death by the same assassin (826–31). In parallel with *Cicero*,

---

[1] Brian Vickers, *In Defence of Rhetoric* (Oxford: Clarendon Press, 1988), pp. 74–80.
[2] In addition to Vickers, see Neil Rhodes, *The Power of Eloquence and English Renaissance Literature* (Basingstoke: Palgrave Macmillan, 1992); Skinner, *Reason and Rhetoric*.

Demosthenes presents the Athenian orator defending the city against monarchs whose power is based on military conquest, the Macedonian kings Philip and Alexander the Great, and connects the loss of the democratic self-rule of Athens with the death of the rhetor: just as Cicero is said to have 'undone himself and together also lost the liberty [*eleutheria*] of his country' (*Cicero*, 1421–22), the beginning of the end of *Demosthenes* is introduced by the phrase: 'But some fatal destiny and the revolution of times had determined the final end of the liberty [*eleutheria*] of Greece at that time' (515–16). As Plutarch notes, Cicero self-consciously invoked these correspondences by naming his orations against Mark Antony *Philippics* in imitation of Demosthenes' speeches against Philip of Macedon, and thus modelling his struggle for political liberty in Rome on Demosthenes' fight against Athens' domination by foreign despots (723–27).

While the Lives of Demosthenes and Cicero validate the power of oratory and its association with political liberty, their presentation of the moral dimension of eloquence is less straightforwardly positive. Plutarch acknowledges the value of eloquence in making honest political advice pleasing, and therefore acceptable to the audience, in *Cicero*:

> For Cicero only of all men in Rome made the Romans know how much eloquence doth grace and beautify that which is honest, and how invincible right and justice are, being eloquently set forth, and also how that a man that will be counted a wise governor of a commonweal should always in his doings rather prefer profit than to seek to curry favour with the common people, yet so to use his words that the thing which is profitable may not be also unpleasant. (369–74)

While this passage presents the union of oratory and moral philosophy, whose object is 'that which is honest' (*to kalon*), as an ideal, the former is clearly subordinate to the latter for Plutarch. Moreover, the passage warns that the orator-statesman should be guided by 'profit' (*to kalon* again, i.e. an absolute standard of moral rectitude) instead of popular opinion, which is contingent and untrustworthy. The hazards of the popular politician's involvement with 'the common people' are elaborated in a key passage later in the Life, which contrasts the orator-statesman to the philosopher:

> Yet Cicero [...] took this adversity more basely than was looked for of one so well studied and learned as he. And yet he oftentimes prayed his friends not to call him orator but rather philosopher, saying that philosophy was his chiefest profession and that for his eloquence he did not use it but as a necessary instrument to one that pleadeth in the commonwealth. But glory and opinion hath great power to take man's reason from him, even like a colour, from the minds of them that are common pleaders in matters of state, and to make them feel the selfsame passions that common people do by daily frequenting their company unless they take great heed of them and that they come to practise in the commonwealth with this resolute mind to

have to do with the like matters that the common people have but not to entangle themselves with the like passions and moods by the which their matters do rise. (*Cicero*, 993–1009)

Plutarch attributes Cicero's failure to bear his exile with equanimity to the victory of 'glory and opinion' (*doxa*) over reason (*logos*), for exile is shameful only if it is the result of a moral transgression. Instead, Cicero is guided by the wrongful opinion of 'the common people', who hold that exile is dishonourable in itself, and the consequent damage to his reputation (the secondary meaning of both the Greek *doxa* and early modern English 'opinion'). What is more, Plutarch relates Cicero's moral failure to his role as an orator-statesman. Because of his participation in popular politics, and consequent need to adapt his speech to the disposition of his audience, the orator risks becoming tainted by the opinions and passions (*pathē*) of the people unless he has a 'resolute mind' (*phylattomenos*, being on his guard, in Plutarch's Greek). Plutarch thus suggests that despite Cicero's own claims to be more of a philosopher than an orator, as the author of a number of treatises on moral philosophy, the opposite is in fact the case (although elsewhere he offers a more positive assessment of the relationship between Cicero's 'two lives', notably when in the Comparison he presents Cicero as the fulfilment of Plato's ideal of the philosopher-king, the ruler who is educated in, and guided by, philosophy).

The desire for honour associated with the orator-statesman's involvement in popular politics is, in fact, the first of the three main shared characteristics of Demosthenes and Cicero identified by Plutarch in the introduction to the pair of Lives: loving honour (*philotimos*), loving freedom (*phileleutheros*), and lacking courage in dangers and war (*kindynous kai polemous atolmos*) (the latter two considered above).[3] *Philotimia* can be virtuous, as Aristotle explains in the *Nicomachean Ethics*, if not pursued too much, nor indeed too little, nor from the wrong source.[4] Both Demosthenes and Cicero enter into public life motivated by a desire for honour. Demosthenes decides to become an orator after he comes to be 'greatly in love with the honour [*doxa*] which the orator [Callistratus, whom he observed as a schoolboy] had gotten' (*Demosthenes*, 115–16) and Cicero 'being by nature ambitious of honour [*philotimos*] [...], in the end [...] began to plead' (*Cicero*, 129–31). In his encounter with Catiline, Cicero is likewise spurred on by his concern for honour and reputation, which overcomes his timorousness.[5] In *Cicero*, however, *philotimia* is more often a

---

[3] As noted in *Plutarch: 'Demosthenes and Cicero'*, ed. by Andrew Lintott (Oxford: Oxford University Press, 2013), p. 58, Cicero himself discusses oratory under *gloria* (the Latin equivalent of *philotimia*) in *De officiis* ('Of Duties').
[4] Aristotle, *Nicomachean Ethics*, 1125B.
[5] E.g. 'he himself should be thought a coward and timorous man, whereas they had already not much better opinion [*dokōn*] of him' (*Cicero*, lines 577–78); 'the goddess had raised this great flame to show him that he should have great honour [*doxa*] by doing of it' (*Cicero*, lines 586–87).

weakness than it is a strength, reflected in North's consistent translation of the term as 'ambition' in *Cicero*, even when Amyot offers a more neutral translation of the Greek (as in the passage quoted above, where Amyot has 'desireux d'honneur').[6] In particular, Cicero's excessive ambition eventually becomes not only the cause of his own death but also a catalyst for the transformation of Rome from the republic into the principate and thus comes into direct conflict with the supposed guiding thread of his political career, the love of the freedom of his country (the relationship between the two highlighted by the likeness of the Greek terms: *philo-timos* and *phil-eleutheros*). Plutarch writes that Octavian 'finely served his turn by Cicero's ambition, having persuaded him to require the consulship through the help and assistance that he would give him' (*Cicero*, 1415–17); as soon as he has secured the consulship, Octavian abandons Cicero and bargains away his life in the negotiations with the other triumvirs, Mark Antony and Lepidus.

Excessive ambition is related to Cicero's other major moral flaw: the tendency for his passions to overcome reason. Because Cicero places himself at the mercy of his unruly passions and the opinions of others, he is unable to follow his reason and political principles consistently, and the Life presents Cicero changing his mind time after time: he vacillates when the senate discusses the punishment for the Catilinarian conspirators; he first joins Caesar to defend himself against Clodius and then abandons him when Clodius makes overtures; he is irresolute when Caesar advances on Rome and Pompey flees, eventually joining Pompey before abandoning his cause in turn; even when fleeing his death, he changes course. Cicero's changeability is contrasted with Demosthenes' consistency in moral and political action (as well as his lack of ambition, a word used not once in reference to Demosthenes in North's translation).[7] The *synkrisis* juxtaposes Demosthenes' unswerving commitment to the public good of Athens, and his implacable opposition to the Macedonian kings who threatened its liberty, with Cicero's failure to oppose Octavian. Although the cause of Cicero's banishment was much more honourable than Demosthenes', the Roman orator 'idly passed his time of banishment and did nothing' while 'one of the chiefest acts that Demosthenes did in all the time that he dealt in the affairs of the commonwealth was in his banishment' (*Comparison of Demosthenes and Cicero*, 105–08). Likewise, on his return to Athens, Demosthenes immediately resumed his former policy of opposing the Macedonian invaders, but Cicero 'sat still and said nothing' when Octavian sued for the consulate and so 'maintained and nourished a more grievous and greater tyranny than that which they had put down' (*Comparison of Demosthenes and Cicero*, 114, 118–19). In the Life itself, Plutarch defends Demosthenes

---

[6] Amyot, *Vies* (1574), p. 1038.
[7] See Moles, *Cicero*, p. 22.

against the criticism of the historian Theopompus that Demosthenes lacked consistency in his politics and approvingly cites the philosopher Panaetius saying that the reason is his adherence to unchanging moral rectitude (*to kalon*; North: 'honesty') for its own sake instead of 'that which is most pleasant, easiest, or most profitable' (*Demosthenes*, 380–81), which are all contingent.[8] North gives further prominence to this aspect of his character through his use of the language of 'constancy'.[9] In the section on Theopompus, he twice repeats 'constant' (359, 374) and highlights it in the marginal note (362 **Marg.**), combining it with a series of related terms to emphasise the orator's persistence in the same policy: 'he ever continued firm and constant in one mind' (374). Likewise, in the episode in which Plutarch defends Demosthenes against the orator Aeschines, who accused him of 'having little love or charity unto his own children' (604–05) because he 'came abroad in his best gown and crowned with flowers' (602–03) within a week of his daughter's death when news arrived of the death of Philip of Macedon, the narrative voice (in North's words) instead commends his 'patience and constancy' (607–08) in bearing adversity and his 'constancy and courage' (619) in putting the good of the commonwealth before his private grief, a point reinforced in a marginal note using the same term (621 **Marg.**). In neither episode does Plutarch in fact use the term *constant*, except once in its negative form (*a-bebaios*).[10] North instead expands on Amyot, who uses variants of the word in three of the five instances, and Cruser, who includes *constantia* in his note to the first, but not the second, episode.

The actual narratives of the Lives of the two orators are, however, more complex and ambiguous than the neat dichotomies of the Comparison suggests.[11] Nowhere is this more obvious than in the descriptions of their exiles, where the actions of Demosthenes and Cicero are linked to each other through the repetition of words and images:

> So he took his banishment unmanly and remained the most part of his banishment in the city of Aegina or at the city of Troezen, where oftentimes he would cast his eyes towards the country of Attica and weep bitterly. (*Demosthenes*, 755–58)

> [Cicero] was always sad and could not be merry, but cast his eyes still towards Italy, as passioned lovers do towards the women they love, showing

---

[8] *Demosthenes*, 13. 4. The term is repeated twice in this passage by Plutarch; on its significance, see Lintott, pp. 5–8. North (who repeats 'honest' and 'honesty' thrice and a further time in a marginal note on the passage) follows Amyot, who in turn echoes Cicero's *De officiis*, which renders *kalon* as *honestum*.

[9] On 'constant' and 'constancy' in North's translation of Plutarch's *Brutus*, *Antony*, and *Coriolanus*, see Miles, pp. 110–22.

[10] *Demosthenes*, 13. 1.

[11] See Moles, *Cicero*, pp. 24–26 (but contrast the general comments on the formal comparisons in Duff, pp. 243–86).

himself faint-hearted, and took this adversity more basely than was looked for of one so well studied and learned as he. (*Cicero*, 995–99)

Both men demonstrate excessive sorrow and piningly 'cast [their] eyes' to their homeland (two different verbs in Plutarch's Greek, but North's translation brings out the correspondence in their meaning).[12] Plutarch uses gendered imagery ('unmanly': *malakōs*) to express the failure of reason to exercise control over the passions, in accordance with the common equation of masculinity with self-control and femininity with the passions. The Greek author specifically notes that Demosthenes' statements during his banishment contradicted the tenor of his politics: they 'were [not] answerable to the noble things he was wont to persuade in his orations' [*tois en tē politeia neanieumasin*] (lines 759–60). During his exile, Demosthenes also counsels young men to turn their back on politics, in conflict with his characteristic commitment to public life. Elsewhere, his weaknesses likewise come into direct conflict with the alleged guiding thread of his life, his defence of Greek liberty against Macedonian tyranny. Demosthenes 'plied the pulpit no more as he was wont' (651) after Alexander the Great's military successes in Greece; he fails to warn the Athenians against the threat of Macedon as a result of a bribe (paragraph 25); and flees from the battle against Philip, when Plutarch specifically describes his conduct as the opposite of *kalos* (North too contrasts his cowardly behaviour in battle with his former conduct as 'an honest man', line 550). Though *Demosthenes* is often read as more one-dimensional than *Cicero*, the Greek orator, in fact, emerges as a similarly complex figure, and in many cases the parallels with his Roman counterpart bring out the contradictions in his character.

Translation

Translator

Thomas North was born the second son of Edward North, first Baron North, and his first wife, Alice Murfyn, in London in 1535.[13] He may have attended Peterhouse, Cambridge, and was admitted to Lincoln's Inn in 1556. His membership of the Inns of Court, which not only offered legal education but were also centres of literary activity, likely prompted the publication of his first translation, Antonio de Guevara's *The Dial of Princes* (1557).[14] *The Dial*

---

[12] *Demosthenes*, 26. 4; *Cicero*, 32. 4.
[13] The most reliable and up-to-date account of North's life is Tom Lockwood's entry in *ODNB*. See also Matthiessen, pp. 58–65; Harold H. Davis, 'The Military Career of Thomas North', *Huntington Library Quarterly*, 12 (1948–1949), 315–21.
[14] North's translation of *The Dial* is referenced in Jasper Heywood's well-known account of the blossoming of literary activity at the Inns of Court in the preface to his translation of

is a sprawling collection of historical anecdotes, not a few from Plutarch, that serve as a mirror for princes. The title page advertises that the translation is 'Englished oute of the Frenche', although the final section of the book claims to contain 'the letters (which were not in the Frenche Copie) conferred with the originall Spanishe copie'.[15] An expanded second edition was published in 1568; a third edition, in 1582; in the early 1590s North revised the work, but when a fourth edition was eventually published posthumously in 1619, it did not include his corrections, but those of Anthony Munday instead.[16]

North's second major publication, *The Moral Philosophy of Doni*, was published in 1570, with a second edition in 1601. The work comprises a collection of beast fables known as *The Fables of Bidpai*, which originated from India but which North translated from the Italian of Anton Francesco Doni. As the title suggests, the collection presents the tales as moral and political instruction for rulers, counsellors, and courtiers — a mirror for princes similar to Guevara's *Dial* and to Plutarch's *Lives* (as it was interpreted in the Renaissance). North dedicated his translation to the Italophile patron of letters Robert Dudley, Earl of Leicester, a close friend of his brother Roger. A few years after the publication of *The Moral Philosophy of Doni*, in 1574, North had the opportunity to put his skills in modern languages into practice when he accompanied his brother Roger on an embassy to the French court at Lyon to congratulate the new king Henri III on his accession to the throne. The embassy may have also prompted his next publication, the translation of Plutarch's *Lives* from the French of Jacques Amyot, published in 1579 (see below).

North married twice, first to Elizabeth Colville, with whom he had two children (Edward and Elizabeth), and then to Judith Vesey. He received the freedom of the city of Cambridge, where he appears to have been mainly resident, in 1568 and served as a justice of the peace in the city in the 1590s. As a second son, however, he lacked financial independence and security, and he spent the final two-and-a-half decades of his life largely in military service. He served as a captain in Ireland at the time of the rebellions of the earls of Desmond (from 1580 to 1582) and Tyrone (in 1596), when he was accused of neglecting his men. He also took a company of soldiers to the Netherlands to fight the Spanish under Leicester in 1587 and trained and commanded men from Ely to defend England against the Spanish invasion in 1588; he was knighted shortly afterwards. He helped to put down the rebellion of the Earl

---

Seneca's *Thyestes* (1560). See Jessica Winston, *Lawyers at Play: Literature, Law, and Politics at the Early Modern Inns of Court, 1558–1581* (Oxford: Oxford University Press, 2016), pp. 46–47.

[15] Antonio de Guevara, *The diall of princes*, trans. by Thomas North (1557), sig. X5r. See further *The Diall of Princes: by Don Anthony of Guevara, Translated by Sir Thomas North*, ed. by K. N. Colvile (London: Philip Allan, 1919).

[16] Kelly A. Quinn, 'Sir Thomas North's Marginalia in his *Dial of Princes*', *Publications of the Bibliographical Society of America*, 94 (2000), 283–87.

of Essex in 1601 and received an annual pension of £40 from the queen in the same year. In the dedication to his translation of fifteen non-Plutarchan *Lives* of ancient Greeks and Romans in the following year (1602), North thanked the queen for 'comforting and supporting my poore old decaying life', and he seems to have died shortly afterwards.

Historical Context

North's translation of Amyot's French version of Plutarch's *Lives* is likely to have its origin in the embassy to the French court, at that time resident in Lyon, in 1574. In October and November of that year, Thomas accompanied his elder brother Roger North on a mission to congratulate the new king, Henri III, on his accession to the throne following the death of his elder brother Charles IX. North may well have met Amyot there, as the French translator of Plutarch had acted as a tutor to both the old and the new kings in their youth. Even if he did not, North would have undoubtedly heard of the king's tutor and his translation. Moreover, it is almost certain that he purchased his copy of Amyot's *Vies* on his visit to Lyon because, as demonstrated below, North relied for his translation on the edition printed in nearby Lausanne in the exact year of the embassy (1574).[17]

North followed Amyot in dedicating his translation to the reigning monarch, replacing Amyot's dedication to Henri II (the father of the later kings Charles IX and Henri III) with one to Queen Elizabeth. He conventionally praised Elizabeth's virtues and learning, and expressed the hope that 'the common sorte of [her] subjects, shall not onely profit themselves hereby, but also be animated to the better service of your Majestie'.[18] North also added an address to the readers, in which he famously declared that

> there is no prophane studie better then Plutarke. All other learning is private, fitter for Universities then cities, fuller of contemplacion than experience, more commendable in the students themselves, than profitable unto others. Whereas stories [histories] are fit for every place, reache to all persons, serve for all times, teache the living, revive the dead, so farre excelling all other bookes, as it is better to see learning in noble mens lives, than to reade it in Philosophers writings.[19]

As well as dedicating the book to Elizabeth, North arranged for a physical

---

[17] Dennis McCarthy, 'Thomas North Was the "T. N." Who Prefaced Belleforest's *Tragicall Hystories*', *Notes and Queries*, 54 (2007), 244–48, argues that North echoed the phrasing of his translation of Amyot's address to the reader in a preface to the English translation of Belleforest printed in 1577, and had thus at least started on his translation of the *Lives* by this date, and notes that copies of Amyot's *Vies* were not always easy to get hold of for Englishmen at the time.

[18] North, *Lives* (1579), sig. *2r.

[19] Ibid., sig. *3r.

presentation of his translation to the queen and received a reward of unknown value, which was however enlarged by £10 at the instigation of her principal secretary William Cecil, Lord Burghley.

The printer of North's translation was a French Huguenot immigrant, Thomas Vautrollier. Vautrollier specialised in the publication of translations from the French and produced several books in French or about France during the 1570s. Another specialism of Vautrollier was Protestant theology, including the first English translation of Calvin's *Institutes* (1574).[20] North's brother Roger was a staunch Protestant and close friend of the most prominent supporter of the puritans, Robert Dudley, Earl of Leicester, although there is little direct evidence of North's own religious views.

Sources

The title page of North's *Lives* states that it is a translation of Jacques Amyot's French version, first published in 1559, rather than of the original Greek:

> The lives of the noble Grecians and Romanes, compared together by that grave learned Philosopher and Historiographer, Plutarke of Chaeronea: Translated out of Greeke into French by James Amyot, Abbot of Bellozane, Bishop of Auxerre, one of the Kings privy counsel, and great Amner of Fraunce, and out of French into Englishe, by Thomas North.[21]

Amyot's translation enjoyed high repute in sixteenth-century Europe due to its philological and stylistic accomplishments. Amyot consulted numerous manuscripts in France and Italy in an attempt to improve the text of the existing Greek editions of Plutarch's *Lives*, and the superiority of his text is acknowledged by the mid-sixteenth-century Latin translators Xylander and Cruser, who adopted numerous variants from his French version. Cruser equally commended the elegance of his prose, while Montaigne famously praised the 'simplicity and purity of his language' as well as the 'profundity of his knowledge', bestowing on Amyot the accolade of the greatest writer (not just translator) in French.[22]

Amyot's philological labours in establishing the correct Greek text of Plutarch's *Lives* were part and parcel of a wider humanist endeavour to render the meaning of the original faithfully. This is reflected in his multiple revisions to the translation of the *Lives*, which made the text progressively more accurate

---

[20] Andrew Pettegree, 'Vautrollier, Thomas', *ODNB*.
[21] North, *Lives* (1579), title page.
[22] MacCallum, p. 134; John Denton, 'Renaissance Translation Strategies and the Manipulation of a Classical Text: Plutarch from Jacques Amyot to Thomas North', in *Europe et traduction*, ed. by Michel Ballard (Arras: Artois Presses Université, 1998), pp. 67–78 (pp. 69–70); Montaigne, *Essais*, II. 4 (p. 382), trans. by Screech, p. 408.

and precise.²³ In addition to this — and sometimes in tension with it — Amyot aimed to make Plutarch's text clear and comprehensible to his sixteenth-century audience, including countless small glosses and explanatory comments to the Greek text. Many of these are of a historical nature. When Plutarch refers to rhetorical *actio* ('l'action') in *Demosthenes*, for example, Amyot adds 'c'est à dire, la belle maniere de prononcer avec geste de mesme' ('to wit, the comely manner and gesture in his oration', *Demosthenes*, 188), marked clearly as an explanatory gloss by the phrase 'c'est à dire'.²⁴ Likewise, he explains that Antiphanes is a poet and Tesmophoria the feast of Ceres.²⁵ Amyot also includes additions that clarify the narrative, for instance (Amyot's additions in italics):

> First, touching the stammering of his tongue, *which was very fat* and made him that he could not pronounce all syllables distinctly, he did help it by putting of little pebble stones into his mouth *which he found upon the sands by the river's side* and so pronounced *with open mouth* the orations *he had without book*. And for his *small and soft* voice, he made that louder by running up steep and high hills, uttering even with full breath some orations or verses *that he had without book*. (*Demosthenes*, 292–98)²⁶

In some cases, elucidations or modernizations shade into interpretations reflecting or imposing the translator's ideology. Thus, Plutarch's 'priestess' (*hiereia*) is consistently translated by Amyot as 'religieuse' (North: 'nun'), which (like its English equivalent) could refer to a priestess, but had strong Christian connotations.²⁷ When Plutarch refers to 'strife betwixt the debtors and creditors', Amyot adds 'which grew by reason of usury' ('à raison des usures', *Caesar*, 327–28), a practice proscribed by Christianity.²⁸ Although Amyot claimed (in North's translation) that 'the office of a fit translater, consisteth not onely in the faithfull expressing of his authors meaning, but also in a certaine resembling and shadowing out of the forme of his style and the maner of his speaking', a style which he described as 'rather sharpe, learned, and short, than plaine, polished, and easie', he adapted his style to the expectations of early modern readers in various ways.²⁹ Amyot's frequent addition of doublets is the most notable element of his style, but he equally included various other forms of rhetorical embellishment to and expansions of Plutarch's Greek.³⁰ All of these

---

²³ René Sturel, *Jacques Amyot: traducteur des 'Vies parallèles' de Plutarque* (Paris: Champion, 1908), esp. pp. 308–22, 524–51.
²⁴ *Demosthenes*, 7. 2; Amyot, *Vies* (1574), p. 1021.
²⁵ *Demosthenes*, 9. 5, 30. 4; Amyot, *Vies* (1574), pp. 1022, 1034.
²⁶ *Demosthenes*, 11. 1; Amyot, *Vies* (1574), p. 1023.
²⁷ *Demosthenes*, 14. 4. *Dictionnaire de la langue française du seizième siècle*, ed. by Edmond Huguet, 7 vols (Paris: Champion; Didier, 1925–1973), s.v. religieuse; *OED*, nun, n.¹, 1. b.
²⁸ *Caesar*, 12. 1; Amyot, *Vies* (1574), p. 865. See below for further examples.
²⁹ North, *Lives* (1579), sig. *7r; Amyot, *Vies* (1574), p. 865.
³⁰ These features of Amyot's translation were famously censured by Claude-Gaspar

features of Amyot's translation are, to a greater or a lesser extent, reflected in North's English version.

There has been no systematic scholarly attempt to establish the edition of Amyot used by North, unsurprisingly perhaps given the extremely large number of editions on the market — USTC records about forty by 1579 — and the absence of a critical edition of the *Vies* to assist with the task of distinguishing between the different editions.[31] The question is significant, however, because in addition to minor textual variations North's translation borrows a substantial number of components from the French source edition.[32] In particular, it includes Donato Acciaiuoli's *Lives of Scipio and Hannibal*, as all editions published after 1567 do (but not the authorised first three editions of Amyot, published by Michel de Vascosan in Paris in 1559, 1565, and 1567); the majority of the (relatively few) printed marginal notes that had been included in editions since the second authorised edition of 1565 (generally marked by an asterisk in the text); and the medallions of the Greeks and Romans that are the subject of Plutarch's work first included in Jean Le Preux's editions of 1572.[33] One indicator of the edition used by North is the phrasing of the title page, which distinctively combines Amyot's position as Bishop of Auxerre (created in 1570) with his former position as Abbot of Bellozanne, but not his present benefice of Saint-Corneille près de Compiègne. The word-for-word correspondence of North's title with a small cluster of editions published in the mid to late 1570s strongly suggests that he used one of three editions of Amyot's *Vies* published in Lausanne by François Le Preux in 1574 and 1575.[34] This is confirmed by textual evidence. North erroneously names the conspirator and close friend of Caesar who convinced him to come to the senate on the Ides of March as Decius Brutus instead of Decimus Brutus (*Caesar*, 1868). Le Preux's editions of 1574 and 1575 have 'Decius' too, but all other editions that I have consulted have the

Bachet in his address to the Académie française in 1635. See Denton, *Translation and Manipulation*, p. 49 n. 20.

[31] Sturel, Appendix III, sets out the relationship between some of the main editions of Amyot's *Vies* between 1559 and 1619.

[32] *Pace Shakespeare's Plutarch*, ed. by C. F. Tucker Brooke, 2 vols (London: Chatto & Windus, 1909), I, 19: 'It seems hardly possible to ascertain which of these versions was used by North, nor is the matter of any real consequence.'

[33] The significance of the medallions in determining North's source edition is pointed out in Vanna Gentili, *La Roma antica degli elisabettiani* (Bologna: Il Mulino, 1991), p. 36 n. 22, though John Denton, 'Renaissance Translation Strategies', p. 70 n. 6, rightly notes that they appeared in editions from 1572.

[34] Editions that include 'lors Abbé de Bellozane, à present Evesque d'Auxerre', while omitting 'maintenant Abbé de saincte Corneille de Compiegne', on the title page, and that are published before 1579, are USTC, 564264 (Lausanne: François Le Preux, 1574); USTC, 47642 (Lausanne: François Le Preux, 1574); USTC, 30106 (Lausanne: François Le Preux, 1575); USTC, 60698 (Paris: Michel de Vascosan et Fédéric Morel, 1577) — the latter less likely because of the proximity of its publication date to that of North's translation.

correct reading, 'Decimus'.³⁵ A further textual detail, finally, points to the exact edition used by North. When Caesar compares himself with Alexander early in the Life, North's translation renders his words as follows: 'King Alexander, being no older than myself is now, had in old time won so many nations and countries and [...] I hitherunto have done nothing worthy of myself' (316-18). In Amyot, this declaration had ended with the phrase 'digne de memoire' (worthy of memory), but in one of the 1574 editions, there is a line-break after 'memoi', without a hyphen (the next line starting with 're').³⁶ Although 'memoi' is not French, it is easy to see how it could have prompted North's 'myself'.

While North generally follows Amyot very closely (as I discuss below), some features of the edition cannot be explained by his translation or its paratexts. The most substantial component of North's translation absent from editions of Amyot published before 1579 is the extensive body of printed marginalia. North generally reproduces the few marginal notes that appear in Amyot's translation, comprised largely of variant readings and historical information on ancient money and dress, but he also adds a large number of summarizing and moralizing comments.³⁷ My research has revealed that the large majority of North's marginalia derive from the Dutch humanist Hermann Cruser's (Cruserius's) Latin translation of Plutarch's *Lives* (1564) (although by no means all: evidently North added some marginal comments himself).³⁸ This explains why there are sometimes contradictions between the main text and the marginal notes; for example when the conspirators go to the forum ('marketplace', 1962) in the main text of *Caesar* but to the Capitol in the side-note.³⁹ Some elements of North's translation also indicate a reliance on Cruser's version. When Caesar raids the monetary reserves in Rome to fund his campaign against Pompey, for instance, North locates the treasury in 'the temple of Saturn' (*Caesar*, 1074). Neither Plutarch nor Amyot make any mention of this building, but Cruser refers to it both in his marginal note (where North presumably came across it)

---

³⁵ E.g. Amyot, *Vies* (1574), p. 895. I have been unable to consult the 1577 edition by Vascosan and Morel, of which USTC records only a single copy, in the Bibliothèque municipale in Châlons-en-Champagne. North repeats 'Decius' in line 1916, and in two marginal notes, so it is not a simple misprint.

³⁶ Amyot, *Vies* (1574), p. 865 (USTC, 47642). The line breaks are located elsewhere in the two other editions printed in 1574-1575 and all other editions of Amyot's *Vies* that I have consulted.

³⁷ See Valerie Worth, 'Les fortunes de Jacques Amyot en Angleterre: une traduction de Sir Thomas North', in *Fortunes de Jacques Amyot: actes du colloque international (Melun, 18-20 avril 1985)*, ed. by Michel Balard ([Paris]: A.-G. Nizet, 1986), pp. 285-95 (pp. 289-91).

³⁸ On Cruser, see Günter Bers, *Die Schriften des niederländischen Humanisten Dr. Hermann Cruser* (Nieuwkoop: De Graaf, 1971).

³⁹ *Caesar*, line 1965 **Marg.**; *Plutarchi* [...] *vitae comparatae illustrium virorum, graecorum et romanorum*, trans. by Hermann Cruser (Basel: Thomas Guarin, 1573), p. 587. The discrepancy between text and notes is noted, but not explained, in Brooke, I, 196.

and in the text itself.⁴⁰ North's otherwise incomprehensible choice to convert a Greek verse quotation in Plutarch's text into Latin, 'sic recepit sicut cepit' (*Demosthenes*, 267), followed by an English equivalent, is similarly explained by his use of Cruser's translation, which renders the phrase in precisely these words.⁴¹ Although the term *stratēgos* was sometimes used by Greek historians to refer to the Roman office of praetor (which involved, in its various manifestations, both military command and political and judicial authority), it is difficult to imagine that North's use of the Roman term *praetor* to describe the fourth-century BCE Greek general Timotheus, labelled a 'Capitaine' by Amyot, was prompted by anything other than Cruser's Latin translation, which uses the expression in this context.⁴² Likewise, when North calls Cicero's executioner Popillius 'tribune of the soldiers (to wit, colonel of a thousand men)' (*Cicero*, 1493–94), it appears that the first part of his description derives from Cruser (who has 'tribunus'), just as the second half comes from Amyot, who renders Plutarch's *chiliarchos* simply as 'Capitaine de mille hommes'.⁴³ It is unlikely that North would have arrived at 'the Corcyriaeians' from Amyot's 'ceux de Corfou', but it corresponds closely to Cruser's 'Corcyraei' (for the Greek *Kerkyraioi*).⁴⁴ The Greek names of the months included by North are not found in Amyot either, and his use of 'Munychion' (*Demosthenes*, 812) for *Metageitniōn* indicates that he relied on Cruser's Latin rather than the original Greek.⁴⁵ The evidence suggests not only that North drew on Cruser's Latin version of Plutarch's *Lives* in addition to Amyot's French translation, but also that, *pace* Brooke, it was the translator, not the printer, who was responsible for the printed marginal notes in the volume — a point further supported by the fact that North supplied marginal headings in the manuscript revisions to *The Dial of Princes*.⁴⁶

F. O. Matthiessen already observed that in a number of places North appears to have consulted the original Greek text of the *Lives*.⁴⁷ Some of these instances may have derived from Cruser (as in the case of the names of the months), but several other features of North's translation cannot be explained from editions of Amyot or Cruser.⁴⁸ Matthiessen refers, for example, to North's attempt to

---

⁴⁰ Cruser, *Vitae* (1573), p. 578.
⁴¹ Cruser, *Vitae* (1573), p. 593. Xylander's Latin translation, in contrast, has 'Ita [...] recepit, ut accepit' (*Parallela*, p. 744).
⁴² *Demosthenes*, line 417; Amyot, *Vies* (1574), p. 1025; Cruser, *Vitae* (1573), p. 595.
⁴³ *Cicero*, 48. 1; Amyot, *Vies* (1574), p. 1063; Cruser, *Vitae* (1573), p. 615.
⁴⁴ *Demosthenes*, line 477 Textual Note; Amyot, *Vies* (1574), p. 1026; Cruser, *Vitae* (1573), p. 595. 'the Corcyriaeians' is the reading of the editions of 1579 and 1595, but in the third edition of 1603 North emends to 'those of Corfu': see Textual Notes p. 259.
⁴⁵ See also *Caesar*, nn. 255, 257.
⁴⁶ Brooke, I, 196; Quinn, p. 284.
⁴⁷ Matthiessen, pp. 71–74.
⁴⁸ Nor are they found, as far as I have been able to determine, in the marginal notes or commentary to any pre-1580 editions of Amyot's translation, the collected Latin *Lives* by

reproduce a Greek pun in the first edition of his translation, published in 1579. When Demosthenes claims to be unable to speak in the Athenian assembly after having been bribed by Harpalus, his opponents quip that 'it was no sinanche that had stopped his weezle [windpipe] that night, as he would make them believe, but it was Harpalus' argentsinanche which he had received that made him in that case' (*Demosthenes*, 724–26). North's 'sinanche' and 'argentsinanche' are Anglicizations of the Greek *synanchē* (sore throat) and *argyranchē* (money-throatache, with the Latin and French stem *argent-* the equivalent of the Greek *argyr-*), respectively. Amyot's French rendering ('une esquinance ... l'argent') does not signal the wordplay; instead, North may have been alerted to the pun by Cruser's Latin version ('angina ... argentangina'), whose structure his phrasing echoes; however, he would have needed recourse to the Greek to arrive at 'sinanche'.[49] Other examples are North's inclusion of the Greek terms for the philosophical concepts for which Cicero produced Latin equivalents (1238–42); sums of money that match the Greek but not Amyot's French (in écus) or Cruser's Latin (*Demosthenes*, 125; *Cicero*, 219, 227–28, 1353–54); and Greek quotations in the margin (*Demosthenes*, 268 **Marg.**; *Cicero*, 769 **Marg.**). North, therefore, seems to have consulted a Greek edition of the *Lives* in addition to Amyot and Cruser, most likely the Graeco-Latin edition of Plutarch's works published by Henri Estienne (Stephanus) in 1572, both the most recent Greek edition of the text and the sole original-language edition to include a Latin translation published prior to the publication of North's translation (in separate volumes, but with the corresponding pages of the Greek text keyed in the margin). Although the Latin translation included in Estienne's edition was Cruser's, North cannot have relied exclusively on this edition because it does not incorporate the marginal notes found in other editions.

North thus used both a Latin and a Greek edition of the text in addition to Amyot's French, but he evidently consulted them only very intermittently because (as we shall shortly see) many of the errors and peculiarities of his translation could easily have been prevented through reference to one of these editions. A notable example are the many Greek and Roman names, for which North frequently uses the French form or reconstructs the original, in the words of Matthiessen, 'as it would seem, purely by guess'.[50] Thus, North normally relied exclusively on the French of Amyot, and only in exceptional circumstances had recourse to either the Greek or the Latin.

---

various translators published throughout the first half of the sixteenth century (used by Morley), Xylander's Latin version (first published in 1561), or Estienne's 1572 Graeco-Latin edition (which mostly reproduces the commentary in Xylander's translation).

49 Amyot, *Vies* (1574), p. 1031; Cruser, *Vitae* (1573), p. 598.
50 Matthiessen, p. 71.

Translation Method

North's translation of Plutarch's *Lives* has long enjoyed a reputation as 'one of the great monuments of English prose'.[51] The editor of the late nineteenth-century Tudor Translations edition, Sir George Wyndham, thought it 'worthy to stand with Malory's *Morte Darthur* on either side the English Bible', while F. O. Matthiessen in his study of Elizabethan translation described North's translation as 'after Malory's *Morte D'Arthur* and the *Book of Common Prayer* [...] the earliest great masterpiece of English prose'.[52] Matthiessen credited the excellence of the translation to a 'picturesque vigor' that gave expression to the personality of North and his time.[53] While more recent scholars have rightly questioned Matthiessen's often impressionistic claims and value judgements, they concur that, in the words of Gordon Braden, 'North found a highly credible voice in which ancient civilization might speak with authority and force in a contemporary environment'.[54]

In most respects, North's *Lives* is a very close translation of Amyot's *Vies*. The English translator tends to follow the structure of the French sentences clause by clause and often word for word. Frequently, North uses cognates of Amyot's French words, for instance when he renders 'hasarder son credit et sa reputation à la merci de la fortune' as 'hazard his credit and reputation to the mercy of fortune' (*Demosthenes*, 255–56) or 'c'estoient les plus honestes causes qu'on alleguast de leur divorce' as 'And these were the honestest causes alleged for their divorce' (*Cicero*, 1275–76).[55] Clearly, the similarity of the French language compared to ancient Greek (and Latin), both in terms of grammatical structure and vocabulary, was a major draw for North. Not infrequently, however, North's tendency to mirror the structure of the French clause for clause results in anacoluthon (changing the grammatical structure mid-way through a sentence) or other grammatical inaccuracies, because he fails to retain the exact relationship between the clauses.[56] In the following sentence from *Demosthenes*, for instance, North's addition of the relative 'whereupon' confuses the relationship between the initial subordinate participle clause and the following main clause: 'In fine, wars falling out between them, because Philip, of the one side, could not live in peace and the Athenians, on the other side, were still incensed and stirred up by Demosthenes' daily orations, the Athenians first sent into the Isle of Euboea ...' (*Demosthenes*, 453–56).[57]

---

[51] Robert Adger Law, 'The Text of *Shakespeare's Plutarch*', *Huntington Library Quarterly*, 6 (1943), 197–203 (p. 197).
[52] Quoted in ibid.
[53] Matthiessen, pp. 82, 90.
[54] Braden, 'Classical Translation', p. 111.
[55] Amyot, *Vies* (1574), pp. 1022, 1059.
[56] See Matthiessen, p. 74.
[57] Amyot, *Vies* (1574), p. 1026: 'Mais à la fin les choses estans tournees à la guerre, pource

Likewise, in the introduction to the *Demosthenes-Cicero* pair North reproduces the exact order of the clauses in Amyot, but progressively loses his hold on their connection:

> first of all he must needs remain in some great and famous city throughly inhabited, where men do delight in good and virtuous things, because there are [Amyot: 'so that he has'] commonly plenty of all sorts of books, and that [not in Amyot] perusing them, and hearing talk also of many things besides which other historiographers peradventure have not written of, and which will carry so much more credit because men that are alive may presently speak of them as of their own knowledge, whereby [not in Amyot] he may make his work perfect in every point, having many and divers necessary things contained in it. (*Demosthenes*, 26–34)[58]

North also replicates Amyot's errors in translating the Greek, for example calling Attia the sister of Julius Caesar instead of his niece (*Cicero*, 1381); the temple of Aeacus (*to Aiakeion*), ancestral hero of Aegina, the temple of Ajax (*Demosthenes*, 828–29); and Vibo, Vibone (*Cicero*, 979).[59] In contrast to many classical translators in the period, North adds little to his source text because Amyot had already adapted Plutarch's text for sixteenth-century readers by adding glosses and finding modern equivalents for unfamiliar terms and customs, although he does on occasion expand or clarify Amyot's text further; this was evidently another key attraction of Amyot's translation for North. North is not as precise a translator as Amyot, however, and every now and then he omits details. In many cases, these are relatively trivial, but in some instances North fails to convey an image or leaves out a significant detail. Early in *Caesar*, for instance, North casually omits Plutarch's specific reference to the eminence of Caesar's rivals for the senior public office of *Pontifex maximus* in the senate, translating Amyot's 'deux les plus notables personnages de la ville, et qui avoient plus d'authorité au Senat' (two of the most distinguished men of the city, and of the greatest authority in the senate) as 'two of the notablest men of the city and of greatest authority' (169–70), with the result that his translation fails to convey an important element of Plutarch's characterisation of Caesar as a demagogue, whose rise to power in Rome was based on his popularity with

---

que Philippus d'un costé ne pouvoit demeurer en paix, et les Atheniens de l'autre costé estoient poussez et suscitez par les ordinaires harangues de Demosthenes: les Atheniens envoierent premierement en l'isle d'Eubœe …'.

[58] Amyot, *Vies* (1574), p. 1018: 'premierement et devant toutes choses il soit demeurant en une grosse et noble cité, pleine de peuple et de grand nombre d'hommes, aimant les choses belles et honestes, à fin qu'il ait abondance de toutes sortes de livres, et qu'en cerchant çà et là, et entendant dire de vive voix beaucoup de choses, que les autres historiens auront à l'adventure omis à escrire, et qui seront de tant plus croyables, qu'elles seront encore demeurees en la memoire des hommes vivans, il puisse rendre son œuvre de tout point accomplie, et non defectueuse de plusieurs choses y necessaires'.

[59] Amyot, *Vies* (1574), pp. 1033, 1054, 1061. See further Matthiessen, pp. 74–76.

the people instead of his support in the senate.⁶⁰

Despite relying so closely on Amyot, North's translation makes a very different impression on the reader. Where Amyot writes fluent and balanced literary prose — Montaigne praised his French version of Plutarch for its 'pure elegancy' — North's translation is more colloquial and everyday.⁶¹ When using the idiomatic expression 'having fought beyond their powers', Plutarch adds 'as the saying is' (*tēn legomenēn*), expanded by Amyot to 'ainsi qu'on dit en commun langage' (as it is said in everyday language).⁶² North omits the phrase altogether: to him, it seems, it was evident he was writing 'en commun langage'. In particular, he has a tendency to turn abstract terms into concrete ones: 'heart' (*Demosthenes*, 226) for 'hardiesse' (boldness); 'a light housewife [woman of ill repute]' (*Cicero*, 804) for 'peu honeste'; 'he returned again to his book' (*Cicero*, 55-56) for 'il se remit à l'estude'.⁶³ North further has a penchant for idiomatic and proverbial expressions that use figurative language to express abstractions: 'this worm of ambition' (*Cicero*, 711-12) for 'ceste extreme ambition'; '[he] had almost even worn himself to the bones with study' (*Demosthenes*, 176-77) for 'il eust presque despendu toute sa vigueur et force de son corps à l'estude' (he had almost spent all the vigour and force of his body on study); 'they cast at their heels all fear of danger' (*Demosthenes*, 504-05) for 'ils oublierent toute crainte de danger'; and 'This killed his heart straight' (*Cicero*, 166) for 'Cela le descouragea fort sur l'heure' (This immediately discouraged him considerably).⁶⁴ A phrase such as 'he was no people-pleaser' (*Demosthenes*, 407) — the first recorded use of the expression — likewise is notably more conversational than Amyot's 'il se soucioit bien peu de la commune' (he was very little concerned about the people).⁶⁵ Another key element of North's colloquial style is his use of interjections in direct speech, for example in: '"Yea," replied Demosthenes sharply again, "so is there great difference, Pytheas, betwixt thy labour and mine by lamplight"' (*Demosthenes*, 215-16); '"What," quoth Cicero, "and will he come to supper too?"' (*Cicero*, 775).⁶⁶ At the same time as giving emphasis and point to their witticisms, these interjections mimic the oral nature of the orators' utterances. In sharp contrast to the vast majority of translators in the period, moreover, North reduces rather than increases the number of doublets, the hallmark of a rhetorical style in the period.⁶⁷ Unlike many other

---

⁶⁰ *Caesar*, 7. 1; Amyot, *Vies* (1574), p. 862.
⁶¹ Quoted in Matthiessen, p. 77.
⁶² *Caesar*, 20. 5; Amyot, *Vies* (1574), p. 871.
⁶³ Amyot, *Vies* (1574), pp. 1022, 1036, 1051.
⁶⁴ Amyot, *Vies* (1574), pp. 1021, 1027, 1039, 1049.
⁶⁵ Amyot, *Vies* (1574), p. 1025.
⁶⁶ Amyot, *Vies* (1574), pp. 1021, 1050.
⁶⁷ Matthiessen claims that 'Amyot had not been shy of using doublets for the sake of his rhythm, but North increases their numbers', although he then comments in a footnote that 'North sometimes [...] reduces Amyot's doublets' (p. 78). My count in *Demosthenes*, *Cicero*,

contemporary translators too, North tends to confine himself in his translation to words that are already in common usage rather than introducing new and unfamiliar words from the French or the Latin into the English language.[68]

While Matthiessen and others have offered detailed accounts of the differences in vocabulary and register between Amyot's French and North's English translations, less has been said about syntax and sentence structure. Valerie Worth has commented on North's habit of dividing up Amyot's long sentences by adding full stops.[69] At the start of paragraph 48 of *Caesar*, for example, North uses seven full stops to Amyot's one, replacing colons separating main clauses with full stops and leaving out coordinating conjunctions; elsewhere, he retains co-ordinating conjunctions and relatives and simply starts new sentences with them. This is, however, only one aspect of a much wider tendency to simplify Amyot's grammar. Thus, North commonly uses co-ordination instead of subordination. In the introduction to the *Demosthenes–Cicero* pair, for instance, North converts a subordinate participle clause followed by a main clause in Amyot, 'la fortune *ayant voulu* dés le commencement *former* à un mesme moule, par maniere de dire, Demosthenes et Ciceron, *a imprimé* en leurs natures plusieurs qualitez toutes semblables', into a straightforward coordinated construction: 'fortune even from the beginning *hath framed* in manner one self mould of Demosthenes and Cicero and *hath* in their natures *fashioned* many of their qualities one like to the other' (*Demosthenes*, 61–63).[70] Perhaps the most common and pervasive means by which North's translation reduces the complexity of Amyot's French is by decreasing the number of verbs. Compare for example North's straightforward and direct '[they] called his porter and bad him wake his master presently and tell him how they three were at the gate to speak with him' (*Cicero*, 433–34) with Amyot's 'appellerent le portier, et lui dirent qu'il allast esveiller son maistre, et lui faire entendre comme ils estoient eux trois à la porte, et qu'ils avoient à parler à lui' ([they] called the porter and told him to go wake his master and make him know that they three were [lit. they were them three] at the door and that they had to talk to him).[71] North also makes Amyot's writing simpler and more direct by using active instead of passive constructions: 'After he had said so' (*Demosthenes*, 850) for 'Ces paroles dites'; 'following a decree Demosthenes

and *Caesar* indicates that while he sometimes added doublets to Amyot, North considerably decreased their number overall.

[68] See John Denton, 'Wearing a Gown in the Market Place or a Toga in the Forum: Coriolanus from Plutarch to Shakespeare via Renaissance Translation', in *Shakespeare e la sua eredità*, ed. by Grazia Caliumi (Parma: Zara, 1993), pp. 97–109 (p. 100).

[69] Worth, p. 292. I have generally followed North's punctuation in this respect, although I have on occasion combined two sentences separated by a full stop into one or, conversely, divided a long sentence by introducing a full stop.

[70] Amyot, *Vies* (1574), p. 1018 (italics mine).

[71] Amyot, *Vies* (1574), pp. 1043–44.

had preferred' (*Demosthenes*, 457–58) for 'suivant un decret qui fut mis en avant par lui'; 'whom Sulla had by his ordinances deposed from their dignities and offices in Rome' (*Cicero*, 334–35) for 'il estoit defendu par les ordonnances de Sylla de tenir magistrats à Rome' (accompanied by a reduced number of verbs: 'had [...] deposed' for 'estoit defendu [...] de tenir').[72]

As with his choice of words, the effect of North's simplification of Amyot's grammar is a more direct and straightforward form of writing that is closer to everyday speech than Amyot's more literary style. This also results in a reduction in the literary effects of balance, suspense, and climax that the carefully constructed periods of Amyot's translation had been able to achieve (which had, in turn, repeatedly broken the periodic structure and balance of Plutarch's Greek).[73] A notable example is the final sentence of *Caesar*, which Plutarch and Amyot, each in their own way, construct to reflect the fact that the Life comes full circle with the death of Caesar's assassin Brutus. Plutarch's Greek is characteristically economical: following a parenthetical comment on how a friend helped to push the sword into his breast that delays the climax, he ends with a simple *apethanen* (he died): '[Brutus] retired to a crest of ground, put his naked sword to his breast (while a certain friend, as they say, helped to drive the blow home), and so died' (the last three words of the English translation rendering the Greek *apethanen*). Amyot's French is typically copious and balanced, ending after the digression on the friend who assisted Brutus's suicide: 'il se perça le corps d'outre en outre, et mourut sur le champ' (he pierced his own body right through and died on the spot). North joins the two logically related actions (falling on his sword and dying) by removing the digression on Brutus's companion and putting it at the end instead, but in doing so loses the pattern of suspense and climax that animates the other two versions: 'he ran unto a little rock not far off, and there setting his sword's point to his breast, fell upon it and slew himself, but yet, as it is reported, with the help of his friend that dispatched him' (2046–49).[74]

North, as has often been observed, makes the cultures of ancient Greece and Rome described in Plutarch's *Lives* sound very much like Elizabethan England, a result of his habit to substitute ancient Greek and Roman terms with contemporary English ones. In many cases, he simply follows Amyot, who substitutes 'hell' (*Caesar*, 113) for 'Hades' and 'the governors [...] of Thebes and of all the country of Boeotia' ('les gouverneurs de Thebes et du pays de la Bœoce', *Demosthenes*, 510) for the *boiōtarchai* (Thebes being the dominant member of the Boeotian League), and so on.[75] Elsewhere, though, North goes

---

[72] Amyot, *Vies* (1574), pp. 1026, 1033, 1042. On North's mistranslation of 'defendu' see n. ad loc.
[73] On Amyot's simplification of the structure of Plutarch's Greek, see Russell, pp. 150–58.
[74] *Caesar*, 69. 8; Amyot, *Vies* (1574), p. 898.
[75] Amyot, *Vies* (1574), pp. 861, 1027.

well beyond Amyot in domesticating Plutarch's language. Amyot on many occasions retains original Greek and Roman terms with an explanatory gloss introduced by the marker 'c'est à dire' (that is to say), but North often favours substitutions in such cases. Amyot's 'Quæsteur, c'est à dire, superintendant des finances' and 'Quæsteur, c'est à dire, Thresorier' are replaced with 'treasurer', the term consistently used by North throughout *Cicero* and *Caesar*.[76] Amyot's 'gladiateurs, c'est à dire, escrimeurs à outrance' is rendered as 'sword players' (*Caesar*, 132), 'Satrapes' become 'governors' (*Demosthenes*, 567), and an ancient Athenian publishes a work 'in print' (*Demosthenes*, 57; Amyot just has 'mettre hors en lumiere').[77] Domestication has been seen as a form of ethnocentrism, reflecting and reinforcing the values of translators and their societies.[78] This is indicated, for example, in North's reference to the Pontifex maximus (*archiereus*), the head of Rome's state religion, as the 'chief bishop' (*Caesar*, 169, 179) of Rome. On the one hand, this appellation elides the historical difference between the pagan religion of ancient Rome and early modern Christianity (whereas Amyot's 'le souverain Pontife' can refer to either); on the other hand, it introduces negative connotations to early modern English Protestant readers due to the Catholic undertones of the term 'bishop' and the conflation of ancient Rome with contemporary Rome as the centre of Catholicism and the seat of the pope (also known as the Pontifex maximus).[79]

Domestication is not confined to individual words or phrases. It is equally pertinent to literary genres and the philosophical and religious values they reflect. Thus, drawing on the medieval genre of *de casibus* tragedy, Amyot and especially North amplify the pity of the death of Cicero.[80] Plutarch had employed tragic patterning that evokes pity for the protagonists in the final sections of both *Demosthenes* and *Cicero*. In particular, there is a 'characteristically tragic [...] disproportion between suffering and error, the hero suffering more than his deserts'.[81] The tragic pathos of the death of Cicero is heightened in Amyot's and North's translations of the Comparison (starting with the fairly literal modern Loeb translation of the Greek, followed by North's):

ἐπὶ πᾶσι δὲ τῆς τελευτῆς τὸν μὲν οἰκτείραι τις ἄν, ἄνδρα πρεσβύτην δι'

[76] *Cicero*, line 17; *Caesar*, line 120; Amyot, *Vies* (1574), pp. 861, 1036.
[77] *Demosthenes*, 20. 4; Amyot, *Vies* (1574), pp. 862, 1018, 1028. On the gladiators, glossing, and modernisation in Amyot and North, see Denton, *Translation and Manipulation*, pp. 49–50.
[78] Lawrence Venuti, *The Translator's Invisibility: A History of Translation* (London: Routledge, 1995), p. 20 and passim.
[79] Amyot, *Vies* (1574), pp. 862, 863. See Burrow, p. 235; Denton, *Translation and Manipulation*, pp. 51–52.
[80] Cf. the analysis of North's translation of Plutarch's account of the death of Alcibiades in Plutarch, *The Lives of the Noble Grecians and Romans, Translated by Thomas North*, ed. by Judith Mossman (Ware: Wordsworth, 1998), pp. xviii–xix.
[81] Moles, *Cicero*, p. 199.

ἀγένvειαν ὑπὸ οἰκετῶν ἄνω καὶ κάτω περιφερόμενον καὶ περιφεύγοντα τὸν θάνατον καὶ ἀποκρυπτόμενον τοὺς οὐ πολὺ πρὸ τῆς φύσεως ἥκοντας ἐπ' αὐτόν, εἶτ' ἀποσφαγέντα.

[And after all, the one [i.e. Cicero] is to be pitied for the manner of his death — an old man ignobly carried up and down by servants, trying to escape death, hiding himself from those who were coming after him not much in advance of nature's final summons, and then beheaded.]

Et apres tout, la mort de Ciceron est miserable, de voir un povre vieillard, que par bonne affection envers leur maistre ses serviteurs trainoient çà et là, cerchant tous moyens de pouvoir eschapper et fuir la mort, laquelle ne le venoit trouver gueres de temps avant son cours naturel, et puis encore à la fin lui voir tout vieil qu'il estoit, ainsi piteusement trencher la teste.

And last of all, methinks the death of Cicero most pitiful, to see an old man carried up and down with tender love of his servants, seeking all the ways that might be to fly death, which did not long prevent his natural course, and in the end, old as he was, to see his head so pitifully cut off. (*Comparison of Demosthenes and Cicero*, 120-23)[82]

Plutarch's original says that Cicero's death 'is to be pitied' (οἰκτείραι), but North follows Amyot in adding a second reference to his pitiful state at the end of the sentence and strengthens the first by turning it into a superlative ('most pitiful'). This is reinforced by the addition of vivid narrative details that invoke sympathy to Plutarch's description of Cicero's death (all based on Amyot): the love of his servants, the additional reference to his old age, and the multiplicity of his doomed attempts to escape death. A similar pattern is on view in North's translation of Plutarch's earlier account of Cicero's death towards the end of the Life:

αὐτὸς δ', ὥσπερ εἰώθει, τῇ ἀριστερᾷ χειρὶ τῶν γενείων ἁπτόμενος ἀτενὲς ἐνεώρα τοῖς σφαγεῦσιν, αὐχμοῦ καὶ κόμης ἀνάπλεως καὶ συντετηκὼς ὑπὸ φροντίδων τὸ πρόσωπον, ὥστε τοὺς πλείστους ἐγκαλύψασθαι τοῦ Ἐρεννίου σφάζοντος αὐτόν.

[Then he himself, clasping his chin with his left hand, as was his wont, looked steadfastly at his slayers, his head all squalid and unkempt, and his face wasted with anxiety, so that most of those that stood by covered their faces while Herennius was slaying him.]

Penant sa barbe avec la main gauche, comme il avoit accoustumé, regarda franchement les meurtriers au visage, ayant les cheveux et la barbe tous herissez et poudreux, et le visage desfait et cousu pour les ennuis qu'il avoit supportez, de maniere que plusieurs des assistans se boucherent les yeux pendant que Herennius le sacrifioit.

Taking his beard in his left hand, as his manner was, he stoutly looked the

[82] *Comparison of Demosthenes and Cicero*, 5. 1; Amyot, *Vies* (1574), pp. 1066-67.

murderers in the faces, his head and beard being all white and his face lean and wrinkled for the extreme sorrows he had taken. Divers of them that were by held their hands before their eyes whilst Herennius did cruelly murder him. (1506–10)[83]

As in his translation of Plutarch's descriptions of the murders of Cicero's brother (*Cicero*, 1457–59) and Demosthenes, where the orator protests that his executioners defiled the temple 'with *blood and cruel* murder' (*Demosthenes*, 864; my italics), North adds a reference to the cruelty of the assassins.[84] He amplifies Cicero's sorrow by inserting the adjective 'extreme' and enhances his dignity and purity by converting Amyot's 'herissez et poudreux' (tousled and dusty) hairs and beard, which broadly follows the sense of Plutarch's original, into 'all white'. Once again, North's translation calls on the empathy of the reader for the tragic death of the protagonist. His changes reflect a conception of tragedy in which pity is the appropriate response to the condition of humanity governed by the wheel of fortune, which arbitrarily raises men to prosperity before bringing them low once again. Originating in Chaucer's reading of Boethius, who the medieval English poet translated as saying that 'What other thynge bywaylen the cryinges of tragedyes but oonly the dedes of Fortune, that with an unwar strook overturneth the realmes of greet nobleye?', this interpretation of tragedy was central to Lydgate's *Fall of Princes* and its sixteenth-century descendant, *A Mirror for Magistrates*.[85] As one of the most popular works of fiction of the mid-Tudor period and one of few native literary models of biographical history available to North, *A Mirror* in particular is likely to have influenced his ideas about the role of tragic patterning in life writing. The prominence given to fortune and pity in North's translation is combined, however, with a stress on divine retribution following the deaths of the protagonists, which derives from Amyot. Thus, the French translator (and hence North) turns Plutarch's mention of the agency of the divine power (*to daimonion*) into a specific allusion to the providence of the one Christian God in the final sentence of Plutarch's *Cicero*, rendering 'Thus the heavenly powers [*to daimonion*] devolved upon the family of Cicero the final steps in the punishment of Antony' as 'So God's justice [*la justice divine*] made the extreme revenge and punishment of Antonius to fall into the house of Cicero' (1539–41), with North adding the explicit reference to the concept of revenge.[86] Where Plutarch omits to comment on the involvement of the gods in the retribution for the death of Demosthenes in the final paragraph of the parallel Life, Amyot (and hence North) simply puts in a reference to divine justice,

---

[83] *Cicero*, 48. 3; Amyot, *Vies* (1574), p. 1064.
[84] Amyot, *Vies* (1574), pp. 1034, 1063.
[85] See Budra, pp. 39–59 (quotation on p. 44).
[86] *Cicero*, 49. 4; Amyot, *Vies* (1574), p. 1064.

turning 'vengeance for Demosthenes [*hē Dēmosthenous dikē*] brought him into Macedonia, whose people he had disgracefully flattered, only to be by them justly put to death' into 'For the justice of the gods, revenger of the death of Demosthenes [*la justice divine, vengeresse de la mort de Demosthenes*], brought him into Macedon to receive just punishment by death of those whom he dishonestly flattered' (908–10).[87]

These examples further point to the ways in which North's translation choices reflect his ideology, particularly in the realm of religion. Where Amyot neutrally translates Plutarch's verb *ioudaizein* (to Judaise) as 'adherer à la loi des Juifs' (to adhere to the law of the Jews), North introduces heavily negative lexis: 'to hold with the superstition of the Jews' (*Cicero*, 204).[88] North's treatment of politics in Plutarch's *Lives* is equally coloured by the values of Elizabethan England. John Denton has noted, for instance, the negative lexis often associated with the tribunes of the people and the increased separation between the popular politics of the marketplace (North's translation, as we have seen, of the forum) and the aristocratic government of the senate on the Capitol.[89] Likewise, North repeatedly turns to the language of sedition when dealing with challenges to authority, reflecting an abiding concern with rebellion in Tudor England. Thus he describes the followers of Catiline as 'these seditious persons that sought nothing but rebellion' (*Cicero*, 300–01), further reinforcing Amyot's expansion of Plutarch's simple *neōterizontes* (revolutionaries): 'ces seditieux, qui cerchoient de faire quelque nouvelleté' (these seditious men, who looked to effect some change [i.e. to the state, albeit with connotations of revolt]); the noun form of the same term used later in the same life (*neōterismos*), rendered neutrally by Amyot as 'mouvemens' (movements, with potential military, social, and political connotations), is likewise translated as 'rising and rebellion' (*Cicero*, 1100–01) by North; when Pharnaces, the king of Bosporus, is said to have made the Armenians rise up against the Romans (*anistanai*; 'suscitant [...] à l'encontre des Romains'), North writes that he 'procur[ed] all those kings, princes, and governors of the provinces thereabouts to rebel against the Romans' (*Caesar*, 1479–80); finally, North adds the adjective 'seditious' (*Caesar*, 1817) to describe Cassius's writings (Amyot 'escriteaux'; Plutarch has a relative pronoun) encouraging Brutus to join the conspiracy against Caesar.[90]

Many of North's translation choices not only reflect religious dogma and orthodox political doctrine; they equally reflect wider cultural values, such as those of gender and nation. Thus, North makes Plutarch's account of Caesar's

---

[87] *Demosthenes*, 31. 3; Amyot, *Vies* (1574), p. 1035.
[88] Amyot, *Vies* (1574), p. 1039. John Denton, 'Plutarch, Shakespeare, Roman Politics and Renaissance Translation', *Poetica*, 48 (1997), 187–209 (pp. 187–91), gives further examples and argues for the specifically Puritan orientation of the translation.
[89] Denton, 'Wearing a Gown'.
[90] *Cicero*, 10. 1, 36. 2; *Caesar*, 50. 1, 62. 4; Amyot, *Vies* (1574), pp. 887, 894, 1041, 1056.

conquest of England more complimentary in a variety of ways. The explicit reference to conquest, and thus subjection, is omitted altogether (Amyot has 'lui fut le premier, qui commença à la conquerir'); Amyot's statement that it was 'd'une hardiesse grandement recommandable' (of a greatly commendable bravery) is amplified to 'a noble enterprise and very commendable' (*Caesar*, 691); and 'ceste isle si grande, que plusieurs des anciens n'ont pas voulu croire, qu'elle fust en nature' (that island so large that many ancients did not want to believe that it existed in nature) is ingeniously reworked into 'that so great and famous island (which many ancient writers would not believe that it was so indeed …)' (693–94).[91] A more complex example is North's translation of Plutarch's account of Caesar's victory over the Germans in 58 BCE in paragraph 19 of his Life. The section has two key elements, which North connects through a focus on the relationship between war and masculinity. In the second half of the paragraph, Plutarch locates the cause of the German defeat in their reluctance to fight as a result of a prophecy by the holy women. Amyot describes this as 'superstition', a word not used by Plutarch (although it is plainly implied in his narration), and refers to the Germans as 'barbarous', a term for foreign others with strong implications of cultural inferiority used by Plutarch earlier in the paragraph, but not in this sentence.[92] North not only follows Amyot in referring to the 'superstitious fear' (571) of 'the barbarous people' (570); he also calls the female prophets 'foolish' (566). There is a clear link here with the first half of the paragraph, which describes the effete young Roman noblemen who had accompanied Caesar on his campaign 'only for their pleasure and gain' (549–50). North makes the general rebuke these soldiers for having 'womanish faint hearts' (552), gendering their lack of valour in a way that is not explicit in Amyot (who has 'les cœurs si lasches et si foibles': 'hearts so cowardly and weak'), although it is in Plutarch's *anandrōs kai malakōs* (unmanly and soft). North's and Amyot's translation choices thus present the Roman victory as the natural outcome of their religious, cultural, and moral superiority over their foreign opponents, located specifically in a rejection of the feminine.

Reception

North's translation of Plutarch's *Lives* was widely influential. It went through six further editions in the century after its initial publication, an impressive number for a large and expensive folio volume. Recent studies have started to uncover some of the readers of these editions, but the best-known student of North's translation remains, of course, William Shakespeare.[93] In his Roman plays (*Julius Caesar*, *Antony and Cleopatra*, *Coriolanus*), the playwright not only

[91] Amyot, *Vies* (1574), pp. 872–73.
[92] Amyot, *Vies* (1574), p. 870. On Plutarch's account, see Pelling, *Caesar*, pp. 232–33.
[93] See particularly Dodds.

imitated the plot and character of the protagonists in Plutarch, but also copied passages from North's translation almost word for word. Enobarbus's famous account of Cleopatra when she is first seen by Antony ('The barge she sat in, like a burnished throne …'), for instance, closely resembles North's Plutarch both in the details of its description and in its language.[94] Such examples indicate that Shakespeare was attracted by North's phrasing as well as by Plutarch's narratives.[95]

Perhaps the most extensive, and revealing, example of the influence of Plutarch's *Demosthenes and Cicero* in Renaissance England is *The life and doings of Demosthenes* that accompanies Thomas Wilson's translation of Demosthenes' *Philippics* and *Olynthiacs* (1570). *The life* is essentially a free translation of Plutarch's *Demosthenes*, with some omissions and transpositions and a few substantial additions from other sources (notably Pseudo-Lucian's *In Praise of Demosthenes* and Erasmus's *Apophthegmata*).[96] Wilson translated Demosthenes' orations against Philip of Macedon as a thinly-veiled warning against the Spanish King Philip II and, in consequence, highlights Demosthenes' defence of the liberty of his country against foreign invasion in *The life*.[97] In one of his additions to Plutarch, Wilson further stresses how it was the Greek rhetor's skill in oratory instead of warfare that enabled him to come to the defence of his country: 'For I thinke the might of a wise Orator, and the gravitie of an eloquent speaker, is nothing inferiour at all to the force of armor, and manhoode whatsoever.'[98] Throughout *The life*, Wilson uses the language of counsel in relation to Demosthenes' oratory, and in the dedication to the queen's principal secretary William Cecil, Lord Burghley, he draws a parallel between Demosthenes and Burghley (and, by extension, himself as the translator of Demosthenes) as political advisers to their states.[99] Demosthenes is thus presented as an exemplar for those Tudor humanists who put their training in rhetoric and the language arts in the service of the commonwealth, in particular the influential group of Elizabethan counsellors educated in the newly-established humanist curriculum at Cambridge in the 1530s and 1540s, to which both Cecil and Wilson belonged.[100]

Wilson's presentation of Demosthenes as a model for humanist counsellors goes back to the initial reception of Plutarch's pair of Lives in fifteenth-century

---

[94] *Antony and Cleopatra*, II. 2. 198–212.
[95] On Shakespeare's use of North, see further the Introduction to North's *The Life of Julius Caesar* and the General Introduction.
[96] See Blanshard and Sowerby, pp. 54–55, who note the presence of the material from Pseudo-Lucian, but not from Erasmus, in *The life*.
[97] On the politics of Wilson's translation, see Peter E. Medine, *Thomas Wilson* (Boston: Twayne, 1986), pp. 127–54; Blanshard and Sowerby.
[98] Wilson, *Orations of Demosthenes*, sig. S3v.
[99] Ibid., sig. *2r and passim.
[100] See Winthrop S. Hudson, *The Cambridge Connection and the Elizabethan Settlement of 1559* (Durham, NC: Duke University Press, 1980).

Italy. Under the influence of the republican ideal of the *vita activa*, the Florentine humanist Leonardo Bruni composed a new, more favourable, biography of Cicero on the model of Plutarch, *Cicero novus* (1415), which 'glorifies the prototype of the civic humanist who served his country, the Roman republic, through direct participation in politics as well as through his scholarship. Bruni often made the connection between Cicero's literary excellence and the well-being of the state.'[101] Although Bruni's *Cicero novus* was not translated in early modern England, similar attitudes prevailed. The German schoolmaster Reinhard Lorich's edition of the ancient rhetorician Aphthonius's manual *Progymnasmata* ('Preliminary exercises'), studied by almost all grammar school boys in Renaissance England, includes a comparison of Demosthenes and Cicero as an example of *synkrisis* or *comparatio*, indebted to Plutarch in form and content.[102] Demosthenes and Cicero, both of modest background but hard-working, are presented to students of rhetoric as models of how they can save their country through eloquence. Likewise, the brief life of Cicero in the grammarian Robert Whittington's translation of *De officiis* ('On Duties', 1534), which acknowledges Plutarch as one of its sources, throughout relates his eloquence and learning in the Greek and Latin language to the political service to the city of Rome that Cato praised by calling him father of his country.[103] As orators rather than soldiers, Demosthenes and Cicero offered a powerful model to Renaissance humanists of how to put their rhetorical skills to the service of the commonwealth, and their example helped to put rhetoric at the heart of political theory and practice in early modern England.[104]

Further Reading

Demosthenes and Cicero: Hartmut Erbse, 'Die Bedeutung der Synkrisis in den Parallelbiographien Plutarchs', *Hermes*, 84 (1956), 398–424; Lintott; Moles, *Cicero*.

Sources: *Fortunes de Jacques Amyot: actes du colloque international (Melun, 18–20 avril 1985)*, ed. by Michel Balard ([Paris]: A.-G. Nizet, 1986); Sturel; Plutarch, *Les Vies des hommes illustres*, trans. by Jacques Amyot, ed. by Gérard Walter, 2 vols (Paris: Nouvelle revue française, 1937).

[101] Pade, *Reception*, I, 156. See also Howard Jones, *Master Tully: Cicero in Tudor England* (Nieuwkoop: De Graaf, 1998), pp. 65–81.
[102] Aphthonius, *Progymnasmata*, trans. by Rudolph Agricola and Giovanni Maria Cataneo, ed. by Reinhard Lorich (1572), sigs Y5v–8r. See Manfred Kraus, 'Progymnasmata, Gymnasmata', in *Historisches Wörterbuch der Rhetorik*, ed. by Gert Ueding, 10 vols (Tübingen: Niemeyer, 1992–2011), VII, 159–91.
[103] *The thre bookes of Tullies offices*, trans. by Robert Whittington (1534), sig. b5r–v.
[104] See Skinner, *Reason and Rhetoric*, Part I.

Translation: Denton, *Translation and Manipulation*; Matthiessen; Worth.

Reception: Blanshard and Sowerby; Jones, *Master Tully*; Pade, *Reception*.

Abbreviations and References

N. North.

P. Plutarch. Quoted from LCL, 99 (*Plutarch's 'Lives'*, VII).

A. Amyot. Quoted from *Les Vies des hommes illustres grecs et romains*, trans. by Jacques Amyot (Lausanne: François Le Preux, 1574). Available online at <https://doi.org/10.3931/e-rara-6943>.

C. Cruser. Quoted from *Plutarchi* [...] *vitae comparatae illustrium virorum, graecorum et romanorum*, trans. by Hermann Cruser (Basel: Thomas Guarin, 1573). Available online at <http://mdz-nbn-resolving.de/urn:nbn:de:bvb:12-bsb10139851-5>.

The life of Demosthenes.

[1] He that made the little book of the praise of Alcibiades touching the victory he won at the horse race of the Olympian games, were it the poet Euripides (as some think) or any other, my friend Sossius, said that to make a man happy he must of necessity be born in some famous city.¹ But to tell you what I think hereof, doubtless true happiness chiefly consisteth in the virtue and qualities of the mind, being a matter of no moment whether a man be born in a pelting° village or in a famous city, no more than it is for one to be born of a fair or foul mother.² For it were a madness to think that the little village of Iulide, being the least part of the isle of Ceo (the whole island of itself being but a small thing), and that the isle of Aegina (which is of so small a length that a certain Athenian on a time made a motion it might be taken away, because it was but as a straw in the sight of the haven of Piraea) could bring forth famous poets and excellent comedians and not breed an honest, just, and wise man, and of noble courage.³ For, as we have reason to think that arts and sciences which were first devised and invented to make some things necessary for men's use or otherwise to win fame and credit are drowned and cast away in little poor villages, so are we to judge also that virtue, like a strong and fruitful plant, can take root and bring forth in every place where it is graffed° in a good nature and gentle person that can patiently away° with pains. And therefore if we chance to offend and live not as we should, we cannot accuse the meanness of our country where we were born, but we must justly accuse ourselves.

[2] Surely, he that hath taken upon him to put forth any work or to write any history into the which he is to thrust many strange things unknown to his country and which are not ready at his hand to be had but dispersed abroad in divers places and to be gathered out of divers books and authorities, first of all he must needs remain in some great and famous city throughly° inhabited, where men do delight in good and virtuous things, because there are commonly plenty of all sorts of books, and that perusing them, and hearing talk also of many things besides which other historiographers peradventure° have not written of, and which will carry so much more credit because men that are alive may presently speak of them as of their own knowledge, whereby he may make his work perfect in every point, having many and diverse necessary things contained in it.⁴ But I myself, that dwell in a poor little town, and yet do remain

---

¹   Sossius] Q. Sosius Senecio: see General Introduction, I, 6, 22. The first three paragraphs constitute P.'s introduction to the *Demosthenes–Cicero* pair.
²   **Marg.** 'True happiness consisteth in the mind and manners of man, not in any place or country.'
³   Iulide] Iulis.   Ceo] Ceos.   Piraea] Piraeus.
⁴   **Marg.** 'Expedient for an historiographer to be in a famous city.' N. loses hold of A.'s

THE LIFE OF DEMOSTHENES 75

there willingly lest it should become less, whilst I was in Italy and at Rome, I had no leisure to study and exercise the Latin tongue, as well for the great business I had then to do, as also to satisfy them that came to learn philosophy of me.[5] So that even somewhat too late and now in my latter time I began to take Latin books in hand. And thereby (a strange thing to tell you, but yet true) I learned not, nor understood, matters so much by the words, as I came to understand the words by common experience and knowledge I had in things. But furthermore, to know how to pronounce the Latin tongue well, or to speak it readily, or to understand the figures, translations, and fine joining of the simple words one with another, which do beautify and set forth the tongue, surely I judge it to be a marvellous pleasant and sweet thing, but withal it requireth a long and laboursome study, meet for those that have better leisure than I have and that have young years on their backs to follow such pleasure.[6]

[3] Therefore in this present book, which is the fifth of this work where I have taken upon me to compare the lives of noble men one with another, undertaking to write the lives of Demosthenes and Cicero, we will consider and examine their nature, manners, and conditions by their acts and deeds in the government of the commonwealth, not meaning otherwise to confer their works and writings of eloquence, neither to define which of them two were sharper or sweeter in his oration.[7] For, as the poet Ion saith, 'In this behalf a man may rightly say, | The dolphins in their proper soil° do play.'[8] The which Caecilius little understanding, being a man very rash in all his doings, hath unadvisedly written and set forth in print a comparison of Demosthenes' eloquence with Cicero's.[9] But if it were an easy matter for every man to know himself, then the gods needed have given us no commandment, neither could

grammatical structure in this overlong sentence when he gets to 'and that perusing them' (which in the French depends on the same conjunction as the preceding clause: 'à fin qu'il ait abondance de toutes sortes de livres, et qu'en cerchant çà et là, et entendant [...], il puisse rendre ...', p. 1018), which results in anacoluthon. See Introduction, p. 62.
[5] Marg. 'Plutarch's country very little.' P. lived in the small town of Chaeronea in Boeotia. See General Introduction, 1, 5–6.
[6] But [...] readily] P. 'But to appreciate the beauty and quickness of the Roman style.' N. follows A., who takes 'quickness' (τάχος) to apply to speech: 'Mais au demeurant, de scavoir bien gouster en quoi gist la beauté de la langue Romaine, ou la parler promptement' (p. 1018).
[7] This statement provides important evidence of the composition of P.'s Lives. See Pelling, Plutarch and History, p. 2.
[8] In [...] play] P. 'useless is a dolphin's might upon dry ground' (Nauck, fr. 58). A. (apparently relying on a different manuscript reading: κἀκεῖ (there also) instead of κακὴ (useless)) states virtually the opposite ('Là le Dauphin courant grand erre; | A force mesme sur la terre', p. 1018), but N. (presumably relying on the context, which makes clear what the sense should be) is closer to the original.
[9] Marg. 'Demosthenes compared with Cicero.'   set forth in print] The anachronism is N.'s.

men have said that it came from heaven.¹⁰ But for my opinion, methinks fortune even from the beginning hath framed in manner one self° mould of Demosthenes and Cicero and hath in their natures fashioned many of their qualities one like to the other, as both of them to be ambitious, both of them to love the liberty of their country, and both of them very fearful in any danger of wars. And likewise their fortunes seem to me to be both much alike. For it is hard to find two orators again, that being so meanly born as they, have come to be of so great power and authority as they two, nor that have deserved the ill will of kings and noblemen so much as they have done, nor that have lost their daughters, nor that have been banished their countries and that have been restored again with honour, and that again have fled and have been taken again, nor that have ended their lives with the liberty of their country.¹¹ So that it is hard to be judged whether nature have made them liker in manners or fortune in their doings, as if they had both, like cunning workmasters,° strived one with the other to whom they should make them best resemble.¹² But first of all we must write of the elder of them two.

[4] Demosthenes, the father of this orator Demosthenes, was (as Theopompus writeth) one of the chief men of the city, and they called him Machaeropoeus, to wit, a maker of sword-blades, because he had a great shop where he kept a number of slaves to forge them.¹³ But touching Aeschines the orator's report of his mother, who said that she was the daughter of one Gelon, that fled from Athens being accused of treason, and of a barbarous° woman that was her mother, I am not able to say whether it be true or devised of malice to do him despite.¹⁴ Howsoever it was, it is true that his father died, leaving him but seven years old, and left him reasonable° well, for his goods came to little less than the value of fifteen talents.¹⁵ Howbeit, his guardians did him great wrong, for they stole a great part of his goods themselves and did let the rest run to naught, as having little care of it, for they would not pay his schoolmasters their wages. And this was the cause that he did not learn the liberal sciences, which are usually taught unto honest men's sons, and to further that want also, he was but a weakling and very tender, and therefore his mother would not much let him go to school, neither his masters also durst keep him too hard

---

¹⁰ 'Know thyself' was inscribed on the temple of Apollo at Delphi.
¹¹ with the liberty of their country] at the same time as…
¹² strived one with the other to whom they should make them best resemble] A. 'eussent fait à l'envy l'une de l'autre […] à qui les feroit mieux ressembler' (competed with one another as to who [nature or fortune] would make them [Demosthenes and Cicero] best resemble each other, p. 1019).
¹³ Marg. 'The parentage of Demosthenes.'
¹⁴ Aeschines, *Against Ctesiphon*, 171.   Gelon] Gylon.
¹⁵ Marg. 'The patrimony of Demosthenes.'

to it, because he was but a sickly child at the first and very weak.¹⁶ And it is reported also that the surname of Battalus was given him in mockery by other schoolboys his companions because of his weakness of body.¹⁷ This Battalus (as divers men do report) was an effeminate player on the flute, against whom the poet Antiphanes to mock him devised a little play. Others also do write of one Battalus, a dissolute orator, and that wrote lascivious verses.¹⁸ And it seemeth that the Athenians at that time did call a certain part of man's body uncomely to be named, Battalus. Now for Argas, which surname men say was also given him, he was so called either for his rude and beastly manners, because some poets do call a snake Argas, or else for his manner of speech, which was very unpleasant to the ear; for Argas is the name of a poet that made always bawdy and ill-favoured songs.¹⁹ But hereof enough, as Plato said.

[5] Furthermore, the occasion (as it is reported) that moved him to give himself to eloquence was this. Callistratus the orator was to defend the cause of one Oropus before the judges, and every man longed greatly for this day of pleading, both for the excellency of the orator, that then bore the bell for eloquence, as for the matter and his accusation, which was manifestly known to all.²⁰ Demosthenes, hearing his schoolmasters agree together to go to the hearing of this matter, he prayed his schoolmaster to be so good as to let him go with him. His master granted him, and being acquainted with the keepers of the hall-door where this matter was to be pleaded, he so entreated them that they placed their scholar in a very good place, where, being set at his ease, he might both hear and see all that was done, and no man could see him. Thereupon, when Demosthenes had heard the case pleaded, he was greatly in love with the honour which the orator had gotten, when he saw how he was waited upon home with such a train of people after him, but yet he wondered more at the force of his great eloquence, that could so turn and convey all things at his pleasure. Thereupon he left the study of all other sciences and all other exercises of wit and body which other children are brought up in, and began to labour continually and to frame himself to make orations, with intent one day to be an orator among the rest.²¹ His master that taught him rhetoric was Isaeus, notwithstanding that Isocrates also kept a school of rhetoric at that time, either because that being an orphan he was not able to pay the wages that Isocrates demanded of his scholars, which was ten minas, or rather for that° he found

---

¹⁶ go to school] P.'s τοῖς πόνοις indicates physical exercise rather than study, as A. has it ('à l'estude', p. 1019).
¹⁷ Marg. 'Demosthenes, why he was called Battalus.'
¹⁸ orator] P. and A. 'poet'.
¹⁹ Marg. 'Demosthenes, why surnamed Argas.'
²⁰ Marg. 'Callistratus the orator.'   bore the bell] was the best.
²¹ Marg. 'The earnest desire of Demosthenes to learn eloquence.'

Isaeus' manner of speech more proper for the use of the eloquence he desired, because it was more fine and subtle.[22] Yet Hermippus writeth notwithstanding that he had read certain books, having no name of any author, which declared that Demosthenes had been Plato's scholar and that by hearing of him he learned to frame his pronunciation and eloquence. And he writeth also of one Ctesibius, who reporteth that Demosthenes had secretly read Isocrates' works of rhetoric and also Alcidamus' books by means of one Callias Syracusan and others.[23]

[6] Wherefore, when he came out of his wardship, he began to put his guardians in suit and to write orations and pleas against them, who in contrary manner did ever use delays and excuses to save themselves from giving up any account unto him of his goods and patrimony left him.[24] And thus, following this exercise (as Thucydides writeth), it prospered so well with him that in the end he obtained it, but not without great pains and danger. And yet, with all that he could do, he could not recover all that his father left him by a good deal. So, having now gotten some boldness, and being used also to speak in open presence, and withal having a feeling and delight of the estimation that is won by eloquence in pleading, afterwards he attempted to put forward himself and to practise in matters of state. For, as there goeth a tale of one Laomedon an Orchomenian, who having a grievous pain in the spleen, by advice of the physicians was willed to run long courses to help him, and that following their order he became in the end so lusty and nimble of body that afterwards he would needs make one to run for games and indeed grew to be the swiftest runner of all men in his time, even so the like chanced unto Demosthenes.[25] For at the first beginning to practise oratory for recovery of his goods, and thereby having gotten good skill and knowledge how to plead, he afterwards took upon him to speak to the people in assemblies touching the government of the commonwealth, even as he should have contended for some game of price, and at length did excel all the orators at that time that got up into the pulpit° for orations, notwithstanding that when he first ventured to speak openly, the people made such a noise that he could scant be heard, and besides they mocked him for his manner of speech that was so strange, because he used so many long confused periods and his matter he spoke of was so intricate with arguments one upon another that they were tedious and made men weary to hear him.[26] And furthermore, he had a

---

[22] Marg. 'Isaeus, Demosthenes' schoolmaster of rhetoric.'   ten minas] A. 'cent escus' (p. 1020); N. follows P. See Introduction, p. 60.
[23] Alcidamus] Alcidamas of Elaia.
[24] Marg. 'Demosthenes' first practice in drawing and penning of orations.' In 364/363 BCE.
[25] Marg. 'A remedy for the pain of the spleen.'
[26] Marg. 'Demosthenes mocked of the people for his long orations.'

The Life of Demosthenes

very soft voice, an impediment in his tongue, and had also a short breath, the which made that men could not well understand what he meant, for his long periods in his oration were oftentimes interrupted before he was at the end of his sentence, so that at length perceiving he was thus rejected, he gave over to speak any more before the people and half in despair withdrew himself into the haven of Piraea.[27] There Eunomus the Thessalian,[28] being a very old man, found him, and sharply reproved him, and told him that he did himself great wrong, considering that having a manner of speech much like unto Pericles, he drowned himself by his faint heart, because he did not seek the way to be bold against the noise of the common people and to arm his body to away with the pains and burden of public orations, but suffering it to grow feebler for lack of use and practice.

[7] Furthermore, being once again repulsed and whistled at as he returned home, hanging down his head for shame and utterly discouraged, Satyrus, an excellent player of comedies, being his familiar friend, followed him and went and spoke with him. Demosthenes made his complaint unto him that, where he had taken more pains than all the orators besides and had almost even worn himself to the bones with study, yet he could by no means devise to please the people, whereas other orators, that did nothing but bib° all day long, and mariners that understood nothing were quietly heard and continually occupied the pulpit with orations, and on the other side that they made no account of him. Satyrus then answered him: 'Thou sayest true, Demosthenes, but care not for this. I will help it straight and take away the cause of all this, so thou wilt but tell me without book certain verses of Euripides or of Sophocles.' Thereupon Demosthenes presently rehearsed some unto him that came into his mind. Satyrus, repeating them after him, gave them quite another grace, with such a pronunciation, comely gesture, and modest countenance° becoming the verses that Demosthenes thought them clean changed. Whereby perceiving how much the action (to wit, the comely manner and gesture in his oration) doth give grace and comeliness in his pleading, he then thought it but a trifle and almost nothing to speak of to exercise to plead well unless therewithal he do also study to have a good pronunciation and gesture. Thereupon he built him a cellar under the ground, the which was whole even in my time, and he would daily go down into it to fashion his gesture and pronunciation, and also to exercise his voice, and that with such earnest affection that oftentimes he would be there two or three months, one after another, and did shave his head of purpose because he durst not go abroad in that sort, although his will was good.[29]

---

[27] Marg. 'Demosthenes' impediments of nature.'
[28] Thessalian] P. 'Thriasian' (i.e. from Thria, one of the districts of Athens). N. follows A.
[29] Marg. 'Demosthenes' cellar.'   his head] P. and A. 'one side of his head' ('la moitié de la teste', p. 1021).

[8] And yet he took his theme and matter to declaim upon and to practise to plead of the matters he had had in hand before, or else upon occasion of such talk as he had with them that came to see him while he kept his house. For they were no sooner gone from him, but he went down into his cellar and repeated from the first to the last all matters that had passed between him and his friends in talk together and alleged° also both his own and their answers. And if peradventure he had been at the hearing of any long matter, he would repeat it by himself and would finely couch and convey it into proper sentences, and thus change and alter every way any matter that he had heard or talked with others. Thereof came the opinion men had of him that he had no very quick capacity by nature and that his eloquence was not natural but artificially gotten with extreme labour. And for proof hereof, they make this probable reason, that they never saw Demosthenes make any oration on the sudden, and that oftentimes when he was set° in the assembly, the people would call him by his name to say his opinion touching the matter of counsel then in hand, howbeit that he never rose upon their call unless he had first studied the matter well he would speak of.[30] So that all the other orators would many times give him a taunt for it, as Pytheas among other, that taunting him on a time told him his reasons smelled of the lamp. 'Yea,' replied Demosthenes sharply again, 'so is there great difference, Pytheas, betwixt thy labour and mine by lamplight.' And himself also speaking to others did not altogether deny it, but told them plainly that he did not always write at length all that he would speak, neither did he also offer to speak before he had made briefs° of that he would speak. He said furthermore that it was a token the man loved the people well that he would be careful before what he would say to them.[31] For this preparative, quoth he, doth show that he doth honour and reverence them. In contrary manner also he that passeth° not how the people take his words, it is a plain token that he despiseth their authority and that he lacketh no good will, if he could, to use force against them rather than reason and persuasion.[32] But yet further to enlarge the proofs that Demosthenes had no heart to make any oration on the sudden, they do allege this reason, that Demades many times rose up on the sudden to maintain Demosthenes' reasons when the people otherwhile° did reject him, and that Demosthenes, on the other side, did never rise to make Demades' words good which he had spoken in his behalf.

---

[30] **Marg.** 'Demosthenes seldom pleaded on the sudden.'
[31] **Marg.** 'Demosthenes in his oration studieth to please the people.'
[32] he despiseth their authority] The specific opposition P. makes between those supporting democracy (δημοτικός), translated as 'the man [who] loved the people well' by N. two sentences earlier, and oligarchy (ὀλιγαρχικός), paraphrased here, is progressively obscured in both A.'s translation ('homme populaire [...] homme mesprisant l'authorité du peuple', p. 1021) and N.'s.

[9] But now might a man ask again, if Demosthenes was so timorous to speak before the people upon the sudden, what meant Aeschines then to say that he was marvellous bold in his words? And how chanceth it that he, rising upon the sudden, did presently answer the orator Python Byzantine in the field, that was very lusty in speech and rough like a vehement running stream against the Athenians?³³ And how chanced it that Lamachus Myrrinaeian, having made an oration in the praise of Philip and Alexander, kings of Macedon, in the which he spoke all the ill he could of the Thebans and of the Olynthians, and when he had read and pronounced it in the open assembly of the Olympian Games, Demosthenes, upon the instant rising up on his feet, declared as if he had read some history and pointed,° as it were with his finger, unto all the whole assembly the notable great service and worthy deeds the which the Chalcidians had done in former times for the benefit and honour of Greece and in contrary manner also what mischief and inconvenience came by means of the flatterers that altogether gave themselves to curry favour with the Macedonians?³⁴ With these and such like persuasions Demosthenes made such stir amongst the people that the orator Lamachus, being afraid of the sudden uproar, did secretly convey himself out of the assembly.³⁵ But yet to tell you what I think, Demosthenes in my opinion fashioning himself even from the beginning to follow Pericles' steps and example, he thought that for other qualities he had, they were not so requisite for him, and that he would counterfeit his gravity and sober countenance, and to be wise not to speak over-lightly to every matter at all adventures, judging that by that manner of wisdom he came to be great.³⁶ And like as he would not let slip any good occasion to speak where it might be for his credit, so would he not likewise over-rashly hazard his credit and reputation to the mercy of fortune.³⁷ And to prove this true, the orations which he made upon the sudden without premeditation before do show more boldness and courage than those which he had written and studied long before, if we may believe the reports of Eratosthenes, Demetrius Phalerian, and of the other comical poets.³⁸ For Eratosthenes said that he would be often carried away with choler and fury. Demetrius also saith that speaking one day to the people, he swore a great oath in rhyme, as if he had been possessed with some divine spirit, and said, 'By sea and land, by rivers, springs, and ponds.' There are also certain comical

³³ in the field] N.'s literal rendering of A.'s idiomatic 'sur le champ' (p. 1022), which had already been correctly translated as 'presently'.
³⁴ the Chalcidians] P. 'Thebans and Chalcidians'. N. follows A.
³⁵ Marg. 'Demosthenes terrified Lamachus in his oration.'
³⁶ gravity] P. 'style' (πλάσμα). N. follows A. ('gravité', p. 1022).
³⁷ let slip] Modern editions accept the sixteenth-century French scholar Denys Lambin's emendation of προίεσθαι in the manuscripts (translated by A. and N.) to προσίεσθαι (seek), which yields exactly the opposite meaning.
³⁸ other] N.'s addition. Neither Eratosthenes nor Demetrius of Phalerum was a writer of comedies.

poets that do call him Ropoperperethra, as who would say, a great babbler that speaketh all things that cometh to his tongue's end. Another mocked him for too much affecting a figure of rhetoric called antitheton, which is opposition, with saying: 'sic recepit sicut cepit' (which signifieth: 'he took it as he found it').[39] In the use of this figure, Demosthenes much pleased himself, unless the poet Antiphanes speaketh it of pleasure, deriding the counsel he gave the people not to take the Isle of Halonesus of King Philip as of gift, but to receive it as their own restored.[40]

[10] And yet everybody did grant that Demades of his own natural wit, without art, was invincible and that many times speaking upon the sudden he did utterly overthrow Demosthenes' long-studied reasons.[41] And Aristo of the Isle of Chio hath written Theophrastus' judgement of the orators at that time, who being asked what manner of orator he thought Demosthenes, he answered: 'worthy of this city'.[42] Then again, how he thought of Demades: 'above this city', said he. The same philosopher writeth also that Polyeuctus Sphettian, one of those that practised at that time in the commonwealth, gave this sentence, that Demosthenes indeed was a great orator, but Phocion's tongue had a sharper understanding, because in few words he comprehended much matter.[43] And to this purpose, they say that Demosthenes himself said also that as oft as he saw Phocion get up into the pulpit for orations to speak against him, he was wont to say to his friends: 'See, the axe of my words riseth.'[44] And yet it is hard to judge whether he spoke that in respect of his tongue, or rather for the estimation he had gotten because of his great wisdom, thinking (as indeed it is true) that one word only, the twinkling of an eye, or a nod of the head of such a man that through his worthiness is attained to that credit hath more force to persuade

---

[39] **Marg.** ‘Οὕτως ἀπέλαβεν ὥσπερ ἔλαβεν. Μὴ λαμβάνειν ἀλλὰ ἀπολαμβάνειν παρὰ Φιλίππου.’ The marginal note supplies the original Greek of the phrase in the main text translated by N. as 'sic recepit sicut cepit' (from Cruser's Latin version; see Introduction, p. 59) and of the final clause of the paragraph, translated by N. as 'not to take [the Isle of Halonesus] of King Philip as of gift, but to receive it as their own restored'.

[40] In [...] himself] 'This sentence is really part of the verse quotation [which starts with 'he took it as he found it']. A second character comments: "Demosthenes would like to take over that remark" (the word for *take over* continuing the jingle: *paralabōn*). Amyot takes it as Plutarch's comment, and further confuses the issue by interpreting *paralabōn* as the name of a rhetorical figure. Fortunately North leaves the word out.' (*Selected Lives from 'The Lives of the Noble Grecians and Romans'*, ed. by Paul Turner, 2 vols (Fontwell: Centaur Press, 1963), II, 53 n. 2).

[41] **Marg.** 'The natural eloquence of Demades the orator.'

[42] **Marg.** 'Theophrastus' judgement of orators.' Aristo of the Isle of Chio] Ariston of Chios.

[43] Phocion's [...] understanding] P. 'Phocion was the most effective speaker' (A. 'le parler de Phocion avoit [...] plus [more] d'efficace', p. 1023).

[44] **Marg.** 'Phocion called the axe of Demosthenes' orations.'

than all the fine reasons and devices of rhetoric.

[11] But now for his bodily defects of nature, Demetrius Phalerian writeth that he heard Demosthenes himself say, being very old, that he did help them by these means.⁴⁵ First, touching the stammering of his tongue, which was very fat and made him that he could not pronounce all syllables distinctly, he did help it by putting of little pebble stones into his mouth which he found upon the sands by the river's side and so pronounced with open mouth the orations he had without book. And for his small and soft voice, he made that louder by running up steep and high hills, uttering even with full breath some orations or verses that he had without book. And further it is reported of him that he had a great looking-glass in his house and, ever standing on his feet before it, he would learn and exercise himself to pronounce his orations. For proof hereof it is reported that there came a man unto him on a time and prayed his help to defend his cause and told him that one had beaten him, and that Demosthenes said again unto him: 'I do not believe this is true thou tellest me, for surely the other did never beat thee.' The plaintiff then thrusting out his voice aloud said: 'What, hath he not beaten me?'. 'Yes, indeed,' quoth Demosthenes then, 'I believe it now, for I hear the voice of a man that was beaten indeed.' Thus he thought that the sound of the voice, the pronunciation, or gesture in one sort or other were things of force to credit or discredit that a man saith. His countenance when he pleaded before the people did marvellously please the common sort, but the noble men and men of understanding found it too base and mean, as Demetrius Phalerius said amongst others.⁴⁶ And Hermippus writeth that one called Aesion, being asked of the ancient orators and of those of his time, answered that every man that had seen them would have wondered with what honour, reverence, and modesty they spoke unto the people, howbeit that Demosthenes' orations (whosoever read them) were too artificial and vehement.⁴⁷ And therefore we may easily judge that the orations Demosthenes wrote are very severe and sharp. This notwithstanding, otherwhiles° he would give many pleasant and witty answers upon the sudden.⁴⁸ As when Demades one day said unto him, 'Demosthenes will teach me; after the common proverb, "the sow will teach Minerva"', he answered straight again: 'This Minerva not

---

⁴⁵ Marg. 'Demosthenes by industry reformeth his defects of nature.'
⁴⁶ Marg. 'Demosthenes' countenance and gesture misliked of the nobility.'
⁴⁷ P.'s comparison between the ancient orators, whose graceful and magnificent manner of speaking (εὐκόσμως καὶ μεγαλοπρεπῶς) would (in Aesion's opinion) have been heard with admiration, and Demosthenes, whose orations were superior in arrangement and force (τῇ κατασκευῇ καὶ δυνάμει), gets progressively lost in A. ('il n'estoit homme, qui ne se fust esmerveillé s'il eust veu, avec quelle dignité, reverence et gravité ils [les anciens orateurs] parloient au peuple: mais que les oraisons de Demosthenes à qui les lisoit à part, avoient trop plus d'artifice et trop plus de vehemence', p. 1023) and N.
⁴⁸ Marg. 'Demosthenes' witty answers.'

long since was in Collytus' street taken in adultery.'⁴⁹ A certain thief also called Chalcus (as much to say as 'of copper') stepping forth to say somewhat of Demosthenes late sitting up a nights, and that he wrote and studied the most part of the night by lamplight, 'Indeed,' quoth Demosthenes, 'I know it grieves thee to see my lamp burn all night. And therefore, my lords of Athens, methinks you should not wonder to see such robberies in your city, considering we have thieves of copper and the walls of our houses be but of clay.' We could tell you of divers others of his like pleasant and witty answers, but these may suffice for this present, and therefore we will proceed to consider further of his nature and conditions by his acts and deeds in the affairs of the commonwealth.

[12] Now Demosthenes' first beginning when he came to deal in the affairs of the state was in the time of the war made with the Phocians, as himself reporteth and as appeareth further in his orations which he made against Philip, of the which the last were made after the war was ended and the first do touch also some particular doings of the same.⁵⁰ He made the oration against Midias when he was but 32 years old and was of small countenance° and reputation in the commonwealth, the want whereof was the chiefest cause (as I think) that induced him to take money for the injury he had done him and to let his action fall against him: 'He was not of a mild and gentle mind, | But fierce and hasty to revenge by kind.'⁵¹ But knowing that it was no small enterprise, nor that could take effect by a man of so small power and authority as himself, to overthrow a man so wealthy, so befriended, and so eloquent as Midias, he therefore yielded himself unto those that did speak and entreat for him. Neither do I think that the three thousand drachmas which he received could have bridled the bitterness of his nature if otherwise he had seen any hope or likelihood that he could have prevailed against him. Now at his first coming unto the commonwealth taking a noble matter in hand, to speak against Philip for the defence and maintenance of the laws and liberties of the Grecians, he behaved himself so worthily that in short space he won him marvellous fame for his great eloquence and plain manner of speech.⁵² Thereby he was marvellously honoured also through all Greece, and greatly esteemed with the king of Persia, and Philip himself made more account of him than of all the orators in Athens,

---

⁴⁹ Demosthenes' pun refers to an intimate of Demades by the same name as the Roman goddess of wisdom and arts. Collytus was, in fact, one of the demes (districts) of Athens, but N. follows A. ('la rue de Collytus', p. 1023).
⁵⁰ Marg. 'The time of Demosthenes coming to practise in the affairs of the state.'
⁵¹ Marg. 'Displeasure betwixt Demosthenes and Midias.' The first line is Homer, *Iliad*, xx. 467 (of Achilles); the second line is N.'s rendering of P.'s subsequent prose clause. If Demosthenes was 32 when he wrote *Against Midias*, the date of the oration would be *c.* 352 BCE; a more likely date is *c.* 348.
⁵² Marg. 'Demosthenes an enemy to the Macedonians.'

THE LIFE OF DEMOSTHENES 85

and his greatest foes which° were most against him were driven to confess that they had to do with a famous man. For in the orations which Aeschines and Hyperides made to accuse him, they write thus of him.

[13] And therefore I marvel what Theopompus meant when he wrote that Demosthenes had a subtle, unconstant mind and could not long continue with one kind of men, nor in one mind for matters of state. But in contrary manner, in my judgement, he continued constant still° to the end in one self manner and order unto the which he had betaken himself at the beginning, and that not only he never changed all his lifetime, but to the contrary he lost his life because he would be no changeling.'[53] For he did not like Demades,[54] who, to excuse himself for that he had oft turned coat in matters of government, said that he went oftentimes against his own sayings as matters fell out, but never against the benefit of the commonwealth.[55] And Melanopus also, who was ever against Callistratus, having his mouth many times stopped with money, he would up to the pulpit for orations and tell the people that 'indeed Callistratus, which maintaineth the contrary opinion against me, is my enemy, and yet I yield unto him for this time, for the benefit of the commonwealth must carry it'. And another also, Nicodemus Messenian, who, being first of Cassander's side, took part afterwards with Demetrius, and then said that he did not speak against himself but that it was meet he should obey his superiors. They cannot detect Demosthenes with the like, that he did ever halt or yield, either in word or deed, for he ever continued firm and constant in one mind in his orations,[56] insomuch that Panaetius the philosopher saith that the most part of all his orations are grounded upon this maxim and principle, that for itself nothing is to be taken or accepted but that which is honest, as the oration of the crown, the which he made against Aristocrates, that also which he made for the franchise° and freedom,° and, in fine,° all his orations against Philip of Macedon.[57] And in all those he doth not persuade his countrymen to take that which is most

---

[53] **Marg.** 'The constancy of Demosthenes, against Theopompus.' manner and order] P. is explicitly political, 'a party and a line of policy in the conduct of the city's affairs' (μερίδα καὶ τάξιν […] ἐν τῇ πολιτείᾳ); A. interprets τάξις as 'reng' (rank, p. 1024).
[54] i.e. he did not act like Demades.
[55] **Marg.** 'Note the inconstancy and subtle evasion of these orators.'
[56] in his orations] P. twice refers to politics in this clause (ἀλλ' ὥσπερ ἀφ' ἑνὸς καὶ ἀμεταβλήτου διαγράμματος τῆς πολιτείας ἕνα τόνον ἔχων ἐν τοῖς πράγμασιν ἀεὶ διετέλεσε); A. omits the first reference (τῆς πολιτείας), but translates the second (ἐν τοῖς πράγμασιν: 'en l'administration des affaires', p. 1024); N. changes to 'orations'.
[57] **Marg.** 'Demosthenes preferreth honesty as a special rule in his orations.' Contrary to what N.'s translation may imply, *On the Crown* (330/29 BCE) and *Against Aristocrates* (352/51 BCE) are two separate orations; the other speeches to which P. refers here are *Against Leptines* (355/54 BCE) (which deals with immunities from taxes) and *Philippics* (351–341/40 BCE).

pleasant, easiest, or most profitable, but he proveth that oftentimes honesty is to be preferred above safety or health, so that had he in all his orations and doings joined to his honesty, courtesy, and frank speech, valiantness in wars and clean hands from bribery, he might deservedly have been compared not with Myrocles, Polyeuctus, Hyperides, and such other orators, but even with the highest, with Cimon, Thucydides, and Pericles.[58]

[14] For Phocion, who took the worst way in government of the commonwealth, because he was suspected that he took part with the Macedonians, yet for valiantness, wisdom, and justice, he was ever thought as honest a man as Ephialtes and Aristides.[59] But Demosthenes on the other side (as Demetrius saith) was no man to trust to for wars, neither had he any power to refuse gifts and bribes. For, though he would never be corrupted by Philip, king of Macedon, yet he was bribed with gold and silver that was brought from the cities of Susa and Ecbatana, and was very ready to praise and commend the deeds of their ancestors, but not to follow them.[60] Truly, yet was he the honestest man of all other orators in his time, excepting Phocion, and besides he did ever speak more boldly and plainly unto the people than any man else and would openly contrary° their minds and sharply reprove the Athenians for their faults, as appeareth by his orations.[61] Theopompus also writeth that the people on a time would have had him to accuse a man whom they would needs have condemned, but he refusing to do it, the people were offended and did mutine° against him. Thereupon he, rising up, said openly unto them: 'My lords Athenians, I will always counsel you to that which I think best for the benefit of the commonwealth, although it be against your minds, but falsely to accuse one to satisfy your minds, though you command me, I will not do it.'[62] Furthermore, that which he did against Antiphon showeth plainly that he was no people-pleaser and that he did lean more unto the authority of the senate.[63] For when Antiphon was quit° by the people in an assembly of the city, Demosthenes notwithstanding took him, and called him again into the

---

[58] **Marg.** 'Demosthenes a timorous man and given to bribes.'   Myrocles] Moerocles.
[59] N. follows A. in leaving out Cimon.
[60] A.'s introduction of the personal pronoun 'leurs' (their, p. 1025) is confusing: Demosthenes fails to live up to the example of his ancestors, not that of the people of Susa and Ecbatana.
[61] **Marg.** 'Demosthenes' frank speech in his orations.'   their minds] A. adds 'fols' (foolish, p. 1025) to P.'s 'the desires of the multitude' (τὰς ἐπιθυμίας τῶν πολλῶν), but he is not followed by N.
[62] to that [...] commonwealth] A.'s addition.
[63] showeth [...] senate] P. writes simply that his conduct of the case was 'exceedingly aristocratic in [...] spirit' (σφόδρα [...] ἀριστοκρατικὸν); N. follows A. ('monstra bien clairement qu'il se soucioit bien peu de la commune, et qu'il deferoit beaucoup plus à l'authorité du Senat', p. 1025).

Court of the Areopagites, and did not pass° for the people's ill will, but there convinced° him for promising Philip of Macedon to burn the arsenal of Athens, so by sentence of that court he was condemned and suffered for it. He did also accuse the nun Theorides for many lewd° parts committed, and amongst others for that she taught slaves to deceive their masters, and so following° the matter against her to death, she was condemned and executed.[64]

[15] It is thought also that he made the oration Apollodorus spoke against the praetor Timotheus, and proved thereby that he was a debtor to the commonwealth and so a naughty° man, and that he wrote those orations also intituled to Formio and Stephanus, for the which he was justly reproved.[65] For Formio pleaded against Apollodorus with the oration which Demosthenes self had made for him, which was even alike as if out of one self cutler's shop he had sold his enemies swords one to kill another.[66] And for his known orations, those which he made against Androtion, Timocrates, and Aristocrates, he caused them to give them unto others when he had not yet dealt in matters of state.[67] For indeed, when he did put them forth, he was not passing seven or eight and twenty years old. The oration which he made against Aristogiton, and the other also of liberty against Ctesippus the son of Chabrias, he spoke them (as he saith himself or as others write) openly unto the people because he intended to marry Chabrias' mother.[68] Howbeit he did not, but married a Samian woman, as Demetrius Magnesian writeth in his book he made intituled *Synonyma* and in that he wrote against Aeschines, where he accuseth him that he dealt falsely when he was ambassador.[69] It is not known whether it was

---

[64] the nun Theorides] Theoris. N. follows A. in using the inflected form ('Theoride', p. 1025; the Greek has the genitive Θεωρίδος) and introduces further confusion by adding an 's' at the end.
[65] Marg. 'Demosthenes' orations, which were true and which false.'   praetor] from Cruser; P. 'general' (στρατηγός); A. 'Capitaine' (p. 1025). See Introduction, p. 59.
[66] his] N.'s addition, which confuses the meaning: they were not his enemies but each other's, as A.'s translation makes clear: 'ce qui estoit tout autant comme si d'une mesme boutique d'armurier, il eust vendu à des ennemis des espees, pour s'entretuer' (p. 1025).
[67] The reference is to *Against Androtion* (355/54 BCE); *Against Aristocrates* (352/51 BCE); *Against Timocrates* (353/52 BCE).   known] N.'s translation of A.'s 'publiques' (p. 1025), which refers to speeches in public (rather than private) cases.   caused [...] others] P. declares that Demosthenes 'wrote' these orations to be delivered by others (followed by A. 'il les composa pour les bailler à d'autres', p. 1025).
[68] P. 'But he himself delivered the speech against Aristogeiton [c. 325–324 BCE], as well as the one "On the Immunities" [i.e. *Against Leptines*], at the instance of Ctesippus the son of Chabrias, as he himself says, but as some say, because he was wooing the mother of this young man.' A. (followed by N.) translates 'at the instance' (διὰ) by its opposite 'contre' (against, p. 1025) and hence confuses the opposition between what Demosthenes said and what others claimed.
[69] that [...] ambassador] In P., this phrase goes with the next sentence, i.e. it is uncertain whether Demosthenes' (not Demetrius') speech against Aeschines, *On the False Embassy*

recited or not, although Idomeneus writeth that there lacked but thirty voices only to have quit Aeschines. But in this methinks he spoke not truly and doth but conjecture it by that the one and the other have said in their orations against the crown, in the which neither the one nor the other do say precisely that this accusation proceeded to judgement.⁷⁰ But let other that list decide this doubt.

[16] Now, before the war began, it was evident enough to which part Demosthenes would incline in the commonwealth, for he would never leave to reprove and withstand Philip's doings.⁷¹ Therefore, he being more spoken of in Philip's court than any man else, he was sent unto him the tenth person with nine others in ambassade.°⁷² Philip gave them all audience one after another, howbeit he was more careful and circumspect to answer Demosthenes' oration than all the rest. But otherwise, out of that place, he did not Demosthenes so much honour nor gave him so good entertainment as to his other companions. For Philip showed more kindness and gave better countenance unto Aeschines and Philocrates than unto him. Wherefore, when they did highly praise Philip and said that he was a well-spoken prince, a fair man, and would drink freely and be pleasant in company, Demosthenes smiled at it and turned all things to the worst, saying that those qualities were nothing commendable nor meet for a king. For the first was a quality meet for a pleader, the second for a woman, and the third for a sponge.

[17] In fine, wars falling out between them, because Philip, of the one side, could not live in peace and the Athenians, on the other side, were still incensed and stirred up by Demosthenes' daily orations, the Athenians first sent into the Isle of Euboea, the which by means of certain private° tyrants that had taken the towns became subject again unto Philip, following a decree Demosthenes had preferred,° and so went to expulse the Macedonians again.⁷³ After that also he caused them to send aid unto the Byzantines and to the Perinthians, with whom Philip made war. For he so persuaded the Athenians that he made them forget the malice they did bear unto those two nations and the faults which either of

(343/42 BCE), was delivered or not. In A. the phrase is the object of 'spoke' in the previous sentence ('il prononça lui-mesme celle contre Aristogiton, et celle aussi des immunitez contre Ctesippus [...], et celle qu'il fit à l'encontre d'Aeschines', pp. 1025-26), but this is obscured by the long intervening clause about Demosthenes' love life; N.'s addition of 'in' and changes to the punctuation confuse the meaning further.

⁷⁰ the one [...] the crown] The reference is to the opposing speeches of Aeschines (*Against Ctesiphon*) and Demostenes (*On the Crown*), both dating from 330 BCE.

⁷¹ **Marg.** 'Demosthenes' doings against Philip.' A. (and hence N.) omits the following clause in P.: 'but on every occasion kept rousing and inflaming the Athenians against him' (ἀλλ' ἐφ' ἑκάστῳ ταράττοντος τοὺς Ἀθηναίους καὶ διακαίοντος ἐπὶ τὸν ἄνθρωπον).

⁷² In 346 BCE.

⁷³ The events in this paragraph took place between 342 and 338 BCE.

both the cities had committed against them in the wars touching the rebellion of their confederates, and he caused them to send them aid, which kept them from Philip's force and power.[74] Furthermore, going afterwards unto all the great cities of Greece as ambassador, he did so solicit and persuade them that he brought them all in manner to be against Philip, so that the army which their tribe should find at their common charge was fifteen thousand footmen, all strangers, and two thousand horsemen, besides the citizens of every city which should also serve in the wars at their charge, and the money also levied for the maintenance of this war was very willingly disbursed.[75] Theophrastus writeth that it was at that time their confederates did pray that they would set down a certain sum of money what every city should pay and that Crobylus, an orator, should make answer that the war had no certain maintenance, inferring that the charges of war was infinite.[76] Now all Greece being in arms, attending° what should happen, and all these people and cities being united in one league together, as the Euboeians, the Athenians, the Corinthians, the Megarians, the Leucadians, and those of Corfu, the greatest matter Demosthenes had to do was to persuade the Thebans also to enter into this league, because their country confined and bordered with Attica;[77] besides, their force and power was of great importance, for that they carried the fame of all Greece at that time for the valiantest soldiers. But it was no trifling matter to win the Thebans and to make them break with Philip, who but lately before had bound them unto him by many great pleasures which he had done to them in the war of the Phocians, besides also that betwixt Athens and Thebes by reason of vicinity there fell out daily quarrels and debates,° the which with every little thing were soon renewed.

[18] This notwithstanding, Philip, being proud of the victory he had won by the city of Amphisse, when he came and invaded the country of Elatia and was entered into Phocide, the Athenians were then so amazed° with it that no man durst occupy the pulpit for orations, neither could they tell what way to take.[78] Thus the whole assembly standing in a doubt with great silence, Demosthenes only stepped up and did again give them counsel to seek to make league and

---

[74] The reference is to the War of the Allies, also known as the Social War (357–355 BCE) between Athens and its allies in the Second League, including Perinthus, who successfully revolted against Athenian supremacy with the support of Byzantium.
[75] Marg. 'Demosthenes stirreth up Greece against the Macedonians.'
[76] Crobylus] The nickname ('Topknot') of the orator Hegesippus.   the war had no certain maintenance, inferring that the charges of war was infinite] P. 'War has no fixed rations' (οὐ τεταγμένα σιτεῖται πόλεμος); A. adds the explanation ('La guerre ne se nourrit pas à mesure certaine, voulant dire, que la despense de la guerre ne se peut mesurer ne definir', p. 1026), but the idea becomes less distinct in N.
[77] Euboeians] Euboeans.
[78] In 339 BCE.   Amphisse] Amphissa.   Phocide] Phocis.

alliance with the Thebans, and so did further encourage the people and put them in good hope as he was always wont to do. Then with others he was sent ambassador unto Thebes, and Philip also for his part sent ambassadors unto the Thebans, Amyntas and Clearchus, two gentlemen Macedonians, and with them, Daochus, Thessalus, and Thrasydaeus, to answer and withstand the persuasions of the Athenian ambassadors.[79] Thereupon the Thebans began to advise themselves for the best and laid before their eyes the miserable fruits and calamities of war, their wounds being yet green and uncured which they got by the wars of Phocide. Notwithstanding, the great force of Demosthenes' eloquence (as Theopompus writeth) did so inflame the Thebans' courage with desire of honour that it trod under their feet all manner of considerations and did so ravish them with the love and desire of honesty that they cast at their heels all fear of danger, all remembrance of pleasures received, and all reason persuading the contrary.[80] This act of an orator was of so great force that Philip forthwith sent ambassadors unto the Grecians to entreat for peace, and all Greece was up to see what would become of this stir. Thus, not only the captains of Athens obeyed Demosthenes, doing all that he commanded them, but the governors also of Thebes and of all the country of Boeotia besides. And the assemblies also of the council of Thebes were as well governed by him as the assemblies of Athens, being alike beloved both of the one and the other and having alike authority to command both, and not undeservedly (as Theopompus saith) but by just desert.

[19] But some fatal destiny and the revolution of times had determined the final end of the liberty of Greece at that time, clean contrary to his purpose and intent. There were also many celestial signs that did foreshow and prognosticate what end should ensue thereof, and amongst others Apollo's nun gave these dreadful oracles, and this old prophecy of the Sibyl's was commonly sung in everybody's mouth:[81]

> What time the bloody battle shall be fought at Thermodon,
> God grant I may be far away, or else (to look thereon)
> Have eagle's wings to sore above, among the clouds on high,
> For there the vanquished side shall weep, and conqueror shall die.

Men do report that this Thermodon is a little river of our country of Chaeronea,

---

[79] P. adds a reference to his source ('as Marsyas tells us'), but this is omitted by A. Daochus, Thessalus] The reference in P. is to a single person ('Daochus of Thessaly'), but A. (followed by N.) has confused Θεσσαλὸν (of Thessaly) for the name of a second man.

[80] Marg. 'Demosthenes' force of eloquence joined the Thebans with the Athenians and won them from Philip, king of Macedon.'

[81] Marg. 'The overthrow of the Grecians foreshowed at Chaeronea by signs and ancient oracles.'   Apollo's nun] P. 'the Pythian priestess' (ἡ Πυθία); A. 'la prophetisse Pythia' (p. 1027). Pythia was the priestess of Apollo at Delphi.

which falleth into the river of Cephisus; howbeit at this present time there is never a river nor brook in all our country that I know called Thermodon. And I think that that river which we call now Haemon was in old time Thermodon, for it runneth by the temple of Hercules, where the Grecians lay in camp.[82] And it may be that because it was filled with dead bodies and that it ran blood at the day of the battle, it changed her name and was surnamed Haemon, because *haema* in the Greek tongue signifieth blood. Yet Duris writeth notwithstanding that this Thermodon was no river, but that certain men setting up their tent and trenching it about found a little image of stone whereupon were engraven these letters, whereby it appeareth that it was a man called Thermodon who carried an Amazon hurt in his arms, and that for this image of Thermodon they do sing such another old oracle as this: 'Ye ernes° and ravens tarry till the field° of Thermodon: | There will be store of carcasses of men to feed upon.'[83]

[20] This notwithstanding, it is very hard to tell the troth° of these things. But Demosthenes, trusting to the valiantness and power of the Graecians and being marvellously encouraged to see such a great number of valiant and resolute men so willing to fight with the enemy, he bad them be of good courage and not to buzz about such oracles and to give ear to such prophecies.[84] And furthermore he told them plainly that he did mistrust° the nun Pythia did lean unto Philip, as favouring him, and did put the Thebans in mind of their captain Epaminondas and the Athenians of Pericles, and persuaded them that those two famous men were always of opinion that such prophecies were no other but a fine cloak for cowards, and that taking no heed to them they did dispatch their matters according to their own discretion. Until this present time, Demosthenes showed himself always an honest man, but when it came to the battle, he fled like a coward and did no valiant act anything answerable to the orations whereby he had persuaded the people.[85] For he left his rank and cowardly cast away his weapons to run the lighter and was not ashamed at all (as Pythias said) of the words written upon his shield in golden letters, which were: 'Good fortune.'[86] Now Philip, having won the battle, he was at that present so joyful that he fell to commit many fond parts.[87] For after he had drunk well with his friends, he went into the place where the overthrow was given and

---

[82] Marg. 'The river of Thermodon (or Haemon) in the country of Chaeronea.'
[83] Marg. 'Another opinion of Thermodon.'
[84] he [...] prophecies] In the first edition of 1579, N. had mistranslated A.'s 'se [...] amuser' (to occupy themselves with trifles, p. 1028) as 'to buff' (to burst into laughter); in the third edition of 1603 this is corrected, evidently without reference to the original text, to 'buzz', apparently in the sense of 'to spread as a rumour, with whispering or busy talk' (*OED, v.*¹, 5) or possibly 'to move about busily' (*OED, v.*¹, 2. a). 'Be of good courage' is N.'s addition.
[85] Marg. 'Demosthenes flieth from the battle.' In the Battle of Chaeroneia in 338 BCE.
[86] Marg. 'Demosthenes' word and device upon his shield.'
[87] fond parts] foolish acts.

there in mockery began to sing the beginning of the decree which Demosthenes had preferred, by the which the Athenians accordingly proclaimed wars against him, rising and falling with his voice and dancing it in measure with his foot: 'Demosthenes, the son of Demosthenes Paeanian, did put forth this.'[88] But afterwards, beginning to wax sober and leaving his drunkenness, and that he had remembered himself what danger he had been in, then his hair stood bolt upright upon his head, considering the force and power of such an orator that in a piece of a day had enforced him to hazard his realm and life at a battle. Now Demosthenes' fame was so great that it was carried even to the great king of Persia's court, who wrote unto his lieutenants and governors that they should feed Demosthenes with money and should procure° to entertain him above all the men in Greece, as he that could best withdraw Philip and trouble him with the wars and tumults of Greece. And this was afterwards proved by letters found of Demosthenes himself, the which came to King Alexander's hands in the city of Sardis, and by other writings also of the governors and lieutenants of the king of Persia, in the which were named directly the express sums of money which had been sent and given unto him.[89]

[21] Now the Grecians being thus overthrown by battle, the other orators, adversaries unto Demosthenes in the commonwealth, began to set upon him and to prepare to accuse him. But the people did not only clear him of all the accusations objected against him, but did continue to honour him more than before and to call him to assemblies, as one that loved the honour and benefit of his country. So that when the bones of their countrymen which were slain at the battle of Chaeronea were brought to be openly buried according to the custom, the people gave him the honour to make the funeral oration in praise of the dead and made no show of sorrow or grief for the loss they had received (as Theopompus witnesseth and doth nobly declare), but rather in contrary manner showed that they did not repent them in following of his counsel but did honour him that gave it.[90] Demosthenes then did make the funeral oration. But afterwards in all the decrees he preferred to the people he would never subscribe any, to prevent the sinister luck and misfortune of his name, but did pass it under his friends' names one after another, until he grew courageous again shortly after that he understood of the death of Philip, who was slain immediately after the victory he won at Chaeronea.[91] And it seemeth this was the meaning of the prophecy or oracle in the two last verses: 'The vanquished

---

[88] This verse quotation is set apart from the main text in N., as in Cruser, but not in A.
dancing [...] foot] N. is misled by A.'s use of 'pied' for metrical foot: 'batant la mesure à chasque pied' (beating the measure at each foot, p. 1028).
[89] Marg. 'Demosthenes corrupted with money of the king of Persia.'
[90] Marg. 'Demosthenes praiseth them that were slain at the battle of Chaeronea.'
[91] Marg. 'The death of Philip, king of Macedon.' In 336 BCE.

bewails his luckless lot, | And he that wins, with life escapeth not.'⁹²

[22] Now Demosthenes, hearing of Philip's death before the news were openly known, to prevent° them, he would put the people again into a good hope of better luck to come. Thereupon he went with a cheerful countenance into the assembly of the council and told them there that he had a certain dream that promised great good hap, and that out of hand, unto the Athenians, and immediately after the messengers arrived and brought certain news of King Philip's death. Thereupon the Athenians made sacrifices of joy to the gods for this happy news and appointed° a crown unto Pausanias that had slain him. Demosthenes also came abroad in his best gown and crowned with flowers, seven days after the death of his daughter, as Aeschines reporteth, who reproveth him for it and noteth him to be a man having little love or charity unto his own children.⁹³ But indeed Aeschines self deserveth more blame to have such a tender womanish heart as to believe that weeping and lamenting are signs of a gentle and charitable nature, condemning them that with patience and constancy do pass away such misfortunes.⁹⁴ But now to the Athenians again. I can neither think nor say that they did wisely to show such open signs of joy as to wear crowns and garlands upon their heads, nor also to sacrifice unto the gods for the death of a prince that behaved himself so princely and courteously unto them in the victories he had won of them. For though indeed all cruelty be subject to the revenge of the gods, yet is this an act of a vile and base mind,⁹⁵ to honour a man while he lived and to make him free of their city, and now that another hath slain him, they to be in such an exceeding jollity withal and to exceed the bounds of modesty so far as to ramp° in manner with both their feet upon the dead and to sing songs of victory, as if they themselves had been the men that had valiantly slain him. In contrary manner also, I praise and commend the constancy and courage of Demosthenes, that he, leaving the tears and lamentation of his home trouble unto women, did himself in the meantime that he thought was for the benefit of the commonwealth,⁹⁶ and in my opinion I think he did therein like a man of courage and worthy to be a governor of

---

⁹² N.'s couplet translates the same line of Greek poetry as 'For there the vanquished side shall weep, and conqueror shall die' (line 524), but unlike A., N. offers a different version here.
⁹³ Marg. 'Demosthenes preferreth the joy of his country before the sorrow of his own daughter.'
⁹⁴ Marg. 'Aeschines reproved by Plutarch for his fond belief that blubbering and sorrowing are signs of love and charity.'   pass away] The meaning seems to be 'To cause to abate; to dispel' (*OED*, v., 11. d); the only other example cited by *OED* (without 'away') is from Thomas Cooper's *Dictionary* (1565). A. has 'portent' (bear, p. 1029).
⁹⁵ though ... yet] A. 'besides that [...] also' ('outre ce qu' [...] encore', p. 1029).
⁹⁶ Marg. 'Plutarch praiseth Demosthenes' constancy for leaving off his mourning to rejoice for his common country benefit.'

a commonwealth, never to stoop nor yield, but always to be found stable and constant for the benefit of the commonwealth, rejecting° all his troubles, cares, and affections in respect of the service of his country,[97] and to keep his honour much more carefully than common players use to do when they play the parts of kings and princes, whom we see neither weep nor laugh when they list, though they be on the stage, but when the matter of the play falleth out to give them just occasion. But omitting those reasons, if there be no reason (as indeed there is not) to leave and forsake a man in his sorrow and trouble without giving him some words of comfort and rather to devise some matter to assuage his sorrow and to withdraw his mind from that to think upon some pleasanter things, even as they should keep sore eyes from seeing bright and glaring colours in offering them green and darker.[98] And from whence can a man take greater comfort for his troubles and griefs at home, when the commonwealth doth well, than to join their private griefs with common joys, to the end that the better may obscure and take away the worse? But thus far I digressed from my history, enlarging this matter because Aeschines in his oration touching this matter did move the people's hearts too much unto womanish sorrow.

[23] But now to the rest.[99] The cities of Greece, being again stirred up by Demosthenes, made a new league again together, and the Thebans also, having armed themselves by his practice,° did one day set upon the garrison of the Macedonians within their city and slew many of them.[100] The Athenians prepared also to maintain war on the Thebans' behalf, and Demosthenes was daily at all the assemblies of council in the pulpit, persuading the people with his orations, and he wrote also into Asia unto the king of Persia's lieutenants and captains to make war with Alexander on their side, calling him child and Margites, as much to say as fool.[101] But after that Alexander, having set all his things at stay within his realm, came himself in person with his army and invaded the country of Boeotia, then fell the pride of the Athenians greatly, and Demosthenes also plied the pulpit no more as he was wont. At length, the poor Thebans being left unto themselves, forsaken of every man, they were compelled themselves alone to bear the brunt of this war, and so came their city to utter ruin and destruction. Thereby the Athenians, being in a marvellous

---

[97] rejecting [...] country] N.'s phrasing is rather stronger than A.'s: 'en remettant toutes ses adventures, toutes ses affections et passions à celles de la chose publique' (setting aside all his own fortunes, all his own desires and feelings in favour of those of the commonwealth, p. 1029). P., in contrast, has 'to find support for domestic sorrows and concerns in the public welfare' (τὰ οἰκεῖα πάθη καὶ πράγματα τοῖς δημοσίοις ἐπανέχοντα).
[98] N.'s addition of 'And' at the start of the following sentence makes this clause incomplete.
[99] The events described in this paragraph span the period 336 to 335 BCE.
[100] **Marg.** 'Demosthenes raiseth up the Grecians against Alexander.'
[101] Margites] The foolish hero of a lost poem attributed to Homer.

fear and perplexity, did suddenly choose ambassadors to send unto this young king, and Demosthenes chiefly among others, who, being afraid of Alexander's fury and wrath, durst not go to him, but returned from Mount Cithaeron and gave up the ambassade. But Alexander sent to summon the Athenians to send unto him ten of their orators (as Idomeneus and Duris both do write) or eight (as the most writers and best historiographers do report), which were these: Demosthenes, Polyeuctus, Ephialtes, Lycurgus, Myrocles, Damon, Callisthenes, and Charidemus.[102] At which time they write that Demosthenes told the people of Athens the fable of the sheep and wolves, how that the wolves came on a time and willed° the sheep, if they would have peace with them, to deliver them their mastiffs that kept them.[103] And so he compared himself and his companions that travailed° for the benefit of the people unto the dogs that keep the flocks of sheep, and called Alexander the wolf. Moreover, said he, like as you see these corn-masters bringing a sample of their corn in a dish or napkin to show you, and by that little do sell all that they have, so I think you will all wonder that delivering of us, you shall also deliver yourselves into the hands of your enemies. Aristobulus of Cassandria reporteth this matter thus. Now the Athenians being in consultation, not knowing how to resolve, Demades, having taken five talents of them whom Alexander demanded, did offer himself and promised to go in this ambassage unto Alexander and to entreat for them, either because he trusted in the love the king did bear him or else for that he thought he hoped he should find him pacified, as a lion glutted with the blood of beasts which he had slain.[104] Howsoever it happened, he persuaded the people to send him unto Alexander, whom he so handled that he got their pardon and did reconcile him with the city of Athens.

[24] Thereupon Alexander being retired, Demades and his fellows bore all the sway and authority, and Demosthenes was under foot. Indeed when Agis, king of Lacedaemon, came with his army into the field, he began a little to rouse himself and to lift up his head, but he shrunk collar again soon after because the Athenians would not rise with the Lacedaemonians, who were overthrown, and Agis slain in battle.[105] At that time was the cause of the crown pleaded against Ctesiphon, and the plea was written a little before the battle of Chaeronea, in

---

[102] Marg. 'Alexander required certain orators of Athens.'   Myrocles] Moerocles; N. follows A., who (in accordance with the manuscripts) has Myrocles.   Damon] Demon of Paeania.
[103] Marg. 'Demosthenes' tale of the sheep and wolves.'
[104] he thought he hoped] It appears that N. or the compositor failed to delete an earlier version here as this is both redundant and inelegant ('he [verb] he [verb] he [verb]'), but it is not corrected in any of the later editions.
[105] In 330 BCE.   shrunk collar] '[drew] back from a task or undertaking' (*OED*, *n*., 8. a, citing this passage alone).

the year when Charondas was provost of Athens, howbeit no sentence was given till ten years after, when Aristophon was provost.¹⁰⁶ This was such an open° judgement, and so famous, as never was any, as well for the great fame of the orators that pleaded in emulation one of the other as also for the worthiness of the judges that gave sentence thereof, who did not leave Demosthenes to his enemies, although indeed they were of greater power than he and were also supported with the favour and goodwill of the Macedonians, but they did notwithstanding so well quit° him that Aeschines had not so much as the fifth part of men's voices and opinions on his side. Wherefore immediately after the sentence given, he went out of Athens for shame and travelled into the country of Ionia and unto the Rhodes, where he did teach rhetoric.¹⁰⁷

[25] Shortly after, Harpalus, flying out of Alexander's service, came unto Athens, being to be charged with many foul matters he had committed by his exceeding prodigality, and also because he feared Alexander's fury, who was grown severe and cruel unto his chiefest servants.¹⁰⁸ He coming now amongst the Athenians with store of gold and silver, the orators, being greedy and desirous of the gold and silver he had brought, began straight to speak for him and did counsel the people to receive and protect a poor suitor that came to them for succour.¹⁰⁹ But Demosthenes gave counsel to the contrary, and bad them rather drive him out of the city and take heed they brought not wars upon their backs for a matter that not only was not necessary but furthermore merely° unjust. But within few days after, inventory being taken of all Harpalus' goods, he perceiving that Demosthenes took great pleasure to see a cup of the kings and considered very curiously the fashion and workmanship upon it, he gave it him in his hand to judge what it weighed.¹¹⁰ Demosthenes peising° it wondered at the great weight of it, it was so heavy, so he asked how many pound weight it weighed. Harpalus smiling answered him: 'It will bring thee twenty talents.'¹¹¹ So when

---

¹⁰⁶ **Marg.** 'The judgement of the crown unto Ctesiphon.' Aeschines had indicted Ctesiphon for having proposed that Demosthenes be crowned for his services to Athens in 337–336 BCE (not in 338–337, the year that Chaerondas [N. 'Charondas'] was archon [N. 'provost'], as P. thought). Aeschines' oration *Against Ctesiphon* and Demosthenes' reply *On the Crown* survive.

¹⁰⁷ the Rhodes] Rhodes. N. appears to have interpreted the 's' at the end of the name as signifying a plural and hence added a definite article.

¹⁰⁸ **Marg.** 'Harpalus a great monied man came to Athens, flying from Alexander.' In 324 BCE. being to be charged with] P. 'he was conscious that' (συνειδὼς); A. 'se sentant coulpable de' (feeling guilty of, p. 1031).

¹⁰⁹ the gold and silver] N. omits P. and A. 'and ships' ('et ses galeres', p. 1031).

¹¹⁰ of the kings] As A. points out in a marginal note (not included by N.), other manuscripts have 'foreign' (βαρβαρικῇ), the reading adopted by modern editions.

¹¹¹ Harpalus' response puns on the double meaning of the verb ἄγειν as both *weigh* and *bring*: Demosthenes asks how much the cup *weighs* (and thus, as it is made of gold, how much it is worth); Harpalus' reply is that it will *bring* him (with a secondary meaning

night was come, he sent him the cup with the twenty talents. This Harpalus was a very wise man and found straight by Demosthenes' countenance that he loved money and could presently judge his nature by seeing his pleasant countenance and his eyes still upon the cup. So Demosthenes refused not his gift and being overcome withal, as if he had received a garrison into his house, he took Harpalus' part.[112] The next morning he went into the assembly of the people having his neck bound up with wool and rolls.° So when they called him by his name to step up into the pulpit to speak to the people as he had done before, he made a sign with his head that he had an impediment in his voice and that he could not speak. But wise men, laughing at his fine excuse, told him it was no squinance° that had stopped his weezle° that night, as he would make them believe, but it was Harpalus' money which he had received that made him in that case.[113] Afterwards, when the people understood that he was corrupted, Demosthenes going about to excuse himself, they would not abide to hear him but made a noise and exclamation against him. Thereupon there rose up a pleasant conceited man and said: 'Why, my masters, do ye refuse to hear a man that hath such a golden tongue?'.[114] The people thereupon did immediately banish Harpalus, and fearing lest King Alexander would require an account of the gold and silver which the orators had robbed and pilfered away among them, they made very diligent search and inquiry in every man's house, excepting Callicles' house, the son of Arrenidas, whose house they would by no means have searched because he was but newly married and had his new spouse in his house, as Theopompus writeth.[115]

[26] Now Demosthenes, desiring to show that he was in no fault, preferred a

---

of weighing and thus being worth to him) twenty talents (which is both a weight and a currency). A. uses the verb *emporter* (p. 1031), which can mean both *weigh down* (scales) and *bring*. The first edition of 1579 has 'wey' (weigh) for 'bring' in an attempt to reproduce P.'s (and A.'s) word play.

[112] Marg. 'Demosthenes bribed by Harpalus with twenty talents.'

[113] In the first edition of 1579 N. attempted to reproduce the pun in the Greek, anglicizing P.'s συνάγχη (sore throat) as 'sinanche' and combining it with the Latin and French 'argent-' (money) to produce an equivalent of the Greek ἀργυράγχη (money-throat-ache): 'argentsinanche'. The third edition of 1603 abandons the endeavour to find an equivalent for the word-play in the Greek and aims for clarity instead, changing 'sinanche' (which is not English) to 'squinance' (which is English and means tonsillitis) and 'argentsinanche' to 'money' (as A. has: 'esquinance [...] argent', p. 1031). See Introduction, p. 60.

[114] Marg. '* This conceit can hardly be expressed in any other language than in Greek. For he saith, οὐκ ἀκούσατε τοῦ τὴν κύλικα ἔχοντος: alluding to the verb κηλεῖν, which signifieth to delight by pleasant speech or sound.' The Greek quotation translates 'did ['will' in P.] you not listen to the man who holds the cup [κύλιξ]?'. It refers to the custom that the guest who held the drinking cup had the right to sing or speak without interruption.

pleasant conceited] inclined to wit.

[115] Arrenidas] Arrheneides.

decree that the court of the Areopagites should hear the matter and punish them that were found faulty and therewithal straight offered himself to be tried. Howbeit, he was one of the first whom the court condemned in the sum of fifty talents, and for lack of payment they put him in prison, where he could not endure long, both for the shame of the matter for the which he was condemned as also for his sickly body. So he broke prison, partly without° the privity° of his keepers and partly also with their consent, for they were willing he should make a scape.° Some do report that he fled not far from the city, where it was told him that certain of his enemies followed him, whereupon he would have hidden himself from them, but they themselves first called him by his name and, coming to him, prayed him to take money of them, which they had brought him from their houses to help him in his banishment, and that therefore they ran after him.[116] Then they did comfort him the best they could, and persuaded him to be of good cheer, and not to despair for the misfortune that was come unto him. This did pierce his heart the more for sorrow, that he answered them: 'Why, would you not have me be sorry for my misfortune, that compelleth me to forsake the city where indeed I have so courteous enemies that it is hard for me to find anywhere so good friends?'. So he took his banishment unmanly and remained the most part of his banishment in the city of Aegina or at the city of Troezen, where oftentimes he would cast his eyes towards the country of Attica and weep bitterly.[117] And some have written certain words he spoke which showed no mind of a man of courage nor were answerable to the noble things he was wont to persuade in his orations. For it is reported of him that as he went out of Athens, he looked back again and, holding up his hands to the castle, said in this sort:[118] 'O Lady Minerva, lady patroness of this city, why doest thou delight in three so mischievous beasts: the owl, the dragon, and the people?'.[119] Besides, he persuaded the young men that came to see him and that were with him never to meddle in matters of state, assuring them that if they had offered him two ways at the first, the one to go into the assembly of the people to make orations in the pulpit and the other to be put to death presently, and that he had known as he did then the troubles a man is compelled to suffer that meddleth with the affairs of the state — the fear, the envy, the accusations, and troubles in the same — he would rather have chosen the way to have suffered death.

[27] So Demosthenes continuing in his exile, King Alexander died, and all Greece was up again, insomuch as Leosthenes, being a man of great valour, had shut up Antipater in the city of Lamea and there kept him straightly besieged.[120] Then Pytheas and Callimedon, surnamed Carabos, two orators and both of

[116] Marg. 'Demosthenes' banishment.'
[117] Marg. 'Demosthenes took his banishment grievously.'
[118] castle] The Acropolis, the citadel of Athens, which included a temple to the goddess Athena (whose Roman equivalent was Minerva).
[119] Marg. 'Three mischievous beasts.'
[120] Marg. 'Antipater besieged of the Athenians.' In 323 BCE.   Lamea] Lamia.

them banished from Athens, they took part with Antipater and went from town to town with his ambassadors and friends, persuading the Grecians not to stir, neither to take part with the Athenians.[121] But Demosthenes, in contrary manner, joining with the ambassadors sent from Athens into every quarter to solicit the cities of Greece to seek to recover their liberty, he did aid them the best he could to solicit the Grecians to take arms with the Athenians to drive the Macedonians out of Greece. And Phylarchus writeth that Demosthenes encountered with Pytheas' words in an open assembly of the people in a certain town of Arcadia. Pytheas, having spoken before him, had said: 'Like as we presume always that there is some sickness in the house whither we do see ass's milk brought, so must that town of necessity be sick wherein the ambassadors of Athens do enter.' Demosthenes answered him again, turning his comparison against him, that indeed they brought ass's milk where there was need to recover health, and even so the ambassadors of Athens were sent to heal and cure them that were sick. The people at Athens understanding what Demosthenes had done, they so rejoiced at it that presently they gave order in the field that his banishment should be revoked.[122] He that persuaded the decree of his revocation was called Daemon Paeanian, that was his nephew, and thereupon the Athenians sent him a galley to bring him to Athens from the city of Aegina.[123] So Demosthenes being arrived at the haven of Piraea, there was neither governor, priest, nor almost any townsman left in the city but went out to the haven to welcome him home. So that Demetrius Magnesian writeth that Demosthenes then, lifting up his hands unto heaven, said that he thought himself happy for the honour of that journey, that the return from his banishment was far more honourable than Alcibiades' return in the like case had been. For Alcibiades was called home by force, and he was sent for with the goodwill of the citizens. This notwithstanding, he remained still condemned for his fine, for by the law the people could not dispense withal nor remit it. Howbeit, they devised a way to deceive the law, for they had a manner to give certain money unto them that did prepare and set out the altar of Jupiter Saviour for the day of the solemnity of the sacrifice, the which they did yearly celebrate unto him, so they gave him the charge to make this preparation for the sum of fifty talents, being the sum of the fine aforesaid wherein he was condemned.[124]

[28] Howbeit, he did not long enjoy the good hap of his restitution to his country and goods, for the affairs of the Grecians were immediately after brought

---

[121] Carabos] Greek for 'Stag Beetle'.
[122] Marg. 'Demosthenes called home from exile.' N. translates A.'s idiomatic expression 'sur le champ' (immediately, p. 1032) twice, once correctly ('presently') and once literally ('in the field'), having seemingly failed to remember to delete the latter once he included the former.
[123] Daemon] Demon.
[124] Marg. 'Demosthenes' fine of fifty talents remitted.'

to utter ruin. For the battle of Cranon, which they lost, was in the month Munychion (to wit, July), and in the month Boedromion next ensuing (to wit, August) the garrison of the Macedonians entered into the fort of Munychia.[125] And in the month Pyanepsion (to wit, the October following) Demosthenes died in this manner. When news came to Athens that Antipater and Craterus were coming thither with a great army, Demosthenes and his friends got out of the town a little before they entered, the people (by Demades' persuasion) having condemned them to die. So every man making shift for himself, Antipater sent soldiers after them to take them, and of them Archias was captain, surnamed Phygadotheras, as much to say as a hunter of the banished men.[126] It is reported that this Archias was born in the city of Thuries, and that he had been sometimes° a common player of tragedies, and that Polus also, who was born in the city of Aegina, the excellentest craftsmaster in that faculty of all men, was his scholar.[127] Yet Hermippus doth place him[128] amongst the number of the scholars of Lacritus the orator, and Demetrius also writeth that he had been at Anaximenes' school. Now this Archias having found the orator Hyperides in the city of Aegina, Aristonicus Marathonian and Himeraeus the brother of Demetrius the Phalerian, which had taken sanctuary in the temple of Ajax, he took them out of the temple by force and sent them unto Antipater, who was at that time in the city of Cleones, where he did put them all to death, and some say that he did cut off Hyperides' tongue.[129]

[29] Furthermore, hearing that Demosthenes had taken sanctuary in the Isle of Calauria, he took little pinnaces° with a certain number of Thracian soldiers, and being come thither, he sought to persuade Demosthenes to be contented to go with him unto Antipater, promising him that he should have no hurt.[130] Demosthenes had a strange dream the night before and thought that he had played a tragedy contending with Archias and that he handled himself so well that all the lookers-on at the theatre did commend him and gave him the honour to be the best player, howbeit that otherwise he was not so well furnished° as Archias and his players and that in all manner of furniture° he did far exceed

[125] In 322 BCE. Cranon] Crannon. in the month [...] August)] N. combines A. and Cruser here: A. solely gives the French names of the month ('Juillet', 'Aoust', p. 1033); Cruser, Latinized versions of the Greek names ('mense Munichione', 'Boedromione', p. 599); the same applies to 'Pyanepsion' in the following sentence and in line 885 (where it is erroneously spelled 'Pynepsion'). The Greek text in Plutarch, *Quae extant opera* (1572), VI, 1574, correctly gives the name of the first month listed here as Μεταγειτνιών instead of Munychion.
[126] Marg. 'Archias Phygadotheras, a hunter of the banished men.'
[127] Thuries] Thurii.
[128] i.e. Archias.
[129] the temple of Ajax] the temple of Aeacus (τὸ Αἰάκειον), ancestral hero of Aegina. N. follows A. Cleones] Cleonae.
[130] in the Isle of Calauria] N. omits P. and A. 'in the temple of Poseidon'.

him.¹³¹ The next morning, when Archias came to speak with him, and using gentle words unto him, thinking thereby to win him by fair means to leave the sanctuary, Demosthenes looking him full in the face, sitting still where he was without removing, said unto him: 'O Archias, thou didst never persuade me when thou playedst a play, neither shalt thou now persuade me, though thou promise me.' Then Archias began to be angry with him and to threaten him. 'O,' said Demosthenes, 'now thou speakest in good earnest, without dissimulation, as the oracle of Macedon hath commanded thee, for before thou spokest in the clouds and far from thy thought.¹³² But I pray thee, stay° a while, till I have written somewhat to my friends.' After he had said so, he went into the temple as though he would have dispatched some letters, and did put the end of the quill in his mouth which he wrote withal,° and bit it as his manner was when he did use to write anything, and held the end of the quill in his mouth a pretty while together; then he cast his gown over his head and laid him down.¹³³ Archias' soldiers seeing that, being at the door of the temple, laughed him to scorn (thinking he had done so for that he was afraid to die), calling him coward and beast. Archias also, coming to him, prayed him to rise and began to use the former persuasions to him, promising him that he would make Antipater his friend. Then Demosthenes, feeling the poison work, cast open his gown and, boldly looking Archias in the face, said unto him: 'Now when thou wilt, play Creon's part and throw my body to the dogs without further grave or burial.¹³⁴ For my part, O God Neptune, I do go out of thy temple being yet alive because I will not profane it with my death, but Antipater and the Macedonians have not spared to defile thy sanctuary with blood and cruel murder.' Having spoken these words, he prayed them to stay him up by his armholes, for his feet began already to fail him, and thinking to go forward, as he passed by the altar of Neptune, he fell down and, giving one gasp, gave up the ghost.¹³⁵

[30] Now touching the poison, Aristo reporteth that he sucked and drew it up into his mouth out of his quill, as we have said before. But one Pappus (from whom Hermippus hath taken his history) writeth that when he was laid on the ground before the altar, they found the beginning of a letter which said 'Demosthenes unto Antipater', but no more. Now his death being thus sudden,

---

¹³¹ Marg. 'Demosthenes' dream.'   he did far exceed him] i.e. Archias had much the better of Demosthenes (in terms of costume and other equipment necessary for dramatic performance).
¹³² thou spokest in the clouds] N.'s translation obscures the reference to play-acting present in the Greek (ὑπεκρίνου) and French ('en masque', p. 1033).
¹³³ Marg. 'Demosthenes taketh poison to kill himself in the temple of Neptune in the Isle of Calauria.'
¹³⁴ Creon in Sophocles' *Antigone* orders the body of Polyneices to remain unburied.
¹³⁵ Marg. 'The death of Demosthenes.'

the Thracian soldiers that were at the temple-door reported that they saw him pluck the poison which he put into his mouth out of a little cloth he had, thinking to them that it had been a piece of gold he had swallowed down. Howbeit, a maid of the house that served him, being examined about it, told him that he had carried it about him a long time for a preservative for him. Eratosthenes writeth that he kept this poison in a little box of gold made hollow within, the which he wore as a bracelet about his arm. There are many writers also that do report his death diversely, but to recite them all it were in vain, saving that there was one called Demochares (who was Demosthenes' very friend said), who said that he died not so suddenly by poison, but that it was the special favour of the gods to preserve him from the cruelty of the Macedonians, that so suddenly took him out of his life and made him feel so little pain.[136] Demosthenes died the sixteenth day of the month Pynepsion (to wit, October), on the which day they do celebrate at Athens the feast of Ceres called Tesmophoria, which is the dolefulest feast of all the year, on the which day also the women remain all day long in the temple of the goddess without meat° or drink.[137] Shortly after, the Athenians to honour him according to his deserts did cast his image in brass, and made a law besides that the oldest man of his house should forever be kept within the palace at the charge of the commonwealth, and engraved these verses also upon the base of his image:[138] 'Hadst thou, Demosthenes, had strength according to thy heart, | The Macedons should not have wrought the Greeks such woe and smart.' For they that think that it was Demosthenes himself that made the verses in the Isle of Calauria before he took his poison, they are greatly deceived.

[31] But yet a little before my first coming to Athens, there went a report that such a thing happened. A certain soldier being sent for to come unto his captain did put such pieces of gold as he had into the hands of Demosthenes' statue, which had both his hands joined together, and there grew hard by it a great

---

[136] (who was Demosthenes' very friend said), who said] The addition of the relative pronoun 'who' before 'said' in the third edition of 1603 fixes the grammatical structure of the sentence, but the repetition of 'said' in the first place appears to have been a compositorial error. Demochares was a nephew of Demosthenes (P. οἰκεῖος: kinsman); N. follows A. ('son familier ami', p. 1034).

[137] Marg. 'The time of Demosthenes' death.' Pynepsion] Pyanepsion. on the which day they do celebrate at Athens the feast of Ceres called Tesmophoria, which is the dolefulest feast of all the year] P. 'on which [date] observing the most gloomy day of the Thesmophoria' (ἐν ᾗ τὴν σκυθρωποτάτην τῶν Θεσμοφορίων ἡμέραν ἄγουσαι); the explanatory addition and the transposition of 'gloomy' from the day to the feast are A.'s ('auquel jour se celebre à Athenes la feste de Ceres, qui s'appelle Thesmophoria, qui est la plus austere et la plus triste solennité de toute l'annee', p. 1034).

[138] Marg. 'The Athenians honoured Demosthenes after his death.' the palace] The prytaneion, the Athenian equivalent of the town hall.

plane tree, divers leaves whereof either blown off by wind, by chance, or else put there of purpose by the soldier covered so this gold that it was there a long time and no man found it until such time as the soldier came again and found it as he left it.[139] Hereupon this matter running abroad in every man's mouth, there were divers wise men that took occasion of this subject to make epigrams in the praise of Demosthenes, as one who in his life was never corrupted. Furthermore, Demades did not long enjoy the honour he thought he had newly gotten. For the justice of the gods, revenger of the death of Demosthenes, brought him into Macedon to receive just punishment by death of those whom he dishonestly flattered, being before grown hateful to them, and afterwards committed a fault whereby he could not escape.[140] For there were letters of his taken, by the which he did persuade and pray Perdiccas[141] to make himself king of Macedon and to deliver Greece from bondage, saying that it hung but by a thread and yet it was half rotten, meaning thereby Antipater. Dinarchus Corinthian accused him that he wrote these letters, the which so grievously offended Cassander that first he slew his own son[142] in his arms and then commanded they should afterwards kill Demades, making him feel then by those miseries (which are the cruellest that can happen unto man) that traitors betraying their own country do first of all betray themselves.[143] Demosthenes had often forewarned him of his end, but he would never believe him. Thus, my friend Sossius, you have what we can deliver you, by reading or report, touching Demosthenes' life and doings.

---

[139] a great plane tree] P. 'not big' (οὐ μεγάλη); N. follows A. ('un grand Platane', p. 1034).
[140] the justice of the gods, revenger of the death of Demosthenes] P. has simply ἡ Δημοσθένους δίκη (vengeance for Demosthenes). N. follows A.'s expansion ('la justice divine, vengeresse de la mort de Demosthenes', p. 1035), which brings out the latent reference to divine retribution in P.
[141] Marg. '* He saith Antigonus in *The Life of Phocion*.'
[142] i.e. Demades' son.
[143] Marg. 'Demades' death and reward for his treason.'

The life of Marcus Tullius Cicero.

[1] As touching Cicero's mother, whose name was Helvia, it is reported she was a gentlewoman born and lived always very honestly, but for his father, the reports of him are diverse and infinite.¹ For some say that he was born and brought up in a fuller's shop;² others report that he came of Tullius Actius, who while he lived was honoured among the Volsces as king and made very sharp and cruel wars with the Romans.³ But surely it seems to me that the first of that name called Cicero was some famous man and that for his sake his offspring continued still that surname and were glad to keep it, though many men scorned it because *cicer* in English signifieth a chickpea. That Cicero had a thing upon the tip of his nose, as it had been a little wart, much like to a chickpea, whereupon they surnamed him Cicero.⁴ But this Cicero whose life we write of now nobly answered certain of his friends on a time giving him counsel to change his name when he first made suit for office and began to practise in matters of state that he would endeavour himself to make the name of Ciceros more noble and famous than the Scauri or Catuli.⁵ After that, Cicero being made treasurer in Sicily, he gave an offering of certain silver plate unto the gods and at large engraved on it his two first names, Marcus Tullius, and in place of his third name he pleasantly commanded the workman to cut out the form and fashion° of a chickpea.⁶ Thus much they write of his name.

[2] Now for his birth, it was said that his mother was brought to bed of him without any pain the third day of January, on which day the magistrates and governors of Rome do use at this present yearly to make solemn prayers and sacrifices unto the gods for the health and prosperity of the emperor.⁷ Further, it is reported that there appeared an image to his nurse that did prognosticate unto her she gave a child suck which in time to come should do great good unto all the Romans.⁸ Now, though such things may seem but dreams and fables unto many,⁹ yet Cicero himself shortly after proved this prophecy true, because

---

¹   Marg. 'Cicero's parentage.'
²   Particularly shameful because fullers used urine to clean clothes.
³   Actius] Attius.   Volsces] Volscians.
⁴   Marg. 'Cicero, why so called.'   as it had been] alike.
⁵   Scauri or Catuli] Prominent consular families whose names have equally dubious significations: 'swollen-ankled' and 'puppy'.
⁶   Marg. 'Cicero quaestor.'   treasurer] quaestor, as the marginal note makes clear. A. explains: 'Quaesteur, c'est à dire, superintendant des finances' (p. 1036).
⁷   Marg. 'Cicero's birth.' In 106 BCE.
⁸   Marg. 'An image appeared to Cicero's nurse.'
⁹   P. is more specific: 'these [presages] were thought to be mere dreams and idle fancies'. A. (followed by N.) presents the belief in prognostications in general as a form of superstition ('telles choses semblent à plusieurs estre songes et resveries', p. 1036).

that when he came of age to learn he grew so toward and won such fame among the boys for his excellent wit and quick capacity.[10] For thereupon came the other boys' fathers themselves to the school to see his face and to be eye witnesses of the report that went of him of his sharp and quick wit to learn. But others, of the rude and baser sort of men, were offended with their sons because to honour Cicero they did always put him in the midst between them as they went in the streets. Cicero indeed had such a natural wit and understanding as Plato thought meet for learning and apt for the study of philosophy.[11] For he gave himself to all kind of knowledge, and there was no art nor any of the liberal sciences that he disdained, notwithstanding in his first young years he was apter and better disposed to the study of poetry than any other.[12] There is a pretty poem of his in verses of eight staves called Pontius Glaucus extant at this day, the which he made when he was but a boy.[13] After that, being given more earnestly unto this study, he was not only thought the best orator but the best poet also of all the Romans in his time. And yet doth the excellency of his eloquence and commendation of his tongue continue even to this day, notwithstanding the great alteration and change of the Latin tongue, but his poetry hath lost the name and estimation of it, because there were many after him that became far more excellent therein than he.

[3] After he had left his childish studies, he became then Philo's scholar, the Academic philosopher, the only scholar of all Clitomachus' scholars whom the Romans esteemed so much for his eloquence and loved more for his gentle behaviour and conversation.°[14] He gave himself also to be a follower of Mucius Scaevola, who at that time was a great man in Rome and prince of the senate and who did also instruct Cicero in the laws of Rome.[15] He did also follow Sulla for a time in the wars of the Marsians.[16] But when he saw that the commonwealth of Rome fell to civil wars, and from civil wars to a monarchy, then he returned again to his book and contemplative life, and frequented the learned men of Greece, and always studied with them until Sulla had gotten the upper hand and that he

---

[10] Marg. 'Cicero's towardness and wit.'
[11] *Republic*, 475B.
[12] Marg. 'Cicero a notable poet.'   Cicero indeed [...] other] P. 'And although he showed himself, as Plato thought a nature should do which was fond of learning and fond of wisdom, capable of welcoming all knowledge and incapable of slighting any kind of literature or training, he lent himself with somewhat greater ardour to the art of poetry.' N. follows A.
[13] of eight staves] 'Staves' can mean either lines of verse or stanzas, but A. refers to the number of feet in a line of verse instead ('iambiques de huict pieds', p. 1036; P. 'tetrameter').
[14] Marg. 'Cicero, Philo's scholar, the Academic philosopher.'
[15] Marg. 'Cicero a follower of Mutius Scaevola.'
[16] In 89 BCE.

saw all the commonwealth again at some stay.¹⁷ About that time, Sulla causing the goods of one that was said to be slain to be sold by the crier (being one of the outlaws and proscripts,° to wit, banished by bills set up on posts), Chrysogonus, one of Sulla's freed bondmen and in great favour with his master, bought them for the sum of two thousand drachms. Therewithal the son and heir of the dead person, called Roscius, being marvellously offended, he showed that it was too shameful an abuse, for his father's goods amounted to the sum of two hundred and fifty talents. Sulla finding himself thus openly touched with public fraud and deceit for the only gratifying of his man, he procured Chrysogonus to accuse him that he had killed his own father.¹⁸ Never an orator durst speak in Roscius' behalf to defend his cause but shrank back fearing Sulla's cruelty and severity. Wherefore poor Roscius, the young man, seeing every man forsake him, had no other refuge but to go to Cicero, whom his friends did counsel and persuade boldly to take upon him the defence of Roscius' cause, for he should never have a happier occasion, nor so noble a beginning, to bring himself into estimation as this. Thereupon Cicero determined to take his cause in hand and did handle it so well that he obtained the thing he sued for, whereby he won him great fame and credit.¹⁹ But yet, being afraid of Sulla's displeasure, he absented himself from Rome and went into Greece, giving it out that his travel was for a disease he had upon him. Indeed Cicero was dog lean, a little eater, and would also eat late because of the great weakness of his stomach, but yet he had a good loud voice, though it was somewhat harsh and lacked grace and comeliness.²⁰ Furthermore, he was so earnest and vehement in his oration that he mounted still° with his voice into the highest tunes, insomuch that men were afraid it would one day put him in hazard of his life.

[4] When he came to Athens, he went to hear Antiochus of the city of Ascalon and fell in great liking with his sweet tongue and excellent grace, though otherwise he misliked his new opinions in philosophy.²¹ For Antiochus had then forsaken the opinions of the New Academic philosophers and the sect of the Carneades,²² being moved thereunto either through the manifest proof of things or by his certain judgement,²³ or (as some say) for that° of an ambition or dissention against the scholars and followers of Clitomachus and Philo he

---

17 In 82 BCE.
18 Marg. 'Roscius put in suit.'
19 In 80 BCE.
20 Marg. 'Cicero a weak man.'
21 Marg. 'Cicero, Antiochus' scholar.'
22 Carneades (as in P. and A.) of Cyrene, founder of the New Academy (214/3–129/8 BCE).
23 the manifest proof of things or by his certain judgement] N.'s 'or' instead of P. and A. 'and' reflects his wider confusion about the philosophical implication of the passage, which is that Cicero (in contrast to the New Academics) accepted the validity of sense perceptions in philosophical enquiry.

had reproved the resolutions of the Academics, which he had of long time defended, only to lean for the most part to the Stoics' opinions. Howbeit, Cicero had most affection unto the Academics and did study that sect more than all the rest, of purpose that if he saw he were forbidden to practise in the commonwealth at Rome, he would then go to Athens (leaving all pleas and affairs of the commonwealth) to bestow the rest of his time quietly in the study of philosophy.[24] At length, when he heard news of Sulla's death, and saw that his body was grown to good state and health by exercise and that his voice became daily more and more to fill men's ears with a sweet and pleasant sound, and yet was loud enough for the constitution of his body,[25] receiving letters daily from his friends at Rome that prayed him to return home and, moreover, Antiochus self also earnestly persuading him to practise in the commonwealth, he began again to fall to the study of rhetoric and to frame himself to be eloquent, being a necessary thing for an orator, and did continually exercise himself in making orations upon any speech or proposition, and so frequented the chief orators and masters of eloquence that were at that time. To this end, therefore, he went into Asia unto Rhodes,[26] and amongst the orators of Asia he frequented Xenocles Adramettin and Dionysius Magnesian and studied also with Menippus Carian; at Rhodes he heard Apollonius Molon and the philosopher Posidonius.[27] And it is reported also that Apollonius, wanting the Latin tongue, he did pray Cicero for exercise sake to declaim in Greek.[28] Cicero was very well contented with it, thinking that thereby his faults should be the better corrected. When he had ended his declamation, all those that were present were amazed to hear him, and every man praised him, one after another. Howbeit, Apollonius all the while Cicero spoke did never show any glad countenance, and when he had ended, he stayed° a great while and said never a word. Cicero misliking withal,° Apollonius at length said unto him: 'As for me, Cicero, I do not only praise thee, but, more than that, I wonder at thee, and yet I am sorry for poor Greece to see that learning and eloquence, which were the two only gifts and honours left us, are by thee obtained with us and carried unto the Romans.'[29]

[5] Now Cicero being very well disposed to go with good hope to practise at Rome, he was a little discouraged by an oracle that was told him. For, inquiring

---

[24] (leaving [...] commonwealth)] N.'s correction in the third edition of 1603 from 'leaving all pleas and orators in the commonwealth' to 'leaving all pleas and affairs of the commonwealth' brings the text in line with A. 'loin de toute plaiderie, et de toute administration de la chose publique' (far from all legal proceedings and from all government of the commonwealth, p. 1037).
[25] Marg. 'The commodity of exercise.'
[26] P. and A. 'to Asia and Rhodes' (as N.'s marginal note correctly has).
[27] Marg. 'Cicero goeth into Asia and to Rhodes.'   Adramettin] P. τῷ Ἀδραμυττηνῷ (of Adramyttium, on the west coast of modern Turkey). N. follows A. to the letter.
[28] Marg. 'Cicero declaimed in Greek.'
[29] Marg. 'Apollonius' testimony of Cicero.'

of the god Apollo Delphian how he might do to win fame and estimation, the nun Pythias answered him he should obtain it so that° in his doings he would rather follow the disposition of his own nature than the opinion of the common people.[30] Wherefore, when he came to Rome, at the first he proceeded very warily and discreetly and did unwillingly seek for any office, and when he did, he was not greatly esteemed, for they commonly called him the Grecian and scholar, which are two words the which the artificers and such base mechanical people at Rome have ever ready at their tongue's end.[31] Now he being by nature ambitious of honour and pricked forward also by the persuasion of his father and friends, in the end he began to plead, and there obtained not the chiefest place by little and little, but so soon as he fell to practise he was immediately esteemed above all the other orators and pleaders in his time and did excel them all. Yet it is reported notwithstanding that for his gesture and pronunciation, having the selfsame defects of nature at the beginning which Demosthenes had, to reform them he carefully studied to counterfeit Roscius, an excellent comedian, and Aesop also, a player of tragedies.[32] Of this Aesop men write that he playing one day Atreus' part upon a stage, who determined with himself how he might be revenged of his brother Thyestes, a servant by chance having occasion to run suddenly by him, he forgetting himself, striving to show the vehement passion and fury of this king, gave him such a blow on his head with the sceptre in his hand that he slew him dead in the place.[33] Even so, Cicero's words were of great force to persuade by means of his grace and pronunciation. For he, mocking the orators that thrust out their heads and cried in their orations, was wont to say that they were like to lame men, who were driven to ride because they could not go on foot: even so, said he, they cry out because they cannot speak. Truly pleasant taunts do grace an orator, and showeth a fine wit, but yet Cicero used them so commonly that they were offensive unto many and brought him to be counted a malicious scoffer and spiteful man.[34]

[6] He was chosen treasurer in the time of dearth, when there was great scarcity of corn at Rome, and the province of Sicily fell to his lot.[35] At his first coming thither, the Sicilians misliked him very much, because he compelled them to send corn unto Rome, but after they had found his diligence, justice, and

---

[30] Marg. 'An Oracle given to Cicero.'   Pythias] Pythia, the priestess of Apollo at Delphi.
[31] Marg. 'Cicero's first practising in the commonwealth.' In 77 BCE.
[32] Marg. 'Roscius and Aesop common players.'
[33] Atreus' wife, Aerope, had handed over to her lover and brother-in-law Thyestes a golden lamb whose owner would be entitled to the kingship of Mycenae. Atreus avenged the adultery by killing Thyestes' sons and serving him their flesh for dinner.
[34] Marg. 'Cicero a fine taunter.'
[35] Marg. 'Cicero chosen quaestor.' In 75 BCE.

lenity, they honoured him above any governor that ever was sent from Rome.³⁶ Now there were divers young gentlemen of Rome of noble houses who, being accused for sundry faults committed in wars against their honour and martial discipline, had been sent back again unto the praetor of Sicily, for whom Cicero pleaded, and did so excellently defend their cause that they were pardoned every man. Thereupon, thinking well of himself, when his time was expired, he went to Rome, and by the way there happened a pretty jest unto him. As he passed through the country of Campania (otherwise called the land of labour), he met by chance with one of the chiefest Romans of all his friends.³⁷ So falling in talk with him, he asked him what they said of him at Rome and what they thought of his doings, imagining that all Rome had been full of the glory of his name and deeds. His friend asked him again: 'And where hast thou been, Cicero, all this while, that we have not seen thee at Rome?'. This killed his heart straight, when he saw that the report of his name and doings, entering into the city of Rome as into an infinite sea, was so suddenly vanished away again, without any other fame or speech. But after that, when he looked into himself and saw that in reason he took an infinite labour in hand to attain to glory, wherein he saw no certain end whereby to attain unto it, it cut off a great part of the ambition he had in his head.³⁸ And yet, the great pleasure he took to hear his own praise and to be overmuch given to desire of honour and estimation, these two things continued with him even to his dying day, and did eftsoons° make him swerve from justice.³⁹

[7] Furthermore, when he began thoroughly to practise in the affairs of the state, he thought it an ill thing that artificers and craftsmen should have many sorts of instruments and tools without life, to know the names of every one of them,⁴⁰ the places where they should take them, and the use whereto they should employ them, and that a man of knowledge and quality (who doth all things with the help and service of men) should be slothful and careless to learn

---

³⁶ Marg. 'Cicero's diligence, justice, and lenity.'
³⁷ labour] N's translation of A.'s 'labour' (p. 1038), which means 'tillage' here. A.'s explanatory addition translated by N. as '(otherwise called the land of labour)' points to the derivation of Campania from Latin *campus*, a plain suitable for agriculture.
³⁸ in reason] N.'s transposition and adaptation of this phrase from the previous clause, where Cicero, in A.'s words, 'vint à considerer en lui-mesme avec discours de raison' (p. 1039; P. λογισμός), obscures the key role of reason (and Cicero's failure to adhere to it) in this passage and the Life. See Introduction, pp. 48–50.
³⁹ swerve from justice] A. 'dévoier du droit chemin de la raison' (deviate from the true path of reason, p. 1039). Again, N.'s translation obfuscates the centrality of the conflict between reason and the emotions in P.'s moral analysis of Cicero's life, reflected in P.'s repetition of the word λογισμός (reason). Marg. 'Cicero ambitious and desirous of praise.'
⁴⁰ to know] i.e. and know.

to know the names of his citizens.⁴¹ Therefore he gave himself to know not only men's names of quality but the streets also they dwelt in, what part of the city soever it was, their goodly houses in the country, the friends they made of, and the neighbours whom they companied with.⁴² So that when he went abroad into Italy, wheresoever he became,° Cicero could show and name his friends' houses. He was not very rich, and yet he had enough to serve his turn, the which made men muse the more at him, and they loved him the better, because he took no fee nor gift for his pleading, what cause soever he took in hand, but then specially when he defended a matter against Verres.⁴³ This Verres had been praetor of Sicilia, and had committed many lewd° parts there, for the which the Sicilians did accuse him. Cicero, taking upon him to defend their cause, made Verres to be condemned, not by pleading, but in manner without pleading, and in this sort. The praetors, being his judges and favouring Verres, had made so many rejournments° and delays that they had driven it off to the last day of hearing. Cicero perceiving then he should not have time to speak all that he had to say against him and that thereby nothing should be done and judged, he rose up and said that there needed no further plea in this matter, but only brought forth the witnesses before the judges and, having caused their depositions to be taken, he prayed they would proceed to sentence according to their evidence given on that behalf. Yet some do report that Cicero gave many pleasant taunts and girds° in pleading the accusation of the Sicilians against Verres. The Romans do call a boar *verres*. There was one Caecilius, the son of a freed bondman, who was suspected to hold with the superstition of the Jews.⁴⁴ This Caecilius would have put by° the Sicilians from following the accusation of Verres and would have had the matter of his accusation only referred to him for the prosecuting of it against him. Cicero, scorning his suit, said unto him: 'What hath a Jew to do with a boar?'.⁴⁵ This Verres had a son somewhat above twenty years of age, who (as the report went) had a very ill name for his beauty, and therefore when Verres one day thought to mock Cicero, saying that he was too effeminate, 'Thy children', said he, 'are to be reproved of that secretly at home.' ⁴⁶ In this accusation Hortensius the orator durst not directly defend Verres, but touching the condemnation of his fine he was then contented

---

⁴¹ man of knowledge and quality] P. and A. 'statesman' ('un homme d'estat', p. 1039).
⁴² Marg. 'Cicero given to know men's names, their lands and friends.'   men's names of quality] i.e. the names of eminent men.
⁴³ Marg. 'Cicero's doings against Verres.' In 70 BCE.
⁴⁴ to hold [...] Jews] P. and A. have more neutral ἰουδαΐζειν (Judaising) and 'adherer à la loi des Juifs' (adhere to the law of the Jews, p. 1039). See Introduction, p. 69.
⁴⁵ Marg. 'He spoke it because the Jews do eat no swine's flesh.'
⁴⁶ This [...] beauty] N. mutes the sexual implications of this passage. Moles notes that P.'s description of Verres's son is 'an eloborate periphrasis for "prostitute"' (*Cicero*, 7. 7 n.). N. also makes the son significantly older; in P., he is ἀντίπαις (little more than a boy) and in A., 'ia à l'entree de son adolescence' (p. 1039).

to answer for him, for he had a sphinx of ivory given him by Verres for his reward. Thereupon Cicero gave him a pretty nip° by the way, but Hortensius not understanding him said he could° no skill of dark speeches. 'Well,' said Cicero, 'yet hast thou a sphinx in thy house.'

[8] In the end Verres being condemned and a fine set on his head to the value of threescore and fifteen myriads,° Cicero notwithstanding was suspected to be bribed with money for agreeing to cast him in so small a sum. But yet when he came to be aedilis, the Sicilians to show themselves thankful to him both brought and sent him many presents out of Sicily.[47] Of all that he took nothing to his own use, but only bestowed their liberality in bringing down the prices of victuals at Rome. He had a goodly house within the confines° of the city of Arpos, a farm also by Naples, and another about the city of Pompeii, but all these were no great things.[48] Afterwards he had also the jointure° of his wife Terentia, which amounted to the sum of twelve myriads, and besides all this there came to him by inheritance eleven myriads of their denarii.[49] Thereupon he lived very honestly and soberly without excess with his familiar friends that loved him, both Grecians and Romans, and would never go to supper till after sunset, not so much for any great business he had, as for the weakness of his stomach.[50] But otherwise he was very curious and careful of his person and would be rubbed and nointed,° and he would use also to walk a certain number of turns by proportion, and so exercising his body in that sort he was never sick and besides was also very strong and lusty of body, able to abide great pains and sorrows which he fell into afterwards. He gave his father's chief mansion house to his brother and went to dwell himself in the mount Palatine because such as came to wait upon him to do him honour should not take the pains to go so far to see him.[51] For he had as many men daily at his gate every morning as either Crassus had for his wealth or Pompey for his estimation among the soldiers, both of them being at that time the chiefest men of Rome. Yea furthermore,

---

[47] Marg. 'Cicero chosen aedilis.' In 69 BCE. Aediles supervised various areas of municipal government.
[48] Marg. 'Cicero's riches.'   Arpos] Arpi.
[49] twelve [...] eleven] The reference to myriads (ten thousands), as in the first sentence of this paragraph, and denarii indicates that N. is working directly from P.'s Greek here: 'a hundred and twenty thousand [lit. 'twelve ten thousands'] denarii [...] ninety thousand [lit. 'nine ten thousands']' (μυριάδων δώδεκα [...] ἐννέα δηναρίων [...] μυριάδας). Some manuscripts and editions (including Loeb) have δέκα (ten) instead of δώδεκα (twelve), but Plutarch, *Quae extant opera* (1572), VI, 1584, has the latter. A. has 'douze mille escus [...] neuf mille escus' (p. 1040) and Cruser 'CCCCLXXX millium nummum [...] CCCLX millia nummum' (p. 602). N. appears to have mixed up ἐννέα (nine) and ἕνδεκα (eleven).
[50] loved him] P. and A. 'loved letters' ('aimoient les lettres', p. 1040), i.e. his friends were scholars.
[51] Marg. 'Cicero's great courtesy and resort.°'

Pompey's self came unto Cicero because his orations stood him to great purpose for the increase of his honour and authority.

[9] Now when Cicero came to make suit to be praetor (which is, to be as an ordinary judge), though he had many competitors and fellow suitors with him, yet was he first chosen afore them all.⁵² And he did so honestly behave himself in that office that they did not so much as once suspect him of bribery or extortion. And for proof hereof, it is reported that Licinius Macer (a man that of himself was of great power and yet favoured and supported besides by Crassus) was accused before Cicero of theft and extortion in his office, but he, trusting much to his supposed credit and to the great suit and labour his friends made for him, went home to his house before sentence pronounced against him (the judges being yet to give their opinions) and there speedily trimmed his beard and put a new gown upon his back, as though he had been sure to have been quit° of his accusation, and then returned again into the marketplace; but Crassus went to meet him and told him all the judges had condemned him.⁵³ Licinius Macer took such a grief and conceit upon it that he went home to his house again, laid him down on his bed, and never rose after. This judgement won Cicero great fame, for they praised him exceedingly for the great pains he took to see justice duly executed. Another called also Vatinius (a bedlam fellow, and one that behaved himself very unreverently° to the magistrates in his pleading, and besides had a swollen neck) came very arrogantly one day unto Cicero, being in his praetorial seat, and asked him a thing which Cicero would not grant him there, but would think of it at better leisure.⁵⁴ Thereupon Vatinius told him that he would not be scrupulous to grant that if he were praetor. Cicero, turning to him, answered him again: 'No more have I', said he, 'such a swollen neck as thou hast.'⁵⁵ Towards the end of his office, two or three days before his time expired, there was one accused Manilius before him that he also had robbed the commonwealth. This Manilius was very well-beloved of the common people, who were persuaded that he was put in suit, not for any fault he had committed, but only to despite Pompey with, whose familiar friend he was. So he required° certain days to answer the matter he was accused of, but Cicero would give him no further respite but to answer it the next day. The people therewith were marvellously offended, because the other praetors in such like cases were wont to give ten days' respite unto others. The next morning, when the tribunes had brought him before the judges and also accused him unto them, he besought Cicero to hear him patiently.⁵⁶ Cicero

---

⁵² Marg. 'Cicero chosen praetor.' In 66 BCE.
⁵³ Marg. 'Licinius Macer condemned.'
⁵⁴ Another called also Vatinius] i.e. another also, called Vatinius.
⁵⁵ *Neck*, in Greek and in Latin, as in English, can refer to impudence.
⁵⁶ brought him] In P. 'him' refers to Cicero, but A. (followed by N.) takes this to refer to

made him answer that, having always used as much favour and courtesy as he possibly might by law unto those that were accused, he thought he should offer Manilius too great wrong if he should not do the like to him, wherefore, because he had but one day more to continue praetor in office, he had purposely given him that day to make his answer before him.[57] For he thought that to leave his accusation to the hearing of another praetor, he could not have been thought a man that had borne him goodwill and meant to pleasure him. These words did marvellously change the people's opinion and affection towards him, and every man speaking well of him, they prayed him to defend Manilius' cause. He willingly granted them, and coming from the bench, standing at the bar like an orator to plead for him, he made a notable oration and spoke both boldly and sharply against the chief men of the city, and those specially that did envy Pompey.

[10] This notwithstanding, when he came to sue to be consul, he found as great favour amongst the nobility as he did with the commonalty.[58] For they did further his suit for the commonwealth's sake upon this occasion.[59] The change and alteration of government the which Sulla brought in was thought strange at the first among the people, but now, men by process of time being used to it, it was throughly° established and no man misliked it. At that time many men practised to subvert the government, not for the benefit of the commonwealth, but to serve their own covetous minds.[60] For Pompey, being then in the east parts, made wars with the kings of Pontus and Armenia, and had not left sufficient force at Rome to resist these seditious persons that sought nothing but rebellion. These men had made Lucius Catiline their captain, a desperate man to attempt any great enterprise, subtle and malicious of nature.[61] He was accused before, besides many other vile faults, for deflowering of his own daughter and killing his brother, and being afraid to be put in suit for it, he prayed Sulla to put his brother amongst the number of the outlaws or proscripts as if he had been then alive. These wicked rebels, having chosen them such a captain, were sworn and bound one to another in this manner. They killed a man and did eat of his flesh together, and had besides corrupted the most part of all the youth. For Catiline, their captain, suffered every man to take his pleasure as his youth was inclined unto, as to banquet, to follow harlots, and gave them money largely°

Manilius and thus makes him address Cicero in the subsequent clause.
57   **Marg.** 'Cicero with one word pacified the offended tribunes.'
58   **Marg.** 'Cicero made consul.'
59   upon this occasion] i.e. for the following reasons.
60   **Marg.** 'The conspiracy of Catiline.'   At that time many men practised to subvert the government] N.'s translation obscures the contrast with the previous sentence: P. and A. 'There were those, however …' ('toutefois il y avoit quelques particuliers qui …', p. 1041).
61   **Marg.** 'Catiline's wickedness.'

to bestow in these vain expenses. Furthermore all Thuscan began to rise, and the most part of Gaul also lying between the Alps and Italy.⁶² The city of Rome itself was also in great danger of rising for the inequality of the goods of the inhabitants. For the noble men and of greatest courage had spent all their lands in plays and feasts or in buildings and common works, which they built at their own charge to curry favour with the common people that° they might obtain the chief offices, so that thereby they became very poor and their goods were in the hands of the mean men and wretches. Thus the state of Rome stood in great hazard of uproar, the which any man might easily have procured that durst have taken upon him any change or alteration of government, there was then such division among them in the state.

[11] Catiline, notwithstanding, to provide him of a strong bulwark to prosecute his intent, came to sue to be consul, hoping that he should be chosen with Caius Antonius, a man that of himself was apt neither to do any great good nor much hurt, and yet that could be a great strength and aid unto him that would attempt anything. Divers noble and wise men, foreseeing that, did procure Cicero to sue for the consulship. The people accepted him and rejected Catiline. Antonius and Cicero thereupon were created consuls, although that Cicero of all the suitors for the consulship was but only a knight's son and not the son of a senator of Rome.⁶³

[12] Now, though the common people understood not the secret practice and meaning of Catiline, yet at the beginning of Cicero's consulship there fell out great trouble and contention in the commonwealth.⁶⁴ For they of the one side whom Sulla had by his ordinances deposed from their dignities and offices in Rome, who were no small men, neither few in number, began to creep into the people's goodwill, alleging many true and just reasons against the tyrannical power of Sulla, howbeit spoken in ill time, when it was out of time to make any change or alteration in the commonwealth.⁶⁵ The tribunes, on the other side, preferred° laws and ordinances to further this device. They preferred the law to choose the decemviri, with sovereign power and authority through all Italy and Syria, and also through all the countries and provinces which Pompey had newly conquered to the empire of Rome, to sell and release all the lands belonging to the state of Rome, to accuse any man whom they thought good, to banish any man, to restore the colonies with people, to take what money they would out of the treasury, to levy men of war, and to keep them in pay as long

---

⁶² Thuscan] Tuscany.
⁶³ Marg. 'C. Antonius and M. T. Cicero created consuls.' In 63 BCE.
⁶⁴ Marg. 'Great troubles at Rome in the time of Cicero's consulship.'
⁶⁵ deposed from] P. and A. 'forbidden' ('ceux à qui il estoit defendu par les ordonnances de Sylla de tenir magistrats à Rome', p. 1042).

The Life of Marcus Tullius Cicero

as they thought good.⁶⁶ For this great and absolute power of the decemviri, there were many men of great account that favoured this law, but Antonius chiefly, being colleague and fellow consul with Cicero, for he had good hope to be chosen one of these ten commissioners, and furthermore it was thought that he was privy unto Catiline's conspiracy and that he misliked it not because he was so much in debt. And this was it that the noblemen most feared of all other things. Thereupon Cicero, to provide first to prevent this danger, granted him⁶⁷ the province of the realm of Macedon, and the province of Gaul being offered unto himself, he refused it. By this good turn he won Antonius like a hired player, making him to promise him that he would assist and aid him for the benefit of the commonwealth and that he would say no more than he should will him. When he had brought him to this and had won him to his mind, he then began to be the bolder and more stoutly to resist them that were authors of this innovation and new laws. Cicero therefore in open senate did one day sharply reprove and inveigh against this law of the decemviri which the tribunes would have established. And thereby he did so terrify the authors thereof that there was not one man durst speak against him. This notwithstanding, the tribunes afterwards attempted once again to have it to pass and appointed the consuls to appear before the people. Howbeit, Cicero being nothing abashed at it, he commanded the senate to follow him. So he did not only overthrow this law of the decemviri which the tribunes did prefer, but furthermore they were utterly discouraged and out of hope to bring any of their matters to pass they intended, he struck them so dead with his eloquence.⁶⁸

[13] For Cicero only of all men in Rome made the Romans know how much eloquence doth grace and beautify that which is honest, and how invincible right and justice are, being eloquently set forth, and also how that a man that will be counted a wise governor of a commonweal should always in his doings rather prefer profit than to seek to curry favour with the common people, yet so to use his words that the thing which is profitable may not be also unpleasant. And to prove his sweet and pleasant tongue may be alleged that which he did in the time of his consulship touching the placing of men at the theatre to see the pastimes.⁶⁹ For before, the knights of Rome did sit mingled one with another amongst the common people and took their place as they came. The first that made the difference between them was Marcus Otho,⁷⁰ at that time praetor, who made a law by the which he appointed several seats for the

---

⁶⁶ Marg. 'A law preferred for the creation and authority of the decemviri.' The decemvirs were a commission of ten men.
⁶⁷ i.e. Antonius.
⁶⁸ Marg. 'Cicero by his eloquence overthrew the law of the decemviri.'
⁶⁹ Marg. 'Cicero's sweet tongue.'
⁷⁰ Marg. '* Others do say Lucius Roscius Otho, tribune of the people.'

knights where they might from thenceforth see the pastimes.[71] The people took this grievously as a thing done to discountenance them, insomuch that Otho coming afterwards into the theatre, all the common people fell a-whistling at him to shame him withal. The knights also in contrariwise made him room amongst them with great clapping of hands in token of honour. Therewith the people fell a-whistling louder than before, and the knights in like manner to clapping of their hands, and so grew to words one with another, that all the theatre was straight in uproar with it. Cicero, understanding it, went thither himself, and calling the people to the temple of the goddess Bellona, he there so sharply reproved them, and therewith so persuaded them, that returning presently to the theatre, they did then welcome and receive Otho with clapping of their hands and contended with the knights which of them should do him greatest honour.

[14] But now again the rebels of Catiline's conspiracy, who were prettily cooled at the first for the fear they stood in, began to be lusty again and to gather together, boldly encouraging one another to broach their practice before Pompey returned, who was said to be on the way towards Rome with his army.[72] But besides them, those soldiers that had served before in the wars under Sulla, being dispersed up and down Italy, but specially the best soldiers among them, dwelling in the good towns of Thuscan, did stir up Catiline to hasten the enterprise, persuading themselves that they should once again have goods enough at home to spoil and ransack at their pleasure.[73] These soldiers, having one Manlius to their captain, that had borne office in the field under Sulla, conspired with Catiline and came to Rome to assist him in his suit, who purposed once again to demand the consulship, being determined at the election to kill Cicero in the tumult and hurly-burly.[74] The gods also did plainly show by earthquakes, lightning, and thunder, and by vision of spirits that did appear, the secret practice and conspiracy. Besides also there fell out manifest conjectures and proofs by men that came to reveal them, howbeit they had no power sufficient to encounter so noble a man and of so great power as Catiline was. Cicero therefore deferring the day of election called Catiline into the senate and there did examine him of that which was reported of

---

[71] Marg. 'Roscius' law for dividing of the Roman knights from the common people.'
[72] broach] The meaning does not accord with any of the senses recorded in *OED*; A. has 'mettre la main à' (to put their hand to, p. 1043) and (in line 430 below) 'executer' (carry out, ibid.).
[73] Marg. 'Sulla's soldiers conspired with Catiline.'   persuading [...] pleasure] The correct reading is evidently 'at hand' (as in the first edition of 1579) instead of 'at home', apparently an editorial emendation in the second edition of 1595 but retained in the third edition of 1603.
[74] Manlius] P. 'Mallius', corrected by A.

him.⁷⁵ Catiline supposing there were many in the senate that had good wills to rebel, and also because he would show himself ready unto them that were of his conspiracy, he gave Cicero a gentle answer and said thus.⁷⁶ 'What do I offend', said he, 'if that being two bodies in this town, the one lean and weak and thoroughly rotten, and hath a head, and the other being great, strong, and of power, having no head, I do give it one?'. Meaning under this dark answer to signify the people and senate. This answer being made, Cicero was more afraid than before, insomuch that he put on a brigantine° for the safety of his body and was accompanied with the chiefest men of Rome and a great number of young men besides, going with him from his house unto the field of Mars, where the elections were made, and had of purpose left open his jacket loose at the collar that his brigantine he had on might be seen, thereby to let every man that saw him know the danger he was in. Every man misliked it when they saw it and came about him to defend him if any offered to assail him. But it so came to pass that by voices of the people Catiline was again rejected from the consulship and Syllanus and Muraena chosen consuls.⁷⁷

[15] Shortly after this election, the soldiers of Thuscan being joined which should have come to Catiline, and the day appointed being at hand to broach their enterprise, about midnight there came three of the chiefest men of Rome to Cicero's house (Marcus Crassus, Marcus Marcellus, and Scipio Metellus) and, knocking at his gate, called his porter and bad him wake his master presently and tell him how they three were at the gate to speak with him about a matter of importance.⁷⁸ At night after supper, Crassus' porter brought his master a packet of letters, delivered him by a stranger unknown, which were directed unto divers persons, among the which one of them had no name subscribed but was only directed unto Crassus himself.⁷⁹ The effect of the letter was that there should be made a great slaughter in Rome by Catiline, and therefore he prayed him that he would depart out of Rome to save himself.⁸⁰ Crassus, having read his own letter, would not open the rest, but went forthwith unto Cicero, partly for fear of the danger, and partly also to clear himself of the suspicion they had of him for the friendship that was betwixt him and Catiline. Cicero, counselling with them what was to be done, the next morning assembled the senate very

---

⁷⁵ Marg. 'Cicero examined Catiline in the senate.'
⁷⁶ gentle] P. 'of a madman' (μανικός). N. follows what appears to be a misprint in A. ('molle', p. 1043, perhaps a misreading of 'folle').
⁷⁷ Marg. 'Syllanus and Muraena consuls.' For the year 62 BCE.   Syllanus] Silanus. Muraena] Murena.
⁷⁸ about a matter of importance] A. 'pour une telle occasion' (for the following reason, p. 1044).
⁷⁹ Marg. 'Letters brought to Crassus of Catiline's conspiracy.'
⁸⁰ to save himself] An unusual explanatory addition by N.

early, and carrying the letters with him, he did deliver them according to their direction and commanded they should read them out aloud. All these letters, and every one of them particularly, did bewray the conspiracy. Furthermore, Quintus Arrius, a man of authority, and that had been praetor, told openly the soldiers and men of war that were levied in Thuscan. And it is reported also that Manlius was in the field with a great number of soldiers about the cities of Thuscan, gaping daily to hear news of some change at Rome. All these things being thoroughly considered, a decree passed by the senate that they should refer the care of the commonwealth unto the consuls to the end that with absolute authority they might, as well as they could, provide for the safety and preservation thereof.[81] Such manner of decree and authority was not often seen concluded of in the senate but in time of present fear and danger.

[16] Now Cicero having this absolute power, he referred all foreign matters to Quintus Metellus' charge and did himself take upon him the care and government of all civil affairs within Rome. On the daytime when he went up and down the town, he had such a troupe of men after him that when he came through the great marketplace, he almost filled it with his train that followed him. Thereupon Catiline would no longer delay time but resolved to go himself unto Manlius where their army lay. But before he departed, he had drawn into his confederacy one Martius and another called Cethegus, whom he commanded betimes in the morning to go to Cicero's house with short daggers to kill him, pretending to come to salute him and to give him a good morrow.[82] But there was a noblewoman of Rome called Fulvia, who went overnight unto Cicero and bad him beware of that Cethegus, who indeed came the next morning betimes unto him, and being denied to be let in, he began to chafe and rail before the gate; this made him the more to be suspected.[83] In the end Cicero, coming out of his house, called the senate to the temple of Jupiter Stator (as much to say as stayer)[84] which standeth at the upper end of the holy street as they go to the Mount Palatine.[85] There was Catiline with others, as though he meant to clear himself of the suspicion that went of him; howbeit, there was not a senator that would sit down by him, but they did all rise from the bench where Catiline had taken his place. And further, when he began to speak, he could

---

[81] a decree passed by the senate] i.e. was passed (as in A. 'il fut fait un arrest et decret au Senat', p. 1044).
[82] Martius] Marcius.
[83] **Marg.** 'Fulvia bewrayeth Catiline's intent to kill Cicero.'
[84] stayer] i.e. one who sustains (P. Στήσιος), although A.'s 'Arresteur' (p. 1044) also suggests the alternative meaning of 'one who restrains'; in either case, symbolically appropriate to the situation.
[85] at the upper end of the holy street] P. and A. 'at the beginning of the Via Sacra' ('à l'entree de la rue sacree', p. 1044).

The Life of Marcus Tullius Cicero

have no audience for the great noise they made against him. So at length Cicero rose and commanded him to avoid° out of Rome, saying that there must needs be a separation of walls between them two, considering that the one used but words and the other force of arms. Catiline, thereupon immediately departing the city with three hundred armed men, was no sooner out of the precinct of the walls but he made his sergeants carry axes and bundles of rods before him, as if he had been a consul lawfully created, and did display his ensigns of war, and so went in this order to seek Manlius.[86] When they were joined, he had not much less than twenty thousand men together, with the which he went to practise° the towns to rebel. Now open war being thus proclaimed, Antonius, Cicero's colleague and fellow consul, was sent against him to fight with him.

[17] In the mean space Cornelius Lentulus, surnamed Sura (a man of a noble house, but of a wicked disposition, and that for his ill life was put off the senate), assembled all the rest which were of Catiline's conspiracy and that remained behind him in Rome and bad them be afraid of nothing. He was then praetor the second time, as the manner is when any man comes to recover again the dignity of a senator which he had lost. It is reported that this surname of Sura was given him upon this occasion.[87] He, being treasurer in Sulla's dictatorship, did fondly° waste and consume a marvellous sum of money of the common treasure. Sulla being offended with him for it and demanding an account of him before the senate, he carelessly and contemptuously stepped forth, saying he could make him no other account but showed him the calf of his leg, as children do when they make a fault at tennis.[88] And thereof it came that ever after that they called him Sura, because Sura in Latin signifieth the calf of the leg. Another time also, being accused for a lewd part he had committed, he bribed some of the judges with money, and being only quit by two voices more which he had in his favour, he said he had lost his money he had given to one of those two judges because it was enough for him to be cleared by one voice more. This man, being of this disposition, was first of all incensed by Catiline and lastly marred by certain wizards and false prognosticators that had mocked him with a vain hope, singing verses unto him which they had feigned and devised, and false prophecies also which they bore° him in hand they had taken out of Sybil's books of prophecy, which said that there should reign three Cornelii at Rome, of the which° two had already fulfilled the prophecy, Cinna and Sulla, and for the third, fortune laid it upon him, and therefore bad him go through withal and not to dream it out, losing opportunity as Catiline had done.[89]

[86] **Marg.** 'Catiline departed.'
[87] **Marg.** 'C. Lentulus was called Sura.'
[88] at tennis] P. 'when they were playing ball' (σφαιρίζειν). N. follows A.'s modernisation ('au jeu de la paume', p. 1045).
[89] **Marg.** 'Oracles of three Cornelii that should reign at Rome.'   Sybil's books of

[18] Now this Lentulus undertook no small enterprise but had an intent with him to kill all the whole senate and as many other citizens as they could murder and to set fire of Rome, sparing none but Pompey's sons, whom they would reserve for pledges to make their peace afterwards with Pompey.[90] For the rumour was very great and certain also that he returned from very great wars and conquests which he had made in the East-countries. So they laid a plot to put their treason in execution in one of the nights of Saturn's feasts.[91] Further, they had brought flax and brimstone and a great number of armours and weapons into Cethegus' house. Besides all this provision, they had appointed a hundred men in an hundred parts of the city to the end that fire being raised in many places at one time, it should the sooner run through the whole city. Other men also were appointed to stop the pipes and water conduits which brought water to Rome and to kill those also that came for water to quench the fire. In all this stir by chance there were two ambassadors of the Allobroges, whose country at that time did much mislike of the Romans and were unwilling to be subject unto them. Lentulus thought these men very fit instruments to cause all Gaul to rebel. Thereupon practising with them, he won them to be of their conspiracy and gave them letters directed to the council of their country and in them did promise them freedom. He sent other letters also unto Catiline and persuaded him to proclaim liberty to all bondmen and to come with all the speed he could to Rome and sent with them one Titus of the city of Crotona to carry these letters.[92] But all their counsels and purposes (like fools that never met together but at feasts, drinking° drunk with light women) were easily found out by Cicero, who had a careful eye upon them and very wisely and discreetly saw through them. For he had appointed men out of the city to spy their doings, which followed them to see what they intended. Furthermore, he spoke secretly with some he trusted (the which others also took to be of the conspiracy) and knew by them that Lentulus and Cethegus had practised with the ambassadors of the Allobroges and drawn them into their conspiracy. At length he watched them one night so narrowly that he took the ambassadors and Titus Crotonian, with the letters he carried, by help of the ambassadors of the Allobroges, which had secretly informed him of all before.[93]

prophecy] 'official oracles uttered by Sybils (ecstatic prophetesses) to be consulted only at the senate's command. But unofficial Sibylline prophecies were often used for political propaganda' (Moles, *Cicero*, 17. 5 n.).
[90] Marg. 'Great treason practised in Rome by C. Lentulus and Cethegus.'
[91] Saturn's feasts] The Saturnalia, a carnivalesque Roman religious festival, celebrated on or around 17 December.
[92] Crotona] Croton.
[93] P. 'laying an ambush by night, he seized the man of Croton and his letters with the secret co-operation of the Allobroges'. N. follows A.'s additions to P.'s Greek and identifies the man of Croton as the previously-named Titus: 'et finalement les fit espier la nuict, si bien qu'il surprit les ambassadeurs, et le Crotoniate avec les letres qu'il portoit, à l'aide

[19] The next morning by break of day, Cicero assembled the senate in the temple of Concord and there openly read the letters and heard the evidence of the witnesses. Further, there was one Iunius Syllanus, a senator, that gave in evidence that some heard Cethegus say that they should kill three consuls and four praetors. Piso, a senator also, and that had been consul, told in manner the selfsame tale. And Caius Sulpitius, a praetor that was sent into Cethegus' house, reported that he had found great store of darts, armour, daggers, and swords new-made.[94] Lastly, the senate having promised Titus Crotonian he should have no hurt, so he would tell what he knew of this conspiracy, Lentulus thereby was convinced° and driven to give up his office of praetor before the senate and, changing his purple gown, to take another meet for his miserable state. This being done, Lentulus and his consorts were committed to ward° to the praetors' houses. Now growing towards evening, the people waiting about the place where the senate was assembled, Cicero at length came out and told them what they had done within. Thereupon, he was conveyed by all the people unto a friend's house of his hard by for that his own house was occupied by the ladies of the city, who were busy solemnly celebrating a secret sacrifice in the honour of the goddess called of the Romans the Good Goddess and of the Grecians Gynaecia, to wit feminine.[95] Unto her this yearly sacrifice is done at the consul's house by the wife or mother of the consul then being, the Vestal Nuns being present at it.[96] Now Cicero, being come into his neighbour's house, began to bethink him what course he were best to take in this matter.[97] For, to punish the offenders with severity according to their deserts, he was afraid to do it, both because he was of a courteous nature as also for that he would not seem to be glad to have occasion to show his absolute power and authority to punish (as he might) with rigour citizens that were of the noblest houses of the city and that had besides many friends. And contrariwise also, being remiss in so weighty a matter as this, he was afraid of the danger that might ensue of their rashness, mistrusting° that if he should punish them with less than death, they would not amend for it, imagining they were well rid of their trouble, but would rather become more bold and desperate than ever they were, adding moreover the sting and spite of a new malice unto their accustomed wickedness, besides that he himself should be thought a coward and timorous man, whereas they had already not much better opinion of him.

---

des ambassadeurs Allobroges, lesquels s'entendirent secretement avec lui' (p. 1046). Marg. 'The conspirators apprehended.'

[94] Caius Sulpitius] Gaius Sulpicius.
[95] i.e. the Roman festival of Bona Dea, celebrated annually in December.
[96] Vestal Nuns] The Vestal Virgins were priestesses to the Roman goddess of the hearth-fire, Vesta.
[97] N. omits P. and A. 'and he had only very few companions' ('ayant bien peu de gens autour de lui', p. 1046). The omission is significant because scenes in which Cicero discusses a problem with friends play a crucial role in P.'s narrative (Moles, *Cicero*, 1. 5 n. and passim).

[20] Cicero being perplexed thus with these doubts, there appeared a miracle to the ladies doing sacrifice at home in his house. For the fire being thought to be clean out upon the altar where they had sacrificed, there suddenly rose out of the embers of the rinds or barks which they had burnt a great bright flame, which amazed° all the other ladies. Howbeit, the Vestal Nuns willed Terentia, Cicero's wife, to go straight unto her husband and to bid him not to be afraid to execute that boldly which he had considered of, for the benefit of the commonwealth, and that the goddess had raised this great flame to show him that he should have great honour by doing of it. Terentia, that was no timorous nor faint-hearted woman but very ambitious, and furthermore had gotten more knowledge from her husband of the affairs of the state than otherwise she had acquainted him with her housewifery in the house, as Cicero himself reporteth, she went to make report thereof unto him and prayed him to do execution of those men. The like did Quintus, Cicero his brother, and also Publius Nigidius, his friend and fellow student with him in philosophy, and whose counsel also Cicero followed much in the government of the commonwealth. The next morning, the matter being propounded to the arbitrement of the senate how these malefactors should be punished, Syllanus, being asked his opinion first, said that they should be put in prison and from thence to suffer execution.[98] Others likewise that followed him were all of that mind but Caius Caesar, that afterwards came to be dictator, and was then but a young man and began to come forward, but yet such a one as by his behaviour and the hope he had took such a course that afterwards he brought the commonwealth of Rome into an absolute monarchy. For at that time Cicero had vehement suspicions of Caesar, but no apparent proof to convince him.[99] And some say that it was brought so near as he was almost convicted, but yet saved himself.[100] Other° write to the contrary that Cicero wittingly dissembled° that he either heard or knew any signs which were told him against Caesar, being afraid indeed of his friends and estimation. For it was a clear case that if they had accused Caesar with the rest, he undoubtedly had sooner saved all their lives than he should have lost his own.[101]

---

[98] Marg. 'Syllanus' sentence of the conspirators.'   execution] P. τὴν ἐσχάτην δίκην (the worst punishment, translated by A. as 'l'extreme supplice' (the greatest torture, p. 1047)). As Turner notes, P.'s phrasing permits Silanus to change his mind subsequently (II, 82 n. 1).
[99] At the start of the sentence, A. (and hence N.) omits P. 'His designs were still unnoticed by the rest, but …'.
[100] Marg. 'Caesar privy to Catiline's conspiracy.'
[101] if […] own] N. follows A., who expands the highly condensed Greek for the sake of clarity, but he confuses the sense of the final clause: 'si on mettoit Caesar au nombre des accusez, il seroit plustost cause de leur faire sauver la vie à eux, que eux de la faire perdre à lui' (if Caesar were included among the accused, he would be more likely to cause the saving of their lives [i.e. of the accused, because of Caesar's power and influential friends], than they would be to cause the loss of his, p. 1047).

[21] Now when Caesar came to deliver his opinion touching the punishment of these prisoners, he stood up and said that he did not think it good to put them to death, but to confiscate their goods, and, as for their persons, that they should bestow them in prison, some in one place, some in another, in such cities of Italy as pleased Cicero best, until the war of Catiline were ended.[102] This sentence being very mild and the author thereof marvellous eloquent to make it good, Cicero himself added thereunto a counterpoise, inclining unto either of both the opinions, partly allowing° the first and partly also the opinion of Caesar.[103] His friends thinking that Caesar's opinion was the safest for Cicero because thereby he should deserve less blame for that he had not put the prisoners to death, they followed rather the second. Whereupon Syllanus also recanted that he had spoken and expounded his opinion, saying that when he spoke they should be put to death, he meant nothing so, but thought the last punishment a senator of Rome could have was the prison.[104] But the first that contraried° this opinion was Catulus Luctatius, and after him Cato, who with vehement words enforced Caesar's suspicion and furthermore filled all the senate with wrath and courage, so that even upon the instant it was decreed by most voices that they should suffer death.[105] But Caesar stepped up again and spoke against the confiscation of their goods, misliking that they should reject the gentlest part of his opinion and that contrariwise they should stick unto the severest only;[106] howbeit, because the greatest number prevailed against him, he called the tribunes to aid him to the end they should withstand it, but they would give no ear unto him. Cicero thereupon, yielding of himself, did remit the confiscation of their goods [22] and went with the senate to fetch the prisoners, who were not all in one house, but every praetor had one of them. So he went first to take C. Lentulus, who was in the mount Palatine, and brought him through the holy street and the marketplace, accompanied with the chiefest men of the city, who compassed him round about and guarded his person.[107] The people seeing that quaked and trembled for fear, passed by, and said never a word, and specially the young men, who thought it had been some solemn mystery for the health of their country that was so accompanied with the chief magistrate and the noblemen of the city with terror and fear.[108] So when he had passed through

[102] Marg. 'Caesar's opinion for the punishment of the conspirators.'
[103] a counterpoise] P. and A. 'no little weight' ('un grand poids', p. 1047). N.'s translation implies that Cicero's speech opposed Caesar's, whereas P.'s phrase indicates support (though both go on to claim that he argued on both sides of the question).
[104] last punishment] Because N. had earlier translated P.'s 'the worst punishment' as 'execution' (line 597), his description of Silanus's evasive manoeuvre here no longer makes sense.
[105] Luctatius] Lutatius.   Caesar's suspicion] The suspicion towards Caesar.
[106] i.e. the senate had decreed both execution (which Caesar had argued against) *and* confiscation of goods (proposed by Caesar as an alternative to the former).
[107] the holy street and the marketplace] i.e. the Via Sacra and Forum (N. follows A.).
[108] that was so accompanied with the chief magistrate and the noblemen of the city] P. 'of

the marketplace and was come to the prison, he delivered Lentulus into the hands of the hangman and commanded him to do execution; afterwards also Cethegus and then all the rest, one after another, whom he brought to the prison himself and caused them to be executed.¹⁰⁹ Furthermore, seeing divers of their accomplices in a troupe together in the marketplace, who knew nothing what he had done and watched° only till night were come, supposing then to take away their companions by force from the place where they were, thinking they were yet alive, he turned unto them and spoke aloud: 'They lived.'¹¹⁰ This is a phrase of speech which the Romans use sometime° when they will finely convey the hardness of the speech to say: 'He is dead.'¹¹¹ When night was come and that he was going homeward, as he came through the marketplace, the people did wait upon him no more with silence as before but with great cries of his praise and clapping of hands in every place he went and called him 'saviour' and 'second founder of Rome'.¹¹² Besides all this, at every man's door there were links° and torches lighted, that it was as light in the streets as at noondays.° The very women also did put lights out of the tops of their houses to do him honour, and also to see him so nobly brought home with such a long train of the chiefest men of the city (of the which many of them had ended great wars, for the which they had triumphed, and had obtained many famous conquests to the empire of Rome, both by sea and land), confessing between themselves one to another that the Romans were greatly bound to many captains and generals of armies in their time for the wonderful riches and spoils and increase of their power which they had won, howbeit that they were to thank Cicero only for their health and preservation, having saved them from so great and extreme a danger; not for that they thought it so wonderful an act to have struck dead the enterprise of the conspirators and also to have punished the offenders by death, but because the conspiracy of Catiline being so great and dangerous an insurrection as ever was any, he had quenched it and plucked it up by the roots with so small hurt and without uproar, trouble, or actual sedition. For the most part of them that were gathered together about Catiline when they heard that Lentulus and all the rest were put to death, they presently forsook him, and Catiline himself also fighting a battle with them he had about him against Antonius, the other consul with Cicero, he was slain in the field and all his army defeated.¹¹³

---

some aristocratic office' (Moles, *Cicero*, and Lintott); A. 'qui se jouast de puissance absolue par les plus gros personnages de la ville' (which was performed with absolute authority by the greatest figures of the city, p. 1048). A. (followed by N.) further omits P.'s reference to the initiation of the young men in the mysteries and adds the phrase that N. translates as 'for the health of their country'.

[109] Marg. 'The execution of the conspirators.'
[110] The perfect tense used in P. and A. ('they have lived') better expresses the meaning.
[111] Marg. 'They lived: a word usurped for the dead.'
[112] Marg. 'Cicero's praise.'
[113] Marg. 'Catiline slain in battle by Antonius.' In 62 BCE.

[23] This notwithstanding, there were many that spoke ill of Cicero for this fact and meant to make him repent it, having for their heads Caesar (who was already chosen praetor for the year to come),[114] Metellus, and Bestia, who should also be chosen tribunes.[115] They, so soon as they were chosen tribunes, would not once suffer Cicero to speak to the people, notwithstanding that he was yet in his office of consul for certain days. And furthermore, to let him that he should not speak unto the people,[116] they did set their benches upon the pulpit for orations which they call at Rome Rostra, and would never suffer him to set foot in it, but only to resign his office and, that done, to come down again immediately. He granted thereunto and went up to the pulpit upon that condition.[117] So silence being made him, he made an oath, not like unto other consuls' oaths when they resign their office in like manner, but strange and never heard of before, swearing that he had saved the city of Rome and preserved all his country and the empire of Rome from utter ruin and destruction. All the people that were present confirmed it and swore the like oath. Wherewithal Caesar and the other tribunes, his enemies, were so offended with him that they devised to breed him some new stir and trouble, and amongst others they made a decree that Pompey should be sent for with his army to bridle the tyranny of Cicero. Cato, who at that time was also tribune, did him great pleasure in the furtherance of the commonwealth, opposing himself against all their practices with the like authority and power that they had, being a tribune and brother with them and of better estimation than they.[118] So that he did not only easily break all their devices, but also in a goodly oration he made in a full assembly of the people he so highly praised and extolled Cicero's consulship unto them, and the things he did in his office, that they gave him the greatest honours that ever were decreed or granted unto any man living.[119] For by decree of the people he was called 'father of the country', as Cato himself had called him in his oration, the which name was never given to any man but only unto him, [24] and also he bore greater sway in Rome at that time than any man beside him.[120]

This notwithstanding, he made himself envied and misliked of many men, not for any ill act he did or meant to do, but only because he did too much boast of himself.[121] For he never was in any assembly of people, senate, or judgement, but every man's head was full still° to hear the sound of Catiline and Lentulus

---

[114] Marg. 'Caesar chosen praetor.'
[115] Marg. 'Metellus and Bestia, tribunes of the people.'
[116] i.e. to prevent him from speaking to the people.
[117] Marg. 'Cicero resigneth his office.'
[118] in the furtherance of the commonwealth] Rather, as P. and A. have it, 'and to the whole state' ('et à toute la chose publique', p. 1049).
[119] Marg. 'Cicero's consulship praised by Cato.'
[120] Marg. 'Cicero the first man called "father of the country".'
[121] Marg. 'Cicero too much given to praise himself.'

brought in for sport, and filling the books and works he compiled besides full of his own praises, the which made his sweet and pleasant style tedious and troublesome to those that heard him, as though this misfortune ever followed him to take away his excellent grace.[122] But now, though he had this worm of ambition and extreme covetous desire of honour in his head, yet did he not malice or envy any other's glory, but would very frankly° praise excellent men, as well those that had been before him as those that were in his time.[123] And this appeareth plainly in his writings. They have written also certain notable words he spoke of some ancient men in old time, as of Aristotle, that he was like a golden flowing river; and of Plato, that if Jupiter himself would speak, he would speak like him; and of Theophrastus, he was wont to call him his delight; and of Demosthenes' orations, when one asked him on a time which of them he liked best, 'the longest', said he. There be divers writers also who, to show that they were great followers of Demosthenes, do follow Cicero's saying in a certain epistle he wrote unto one of his friends, wherein he said that Demosthenes slept in some of his orations,[124] but yet they forget to tell how highly he praised him in that place and that he calleth the orations which he wrote against Antonius (in the which he took great pains and studied more than all the rest) *Philippians* to follow those which Demosthenes wrote against Philip, king of Macedon.[125] Furthermore, there was not a famous man in all his time, either in eloquence or in learning, whose fame he hath not commended in writing or otherwise in honourable speech of him. For he obtained of Caesar, when he had the empire of Rome in his hands, that Cratippus, the Peripatetic philosopher, was made citizen of Rome. Further, he procured that by decree of the court of the Areopagites he was entreated to remain at Athens to teach and instruct the youth there for that° he was a great honour and ornament unto their city. There are extant also of Cicero's epistles unto Herodes, and others unto his son, willing him to follow Cratippus in his study and knowledge. He wrote another letter also unto Gorgias the rhetorician and forbad him his son's company because he understood he enticed him to drunkenness and to other great dishonesty. Of all his epistles he wrote in Greek, there is but that only written in choler, and another which he wrote unto Pelops Byzantine. And for that he wrote to Gorgias, he had great reason to be offended with him and to taunt him in his letter because (as it seemed) he was a man of very lewd life and conversation.° But in contrary manner, writing as he did to Pelops, finding

---

[122] brought in for sport] N.'s over-literal rendering of A.'s 'ramener en jeu' (to bring back into play, p. 1049), which does not imply diversion.
[123] Marg. 'Cicero friendly to praise others.'
[124] Marg. 'Cicero saith Demosthenes sleepeth in his orations.'
[125] Cicero named his fourteen orations against Mark Antony (44–43 BCE) *Philippics* in imitation of Demosthenes' speeches against Philip of Macedon.   in that place] A. 'ailleurs' ('elsewhere', p. 1049).

himself grieved with him for that he was negligent in procuring the Byzantines to ordain some public honours in his behalf, [25] that methinks proceeded of overmuch ambition, the which in many things made him too much forget the part of an honest man, and only because he would be commended for his eloquence. When he had on a time pleaded Munatius' cause before the judges, who shortly after accused Sabinus, a friend of his,[126] it is reported that he was so angry with him that he told him: 'What, Munatius, hast thou forgotten that thou were discharged the last day of thine accusation, not for thine innocency° but for a mist I cast before the judges' eyes that made them they could not discern the fault?'.[127] Another time also, having openly praised Marcus Crassus in the pulpit with good audience of the people, shortly after he spoke to the contrary all the evil he could of him in the same place. 'Why, how now,' said Crassus, 'didst thou not thyself highly praise me in this place the last day?'. 'I cannot deny it,' said Cicero, 'but indeed I took an ill matter in hand to show mine eloquence.' Another time Crassus chanced to say in an open assembly that none of all the Crassi of his house had ever lived above threescore years, and afterwards again repenting himself, he called it in again and said: 'Sure I knew not what I did when I said so.' Cicero answered him again: 'Thou knewest well enough the people were glad to hear it, and therefore thou spokest it to please them.' Another time, Crassus liking the opinion of the Stoic philosophers that said the wise man was ever rich, Cicero answered him and bad him consider whether they meant not thereby that the wise man had all things.[128] Crassus' covetousness was defamed of every man. Of Crassus' sons, one of them did much resemble Actius, and therefore his mother had an ill name by him. One day this son of Crassus made an oration before the senate, which divers of them commended very much. So Cicero being asked how he liked it, 'Methinks', said he, 'it is Actius of Crassus.'[129]

[26] About this time, Crassus being ready to take his journey into Syria, he desired to have Cicero his friend rather than his enemy. Therefore, one night making much of him, he told Cicero that he would come and sup with him. Cicero said he should be welcome. Shortly after some of his friends told him of Vatinius, how he was desirous to be made friends with him, for he was his enemy. 'What,' quoth Cicero, 'and will he come to supper too?'. Thus he used Crassus. Now this Vatinius, having a swollen neck, one day pleading before

---

[126] i.e. Cicero's.
[127] Marg. 'Cicero's subtle and pleasant sayings.'   the last day of thine accusation] A. 'dernierement' (recently, p. 1050).
[128] Marg. 'The Stoics' opinion: a wise man is ever rich.'
[129] Marg. '* Ἄξιος Κράσσου. Actius is a proper name of a Roman, and ἄξιος in Greek signifieth worthy, so the grace of the equivocation cannot be expressed in any other language.'

Cicero, he called him the swollen orator. Another time, when he heard say that he was dead, and then that he was alive again, 'A vengeance on him', said he, 'that hath lied so shamefully.' Another time, when Caesar had made a law for the dividing of the lands of Campania unto the soldiers, divers of the senate were angry with him for it, and among other Lucius Gellius, a very old man, said he would never grant it while he lived. Cicero pleasantly answered again: 'Alas, tarry a little, the good old man will not trouble you long.' Another time, there was one Octavius, supposed to be an African born. He, when Cicero on a time pleaded a matter, said that he heard him not; Cicero presently answered him again: 'And yet hast thou a hole bored through thine ear.'[130] Another time, Metellus Nepos told him that he had overthrown mo° men by his witness than he had saved by his eloquence. 'I grant,' said Cicero, 'for indeed I have more faith° than eloquence in me.' So was there also a young man that was suspected to have poisoned his father with a tart that boasted he would revile Cicero: 'I had rather have that of thee', quoth Cicero, 'than thy tart.' Publius Sextius also, having a matter before the judges, entertained° Cicero with other of his counsellors, but yet he would speak all himself and give none of the orators leave to say anything. In the end, when they saw plainly that the judges would discharge him, being ready to give sentence, Cicero said unto him: 'Bestir thee hardily° today, for tomorrow, Sextius, thou shalt be a private man.'[131] Another, one Publius Cotta, who would fain° have been thought a wise lawyer and yet had little wit and understanding, Cicero appealed to him as a witness in a matter, and being examined, he answered he knew nothing of it.[132] Cicero replied to him again: 'Thou thinkest peradventure° they ask thee touching the law.' Again, Metellus Nepos in a certain disputation he had with Cicero did many times repeat 'Who is thy father?'. Cicero answered him again: 'Thy mother hath made this question harder for thee to answer.' This Nepos' mother was reported to be a light housewife,° and he as subtle-witted° and unconstant.° For he being tribune left in a gere° the exercise of his office and went into Syria to Pompey upon no occasion, and as fondly again he turned thence upon a sudden. His schoolmaster° Philager also being dead, he buried him very honestly and set a crow of stone upon the top of his tomb. Cicero seeing it told him: 'Thou hast done very wisely, for thy master hath taught thee rather to fly than to speak.'[133] Another time, Appius Clodius pleading a matter said in his preamble that his friend had earnestly requested him to employ all his knowledge, diligence, and faith upon this matter. 'O gods,' said Cicero, 'and hast thou showed thyself so hard-hearted to thy friend to perform nothing of all that he requested thee?'

---

[130] Marg. '* Because the Africans have commonly their ears bored through.'
[131] 'While tribune in 57, Sestius had plenty of opportunities for making speeches on his own initiative; as a private citizen, he could only speak, whether in the senate or an assembly or law court, when called on' (Lintott, 26. 8 n.).
[132] Publius Cotta] In fact, Publius Costa; N. follows A.
[133] Cicero's comment refers both to Philager's boisterous speech and volatile character.

[27] Now, to use these fine taunts and girds° to his enemies, it was a part of a good orator, but so commonly to gird every man to make the people laugh, that won him great ill will of many, as shall appear by some examples I will tell you. Marcus Aquinius had two sons-in-law, who were both banished; Cicero therefore called him Adrastus.[134] Lucius Cotta by chance also was censor at that time when Cicero sued to be consul, and following his suit at the day of election, he was athirst° and was driven to drink. But while he drank, all his friends stood about him, and after he had drunk, he said unto them: 'It is well done of ye', said he, 'to be afraid lest the censor should be angry with me because I drink water.' For it was reported the censor loved wine well. Another time, Cicero meeting one Voconius with three foul daughters of his with him, he cried out aloud: 'This man hath gotten children in despite of Phoebus.'[135] It was thought in Rome that Marcus Gellius was not born of free parents by father and mother, who reading certain letters one day in the senate very loud, Cicero said unto them that were about him: 'Wonder not at it,' quoth he, 'for this man hath been a crier in his days.'[136] Faustus, the son of Sulla, dictator at Rome, which set up bills outlawing divers Romans, making it lawful for any man to kill them without danger where they found them, this man after he had spent the most part of his father's goods was so sore in debt that he was driven to sell his household stuff by bills set up on every post. Cicero when he saw them, 'Yea marry,' said he, 'these bills please me better than those which his father set up.'

[28] These taunts and common quips without purpose made divers men to malice him. The great ill will that Clodius bore him began upon this occasion.[137] Clodius was of a noble house, a young man, and very wild and insolent. He being in love with Pompeia, Caesar's wife, found the means secretly to get into Caesar's house, apparelled like a young singing wench, because on that day the ladies of Rome did solemnly celebrate a secret sacrifice in Caesar's house which is not lawful for men to be present at.[138] So there was no man there but Clodius, who thought he should not have been known because he was but a young man without any hair on his face, and that by this means he might come to Pompeia amongst the other women. He being gotten into this great house by night, not knowing the rooms and chambers° in it, there was one of Caesar's mother's maids of her chamber called Aurelia, who seeing him wandering up and down

---

[134] Adrastus, king of Argos, whose daughters married two exiles, Polyneices of Thebes and Tydeus of Calydon.
[135] Euripides, *Oedipus*? (Nauck, p. 911).
[136] Cicero's gibe alludes to the custom whereby Roman slaves receiving their freedom announced: 'I loudly reclaim freedom.' N. (following A.) associates the social stigma with the position of the town crier.
[137] **Marg.** 'The malice betwixt Cicero and Clodius.'
[138] The Roman festival of Bona Dea (the Good Goddess). The incident took place in 62 BCE and is described in greater detail in *Caesar*, 9–10.

the house in this sort asked him what he was and how they called him.¹³⁹ So being forced to answer, he said he sought for Aura, one of Pompeia's maids. The maid perceived straight it was no woman's voice and therewithal gave a great shriek and called the other women, the which did see the gates fast shut and then sought every corner up and down, so that at length they found him in the maid's chamber with whom he came in. His offence was straight blown abroad in the city, whereupon Caesar put his wife away, and one of the tribunes also accused Clodius and burdened° him that he had profaned the holy ceremonies of the sacrifices.

[29] Cicero at that time was yet his friend, being one that had very friendly done for him at all times and had ever accompanied him to guard him if any man would have offered him injury in the busy time of the conspiracy of Catiline. Clodius stoutly denied the matter he was burdened with and said that he was not in Rome at that time but far from thence. Howbeit, Cicero gave evidence against him and deposed that the selfsame day he came home to his house unto him to speak with him about certain matters.¹⁴⁰ This indeed was true, though it seemeth Cicero gave not this evidence so much for the truth's sake as to please his wife Terentia, for she hated Clodius to the death because of his sister Clodia that would have married Cicero and did secretly practise the marriage by one Tullius, who was Cicero's very friend, and because he repaired very often to this Clodia that dwelt hard by Cicero, Terentia began to suspect him.¹⁴¹ Terentia, being a cruel woman and wearing her husband's breeches, allured Cicero to set upon Clodius in his adversity and to witness against him, as many other honest men of the city also did: some that he was perjured, others that he committed a thousand lewd parts, that he bribed the people with money, that he had enticed and deflowered many women.¹⁴² Lucullus also brought forth certain maidens which deposed that Clodius had deflowered the youngest of his own sisters, she being in house with him and married. And there went a great rumour also that he knew his two other sisters, of the which the one was called Terentia¹⁴³ and married unto King Martius and the other Clodia, whom Metellus Celer had married and whom they commonly called quadrantaria because one of her paramours sent her a purse full of quadrines (which are little pieces of copper money) instead of silver.¹⁴⁴ Clodius was slandered more by her than with any

---

¹³⁹   Aurelia] The name of Caesar's mother rather than her maid (as A.'s translation makes clear: 'une des chambrieres d'Aurelia mere de Caesar', p. 1052).
¹⁴⁰   Marg. 'Cicero gave evidence against Clodius.'
¹⁴¹   Tullius] Tullus.
¹⁴²   Marg. 'The wicked parts of Clodius.'
¹⁴³   Marg. '* Some old books do read Tertia.'
¹⁴⁴   King Martius] Martius Rex. N. mistakenly translates the proper name Rex (Latin for 'king').

of the other two.¹⁴⁵ Notwithstanding, the people were very much offended with them that gave evidence against him and accused him. The judges, being afraid of it, got a great number of armed men about them at the day of his judgement for the safety of their persons, and in the tables° where they wrote their sentences their letters for the most part were confusedly set down. This notwithstanding, it was found that he was quit by the greatest number, and it was reported also that some of them were close-fisted.¹⁴⁶ Catulus therefore, meeting with some of them going home after they had given their sentence, told them: 'Surely ye had good reason to be well guarded for your safety, for you were afraid your money should have been taken from you, which you took for bribes.' And Cicero said unto Clodius, who reproved him that his witness was not true he gave against him: 'Clean contrary,' quoth Cicero, 'for five-and-twenty of the judges have believed me, being so many that have condemned thee, and the thirty would not believe thee, for they would not quit thee before they had fingered money.' Notwithstanding, in this judgement Caesar never gave evidence against Clodius and said moreover that he did not think his wife had committed any adultery, howbeit that he had put her away because he would that Caesar's wife should not only be clean from any dishonesty but also void of all suspicion.¹⁴⁷

[30] Clodius being quit of this accusation and trouble and having also found means to be chosen tribune, he began straight to persecute Cicero, changing all things and stirring up all manner of people against him.¹⁴⁸ First he won the goodwill of the common people by devising of new laws which he preferred for their benefit and commodity. To both the consuls he granted great and large provinces: unto Piso, Macedon, and to Gabinius, Syria.¹⁴⁹ He made also many poor men free citizens and had always about him a great number of slaves armed. At that present time there were three notable men in Rome which carried all the sway: Crassus, that showed himself an open enemy unto Cicero; Pompey, the other, made much both of the one and the other; the third was Caesar, who was prepared for his journey into Gaul with an army.¹⁵⁰ Cicero did lean unto him (though he knew him no fast friend of his and that he mistrusted

---

¹⁴⁵ i.e. Clodius was reproached more with (intercourse with) her than with the other two sisters.
¹⁴⁶ some of them were close-fisted] A. 'il y en avoit qui s'estoient laissé gaigner et corrompre par argent' (there were some of them who had let themselves be swayed and bribed by money, p. 1052). N. transposes the reference to bribery to the next sentence, where there is none in A. and P.   Marg. 'Clodius quit and found not guilty.' In 61 BCE.
¹⁴⁷ Marg. 'Caesar's words of the putting away his wife Pompeia.' Cf. *Caesar*, 10.
¹⁴⁸ Marg. 'Clodius chosen tribune of the people.' For the year 58 BCE.
¹⁴⁹ Marg. 'Piso and Gabinius consuls.'
¹⁵⁰ Marg. 'Crassus, Pompey, and Caesar, three of the greatest men in Rome, took part with Clodius against Cicero.'

him for matters passed in Catiline's conspiracy) and prayed him that he might go to the wars with him as one of his lieutenants. Caesar granted him. Thereupon Clodius perceiving that by this means he got him out of the danger of his office of tribuneship for that year, he made fair weather with him (as though he meant to reconcile himself unto him) and told him that he had cause rather to think ill of Terentia for that he had done against him than of himself, and always spoke very courteously of him as occasion fell out, and said he did think nothing in him neither had any malice to him, howbeit it did a little grieve him that being a friend, he was offered unkindness by his friend. These sweet words made Cicero no more afraid, so that he gave up his lieutenancy unto Caesar and began again to plead as he did before. Caesar took this in such disdain that he hardened Clodius the more against him and besides made Pompey his enemy. And Caesar himself also said before all the people that he thought Cicero had put Lentulus, Cethegus, and the rest unjustly to death and contrary to law without lawful trial and condemnation. And this was the fault for the which Cicero was openly accused.[151] Thereupon Cicero seeing himself accused for this fact, he changed his usual gown he wore and put on a mourning gown, and so suffering his beard and hair of his head to grow without any combing, he went in this humble manner and sued to the people. But Clodius was ever about him in every place and street he went, having a sight of rascals and knaves with him that shamefully mocked him for that he had changed his gown and countenance° in that sort, and oftentimes they cast dirt and stones at him, breaking his talk and requests he made unto the people.

[31] This notwithstanding, all the knights of Rome did in manner change their gowns with him for company, and of them there were commonly twenty thousand young gentlemen of noble house which followed him with their hair about their ears and were suitors to the people for him.[152] Furthermore, the senate assembled to decree that the people should mourn in blacks, as in a common calamity, but the consuls were against it. And Clodius, on the other side, was with a band of armed men about the senate, so that many of the senators ran out of the senate, crying and tearing their clothes for sorrow. Howbeit, these men seeing all that were nothing the more moved with pity and shame, but either Cicero must needs absent himself or else determine to fight with Clodius. Then went Cicero to entreat Pompey to aid him, but he absented himself of purpose out of the city because he would not be entreated and lay at one of his houses in the country near unto the city of Alba. So he first of all sent Piso, his son-in-law, unto him to entreat him and afterwards went himself in person to him. But

[151] Marg. 'Cicero accused of Clodius.'
[152] with their hair about their ears] An emblem of mourning.   Marg. 'The knights of Rome and senate changed garments for Cicero's sake.'

Pompey, being told that he was come, had not the heart to suffer him to come to him to look him in the face, for he had been past all shame to have refused the request of so worthy a man, who had before showed him such pleasure and also done and said so many things in his favour.[153] Howbeit Pompey, being the son-in-law of Caesar, did unfortunately (at his request) forsake him at his need, unto whom he was bound for so many infinite pleasures as he had received of him afore, and therefore when he heard say he came to him, he went out at his back gate and would not speak with him. So Cicero seeing himself betrayed of him and now having no other refuge to whom he might repair unto, he put himself into the hands of the two consuls. Of them two, Gabinius was ever cruel and churlish unto him. But Piso, on the other side, spoke always very courteously unto him, and prayed him to absent himself for a time, and to give place a little to Clodius' fury, and patiently to bear the change of the time, for in so doing he might come again another time to be the preserver of his country, which was now for his sake in tumult and sedition. Cicero upon this answer of the consul consulted with his friends, among the which Lucullus gave him advice to tarry and said that he should be the stronger. But all the rest were of contrary opinion and would have him to get him away with speed, for the people would shortly wish for him again when they had once been beaten with Clodius' fury and folly. Cicero liked best to follow this counsel. Whereupon, having had a statue of Minerva a long time in his house, the which he greatly reverenced, he carried her himself and gave her to the Capitol with this inscription: 'Unto Minerva, protector of Rome.' So, his friends having given him safe conduct, he went out of Rome about midnight and took his way through the country of Luke by land, meaning to go into Sicily.[154]

[32] When it was known in Rome that he was fled, Clodius did presently banish him by decree of the people and caused bills of inhibition to be set up that no man should secretly receive him within five hundred miles' compass of Italy. Howbeit, divers men reverencing Cicero made no reckoning of that inhibition, but when they had used him with all manner of courtesy possible, they did conduct him besides at his departure, saving one city only in Luke, called at that time Hipponium and now Vibone,[155] where a Sicilian called Vibius (unto whom Cicero before had done many pleasures and specially among others had made him master of the works in the year that he was consul) would not once receive him into his house but promised him he would appoint him a place in the

---

[153] Cicero had held an oration in support of Manilius's bill giving Pompey the command against Mithridates in 66 and supported him following his return from the East in 61–60 BCE. **Marg.** 'Pompey would not see Cicero being accused.'
[154] the country of Luke] Lucania, a region in Southern Italy now known as Basilicata. **Marg.** 'Cicero's exile.'
[155] **Marg.** 'Hipponium, alias Vibone, a city in Luke.'   Vibone] Vibo. N. follows A.

country that he might go unto. And Caius Virgilius also, at that time praetor and governor of Sicily, who before had showed himself his very great friend, wrote then unto him that he should not come near unto Sicily. This grieved him to the heart. Thereupon he went directly unto the city of Brundusium, and there embarked to pass over the sea unto Dyrrachium, and at the first had wind at will, but when he was in the main sea, the wind turned and brought him back again to the place from whence he came. But after that, he hoised° sail again and the report went that at his arrival at Dyrrachium when he took land, the earth shook under him and the sea gave° back together, whereby the soothsayers interpreted that his exile should not be long, because both the one and the other was a token of change.[156] Yet Cicero, notwithstanding that many men came to see him for the goodwill they bore him and that the cities of Greece contended who should most honour him, he was always sad and could not be merry, but cast his eyes still towards Italy, as passioned lovers do towards the women they love, showing himself faint-hearted, and took this adversity more basely than was looked for of one so well studied and learned as he.[157] And yet he oftentimes prayed his friends not to call him orator but rather philosopher, saying that philosophy was his chiefest profession and that for his eloquence he did not use it but as a necessary instrument to one that pleadeth in the commonwealth. But glory and opinion° hath great power to take man's reason from him, even like a colour, from the minds of them that are common pleaders in matters of state,[158] and to make them feel the selfsame passions that common people do by daily frequenting their company unless they take great heed of them and that they come to practise in the commonwealth with this resolute mind to have to do with the like matters that the common people have but not to entangle themselves with the like passions and moods by the which their matters do rise.[159]

[33] Now Clodius was not contented that he had banished Cicero out of Italy, but further he burnt all his houses in the country and his house also in Rome standing in the marketplace, of the which he built a temple of liberty and caused his goods to be sold by the crier, so that the crier was occupied all day long crying the goods to be sold, and no man offered to buy any of them. The chiefest men of the city beginning to be afraid of these violent parts, and having the common

---

[156] Marg. 'A wonder showed unto Cicero in his exile.'
[157] Marg. 'Cicero's faint heart in his exile.'
[158] to take […] minds] P. 'to wash [A. 'effacer', p. 1054] reason out of the soul, like a dye' (trans. by Moles, *Cicero*). By adding 'man's' and 'from him', N. obscures the construction.
[159] Marg. 'The wonderful power of glory.'   by the which their matters do rise] A. 'que leur engendrent les affaires' (which these affairs engendered in them [i.e. the people], p. 1055).

people at his commandment,¹⁶⁰ whom he had made very bold and insolent, he began to inveigh against Pompey and spoke ill of his doings in the time of his wars, the which every man else but himself did commend. Pompey then was very angry with himself that he had so forsaken Cicero, and repented him of it, and by his friends procured all the means he could to call him home again from his banishment.¹⁶¹ Clodius was against it all he could. The senate notwithstanding with one full consent ordained that nothing should be established for the commonwealth before Cicero's banishment were first repealed. Lentulus was at that time consul, and there grew such an uproar and stir upon it that some of the tribunes were hurt in the marketplace and Quintus Cicero (the brother of Cicero) was slain and hidden under the dead bodies.¹⁶² Then the people began to change their minds. And Annius Milo, one of the tribunes, was the first man that durst venture upon Clodius and bring him by force to be tried before the judges. Pompey himself also, having gotten a great number of men about him, as well of the city of Rome as of other towns adjoining to it, being strongly guarded with them, he came out of his house and compelled Clodius to get him out of the marketplace, and then called the people to give their voices for the calling home again of Cicero. It is reported that the people never passed thing with so great goodwill nor so wholly together as the return of Cicero.¹⁶³ And the senate for their parts also in the behalf of Cicero ordained that the cities which had honoured and received Cicero in his exile should be greatly commended and that his houses which Clodius had overthrown° and razed should be re-edified at the charge of the commonwealth. So Cicero returned the sixteenth month after his banishment, and the towns and cities he came by showed themselves so joyful of his return that all manner of men went to meet and honour him with so great love and affection that Cicero's report thereof afterwards came indeed short of the very truth as it was. For he said that Italy brought him into Rome upon their shoulders. Insomuch as Crassus himself, who before his banishment was his enemy, went then with very good will unto him and became his friend, saying that he did it for the love of his son, who loved Cicero with all his heart.

[34] Now Cicero being returned, he found a time when Clodius was out of the city, and went with a good company of his friends unto the Capitol, and there took away the tables and broke them, in the which Clodius had written all his acts that he had passed and done in the time of his tribuneship.¹⁶⁴ Clodius would afterwards have accused Cicero for it, but Cicero answered him that he was not lawfully created tribune because he was of the patricians and therefore

---

¹⁶⁰ As the pronoun indicates, the subject shifts here from the patricians to Clodius.
¹⁶¹ Marg. 'Pompey, changing mind, doth favour Cicero.'
¹⁶² In 57 BCE.   Marg. 'Lentulus consul.'
¹⁶³ Marg. 'Cicero called home from banishment.'
¹⁶⁴ Marg. 'Cicero taketh away the tables of Clodius' acts out of the Capitol.'

all that he had done in his tribuneship was void and of none effect. Therewith Cato was offended and spoke against him, not for that he liked of Clodius' doings (but to the contrary utterly misliked all that he did) but because he thought it out of all reason that the senate should cancel all those things which he had done and passed in his tribuneship, and specially because amongst the rest that was there which he himself had done in the isle of Cyprus and in the city of Byzantium. Hereupon there grew some strangeness betwixt Cicero and Cato, the which notwithstanding broke not out to open enmity but only to an abstinence of their wonted familiarity and access one to another.

[35] Shortly after, Milo slew Clodius.[165] Milo, being accused of murder, prayed Cicero to plead his cause. The senate fearing that this accusation of Milo (who was a hardy man and of quality besides) would move some sedition and uproar in the city, they gave commission to Pompey to see justice executed, as well in this cause as in other offences, that the city might be quiet and judgement also executed with safety. Thereupon Pompey the night before took the highest places of the marketplace by his soldiers that were armed, whom he placed thereabout. Milo fearing that Cicero would be afraid to see such a number of harnessed men about him, being no usual matter, and that it might peradventure hinder him to plead his cause well, he prayed him he would come betimes in the morning in his litter into the marketplace and there to stay° the coming of the judges till the place were full. For Cicero was not only fearful in wars but timorous also in pleading.[166] For indeed he never began to speak but it was in fear, and when his eloquence was come to the best proof and perfection, he never left his trembling and timorousness. Insomuch that pleading a case for Mutius Muraena (accused by Cato), striving to excel Hortensius, whose pleading was very well thought of, he took no rest all night, and what through watching° and the trouble of his mind he was not very well, so that he was not so well liked for his pleading as Hortensius. So, going to defend Milo's cause, when he came out of his litter and saw Pompey set aloft as if he had been in a camp and the marketplace compassed about with armed men glistering in every corner, it so amated° him that he could scant fashion himself to speak, all the parts of him did so quake and tremble, and his voice could not come to him.[167] But Milo, on the other side, stood boldly by him himself without any fear at all of the judgement of his cause, neither did he let his hair grow as other men accused did, neither did he wear any mourning gown, the which was (as it seemed) one of the chiefest causes that condemned him. Yet many held opinion that this timorousness of Cicero came rather of the goodwill he bore unto his

---

[165] Marg. 'Clodius, the tribune, slain by Milo.' In 52 BCE.
[166] Marg. 'Cicero fearful in wars and timorous in pleading.'
[167] Marg. 'Cicero pleadeth Milo's case.'

friends than of any cowardly mind of himself.

[36] He was also chosen one of the priests of the soothsayers, which they call augurs, in the room of Publius Crassus the younger, who was slain in the realm of Parthia.[168] Afterwards, the province of Cilicia being appointed to him, with an army of twelve thousand footmen and two thousand and five hundred horsemen he took the sea to go thither.[169] So when he was arrived there, he brought Cappadocia again into the subjection and obedience of King Ariobarzanes, according to his commission and commandment given by the senate. Moreover, both there and elsewhere he took as excellent good order as could be devised in reducing of things to quietness without wars. Furthermore, finding that the Cilicians were grown somewhat stout and unruly by the overthrow the Romans had of the Parthians and by reason of the rising and rebellion in Syria, he brought them unto reason by gentle persuasions and never received gifts that were sent him — no, not from kings and princes.[170] Furthermore, he did disburden the provinces of the feasts and banquets they were wont to make other governors before him. On the other side also, he would ever have the company of good and learned men at his table and would use them well, without curiosity° and excess. He had never porter to his gate nor was seen by any man in his bed, for he would always rise at the break of day and would walk or stand before his door. He would courteously receive all them that came to salute and visit him. Further, they report of him that he never caused man to be beaten with rods nor to tear his own garments.[171] In his anger he never reviled any man, neither did despitefully set fine upon any man's head. Finding many things also belonging to the commonwealth which private men had stolen and embezzled to their own use, he restored again unto the cities, whereby they grew very rich and wealthy, and yet did save their honour and credit that had taken them away and did them no other hurt but only constrained them to restore that which was the commonwealth's. He made a little war also and drove away the thieves that kept about the mountain Amanus,[172] for the which exploit his soldiers called him imperator, to say, chief captain.[173] About that time there was an orator called Caecilius, who wrote unto him from Rome to pray him to send him some leopards or panthers out of Cilicia

---

[168] Marg. 'Cicero chosen augur.' In 53 BCE.   Publius Crassus the younger] P. 'the younger Crassus', correctly identified by N. as Publius Crassus, but the combination of the two confuses the matter (the elder Crassus having been named Marcus).
[169] Marg. 'Cicero pro-consul of Cilicia.' In 51 BCE.
[170] Marg. 'Cicero's integrity for the government of his provinces.'
[171] his own] N.'s addition, which confuses the sense, that Cicero had never had anyone's clothes torn off for punishment.
[172] Marg. 'Mons Amanus.'
[173] Marg. 'Cicero called imperator.'

because he would show the people some pastime with them.¹⁷⁴ Cicero, boasting of his doings, wrote to him again that there were no more leopards in Cilicia, but that they were all fled into Caria for anger that, seeing all things quiet in Cilicia, they had leisure now to hunt them. So when he returned towards Rome from the charge of his government, he came by Rhodes and stayed a few days at Athens with great delight to remember how pleasantly he lived there before at what time he studied there. Thither came to him the chiefest learned men of the city and his friends also with whom he was acquainted at his first being there. In fine,° having received all the honourable entertainment in Greece that could be, he returned unto Rome, where at his arrival he found great factions kindled, the which men saw plainly would grow in the end to civil war.¹⁷⁵

[37] Thereupon the senate having decreed that he should enter in triumph into the city, he answered that he would rather (all parties agreed) follow Caesar's coach in triumph. So he travelled very earnestly between Pompey and Caesar, eftsoons° writing unto Caesar and also speaking unto Pompey that was present, seeking all the means he could to take up° the quarrel and misliking betwixt them two.¹⁷⁶ But it was so impossible a matter that there was no speech of agreement would take place. So Pompey hearing that Caesar was not far from Rome, he durst no longer abide in Rome but fled with divers of the greatest men in Rome. Cicero would not follow him when he fled, and therefore men thought he would take part with Caesar, but this is certain, that he was in a marvellous perplexity and could not easily determine what way to take. Whereupon he wrote in his epistles: 'What way should I take? Pompey hath the juster and honester cause of war, but Caesar can better execute and provide for himself and his friends with better safety, so that I have means enough to fly but none to whom I might repair.'¹⁷⁷ In all this stir, there was one of Caesar's friends called Trebatius which wrote a letter unto Cicero and told him that Caesar wished him in any case to come to him and to run with him the hope and fortune he undertook, but if he excused himself by his age, that then he should get him into Greece and there to be quiet from them both. Cicero, marvelling that Caesar wrote not to him himself, answered in anger that he would do nothing unworthy of his acts all the days of his life thitherto, and to this effect he wrote in his letters.

---

¹⁷⁴ Caecilius] Caelius (an emendation by Xylander; Caecilius is the reading of the manuscripts).
¹⁷⁵ In 49 BCE.
¹⁷⁶ **Marg.** 'Cicero seeketh to pacify the quarrel betwixt Pompey and Caesar.'
¹⁷⁷ I have means enough to fly but none to whom I might repair] A. 'j'ai bien qui fuir, mais non pas à qui recourir' (I have someone [i.e. Caesar] to flee for sure, but no one to turn to, p. 1057).   **Marg.** 'Cicero's words of Pompey and Caesar.'

[38] Now Caesar being gone into Spain, Cicero embarked presently to go to Pompey.[178] So when he came unto him, every man was very glad of his coming, but Cato. Howbeit, Cato secretly reproved him for coming unto Pompey, saying that for himself he had been without all honesty at that time to have forsaken that part the which he had always taken and followed from the beginning of his first practice in the commonwealth, but for him, on the other side, that it had been better for the safety of his country and chiefly for all his friends that he had been a neuter to both and so to have taken things as they had fallen out and that he had no manner of reason nor instant cause to make him to become Caesar's enemy and by coming thither to put himself into so great peril.[179] These persuasions of Cato overthrew all Cicero's purpose and determination besides that Pompey himself did not employ him in any matter of service or importance. But hereof himself was more in fault than Pompey because he confessed openly that he did repent him he was come thither. Furthermore, he scorned and disdained all Pompey's preparations and counsels, the which indeed made him to be had in jealousy° and suspicion. Also he would ever be fleering° and gibing at those that took Pompey's part, though he had no list himself to be merry. He would also go up and down the camp very sad and heavy, but yet he would ever have one jest or other to make men laugh, although they had as little lust to be merry as he, and surely it shall do no hurt to call some of them to mind in this place. Domitius being very desirous to prefer a gentleman to have charge of men, to recommend him he said he was an honest, wise, and sober man. Whereto Cicero presently answered: 'Why doest thou not keep him then to bring up thy children?'. Another time when they commended Theophanes Lesbian (that was master of all the artificers of the camp) because he had notably comforted the Rhodians when they had received a great loss of their navy, 'See', said Cicero, 'what a goodly thing it is to have a Grecian master of artificers in the camp?'.[180] When both battles came to join together and that Caesar had in manner all the advantage and kept them as good as besieged, Lentulus told him on a time that he heard say all Caesar's friends were mad and melancholy men.[181] 'Why', quoth Cicero to him again, 'doest thou say that they do envy° Caesar?'. Another, called Martius, coming lately out of Italy, said that there ran a rumour in Rome that Pompey was besieged. 'What', quoth Cicero to him again, 'and didst thou take ship to come and see him thyself because thou mightest believe it when thou hadst seen it?'. Pompey being overthrown, one Nonius said there was yet good hope left because they had taken seven eagles within Pompey's camp.[182] 'Thy persuasion were not ill,' quoth Cicero, 'so we

[178] Marg. 'Cicero goeth unto Pompey.'
[179] for himself [...], but for him, on the other side] i.e. 'for Cato [...], but for Cicero'.
[180] Greeks were supposed to be good at cultural, but not military, pursuits.
[181] mad] A. 'tristes' (sad, p. 1058).
[182] they had taken seven eagles within Pompey's camp] P. 'seven eagles [representing

were to fight but with pies or daws.' Labienus reposed all his trust in certain oracles that Pompey of necessity must have the upper hand. 'Yea,' said Cicero, 'but for all this goodly stratagem of war we have not long since lost our whole camp.'[183]

[39] After the battle of Pharsalia, where Cicero was not by reason of his sickness, Pompey being fled and Cato at that time at Dyrrachium, where he had gathered a great number of men of war and had also prepared a great navy, he prayed Cicero to take charge of all this army as it pertained unto him, having been consul.[184] Cicero did not only refuse it but also told them he would meddle no more with this war. But this was enough to have made him been slain, for the younger Pompey and his friends called him traitor and drew their swords upon him to kill him, which they had done, had not Cato stepped between them and him, and yet had he much ado to save him and to convey him safely out of the camp.[185] When Cicero came to Brundusium, he stayed there a certain time for Caesar's coming, who came but slowly by reason of his troubles he had in Asia as also in Egypt. Howbeit news was brought at length that Caesar was arrived at Tarentum and that he came by land unto Brundusium.[186] Cicero departed thence to go meet him, not mistrusting that Caesar would not pardon him but rather being ashamed to come to his enemy being a conqueror before such a number of men as he had about him.[187] Yet he was not forced to do or speak anything unseemly to his calling.° For Caesar seeing him coming towards him far before the rest that came with him, he lighted° from his horse and embraced him and walked a great way afoot with him, still talking with him only, and ever after he did him great honour and made much of him. Insomuch as Cicero having written a book in praise of Cato, Caesar on the other side wrote another and praised the eloquence and life of Cicero, matching it with the life of Pericles and Theramenes. Cicero's book was intituled *Cato* and Caesar's book called *Anti-Cato*, as much to say as *Against Cato*.[188] They say further that Quintus Ligarius being accused to have been in the field against Caesar, Cicero took upon him to defend his cause, and that Caesar said unto his friends about him: 'What hurt is it for us to hear Cicero speak, whom we have not heard of long time? For otherwise Ligarius (in my opinion) standeth already a condemned

---

legions] were left in the camp of Pompey'. N. follows A.'s error ('on avoit pris sept Aigles dedans le camp de Pompeius', p. 1058).
[183] this goodly stratagem] i.e. blind optimism.
[184] Marg. 'Cato gave place to Cicero and offered him the charge of the navy at Dyrrachium.' In 48 BCE.
[185] the younger Pompey] Gnaeus Pompeius.
[186] In 47 BCE.
[187] not mistrusting that Caesar would not pardon him] i.e. trusting that Caesar would pardon him (double negative for emphasis).
[188] See *Caesar*, lines 1575-78.

man, for I know him to be a vile man and mine enemy.'[189] But when Cicero had begun his oration, he moved Caesar marvellously: he had so sweet a grace and such force in his words that it is reported Caesar changed colour often and showed plainly by his countenance that there was a marvellous alteration in all the parts of him.[190] For, in the end when the orator came to touch the battle of Pharsalia, then was Caesar so troubled that his body shook withal and besides certain books he had fell out of his hands and he was driven against his will to set Ligarius at liberty.

[40] Afterwards, when the commonwealth of Rome came to be a kingdom, Cicero leaving to practise any more in the state, he gave himself to read° philosophy to the young men that came to hear him, by whose access unto him, because they were the chiefest of the nobility in Rome, he came again to bear as great sway and authority in Rome as ever he had done before.[191] His study and endeavour was to write matters of philosophy dialogue-wise and to translate out of Greek into Latin, taking pains to bring all the Greek words which are proper unto logic and natural causes unto Latin.[192] For he was the first man by report that gave Latin names unto these Greek words which are proper unto philosophers, as φαντασία he termed *visio*; κατάθεσις, *assensus*; ἐποχή, *assensus cohibitio*; κατάληψις, *comprehensio*; τὸ ἄτομον, *corpus individuum*; τὸ ἀμερές, *corpus simplex*; τὸ κενόν, *vacuum*; and many other such like words.[193] But though he were not the first, yet was it he that most did devise and use them and turned some of them by translation, others into proper terms, so that at length they came to be well taken, known, and understood of every man.[194] And for his readiness in writing of verses, he would use them many times for his recreation, for it is reported that whensoever he took in hand to make any, he would dispatch 500 of them in a night. Now all that time of his recreation and pleasure, he would commonly be at some of his houses in the country which he had near unto Thusculum, from whence he would write unto his friends that he led Laertes' life, either spoken merrily as his manner was or else pricked forward with ambition, desiring to return again to be a practiser

---

[189] In 46 BCE.
[190] Marg. 'The force of Cicero's eloquence, how it altered Caesar.'
[191] In 46–44 BCE.   Marg. 'Cicero's life under Caesar.'
[192] natural causes] i.e. natural philosophy or science.
[193] The English equivalents are perception, assent, withholding of assent, comprehension, atom, indivisible, void. A. gives French transliterations of the Greek words; N.'s Latin versions do not appear to derive from Cruser either: he for instance has 'assensionis retentionem' (p. 613) instead of 'assensus cohibitio', and does not provide the original Greek terms either.
[194] turned some of them by translation, others into proper terms] 'i.e. some by giving a new metaphorical meaning to an existing Latin word [...], some by adopting for philosophical use a word which already had the appropriate meaning' (Turner, II, 97 n. 2).

in the commonwealth, being weary with the present time and state thereof.¹⁹⁵ Howsoever it was, he came oftentimes to Rome only to see Caesar to keep him his friend and would ever be the first man to confirm any honours decreed unto him and was always studious to utter some new matter to praise him and his doings, as that was he said touching the statues of Pompey, the which being overthrown, Caesar commanded them to be set up again, and so they were.¹⁹⁶ For Cicero said that by that courtesy in setting up of Pompey's statues again, he did establish his own.

[41] So, Cicero being determined to write all the Roman history and to mingle with them many of the Grecians' doings, adding thereunto all the fables and devices which they do write and report, he was hindered of his purpose against his will by many open and private troubles that came upon him at once, whereof notwithstanding he himself was cause of the most of them. For first of all he did put away his wife Terentia because she had made but small account of him in all the wars, so that he departed from Rome having no necessary thing with him to entertain° him out of his country, and yet when he came back again into Italy, she never showed any spark of love or goodwill towards him.¹⁹⁷ For she never came to Brundusium to him, where he remained a long time, and worse than that, his daughter having the heart to take so long a journey in hand to go to him, she neither gave her company to conduct her nor money or other furniture° convenient for her, but so handled the matter that Cicero at his return to Rome found bare walls in his house and nothing in it and yet greatly brought in debt besides. And these were the honestest causes alleged for their divorce. But besides that Terentia denied all these, Cicero himself gave her a good occasion to clear herself because he shortly after married a young maiden, being fallen in fancy with her, as Terentia said, for her beauty or, as Tiro his servant wrote, for her riches, to the end that with her goods he might pay his debts.¹⁹⁸ For she was very rich, and Cicero also was appointed her guardian, she being left sole heir. Now, because he ought° a marvellous sum of money, his parents and friends did counsel him to marry this young maiden, notwithstanding he was too old for her, because that with her goods he might satisfy his creditors. But Antonius speaking of this marriage of Cicero in his answers and orations he made against the Philippians, he doth reprove him for that he put away his wife, with whom he was grown old, being merry with him by the way for that he had been an idle man, and never went from the smoke of

---

¹⁹⁵ Thusculum] Tusculum. Laertes' life] Laertes, Odysseus's elderly father, retreats to the country when the suitors take over his son's home during Odysseus's absence from Ithaca.
¹⁹⁶ oftentimes] P. and A. have the opposite, 'rarely', but N. appears to have overlooked 'peu' in 'bien peu souvent' (lit. very little often, p. 1059).
¹⁹⁷ **Marg.** 'Cicero did put away his wife Terentia.' In 46 BCE.
¹⁹⁸ **Marg.** 'Cicero married a young maiden.'

his chimney, nor had been abroad in the wars in any service of his country or commonwealth. Shortly after that he had married his second wife, his daughter died in labour of child in Lentulus' house, whose second wife she was, being before married unto Piso, who was her first husband.[199] So the philosophers and learned men came of all sides to comfort him, but he took her death so sorrowfully that he put away his second wife because he thought she did rejoice at the death of his daughter.

[42] And thus much touching the state and troubles of his house. Now touching the conspiracy against Caesar, he was not made privy to it, although he was one of Brutus' greatest friends and that it grieved him to see things in that state they were brought unto, and albeit also he wished for the time past as much as any other man did.[200] But indeed the conspirators were afraid of his nature, that lacked hardiness,° and of his age, the which oftentimes maketh the stoutest and most hardiest natures faint-hearted and cowardly. Notwithstanding, the conspiracy being executed by Brutus and Cassius, Caesar's friends being gathered together, every man was afraid that the city would again fall into civil wars. And Antonius also, who was consul at that time, did assemble the senate and made some speech and motion then to draw things again unto quietness. But Cicero having used divers persuasions fit for the time, in the end he moved the senate to decree (following the example of the Athenians) a general oblivion° of things done against Caesar and to assign unto Brutus and Cassius some governments of provinces. Howbeit, nothing was concluded, for the people of themselves were sorry when they saw Caesar's body brought through the marketplace, and when Antonius also did show them his gown all bebloodied, cut, and thrust through with swords, then they were like mad men for anger and sought up and down the marketplace if they could meet with any of them that had slain him, and taking fire-brands in their hands, they ran to their houses to set them afire. But the conspirators, having prevented° this danger, saved themselves, and fearing that if they tarried at Rome they should have many such alarms, they forsook the city.

[43] Then Antonius began to look aloft and became fearful to all men, as though he meant to make himself king, but yet most of all unto Cicero above all others. For Antonius, perceiving that Cicero began again to increase in credit and authority and knowing that he was Brutus' very friend, he did mislike to see him come near him, and besides there was at that time some jealousy betwixt

---

[199] Lentulus'] P. Cornelius Dolabella, apparently adopted into a plebeian family as Lentulus.
[200] **Marg.** 'Cicero not made privy to the conspiracy against Caesar.' The assassination of Caesar took place in 44 BCE.

them for the diversity and difference of their manners and dispositions.²⁰¹ Cicero, being afraid of this, was first of all in mind to go with Dolabella to his province of Syria as one of his lieutenants. But they that were appointed to be consuls the next year following after Antonius, two noble citizens and Cicero's great friends, Hircius and Pansa, they entreated him not to forsake them, undertaking that they would pluck down this over-great power of Antonius, so he would remain with them.²⁰² But Cicero, neither believing nor altogether mistrusting them, forsook Dolabella and promised Hircius and Pansa that he would spend the summer at Athens and that he would return again to Rome so soon as they were entered into their consulship. With this determination Cicero took sea alone to go into Greece.²⁰³ But as it chanceth oftentimes, there was some let that kept him he could not sail,²⁰⁴ and news came to him daily from Rome, as the manner is, that Antonius was wonderfully changed, and that now he did nothing any more without the authority and consent of the senate, and that there lacked nothing but his person to make all things well. Then Cicero, condemning his dastardly fear, returned forthwith to Rome, not being deceived in his first hope. For there came such a number of people out to meet him that he could do nothing all day long but take them by the hands and embrace them, who, to honour him, came to meet him at the gate of the city, as also by the way, to bring him to his house. The next morning Antonius assembled the senate and called for Cicero by name. Cicero refused to go and kept his bed, feigning that he was weary with his journey and pains he had taken the day before, but indeed the cause why he went not was for fear and suspicion of an ambush that was laid for him by the way if he had gone, as he was informed by one of his very good friends. Antonius was marvellously offended that they did wrongfully accuse him for laying of any ambush for him, and therefore sent soldiers to his house and commanded them to bring him by force or else to set his house afire.²⁰⁵ After that time, Cicero and he were always at jar, but yet coldly enough, one of them taking heed of another, until that the young Caesar, returning from the city of Apollonia, came as lawful heir unto Julius Caesar dictator and had contention with Antonius for the sum of two thousand and five hundred myriads,° the which Antonius kept in his hands of his father's goods.²⁰⁶

---

²⁰¹ Marg. 'Private grudge betwixt Antonius and Cicero.'
²⁰² so he would remain with them] i.e. provided that... Hirtius (N.'s 'Hircius') and Pansa were consuls for the year 43 BCE.
²⁰³ Marg. 'Cicero saileth into Greece.'
²⁰⁴ i.e. there was some hitch that prevented him from sailing.
²⁰⁵ N. omits P. and A. 'but since many opposed this course and entreated him to desist, he did so, after merely taking sureties'.
²⁰⁶ Marg. 'Ill will betwixt Cicero and Antonius.'   the young Caesar] i.e. Octavian.
two thousand and five hundred myriads] N. appears to be translating directly from the Greek, as in lines 226–28, above.

[44] Thereupon Philip, who had married the mother of this young Caesar, and Marcellus, who had also married his sister, went with young Caesar unto Cicero and there agreed together that Cicero should help young Caesar with the favour of his authority and eloquence, as well towards the senate as also to the people, and that Caesar in recompense of his goodwill should stand by Cicero with his money and soldiers.[207] For this young Caesar had many of his father's old soldiers about him that had served under him.[208] Now there was another cause that made Cicero glad to embrace the friendship of this young Caesar, and that was this. Whilst Pompey and Julius Caesar were alive and in good case, Cicero dreamed one night that the senators' sons were called into the Capitol because Jupiter had appointed° to show them him that one day should come to be lord and king of Rome, and that the Romans, being desirous to see who it should be, ran all unto the temple, and that all the children likewise were waiting there in their goodly guarded° gowns of purple, until that suddenly the doors of the temple were open, and then that all the children rose one after another and went and passed by the image of Jupiter, who looked upon them all and sent them away discontented, saving this young Caesar, unto whom he put forth his hand as he passed by and said: 'My lords of Rome, this child is he that shall end all your civil wars when he cometh to be lord of Rome.'[209] Some say that Cicero had this vision in his dream and that he carried in good memory the look of this child, howbeit that he knew him not and that the next morning he went of purpose into the field of Mars, where these young boys did exercise themselves, who, when he came thither, had broken up from playing and were going home, and that amongst them he first saw him whom he had dreamed of, and knew him very well, and musing at him the more, asked him whose son he was. The boy answered that he was the son of one Octavius (a man otherwise of no great calling) and of Accia, the sister of Julius Caesar, who having no child, made him his heir by his last will and testament and left him all his lands and goods.[210] After that time, it is reported that Cicero was very glad to speak to him when he met with him and that the boy also liked Cicero's friendship and making of him, for by good hap the boy was born the same year that Cicero was consul.[211]

[45] And these be the reasons alleged why Cicero did favour this young Caesar. But in truth, first of all the great malice he bore unto Antonius and secondly his nature that was ambitious of honour were (in my opinion) the chiefest causes

---

[207] **Marg.** 'Cicero and Octavius Caesar joined in friendship.'   Philip] L. Marcius Philippus.
[208] under him] i.e. under Julius Caesar.
[209] **Marg.** 'Cicero's dream of Octavius, adopted son of Julius Caesar.'
[210] **Marg.** 'Octavius and Accia, the parents of Octavius Caesar.'   Accia] Attia, the niece, rather than the sister, of Julius Caesar; N. follows A.
[211] **Marg.** 'Octavius Caesar was born in the year of Cicero's consulship.'

why he became young Caesar's friend, knowing that the force and power of his soldiers would greatly strengthen his authority and countenance in managing the affairs of the state, besides that the young man could flatter him so well that he called him father. But Brutus being offended with him for it, in his epistles he wrote unto Atticus he sharply reproveth Cicero, saying that for fear of Antonius he flattered this young Caesar, whereby it appeared he did not so much seek for the liberty of Rome as he did procure himself a loving and gentle master.[212] This notwithstanding, Brutus brought with him Cicero's son that studied philosophy at Athens, and gave him charge of men under him and employed him in great affairs, wherein he showed himself very forward and valiant. Now Cicero's authority and power grew again to be so great in Rome as ever it was before.[213] For he did what he thought good, and so vexed Antonius that he drove him out of the city, and sent the two consuls, Hircius and Pansa, against him to fight with him, and caused the senate also to decree that young Caesar should have sergeants to carry rods and axes before him and all other furniture for a praetor, as a man that fighteth for his country. After that Antonius had lost the battle and that both the consuls were slain, both the armies came unto Caesar. The senate then being afraid of this young man that had so great good fortune, they practised by honours and gifts to call the armies from him which he had about him and so to minish° the greatness of his power, saying that their country now stood in no need of force nor fear of defence sith° her enemy Antonius was fled and gone. Caesar, fearing this, sent men secretly unto Cicero to pray him to procure that they two together might be chosen consuls and that when they should be in office, he should do and appoint what he thought good, having the young man at his commandment, who desired no more but the honour only of the name.[214] Caesar himself confessed afterwards that being afraid he should have been utterly cast away to have been left alone, he finely served his turn by Cicero's ambition, having persuaded him to require° the consulship through the help and assistance that he would give him.

[46] But there was Cicero finely colted,° as old as he was, by a young man, when he was contented to sue for the consulship in his behalf and to make the senate agreeable to it, wherefore his friends presently reproved him for it, and shortly after he perceived he had undone himself and together also lost the liberty of his country. For this young man Octavius Caesar, being grown to be very great by his means and procurement, when he saw that he had the consulship upon

---

[212] flattered] The wording in P. (θεραπεύων τὸν Καίσαρα: doing service to Caesar) and A. ('il se soumettoit à ce jeune Ca[e]sar': he submitted himself to this young Caesar, p. 1062) more explicitly anticipates the reference to the master-servant relationship between Augustus and Cicero at the end of the sentence.
[213] Marg. 'Cicero's great power at Rome.'
[214] Marg. 'Octavius Caesar sueth to be consul.'

him, he forsook Cicero and agreed with Antonius and Lepidus.²¹⁵ Then, joining his army with theirs, he divided the empire of Rome with them, as if it had been lands left in common between them, and besides that there was a bill° made of two hundred men and upwards whom they had appointed to be slain. But the greatest difficulty and difference that fell out between them was about the outlawing of Cicero.²¹⁶ For Antonius would hearken to no peace between them unless Cicero were slain first of all; Lepidus was also in the same mind with Antonius; but Caesar was against them both. Their meeting was by the city of Bolonia, where they continued three days together, they three only secretly consulting in a place environed about with a little river.²¹⁷ Some say that Caesar stuck° hard with Cicero the two first days, but at the third that he yielded and forsook him. The exchange they agreed upon between them was this. Caesar forsook Cicero; Lepidus, his own brother Paulus; and Antonius, Lucius Caesar, his uncle by the mother's side.²¹⁸ Such place took wrath in them as they regarded no kindred nor blood, and to speak more properly, they showed that no brute or savage beast is so cruel as man if with his licentiousness he have liberty to execute his will.²¹⁹

[47] While these matters were a-brewing, Cicero was at a house of his in the country by the city of Thusculum, having at home with him also his brother Q. Cicero. News being brought them thither of these proscriptions or outlawries appointing men to be slain, they determined to go to Astyra, a place by the sea-side where Cicero had another house, there to take sea and from thence to go into Macedon unto Brutus.²²⁰ For there ran a rumour that Brutus was very strong and had a great power. So they caused themselves to be conveyed thither in two litters, both of them being so weak with sorrow and grief that they could

---

²¹⁵ Marg. 'Octavius Caesar forsaketh Cicero.'
²¹⁶ Marg. 'Note the fickleness of youth.'
²¹⁷ Marg. 'The meeting of the Triumviri: Antonius, Lepidus, Octavius Caesar.' Bolonia] Bologna (Lat. Bononia).
²¹⁸ Marg. 'Cicero appointed to be slain.'
²¹⁹ There is considerable variation between the three versions in this key passage. A. significantly amplifies P. 'So far did anger and fury lead them to renounce their human sentiments, or rather, they showed that no wild beast is more savage than man when his passion is supplemented by power': 'tant ils se jetterent hors de toute raison et de toute humanité pour servir à la passion de leur furieuse haine et enragé courroux, ou pour mieux dire, ils monstrerent qu'il n'y a beste sauvage au monde si cruelle que l'homme, quand il se trouve en main la licence et le moyen d'executer sa passion' (so far did they leap beyond all reason and all humanity to serve the passion of their furious hate and raging anger or, put better, they showed that there is no wild beast in the world so cruel as man when he has in hand the licence and means to carry out his desire, p. 1062). N.'s translation obscures the key philosophical distinction between the reason proper to humanity and the bestial passions, emphasising instead the violation of family relationships that is more implicit in P. and A.
²²⁰ Astyra] Astura, a coastal town south of Rome.

not otherwise have gone their ways. As they were on their way, both their litters going as near to each other as they could, they bewailed their miserable estate, but Quintus chiefly, who took it most grievously. For, remembering that he took no money with him when he came from his house and that Cicero his brother also had very little for himself, he thought it best that Cicero should hold on his journey whilst he himself made an errand home to fetch such things as he lacked and so to make haste again to overtake his brother. They both thought it best so, and then tenderly embracing one another, the tears falling from their eyes, they took leave of each other. Within few days after, Quintus Cicero being betrayed by his own servants unto them that made search for him, he was cruelly slain, and his son with him.[221] But Marcus Tullius Cicero, being carried unto Astyra and there finding a ship ready, embarked immediately and sailed alongst° the coast unto mount Circe, having a good gale of wind.[222] There, the mariners determining forthwith to make sail again, he came ashore, either for fear of the sea or for that he had some hope that Caesar had not altogether forsaken him, and therewithal returning towards Rome by land, he had gone about an hundred furlongs thence. But then, being at a straight how to resolve and suddenly changing his mind, he would needs be carried back again to the sea, where he continued all night marvellous sorrowful and full of thoughts. For one while he was in mind to go secretly unto Octavius Caesar's house and to kill himself by the hearth of his chimney to make the furies of hell to revenge his blood, but being afraid to be intercepted by the way and cruelly handled, he turned from that determination. Then, falling into other unadvised determinations, being perplexed as he was, he put himself again into his servants' hands to be conveyed by sea to another place, called Capites.[223] There, he had a very proper, pleasant summer-house, where the north winds, called Etesiae, do give a trim fresh air in the summer season. In that place also there is a little temple dedicated unto Apollo, not far from the sea-side. From thence, there came a great shoal of crows, making a marvellous noise, that came flying towards Cicero's ship, which rowed upon the shore-side. This shoal of crows came and lighted upon the yard of their sail, some crying and some pecking the cords with their bills, so that every man judged straight that this was a sign of ill luck at hand.[224] Cicero, notwithstanding this, came ashore and went into his house and laid him down to see if he could sleep. But the most part of these crows came and lighted upon the chamber° window where he lay, making a wonderful great noise, and some of them got unto Cicero's bed where he lay, the clothes being cast over his head, and they never left him till by little

---

[221] cruelly] N.'s addition.   Marg. 'Quintus Cicero slain.'
[222] mount Circe] Circeii, a town built on a mountain on the coast south of Astura.
[223] Marg. '* Some do read Caieta.'
[224] Marg. 'A wondrous matter foreshowed by crows unto Cicero.'

and little they had with their bills plucked off the clothes that covered his face. His men seeing that and saying to themselves that they were too vile beasts if they would tarry to see their master slain before their eyes, considering that brute beasts had care to save his life, seeing him so unworthily entreated,° and that they should not do the best they could to save his life, partly by entreaty and partly by force they put him again into his litter to carry him to the sea.

[48] But in the meantime came the murderers appointed to kill him, Herennius, a centurion, and Popilius Laena, tribune of the soldiers (to wit, colonel of a thousand men), whose cause Cicero had once pleaded before the judges when he was accused for the murder of his own father, having soldiers attending upon them.[225] So Cicero's gate being shut, they entered the house by force, and missing him, they asked them of the house what was become of him. They answered they could not tell. Howbeit, there was a young boy in the house called Philologus, a slave enfranchised by Quintus Cicero, whom Tullius Cicero had brought up in the Latin tongue and had taught him the liberal sciences: he told this Herennius that his servants carried him in a litter towards the sea through dark, narrow lanes, shadowed with wood on either side. Popilius, the colonel, taking some soldiers with him, ran about on the outside of the lanes to take him at his coming out of them, and Herennius on the other side entered the lanes. Cicero, hearing him coming, commanded his men to set down his litter, and taking his beard in his left hand, as his manner was, he stoutly looked the murderers in the faces, his head and beard being all white and his face lean and wrinkled for the extreme sorrows he had taken.[226] Divers of them that were by held their hands before their eyes whilst Herennius did cruelly murder him.[227] So Cicero, being threescore and four years of age, thrust his neck out of the litter and had his head cut off by Antonius' commandment, and his hands also, which wrote the orations (called the Philippians) against him.[228] For so did Cicero call the orations he wrote against him for the malice he bore him, and do yet continue the same name until this present time.

[49] When these poor dismembered members were brought to Rome, Antonius by chance was busily occupied at that time about the election of certain officers, who when he heard of them and saw them, he cried out aloud that now all his

---

[225] Marg. 'Herennius and Popilius sent to kill M. T. Cicero.'   tribune of the soldiers (to wit, colonel of a thousand men)] Apparently a conflation of A.'s 'Capitaine de mille hommes' (p. 1063, a literal translation of P. 'χιλίαρχος') and Cruser's 'tribunus' (p. 615). See Introduction, p. 59. Popilius Laena is Popillius Laenas.
[226] white] A. 'herissez et poudreux' ('tousled and dusty', p. 1064).
[227] cruelly] N.'s addition (like 'extreme' in the previous sentence).   Marg. 'M. T. Cicero slain by Herennius.'
[228] On 7 December 43 BCE.

outlawries and proscriptions were executed, and thereupon commanded his head and his hands should straight be set up over the pulpit for orations in the place called Rostra.²²⁹ This was a fearful and horrible sight unto the Romans, who thought they saw not Cicero's face, but an image of Antonius' life and disposition, who among so many wicked deeds as he committed, yet he did one act only that had some show of goodness, which was this. He delivered Philologus into the hands of Pomponia, the wife of Quintus Cicero, and when she had him, besides other cruel torments she made him abide, she compelled him to cut his own flesh off by little morsels and to broil them and then to eat them.²³⁰ Some historiographers do thus report it. But Tiro, who was a slave enfranchised by Cicero, made no mention of the treason of this Philologus. Howbeit I understood that Caesar Augustus long time after that went one day to see one of his nephews, who had a book in his hand of Cicero's, and he, fearing lest his uncle would be angry to find that book in his hands, thought to hide it under his gown. Caesar saw it, and took it from him, and read the most part of it standing, and then delivered it to the young boy and said unto him: 'He was a wise man indeed, my child, and loved his country well.'²³¹ After he had slain Antonius, being consul, he made Cicero's son his colleague and fellow consul with him,²³² in whose time the senate ordained that the images of Antonius should be thrown down and deprived his memory of all other honours, adding further unto his decree that from thenceforth none of the house and family of the Antonii should ever after bear the christen° name of Marcus.²³³ So God's justice made the extreme revenge and punishment of Antonius to fall into the house of Cicero.

---

²²⁹ Marg. 'Cicero's head and hands set up over the pulpit for orations.'
²³⁰ Marg. 'A strange and cruel punishment taken by Pomponia (Quintus Cicero's wife) of Philologus for betraying of his master.'
²³¹ Marg. 'Augustus Caesar's testimony of Cicero.'
²³² Marg. 'Cicero's son consul with Augustus Caesar.'
²³³ Marg. 'The decree of the senate against Antonius, being dead.' In 30 BCE.

The comparison of Cicero with Demosthenes.

[50/1] This is as much as we could gather by our knowledge touching the notable acts and deeds worthy of memory written of Cicero and Demosthenes. Furthermore, leaving the comparison aside of the difference of their eloquence in their orations, methinks I may say thus much of them, that Demosthenes did wholly employ all his wit and learning (natural or artificial) unto the art of rhetoric, and that in force and virtue° of eloquence he did excel all the orators in his time,¹ and for gravity and magnificent style all those also that only write for show or ostentation, and for sharpness and art all the sophisters° and masters of rhetoric, and that Cicero was a man generally learned in all sciences and that had studied divers books, as appeareth plainly by the sundry books of philosophy of his own making, written after the manner of the Academic philosophers.² Furthermore, they may see in his orations he wrote in certain causes to serve him when he pleaded that he sought occasions in his by-talk to show men that he was excellently well-learned. Furthermore, by their phrases a man may discern some spark of their manners and conditions.³ For Demosthenes' phrase hath no manner of fineness, jests, nor grace in it, but is altogether grave and harsh, and not only smelleth of the lamp, as Pytheas said when he mocked him, but showeth a great drinker of water, extreme pains, and therewith also a sharp and sour nature.⁴ But Cicero oftentimes fell from pleasant taunts unto plain scurrility, and turning all his pleadings of matters of importance to sport and laughter, having a grace in it, many times he did forget the comeliness that became a man of his calling.°⁵ As in his oration for Caelius, where he saith it is no marvel if in so great abundance of wealth and fineness he give himself a little to take his pleasure and that it was a folly not to use pleasures lawful and tolerable, sith the famousest philosophers that ever were did place the chief felicity of man to be in pleasure. And it is reported also that Marcus Cato having accused Muraena, Cicero, being consul, defended his cause and in his oration pleasantly girded° all the sect of the Stoic philosophers for Cato's sake for the

---

¹   **Marg.** 'Demosthenes' eloquence.'
²   **Marg.** 'Cicero's rare and divers doctrines.'   Academic philosophers] Followers of Plato, the founder of the Academy in Athens; Cicero claimed to be an Academic, although his practice was more eclectic. His philosophical treatises include *De finibus bonorum et malorum* ('On the Ends of Good and Evil'), *Tusculanae disputationes* ('Tusculan Disputations'), *De natura deorum* ('On the Nature of the Gods'), *De senectute* ('On Old Age'), *De amicitia* ('On Friendship'), and *De officiis* ('On Duties'), all written in 45–44 BCE.
³   **Marg.** 'Demosthenes' and Cicero's manners.'   phrases] i.e. phrasing or style.
⁴   not only smelleth] The third edition of 1603 follows A. ('ne sent pas seulement', p. 1065), but 'smelleth not' in the first edition of 1579 more accurately renders the original Greek. The smell of lamp-wicks (ἐλλυχνίων) was a sure sign of long nights of study.
⁵   having a grace in it] This appears to be N.'s interpretation of A.'s 'pource qu'il lui venoit à propos' (because it served his purpose (or suited his subject), p. 1065).

strange opinions they hold, which they call paradoxes, insomuch as he made all the people and judges also fall a-laughing a-good.° And Cato himself also smiling a little said unto them that sat by him: 'What a laughing and mocking consul have we, my lords!'. But letting that pass, it seemeth that Cicero was of a pleasant and merry nature, for his face showed ever great life and mirth in it. Whereas in Demosthenes' countenance, on the other side, they might discern a marvellous diligence and care and a pensive man, never weary with pain, insomuch that his enemies (as he reporteth himself) called him a perverse and froward° man.[6]

[51/2] Furthermore, in their writings is discerned that the one speaketh modestly in his own praise, so as no man can justly be offended with him, and yet not always, but when necessity enforceth him for some matter of great importance, but otherwise very discreet and modest to speak of himself.[7] Cicero, in contrary manner, using too often repetition of one self° thing in all his orations, showed an extreme ambition of glory when incessantly he cried out:

> Let spear and shield give place to gown
> And give the tongue the laurel crown.[8]

Yet furthermore, he did not only praise his own acts and deeds but the orations also which he had written or pleaded, as if he should have contended against Isocrates or Anaximenes, a master that taught rhetoric, and not to go about to reform the people of Rome:

> Which were both fierce and stout in arms
> And fit to work their enemies harms.[9]

For, as it is requisite for a governor of a commonwealth to seek authority by his eloquence, so to covet the praise of his own glorious tongue, or as it were to beg it, that showeth a base mind. And therefore, in this point we must confess that Demosthenes is far graver and of a nobler mind, who declared himself that all his eloquence came only but by practice, the which also required the favour of his auditory, and, further, he thought them fools and mad men (as indeed they be no less) that therefore would make any boast of themselves.

---

[6] never weary with pain] Neither in P. nor A.; it seems to correspond to the subordinate clause 'qui ne le laissoit jamais' (which he was never without), governed by 'un chagrin' (a sorrow), in A. (p. 1065).

[7] Marg. 'Demosthenes modest in praising of himself; Cicero too full of ostentation.'

[8] Cicero, *In Pisonem*, 72; *De officiis*, I. 77; *Orationes Philippicae*, II. 20. N.'s phrasing suggests that he may be drawing on the Ciceronian original ('Cedant arma togae; concedat laurea linguae [incorrect reading of 'laudi']') rather than A.'s translation 'Cede la force armee à la prudence | Le triomphal laurier à l'eloquence' (p. 1065).

[9] Aeschylus, unidentified play (Bergk, II, 242). enemies] disyllabic.

[52/3] In this they were both alike, that both of them had great credit and authority in their orations to the people and for obtaining that they would propound, insomuch as captains and they that had armies in their hands stood in need of their eloquence.[10] As Chares, Diopithes, and Leosthenes, they all were helped of Demosthenes; and Pompey, and Octavius Caesar, the young man, of Cicero, as Caesar himself confesseth in his *Commentaries* he wrote unto Agrippa and Moecenas.[11] But nothing showeth a man's nature and condition more (as it is reported, and so is it true) than when one is in authority, for that bewrayeth° his humour and the affections of his mind and layeth open also all his secret vices in him.[12] Demosthenes could never deliver any such proof of himself because he never bore any office nor was called forward. For he was not general of the army which he himself had prepared against King Philip. Cicero, on the other side, being sent treasurer into Sicily and proconsul into Cilicia and Cappadocia in such a time as covetousness reigned most (insomuch that the captains and governors whom they sent to govern their provinces, thinking it villainy and dastardliness to rob, did violently take things by force; at what time also to take bribes was reckoned no shame, but to handle it discreetly he was the better thought of and beloved for it), he showed plainly that he regarded not money and gave forth many proofs of his courtesy and goodness.[13] Furthermore, Cicero being created consul by name, but dictator in deed, having absolute power and authority over all things to suppress the rebellion and conspirators of Catiline, he proved Plato's prophecy true, which was that the cities are safe from danger when the chief magistrates and governors (by some good divine fortune) do govern with wisdom and justice.[14] Demosthenes was reproved for his corruption and selling of his eloquence, because secretly he wrote one oration for Phormio and another in the selfsame matter for Apollodorus, they being both adversaries.[15] Further, he was defamed also for receiving money of the king of Persia and therewithal condemned for the money which he had taken of Harpalus. And though some peradventure° would object that the reports thereof (which are many) do lie, yet they cannot possibly deny this, that Demosthenes had no power to refrain from looking of the presents which divers kings did offer him, praying him to accept them in good part for their sakes, neither was that the part of a man that did take usury

[10] Marg. 'Demosthenes' and Cicero's cunning in their orations in the commonwealth.'
[11] The reference is to a lost memoir by Octavian. Moecenas is Maecenas.
[12] Marg. 'Authority showeth men's virtues and vices.'
[13] Marg. 'Cicero's abstinence from money.'
[14] Plato, *Republic*, 473C–D: 'Unless [...] either philosophers become kings in our states or those whom we now call our kings and rulers take to the pursuit of philosophy seriously and adequately, and there is a conjunction of these two things, political power and philosophic intelligence, [...] there can be no cessation of troubles [...] for our states, nor [...] for the human race either.'
[15] Marg. 'Demosthenes a money taker.'

by traffic on the sea, the extremest yet of all other.¹⁶ In contrary manner (as we have said before) it is certain that Cicero, being treasurer, refused the gifts which the Sicilians offered him there, and the presents also which the king of the Cappadocians offered him whilst he was proconsul in Cilicia, and those especially which his friends pressed upon him to take of them, being a great sum of money, when he went as a banished man out of Rome.

[53/4] Furthermore, the banishment of the one was infamous to him because by judgement he was banished as a thief. The banishment of the other was for as honourable an act as ever he did, being banished for ridding his country of wicked men.¹⁷ And therefore of Demosthenes there was no speech after he was gone, but for Cicero all the senate changed their apparel into black and determined that they would pass no decree by their authority before Cicero's banishment was revoked by the people. Indeed, Cicero idly passed his time of banishment and did nothing all the while he was in Macedon, and one of the chiefest acts that Demosthenes did in all the time that he dealt in the affairs of the commonwealth was in his banishment. For he went into every city and did assist the ambassadors of the Grecians and refused the ambassadors of the Macedonians. In the which he showed himself a better citizen than either Themistocles or Alcibiades in their like fortune and exile. So when he was called home and returned, he fell again to his old trade which he practised before and was ever against Antipater and the Macedonians. Where Laelius in open senate sharply took up Cicero for that he sat still and said nothing when that Octavius Caesar, the young man, made petition against the law that he might sue for the consulship, being so young that he had never a hair on his face. And Brutus self also doth greatly reprove Cicero in his letters for that he had maintained and nourished a more grievous and greater tyranny than that which they had put down.

[54/5] And last of all, methinks the death of Cicero most pitiful, to see an old man carried up and down with tender love of his servants, seeking all the ways that might be to fly death, which did not long prevent his natural course, and in the end, old as he was, to see his head so pitifully cut off.¹⁸ Whereas Demosthenes, though he yielded a little, entreating him that came to take him, yet for that he had prepared the poison long before, that he had kept it long, and also used it as he did, he cannot but be marvellously commended for it. For sith the god Neptune denied him the benefit of his sanctuary, he betook him to a greater, and that was death, whereby he saved himself out of the soldiers' hands of the tyrant and also scorned the bloody cruelty of Antipater.

---

16 neither […] other] The idea is that wealthy moneylenders are not susceptible to bribes.
17 **Marg.** 'Diverse causes of the banishment of Demosthenes and Cicero.'
18 **Marg.** 'The difference betwixt Demosthenes' and Cicero's death.'

THOMAS NORTH

THE LIFE OF JULIUS CAESAR
FROM *THE LIVES* (1579)

Introduction

Caesar

Just as Julius Caesar was unique as a historical figure, so too is Plutarch's *Caesar* one of a kind in the *Lives*. In the preface to the paired Lives of Alexander the Great and Caesar, Plutarch famously distinguishes between his form of writing, biography, and history:

> For they must remember, that my intent is not to write histories, but only lives. For the noblest deeds do not always shew mens vertues and vices, but oftentimes a light occasion, a word, or some sport makes mens naturall dispositions and maners appeare more plaine, then the famous battels won, wherein are slaine ten thousand men, or the great armies, or cities won by siege or assault. For like as painters or drawers of pictures, which make no account of other parts of the body, do take resemblances of the face and favor of the countenance, in the which consisteth the judgement of their maners and disposition: even so they must give us leave to seeke out the signes and tokens of the mind onely, and thereby shew the life of either of them, referring you unto others to write the wars, battels, and other great things they did.[1]

Despite this programmatic opening, however, *Caesar* is largely focused on its protagonist's public life, in particular his military campaigns to secure and expand the Roman Empire and his rise to the monarchy of Rome. We discover little about his personal life, such as his relationship with his wife and his foibles, or about his innermost desires and motivations. In fact, the unremitting pace of the narrative and uncharacteristic lack of digressions of *Caesar* reflect the ruthless ambition and relentless energy of its subject. Even when Caesar has achieved total supremacy in Rome, we are told, his determination does not subside, but rather his former deeds spur him on to ever greater aspirations:

> Caesar being born to attempt all great enterprises and having an ambitious desire besides to covet great honours, the prosperous good success he had of his former conquests bred no desire in him quietly to enjoy the fruits of his labours but rather gave him the hope of things to come, still kindling more and more in him thoughts of greater enterprises and desire of new glory, as if that which he had present were stale and nothing worth. (1680–85)

The remainder of the paragraph comprises a breathless list of grand plans which Caesar makes after becoming dictator for life, but which remain unfulfilled: to extend the Roman Empire by making a grand circle through Parthia (modern-day Iran), Scythia (lands to the north of the Roman empire east of the Danube), and Germany; to divert the course of the river Tiber outside Rome; to drain the Pontine Marshes south of Rome (finally achieved two millennia later in 1930);

---

[1] North, *Lives* (1603), p. 673 (*Alexander*, 1. 2–3).

and so on. The uncommon emphasis on deeds rather than character in *Caesar* is accompanied by a different kind of moralism. Where the preface to this pair of Lives had claimed that personal details expose 'mens vertues and vices', *Caesar*, with its focus on public action, offers little explicit moral comment. That is not to say that the Life is not concerned with moral exploration. Rather, as Christopher Pelling has argued, there is a difference — albeit not an absolute difference but one of degree — between the 'protreptic' moralism of such Lives as *Aemilius Paullus*, which explicitly seek to guide the moral conduct of the reader, and the more 'descriptive' moralism of *Caesar*, which offers little specific guidance on the practical instruction to be drawn from his Life.[2]

The name 'Caesar' was already synonymous with 'emperor' by the time Plutarch was writing the *Lives*, and has of course continued to be so ever since (for instance in German *Kaiser*). Caesar gave his name to his adopted son Octavian, who became the first Emperor Augustus and in turn bequeathed the title to his successors under whom Plutarch lived. *Caesar* offers political analysis of both the causes and effects of his assumption of sole rule. In analysing the sources of Caesar's power, Plutarch persistently focuses on his pursuit of popular support. While his minimization of Caesar's backing from, and involvement in, the senate is historically misleading, it fits a universal pattern of social division as the driving force of political transformation that Plutarch establishes in the *Lives*.[3] The question of how we should judge Rome's transition from republic to empire is raised by Caesar's assassins, who 'called to the people to defend their liberty [*eleutheria*]' (1964), thus presenting the change to monarchy as a loss of the freedom of citizens to exercise their political rights. Plutarch's Life points in different directions in this regard (as does North's translation). On the one hand, following Caesar's appointment as dictator for life, the text unambiguously states: 'This was a plain tyranny [*tyrannis*]' (1639). The words 'tyrant' and 'tyranny' were highly charged at the time North was writing, when questions about the limitations of royal power and the right to resist were prominent, not least due to the religious schisms in the wake of the Reformation.[4] This strain of the Life is perhaps most conspicuous in Caesar's encounters with Pompey. When his opponents convince the senate to appoint Pompey as sole consul, but refuse to let Caesar seek office on equal terms with Pompey for fear that he is striving to become monarch of Rome, Caesar claims that 'they did wrongfully accuse him in going about to make himself a tyrant and, in the meantime, to grant the other [i.e. Pompey] means to be a tyrant [*tyrannos*]' (912–13). After Caesar crossed the Rubicon with his army and marched towards Rome, Pompey decided to flee and 'commanded the senate

---

[2] Pelling, *Plutarch and History*, pp. 237–52, esp. p. 248.
[3] Pelling, *Plutarch and History*, pp. 211–12.
[4] See Skinner, *Foundations*, II, 187–359.

to follow him and not a man to tarry there unless he loved tyranny [*tyrannis*] more than his own liberty [*eleutheria*] and the commonwealth' (1025–26). And at the end of the Life, when Caesar's bloodied corpse falls against the statue of Pompey — a statue Caesar himself had re-erected — the narrator declares, though not without hesitation, and on personal rather than political grounds, that 'it seemed that the image took just revenge of Pompey's enemy, being thrown down on the ground at his feet and yielding up his ghost there for the number of wounds he had upon him' (1947–49).

In a parallel image of revenge in the final paragraph of the Life, however, the narrator less equivocally states that Brutus's vision of the ghost of Caesar shortly before the former's death in the battle of Philippi 'showed plainly that the gods were offended with the murder of Caesar' (2027–28). The supernatural events included in the same, final paragraph of the Life, as well as in the run-up to Caesar's assassination (notably 'the strange and wonderful signs' (1827–28) reported in paragraph 63, including Calpurnia's dream and the warning of the soothsayer to Caesar to beware the Ides of March), likewise point to the involvement of the gods in the momentous alteration of Rome from republic to principate. While the view that the Roman state had need of monarchical rule to put an end to years of civil war is recorded in the Life, however ('there were many that were not afraid to speak it openly that there was no other help to remedy the troubles of the commonwealth but by the authority of one man only that should command them all and that this medicine must be ministered by the hands of him that was the gentlest physician, meaning covertly Pompey', 852–56), it is misdirected towards Pompey, and Plutarch notably declines to locate the events of his subject's life within a wider political and providential perspective in *Caesar*, as he does in the *Comparison of Dion and Brutus*:

> The rule of Caesar, although during its establishment it gave no little trouble to its opponents, still, after they had been overpowered and had accepted it, they saw that it was a tyranny only in name and appearance, and no cruel or tyrannical act was authorized by it; nay, it was plain that the ills of the state required a monarchy, and that Caesar, like a most gentle physician, had been assigned to them by Heaven [*ho daimōn*] itself.[5]

The assassination itself is described by Plutarch in neutral terms as 'a deed of great daring' (*tolmēma megas*), and his characterization of Brutus's motivation as *philotimia*, which can signify both an appropriate and even laudable desire for glory and a reprehensible and excessive ambition, is equally ambivalent.[6] North renders *philotimia* as 'ambition' (1817), even though Amyot has the more

---

[5] *Comparison of Dion and Brutus*, 2. 1. The passage is quoted from the modern Loeb translation as it is significantly altered by North: see I, 78 n. 276. See further Simon Swain, 'Plutarch: Chance, Providence, and History', *American Journal of Philology*, 110 (1989), 272–302; Pelling, *Caesar*, pp. 11–12, 20–21, 31–33, 494–501.

[6] *Caesar*, 62. 4, 66. 4. See Pelling, *Caesar*, 58. 4 n., 62. 8 n.

even-handed 'le desir d'honneur', but it is in his description of the assassination that his deviation from Plutarch becomes fully apparent.[7] Where the Roman author describes the plot as 'the action' (*hē praxis*; Amyot 'l'entreprise') and a 'dreadful attempt' (*to deinon*; Amyot 'l'œuvre'), North calls it 'treason' (1909) and 'their traitorous enterprise' (1912); later in the same paragraph, he renders 'a deed of great daring' (Amyot 'une si hardie et si perilleuse entreprise') as 'such a devilish attempt' (1928–29).[8] Evoking Satan's rebellious endeavour to overthrow God's monarchy of heaven, the latter phrase points to the contemporary religious resonances of North's translation choices here. The Papal Bull 'Regnans in excelsis' (1570) had excommunicated Queen Elizabeth from the Catholic Church and absolved her subjects from allegiance to the queen; this was followed by a series of Catholic plots to assassinate the queen in the following two decades centred on the Catholic claimant to the throne, Mary, Queen of Scots. North's description of Caesar's assassination echoes the language of contemporary accounts of attempts on Elizabeth's life. *A true and plaine declaration of the horrible treasons, practised by William Parry the traitor, against the Queenes Majestie* (1585), for instance, incorporated in full in the second edition of Holinshed's influential *Chronicles* (1587), likewise labels Parry's alleged plot to assassinate the queen as 'that most devilish attempt' and time after time uses the terms 'treason', 'traitorous', and 'enterprise' to refer to Parry's plot.[9]

    Caesar is no less intricate in its treatment of historical and moral questions than of political ones. Plutarch's narrative repeatedly underlines how the same qualities and forces that bring about its protagonist's spectacular rise to power also lead to his downfall. His relentless ambition and irrepressible energy are responsible for his breathtaking military achievements and ascent to political power in Rome, but they also cause the resentment that eventually leads to his assassination. Likewise, the soldiers on whom Caesar relied during the wars turn public opinion against him when he returns to Rome. Plutarch pithily captures his double-bind: 'Caesar knew all this well enough, and would have been contented to have redressed them, but to bring his matters to pass he pretended, he was driven to serve his turn by such instruments' (1499–1501). In the end, moreover, it is Caesar's clemency, not only in sparing Brutus and Cassius following the battle of Pharsalus but even promoting them to the office

---

[7] Amyot, *Vies* (1574), p. 894.
[8] Plutarch, *Caesar*, 66. 4; Amyot, *Vies* (1574), p. 896. In this paragraph, North further heightens Plutarch's language when he translates that danger 'put [Cassius] into a furious passion and made him like a man half besides himself' and Caesar's body was 'hacked and mangled' by the conspirators.
[9] *A true and plaine declaration of the horrible treasons, practised by William Parry the traitor, against the Queenes Majestie* (1585), sig. A2v; Raphael Holinshed and others, *The first and second volumes of Chronicles* (1587), sig. 6Q6v.

of praetor, and his courage in declining the offer of bodyguards in Rome and deciding to come to the capitol on the Ides of March despite many bad omens — precisely the qualities that had created such loyalty in his soldiers — that are responsible for his assassination. Finally, while the *Alexander* and *Caesar* pair does not have a formal Comparison (although Simon Goulart composed one, translated by North in the third edition of *The Lives*, published in 1603, and included in all subsequent editions), the concluding paragraph of *Caesar* offers a quite different perspective on the achievements of the Roman general (and, by extension, his Greek counterpart): 'So he reaped no other fruit of all his reign and dominion, which he had so vehemently desired all his life and pursued with such extreme danger, but a vain name only and a superficial glory that procured him the envy and hatred of his country' (2010–13).[10] The insubstantiality of Caesar's power is much heightened in North's translation, which adds 'vain', 'superficial', and 'hatred' (the first and last from Amyot).[11] The specifically Christian connotations of his version of this passage, which evoke the contrast between the mutability of worldly fame and the eternal glory of heaven, come into view when we note the similarity with the closing stanza of John Higgins's *de casibus* tragedy of Caesar in the additions to *The Mirror for Magistrates*, published in the following decade: 'But sith my whole pretence was glory vaine, | To have renowne and rule above the rest'.[12]

These complexities extend to the framing of the *Life* within the pair and in the sequence of late republican *Lives*.[13] *Caesar* highlights the similarities with the paired *Life of Alexander* (such as their endeavours to circle the known world in its entirety) and the implicit comparisons with Alexander point up some key questions raised by this pair, such as the impact of the boundless conquests of their protagonists on the internal politics of the state (the militarisation of politics and the challenges of accommodating such dominant military figures within existing political structures) and the relative importance of moral and political responsibility and external influences on the fall of these great men. Plutarch further wrote *Caesar* as part of a series of *Lives* dealing with the period in the middle of the first century BCE when a series of military strongmen gradually transformed Rome from a republic to an empire, and the Life is presented as part of this sequence in North's translation (again following Amyot): immediately preceded by *Pompey*, *Caesar* is followed by

---

[10] Goulart's comparison was first published in *Les Vies des hommes illustres grecs et romains*, trans. by Jacques Amyot, ed. by Simon Goulart (Geneva: Jérémie des Planches, 1583). Jacques Pineaux, 'Un continuateur des *Vies Parallèles*: Simon Goulart de Senlis (S.G.S.)', in *Fortunes de Jacques Amyot*, ed. by Balard, pp. 331–42 (pp. 337–38), notes the indebtedness of Goulart's comparison to Montaigne.

[11] Amyot, *Vies* (1574), p. 898.

[12] William Baldwin and others, *The mirour for magistrates* (1587), sig. L3r.

[13] See Pelling, *Caesar*, pp. 23–24, 25–35.

Cato, Cicero, Antony, and Brutus.[14] These Lives are concerned with many of the same historical events and figures, notably Caesar, but from strikingly different perspectives. Thus, the Lives of Caesar's opponents, Cato, Cicero, and Brutus, give more attention to the threat he presents to the Roman republic and its ideals of political participation and liberty, as well as to his less honourable actions, for example his role in the conspiracy of Catiline, a plot to seize power in Rome by deposing the consuls in an armed uprising. They also tackle head-on some of the larger moral and political questions side-stepped in *Caesar*, such as whether his assumption of monarchical rule was beneficial to Rome, as in the passage quoted from the *Comparison of Dion and Brutus* above. It seems no coincidence that for his polyphonic portrayal of the assassination of Caesar and its aftermath in his first Plutarchan play, *Julius Caesar*, Shakespeare chose to focus on a series of events narrated from a range of different perspectives in a variety of *Lives*.

Translation

See Introduction to North's *The Life of Demosthenes*, *The Life of Marcus Tullius Cicero*, and *The Comparison of Cicero with Demosthenes*.

Reception

Caesar was one of the most celebrated historical figures of classical antiquity in early modern England, one of the Nine Worthies and a foundation stone for early modern monarchy. Despite his unassailable status as an icon of Roman power and achievement, however, Caesar was also a controversial figure. Both his political career and his assassination, as well as his moral qualities, were the subject of conflicting interpretations. One reason was that Renaissance accounts of his life went back to a range of different sources, written from varying perspectives, including Caesar's own *Commentaries*, Sallust's *Conspiracy of Catiline*, Suetonius's *Lives of the Caesars*, and Lucan's *Pharsalia*, as well as medieval and Continental Renaissance adaptations, from Lydgate's *Serpent of Division* (1422/3?, reprinted in 1559 and 1590) to *A Brief Chronicle of the Four Principal Empires* (1556; trans. 1563) by Sleidan (Johannes Sleidanus).[15] While it is not always easy to isolate the influence of Plutarch, the distinctive anecdotes, characteristic features, and dicta from his Life had a pervasive presence in early modern English literature and culture. What is more, numerous early modern authors, especially those writing for the stage, responded to the complexity and contradictions of Plutarch's portrait of Caesar.

[14] Pelling, *Caesar*, p. 36; Pelling, *Plutarch and History*, pp. 1–44.
[15] See Cox Jensen, *Reading the Roman Republic*, pp. 45–54.

The political and didactic imperatives of early modern English culture often led to fragmented and polarised accounts of Caesar. Royal iconography is a case in point. Despite his notoriously prudent avoidance of the title — 'he said he was not called king, but Caesar' (1739) — Caesar was commonly considered the first emperor of Rome and, due to his conquest of Britain, the first monarch of England. The title page of John Speed's *The History of Great Britain* (1611), for instance, refers to 'the Successions, Lives, acts and Issues of the English Monarchs from Julius Caesar, to our most gracious Soveraigne King James'.[16] Woodstock Palace was claimed to have been built 'in Julius Caesar's time', and there was a bust of Caesar at the palace at Greenwich and tapestries with stories based on his life at Hampton Court.[17] King James VI of Scotland, who became James I of England following the death of Elizabeth in 1603, particularly encouraged comparisons with Caesar. A key element of the analogy was that James, like Caesar, was a published author as well as a ruler. Early in his life, his prospective military achievements were likened to those of Caesar, while after his ascent to the English throne he was frequently presented as the founder of a British Empire on the model of Caesar as founder of the Roman Empire.[18] In such a context, the calculated ambiguity of Plutarch's *Life* could appear straightforwardly hostile. The French humanist Isaac Casaubon reported in 1610 that 'The king [James I] blamed Plutarch for his partiality against Caesar'.[19]

Early modern commonplace books, and the ubiquitous moral and historical collections based on them, tended to focus attention on individual episodes from Plutarch's *Life* as illustrations of specific virtues and vices. Thus, the story of Caesar's fearlessness when captured by pirates recounted towards the start of the *Life* was entered in a manuscript collection by one early modern English reader under the heading 'Audacia'.[20] Similarly, Lodowick Lloyd's moral-historical compendium *The Pilgrimage of Princes* (1573) draws on Plutarch's account of Caesar's moderate diet and sober living during his campaigns (as the marginal note indicates) to present him as an example 'Of sober and temperate Princes'. Lloyd relates the superior self-control of Caesar, characteristically styled an emperor, to his conquests, and turns him into a political as well as a moral model for modern princes: 'Julius Caesar, that famous Emperour of Rome, for his singuler sobrietie and passing temperaunce, the verie lampe and lantorne of Europe, for his abstinence the onely mirrour of Italy, who by overcomming of himselfe, overcame all Europe'.[21] A more complex assessment

---

[16] John Speed, *The history of Great Britaine* (1611).
[17] James S. Shapiro, *A Year in the Life of William Shakespeare: 1599* (New York: HarperCollins, 2005), pp. 181–82.
[18] See Kewes, pp. 160–69.
[19] Quoted in ibid., p. 161.
[20] Cox Jensen, *Reading the Roman Republic*, p. 102.
[21] Lloyd, sig. N1v; Plutarch, *Caesar*, 17. North's translation of this paragraph draws the

of Caesar's character is offered by Montaigne's *Essais*, translated into English by John Florio in 1603. Reflecting its origins in the commonplace-book method of collecting quotations from classical authors under thematic headings, 'The Tale of Spurina', a consideration of the relative strength and influence of the passions of the body and the mind, draws on Plutarch's *Life*, as well as a range of other sources, to offer a veritable inventory of Caesar's good qualities (his learning, active mind, clemency, courage, prudence, and moderation), while noting two less commendable characteristics, his 'wanton lascivious complexion' and his ambition. Despite his admiration for Caesar's greatness, however, Montaigne in the end comes down decisively on the negative side:

> To conclude, this onely vice [i.e. ambition] (in mine opinion) lost, and overthrew in him the fairest naturall and richest genuitie that ever was; and hath made his memorie abhominable to all honest mindes, insomuch as by the ruine of his countrey, and subversion of the mightiest State and most flourishing Common-wealth, that ever the worlde shall see, he went about to procure his glorie.[22]

Like Lloyd, though arriving at precisely the opposite conclusion, Montaigne parallels Caesar's moral and political accomplishments, equating the subversion of his innate nobility of character through ambition with his destruction of the Roman republic.

It was the drama of the period, an inherently dialogic literary form, however, that responded most fully to the characteristic ambiguities of Plutarch's *Caesar*.[23] Caesar's life was an extremely popular subject of dramatic representation, with over twenty plays produced in England between the middle of the sixteenth and the middle of the seventeenth centuries.[24] Of the surviving playtexts, about half a dozen are primarily based on, or substantially indebted to, Plutarch's *Life*. While by no means all early modern English drama shared the 'descriptive' moralism of the Plutarchan *Life*, most plays for which Plutarch was a major source represented Caesar as a character with a mixture of good and less admirable qualities. Equally complex and, not infrequently, contradictory was their treatment of the political questions raised by Caesar's life and death, and the historical forces that led to his assassination. Dramatists were particularly sensitive to the application of Plutarch's *Life* to the circumstances of early

---

same moral through a marginal note commenting on Caesar's 'temperance' and using the words 'soberly' and 'abstained', which appear nowhere else in the translation.

[22] Montaigne, *Essayes*, sig. 2N6v (II. 33). Montaigne's extensive use of Plutarch's *Caesar* in the essay is traced in Montaigne, *Essais*, pp. 1687–89.

[23] See Julia Griffin, 'Shakespeare's *Julius Caesar* and the Dramatic Tradition', in *A Companion to Julius Caesar*, ed. by Miriam T. Griffin (Oxford: Wiley-Blackwell, 2009), pp. 371–98, who surveys a wide range of plays on Caesar from the sixteenth to the eighteenth centuries in English, French, Italian, German, Dutch, and Neo-Latin.

[24] Lovascio, 'Caesar as a Tyrant', p. 68.

modern England, and developments in the fictional representation of Caesar correlate to political changes. As in Plutarch's Life, historical, moral, and political issues are related and frequently intertwine.

The interplay of ethical and political concerns takes centre stage in *Julius Caesar* by William Alexander (1607), who (as the early twentieth-century editors of his play abundantly illustrate in their notes to the text) 'Ultimately [...], and indeed immediately, for by far the greater part of *Caesar*, [...] gets his material from Plutarch'.[25] From the building blocks of Plutarch's *Lives*, however, Alexander has constructed a *de casibus* tragedy that presents Caesar's fall as a warning against 'Pride' and closes with the Chorus asking 'What fools are those who do repose their trust | On what this masse of misery affords?'.[26] Alexander may well be responding to North's translation in this respect, who (as we have seen) draws on the language of the fall of princes in the final paragraph of *Caesar*: 'So he reaped no other fruit of all his reign and dominion, which he had so vehemently desired all his life and pursued with such extreme danger, but a vain name only and a superficial glory that procured him the envy and hatred of his country' (2010-13). While Alexander's Caesar is not wholly devoid of positive characteristics — though Sally Mapstone's assessment that 'Alexander's presentation of Caesar shows him an admirable figure in many ways' is certainly an exaggeration — these are, as in Montaigne, heavily outweighed by his excessive ambition, captured in Caesar's claim (from Plutarch) 'In emulation of my selfe at last, | I even with envy look on my owne deeds'.[27] Not only does Alexander introduce a chorus that relentlessly harps on Caesar's sinful pride, but a series of changes to the narrative of its main source decisively tilt the balance of sympathy in favour of the opponents of Caesar. In contrast to Shakespeare's play, Alexander omits the providential revenge of Caesar's ghost on Brutus and Cassius, while highlighting the providential nature of Caesar's death. In contrast to Shakespeare too, Antony is met with distrust when he addresses the Roman crowd after Caesar's death, who urge him 'sow not seeds of warre', while the conspirators are praised by the chorus for '(by a Tyrants o're-throw) hav[ing] restor'd | The light of liberty which was put forth' and apportioned no comparable blame for the wars that followed Caesar's death.[28]

Caesar's morality is inseparable from his politics, his 'monstrous pride' from his 'unlimited tyrannicke pow'r' (in Cassius's words), in the play, as in

---

[25] *Poetical Works of Alexander*, I, 474.

[26] *The Tragedy of Julius Caesar*, lines 3127-28, in *Poetical Works of Alexander*, I, 440.

[27] *The Tragedy of Julius Caesar*, lines 603-04; Plutarch, *Caesar*, 58. 2; Sally Mapstone, 'Drunkenness and Ambition in Early Seventeenth-Century Scottish Literature', *Studies in Scottish Literature*, 35-36 (2007), 131-55 (p. 152).

[28] *The Tragedy of Julius Caesar*, lines 2693-94, 2715. This is despite the fact that, as the editors note, Alexander's Antony 'is nobler than Plutarch's' in this scene (*Poetical Works of Alexander*, I, 480).

Plutarch's Life.²⁹ Alexander was a courtier to James I, and his *Julius Caesar* is a closet play written not for performance but as advice to the king. As David Hume of Godscroft wrote in a poem in his *Lusus poetici* (1639) on Alexander's *Monarchical Tragedies*, as part of which his *Caesar* was published, 'Learn, you who rule, since kingdoms are also vanities, let your mind rise up wholly to God alone. Happy the servant who convinces his king of this, and happy the king who believes such a servant.'³⁰ Alexander's portrayal of Caesar as a sinful overreacher frequently leads him to endorse the views of the republican conspirators, so much so that, writing in the wake of the Gunpowder Plot of 1605, he felt compelled to give Brutus a speech distinguishing explicitly between his right to assassinate Caesar, who had unlawfully seized the crown, and the need to obey monarchs who have been lawfully born or elected to the crown (such as James). However, Paulina Kewes's claim that 'the anti-monarchical slant of Alexander's play [...] has been imported wholesale from his chief source, Plutarch' is an overstatement, both with respect to Alexander's play and to Plutarch's Life.³¹ As Sally Mapstone rightly points out, while the play is highly critical of the excesses of monarchy, notably ambition (Cassius's 'unlimited tyrannicke pow'r'), it is not inherently anti-kingship.³² Yet Kewes's assertion does point to the fact that the 'partiality against Caesar' of a play based on Plutarch's Life — though (as I have argued) significantly amplifying its bias — might have become legible as anti-monarchical in the context of the representation of Caesar as an icon of kingship in early modern England, as James's comment to Casaubon (which may have been prompted, in part, by Alexander's Plutarchan tragedy) suggests.

Like Alexander's play, George Chapman's *Caesar and Pompey* (printed in 1631, but probably written in the early years of the seventeenth century) borrows extensively from Plutarch and portrays Caesar as a tyrant who seeks glory in this world and falsely trusts in himself instead of God. Despite the title, Caesar is primarily opposed not to Pompey but to Cato, the 'moral centre' of the play, whose ancient Stoicism is conflated with religious faith in God's providence and a Christian afterlife.³³ The contrast between Cato and Caesar is captured in the play's central paradox of the conqueror conquered, as when the latter confesses: 'All my late conquest, and my life's whole acts, | Most crown'd, most

---

²⁹ *The Tragedy of Julius Caesar*, lines 1027–31.
³⁰ Quoted in Kirsten Sandrock, 'Ancient Empires and Early Modern Colonialism in William Alexander's *Monarchicke Tragedies* (1603–07)', *Renaissance Studies*, 31 (2016), 346–64 (p. 348).
³¹ Kewes, p. 158.
³² Mapstone, p. 150.
³³ Andrew Hadfield, *Shakespeare and Republicanism* (Cambridge: Cambridge University Press, 2005), p. 77.

beautified, are b[l]asted all | With thy grave life's expiring in their scorn'.³⁴ Chapman's antagonism towards Caesar extends to his politics and, drawing on Plutarch's Life, he paints a vivid picture of Cato's opposition in the senate against the insidious practices of Caesar and his agents in their attempt to gain absolute power in Rome in the first act of the play. The play shows little interest in political process or ideology after the opening act, however, and when Cato returns in Act V it is as a moral and religious paragon, not as a spokesman for an alternative political ideology. In the middle acts of the play, where Chapman closely tracks the narrative of Plutarch's *Caesar*, Cato's absence from the action provides the setting for a much more positive portrayal of Caesar as 'the favourite of Fortune [...] eloquent, energetic, generous, loth to spill blood, quick to repair an error, and supremely confident in his destiny'.³⁵ Chapman's reliance on Plutarch's complex portrait of the Roman general in *Caesar*, in combination with a series of other Plutarchan *Lives* with contrasting perspectives on the crucial events of the years 49 to 48 BCE (including *Pompey* and *Cato*), has thus produced a Caesar who is neither wholly good nor wholly bad. Apparently intent on producing a straightforwardly didactic play, however, Chapman makes no attempt to reconcile the different sides of the Roman dictator's character in *Caesar and Pompey*.³⁶

Likewise contradictory is the portrayal of Caesar in John Fletcher and Philip Massinger's *The False One* (printed 1647, but written and performed c. 1620). Drawing on Lucan's *Pharsalia* as well as Plutarch's Life for its account of Caesar's liaison with Cleopatra in the aftermath of the Battle of Pharsalus, the play paints a dark portrait of the corruption of the Egyptian court and of Caesar's tyrannical ambition and loss of self-control, reflecting widely-felt anxieties about the rule of James I at the time the play was written.³⁷ Fletcher and Massinger's Caesar, however, also seems to show genuine remorse for the cost of his recent victory when presented with his adversary Pompey's head, more reflective of the 'clemency' attributed to his response by North's marginal note to this episode than of the dissimulation of Lucan's protagonist, and he is magnanimous and magnificent in his love for Cleopatra. John Curran has recently argued that both sides of Caesar's character emerge from the same impulsiveness that characterises him throughout the play: 'Embracing

---

³⁴ *The Plays and Poems of George Chapman*, ed. by Thomas Marc Parrott, 2 vols (London: Routledge, 1910–1914), I, 399 (v. 2. 180–82; cf. v. 2. 45).
³⁵ *Plays and Poems of Chapman*, I, 659. See Ide, p. 261.
³⁶ See Ide, p. 267.
³⁷ Thomas May's *The Tragedy of Cleopatra* (performed in 1626 but not printed until 1639) similarly drew on both Lucan's epic and Plutarch's *Antony* for its portrayal of the character and reign of Cleopatra. See Denzell S. Smith, 'The Tragoedy of Cleopatra, Queene of Aegypt' by Thomas May: A Critical Edition (New York: Garland, 1979), pp. lxxxi–lxxxv; Paleit, pp. 215–44.

the multivalency of Caesar's history, the play, like Plutarch, creates a unified personality for him. [...] He is not only his truest self — emotional and large-hearted, impulsive and appetitive — when he has given in to his passion for [Cleopatra], but also his best'.[38] But that is to oversimplify both Plutarch's Life and the play. For all his restless energy, Plutarch's Caesar is not obviously typified by emotional impulsiveness, and it would be difficult to imagine the philosopher from Chaeronea approving of such a quality. In fact, Plutarch soberly concludes: 'for the war he made in Alexandria [i.e. Egypt], some say he needed not have done it, but that he willingly did it for the love of Cleopatra, wherein he won little honour and besides did put his person in great danger' (1411–14). In *The False One* too, Caesar's love for Cleopatra is aligned with his avaricious desire for Egyptian wealth and his reckless destruction of the Roman republic by starting a civil war, a link that may go back to North's use of the language of greed ('covetous') in his description of Caesar's yearning for the title of king: 'the chiefest cause that made him mortally hated was the covetous desire [*erōs*; Amyot 'la convoitise'] he had to be called king' (1730–31).[39] What is more, the ineluctable presence of Shakespeare's *Antony and Cleopatra* in the background to Fletcher and Massinger's play calls attention to Caesar's emotional control, which allows him to escape the tragic fate of the impetuous Antony in similar circumstances. By the end of the play, Fletcher and Massinger's Caesar sounds eerily like Antony's nemesis Octavian, Caesar's adopted son and namesake, who has the last word in Shakespeare's play, with the announced return to Rome in both cases pointing to a restoration of the ideals of masculine heroism, cultural supremacy, and political dominion that have come under pressure in the plays. If *The False One* ends with the reunion of the two lovers, Caesar and Rome are firmly back in charge, with the events the audience has witnessed over the course of the play uneasily registered in Caesar's use of the word 'still' ('without change' or 'interruption') in the closing speech of the play: 'and now (my dearest) | Looke upon Caesar, as he still appear'd, | A Conquerour'.[40]

Fletcher and Massinger, the successors of Shakespeare as playwrights for the King's Men, also appear to have inherited his predilection for using North's translation of Plutarch's *Lives* as a major source for their plays, from *Demetrius* for Fletcher's *Demetrius and Enanthe* (c. 1619) and *Timoleon* for Massinger's *The Noble Bondman* (1623) to *Flaminius* for Massinger's *Believe*

---

[38] John E. Curran, 'Fletcher, Massinger, and Roman Imperial Character', *Comparative Drama*, 43 (2009), 317–54 (p. 321).
[39] Amyot, *Vies* (1574), p. 892.
[40] *The Dramatic Works in the Beaumont and Fletcher Canon*, ed. by Fredson Bowers, 10 vols (Cambridge: Cambridge University Press, 1966–1996), VIII, 201 (v. 4. 202–04); *OED*, still, *adv.*, 3. a.

as You List (1631) and *Caesar*, as we have seen, for *The False One*.⁴¹ We might even imagine Fletcher, who collaborated with Shakespeare on *The Two Noble Kinsmen* (1613), which draws on Plutarch's *Theseus* as a narrative source, right towards the end of the latter's career as a dramatist, coming into the possession of Shakespeare's well-thumbed copy of North's *Lives*. *The False One*, besides echoing *Antony and Cleopatra*, also constitutes a response to Shakespeare's *Julius Caesar*, centring on an episode of his life and an aspect of his character overlooked in the earlier play. Fletcher and Massinger's play, however, shares the ambiguity of Shakespeare's portrayal of Caesar and his political import. The different sides of Caesar's character (his bigheartedness towards his enemies and towards Cleopatra versus his reckless ambition in love and war) remain in uneasy tension, as they had been in the earlier plays, inviting the audience to pass judgement on his moral worth and, in conjunction with that, his political significance in a similar manner to Plutarch's *Caesar*. What sets Shakespeare's play apart from the many other dramatic treatments of Caesar's life, and what makes *Julius Caesar* a fitting conclusion to this discussion of the reception of Plutarch's *Life* in early modern English drama despite the fact that it was the earliest play to be written and performed (c. 1599), however, is that the debate over the construction of Caesar's reputation is at its very heart. By showing the different characters of the play actively constructing an image of Caesar that fits their political agenda — even Caesar, as we shall see, is mainly preoccupied with his own Caesar-ness — the play foregrounds the process whereby a figure from history becomes an exemplar whose meaning is appropriated and contested for different ideological ends.⁴² *Julius Caesar* is, we might say, a play about 'Caesar', the Caesar myth, rather than about Caesar, the historical figure.

Thus, Shakespeare does not stage Caesar's triumph on his return to Rome, the first major event in the section of Plutarch's biography on which the play is based, in the opening scene, nor does Caesar even appear as a character there. Instead, the audience is made to witness a humorous but ill-tempered debate between supporters and opponents of Caesar about his impending triumph and, immediately prior to his first appearance on the stage at the start of the second scene, told of the statues of Caesar that have been adorned by his supporters. The statues are not only vital markers of Caesar's growing status in the fictional world of the play; they also point toward Caesar's presence in Shakespeare's own time as a historical figure memorialised in monuments, both artistic and literary, and subject to interpretation and appropriation in the audience's present. This pattern continues in the second scene. Though Caesar now appears on the stage, the key event, the offer of the crown to the Roman general, is not staged but reported within the framework of a debate between

---

⁴¹ Wiggins and Richardson, VI, no. 1724, VII, nos. 1898 and 2074, VIII, no. 2338.
⁴² See General Introduction, I, 65–74.

his republican opponents Brutus and Cassius. In response to the shouts that attend the offer and its rejection, Cassius echoes the image of Caesar as a statue, expressing his frustration to Brutus that 'he doth bestride the narrow world | Like a Colossus' (1. 2. 136–37). The relationship between the offer of the crown and the statues, implicit in Shakespeare's play, is brought out by Plutarch's *Caesar*, which the first two scenes of the play follow closely: 'After that [i.e. the offer of the crown], there were set up images of Caesar in the city with diadems upon their heads like kings' (1785–86). As the adverbial phrase of time indicates, Shakespeare has inverted the order of the two episodes, and relegated the presentation of the insignia of royalty to reports, with the result that the emphasis is less on the historical event (the offer of the crown) than on Caesar's status as a contested icon.

The statues in the opening scene introduce the audience to the vital role of simulacra of Caesar in the play. The image of Caesar as a statue makes a return in Calpurnia's dream in Act II (in a notable change from Plutarch, who has 'a certain pinnacle' (1856)); Caesar's bleeding corpse is both the visual and the rhetorical focal point of the scene at the centre of the play in which Brutus and Antony deliver their rival orations in response to the assassination; and Caesar's ghost has a decisive role in bringing the action of the play to a close in the final two acts. In each case, the simulacrum both invites and resists interpretation by the other characters. Thus, Brutus addresses a series of questions about its nature to the ghost of Caesar on the eve of the battle of Philippi:

> Who comes here?
> I think it is the weakness of mine eyes
> That shapes this monstrous apparition.
> It comes upon me. Art thou any thing?
> Art thou some god, some angel, or some devil,
> That mak'st my blood cold and my hair to stare?
> Speak to me what thou art. (IV. 2. 326–32)

The ghost's response, 'Thy evil spirit, Brutus', serves only to compound the mystery of this supernatural visitation. On the one hand, the stage direction refers to 'the Ghost of Caesar'; the audience likely see the actor who played the character when alive on stage; and the narrative strongly points to Caesar's posthumous involvement in the revenge of his death. On the other hand, the ghost identifies himself as *Brutus*'s spirit. The same confusion had occurred in the final paragraph of Plutarch's *Caesar*, which first states that 'His great guardian spirit [*daimōn*], which had accompanied him in life, continued to avenge his murder', but then has the phantom respond to Brutus's anxious question who he is with the expression that Shakespeare borrowed from North: 'thy ill [i.e. evil] angel [*daimōn*], Brutus' (2037).[43] Although Plutarch does not

[43] *Caesar*, 69. 2, trans. in Pelling, *Caesar*.

explicitly identify the apparition that manifests itself to Brutus as Caesar's, a similar idea 'that Brutus' and Caesar's *daimones* are either identical, or at least inextricably and catastrophically linked' may be present in his Life.[44] This had been less palpable in the translations of Amyot and North, which obfuscate both the religious significance of the concept of the *daimōn* in Plutarch and the relationship between Caesar's and Brutus's *daimones*, with North rendering the first occurrence of the word cited above as Caesar's 'prosperity and good fortune' (2013–14). However, North's reference to Caesar's 'ghost' (2027) a few sentences later — a semantically flexible term in early modern England that could denote a spectre, an angel, and a devil as well as a departed soul appearing in visible shape to the living — combined with the conventions of the genre of the revenge play in which Shakespeare was writing may well have suggested a similar connection between their fates.[45] The self-identification of Caesar's ghost as Brutus's 'ill angel' in North's translation, moreover, appears to have prompted Shakespeare to add a further layer of specifically Christian anxiety about the potentially satanic nature of the spirit, just as the prince in *Hamlet* (probably written shortly after *Julius Caesar*) reflects that 'The spirit that I have seen', the ghost of his father, 'May be the devil'.[46] These ambiguities are compounded when Brutus raises the question whether the apparition may be a trick of his imagination ('I think it is the weakness of mine eyes') instead of an actual supernatural visitation. Whether he appears as a statue or a ghost (and the distinction threatens to collapse in North's final description of Caesar's ghost as an 'image' in line 2037) or something else still, questions of interpretation — ranging from the political to the theological — are at the forefront of Caesar's representation in Shakespeare's play.

While the titular character is symbolically central to *Julius Caesar*, then, his role as a character is extremely limited. He has a mere 1126 words in the play; Brutus has almost five times that number, Cassius more than three times, Mark Antony above two times, and even Casca almost as many.[47] What is more, in contrast to Brutus, whose soliloquies have often been compared to those of the protagonist of what is likely to have been Shakespeare's next play, *Hamlet*, we do not get much sense of Caesar's interiority. As we have seen, this is a feature of many early modern plays on Caesar, and it goes back to Plutarch's *Life*, which shows relatively little interest in the general's inner life. Shakespeare, however, makes Caesar's lack of interiority integral to the play by thematising

[44] Pelling, *Caesar*, p. 496.
[45] *OED*, ghost, *n*. Pace Pelling, *Caesar*, pp. 66–67, and Miola, p. 32, we do not, therefore, have to assume that Shakespeare was somehow able to see through North's translation to the true meaning of Plutarch's text.
[46] Shakespeare, *Hamlet*, II. 2. 600–01.
[47] William Shakespeare, *Julius Caesar*, ed. by David Daniell, The Arden Shakespeare, Third Series (Walton-on-Thames: Nelson, 1998, repr. London: Bloomsbury, 2017), pp. 152–53.

his constructed nature as a historical figure. Caesar's speech and action offer some corroboration for the various interpretations offered by other characters. On the one hand, he is imperious (the imperative is his customary mode of address), warm and amicable to the conspirators, and majestic in his speech and outlook in comments such as 'Cowards die many times before their deaths; | The valiant never taste of death but once' (II. 2. 32–33) or 'What touches us ourself shall be last served' (III. 1. 8). On the other hand, Caesar's majesty sometimes turns into conceit, as when he protests that 'Danger knows full well | That Caesar is more dangerous than he' (II. 2. 44–45) or exclaims 'Hence! Wilt thou lift up Olympus?' (III. 1. 74), and the play in a number of places points to a gap between his rhetoric and actions, notably when Decius persuades him to change his mind and come to the senate by appealing to his vanity and desire for the crown. However, the play reveals little of his motives and intentions, and 'in his few moments onstage', as John E. Curran notes, Caesar 'concerns himself mostly with his own status as a symbol and an idea and with living up to his Caesar-ness, rather than with his own desires'.[48] This is reflected in his 'ille-ism', the pervasive habit of referring to himself in the third person (as the historical Caesar had done in his writings). Although not unique to Caesar, this verbal tic signals both his externalised sense of selfhood and the concern of his character, as of others in the play, with the distinct set of qualities signified by his name.[49] Thus, Caesar in Shakespeare's play self-consciously reflects on the need to embody the quality that his name denotes, valour:

> I fear him not.
> Yet if my name were liable to fear,
> I do not know the man I should avoid
> So soon as that spare Cassius.
> [...]
> I rather tell thee what is to be feared
> Than what I fear, for always I am Caesar. (I. 2. 199–202, 212–13)

As a simulacrum and as a character, Caesar's role in the play is primarily as a focus for debates about his status as exemplary figure, identified by the name destined to become the marker of monarchical authority.

But what does 'Caesar' signify in the play? The references to Caesar as a statue in the opening scene not only bring to the fore his iconic status, but also participate in those debates by pointing to his excessive power and rank in Rome. The original Colossus of Rhodes, one of the Seven Wonders of the Ancient World, was a statue of the god Apollo, and the word retained connotations of

---

[48] Curran, p. 320.
[49] Thus Cassius tells Brutus: 'Brutus and Caesar: what should be in that "Caesar"? | Why should that name be sounded more than yours?' (I. 2. 143–44). See Miles, pp. 140–44.

divinity.⁵⁰ Cassius's simile thus picks up on the repeated references to Caesar's elevated status, from his own earlier contention to Brutus that 'this man | Is now become a god' (I. 2. 117–18) to allusions to idolatry in the opening scene. The first lines of the play combine the homophone 'idle' / 'idol' with a reference to a 'holiday' (I. 1. 1, 2), a holy day traditionally celebrating a saint but rejected by religious reformers as a form of superstition. By conflating Caesar's triumph with the feast of the Lupercal — several months apart in Plutarch's historical narrative — the decoration of his statues with 'ceremonies' becomes similarly sacrilegious, with the tribune of the people, Flavius, commenting that:

> These growing feathers plucked from Caesar's wing
> Will make him fly an ordinary pitch,
> Who else would soar above the view of men
> And keep us all in servile fearfulness. (I. 1. 72–75)

If one set of images (ultimately derived, as we have seen, from Plutarch) associates Caesar with absolute power and divinity, however, an opposing cluster figures him as weak and disabled. Only a few lines before his reference to Caesar as a colossus, Cassius had described him as a 'sick girl' (I. 2. 130): unmanly, immature, and infirm. Cassius's characterisation is the culmination of a passage in which he first recounts a swimming contest in the Tiber 'upon a raw and gusty day', in which he had to rescue Caesar from drowning, and then the Roman general's 'fever' and 'fit' in Spain (I. 2. 102, 121, 122). The feminine weakness and lack of self-control that the conspirators ascribe to Caesar's body reach a climax in Act III. As Gail Kern Paster has argued, 'the assassination [...] discloses the shameful secret of Caesar's bodiliness: by stabbing and displaying his body, the conspirators cause the fallen patriarch to reveal a womanly inability to stop bleeding'.⁵¹

The images of divinity and feminine weakness are, in fact, two sides of the same coin, for both serve the hegemonic attempt by the conspirators to define Caesar in binary opposition to an unarticulated and unexamined normative middle term, 'Rome'. Thus, Brutus justifies the assassination of Caesar in his speech to the Roman people by claiming that: 'If then that friend demand why Brutus rose against Caesar, this is my answer: not that I loved Caesar less, but that I loved Rome more' (III. 2. 20–22). 'Rome' here, as throughout the play, signifies a series of concepts related through ideas of self-control and self-determination: humanity, masculinity, strength, action, republicanism; for to be a man is to be in full control of mind (reason's reign over the passions) and body (whole, impenetrable, well-regulated), and to live under a republic is to have the power to determine one's political fate (frequently contrasted in the

---

⁵⁰ *OED*, colossus, *n*.
⁵¹ Gail Kern Paster, '"In the Spirit of Men There Is No Blood": Blood as Trope of Gender in *Julius Caesar*', *Shakespeare Quarterly*, 40 (1989), 284–98 (p. 285).

INTRODUCTION

play to subjects under a monarchy, who are figured as women and slaves).[52] The play, however, exposes the ideological nature of the conspirators' modus operandi. Brutus's appeal to the Romans shows how the hegemony of the republican faction depends on the consent and complicity of the people of the city: 'Who is here so base that would be a bondman? If any, speak, for him have I offended. Who is here so rude that would not be a Roman? If any, speak, for him have I offended. Who is here so vile that will not love his country?' (III. 2. 29–33). Antony's opposing speech demonstrates, furthermore, how their figuration of Caesar is open to challenge by recasting his bleeding corpse as a source of sympathy, desire, and hostile speech and action.[53] The ensuing war between the followers of Caesar and the defenders of the republic that takes up the second half of the play illustrates how the symbolic dispute over the meaning of 'Caesar' and 'Rome' is bound up with the question of who holds power and dominion within the state. The last word in the play falls to Caesar's adopted son Octavius (Octavian), who took Caesar's name and who the events of the play would eventually propel to become the first Roman emperor.

Many individual elements of the portrayal of Caesar as a 'sick girl' in Shakespeare's play derive from Plutarch, but their overall effect in *Julius Caesar* is quite different: 'The real-life Caesar was anything but frail'.[54] Plutarch's Life had told of Caesar's swimming, but as a token of his bravery and physical strength: Caesar 'with great hazard saved himself by swimming', holding his books above the water while being shot at by the Egyptians (1463–64). His illness in Spain too signifies hardiness and strength of mind in Plutarch: Caesar was

> often subject to headache and otherwhile to the falling sickness (the which took him the first time, as it is reported, in Corduba, a city of Spain), but yet therefore yielded not to the disease of his body, to make it a cloak to cherish him withal, but contrarily took the pains of war as a medicine to cure his sick body, fighting always with his disease, travelling continually, living soberly, and commonly lying abroad in the field. (482–87)

As Christopher Pelling notes, Shakespeare appears to have derived the idea of Caesar's infirmity chiefly from Plutarch's references to his epilepsy, the 'falling sickness'. Pelling highlights the episode in which Caesar invokes his epilepsy as an excuse for failing to rise to his feet to greet the senate, a sign of disrespect that caused great offence to the Romans.[55] However, Caesar's

---

[52] On Romanness, masculinity, and republicanism, see Kahn, pp. 77–109; on disability, self-control, and politics, see Allison P. Hobgood, 'Caesar Hath the Falling Sickness: The Legibility of Early Modern Disability in Shakespearean Drama', *Disability Studies Quarterly*, 29 (2009) <http://dx.doi.org/10.18061/dsq.v29i4.993>.
[53] Paster, pp. 296–98.
[54] Pelling, *Caesar*, p. 71.
[55] Ibid.

epilepsy is twice reported as a fact earlier in the narrative, during his campaign in Spain (quoted above) and at the battle of Thapsacus, and significantly North adds a marginal note drawing further attention to Caesar's condition on both occasions.[56] Pelling relates Shakespeare's change of emphasis in his portrayal of Caesar to what he identifies as the central moral issue of the play. In contrast to Plutarch and other classical authors, for whom the moral question raised by the assassination was principally Brutus's ingratitude towards Caesar, who had spared his life and favoured him as a friend, for Shakespeare:

> The issue is the general one of the justifiability of rebellion: the affront to free persons, whatever their past experience, of having a fellow-human — any fellow-human — who is so powerful; that is where the contrast comes in between the weak, frail old man and the 'Caesar', the position and the idea as much as the person. The more frail the ruler, the sharper the contrast. It is the dramatist's way of presenting the moral question with the clarity of extremes.[57]

But how frail is Caesar actually in Shakespeare's play? A couple of times, he refers to his deafness in one ear, a symptom that contemporary medical literature related to epilepsy.[58] But if, as Pelling claims, Caesar's frailty is primarily a matter of dramatic effect, we might have expected the play to stage an epileptic fit — that would have made for powerful theatre, and indeed Shakespeare used physical deformity and infirmity to great dramatic effect in other plays, such as *Richard III* and *King Lear*. In fact, as we have seen, Caesar's epileptic fits are in all instances reported by his opponents, who construe them as a physical manifestation of the malady to the body politic that he represents, with the involuntary seizure of the body pointing to a lack of self-control. Thus, in the scene following the one where Cassius had highlighted Caesar's shaking as a result of an epileptic seizure ('And when the fit was on him, I did mark | How he did shake. 'Tis true, this god did shake', 1. 2. 122–23), Casca describes the meteorological conditions of Rome in similar terms, demanding from Cicero: 'Are not you moved, when all the sway of earth | Shakes like a thing unfirm?' (1. 3. 3–4). Cicero's response, however, brings to the fore the process whereby the conspirators 'construe' the elements as well as, by extension, Caesar's character:

> Indeed it is a strange-disposèd time;
> But men may construe things after their fashion,
> Clean from the purpose of the things themselves. (1. 3. 33–35)

In Shakespeare's play, then, Caesar's illness is primarily a feature of the othering of Caesar by the conspirators in order to serve their own political agenda, to maintain the political status quo, and, concomitantly, to retain control over the

---

[56] *Caesar*, lines 483 **Marg.**, 1556 **Marg.**
[57] Pelling, *Caesar*, p. 75.
[58] Shakespeare, *Julius Caesar*, ed. by Daniell, p. 163.

symbolic meaning of Rome, masculinity, and able-bodiedness. To reduce the subject matter of *Julius Caesar* to an abstract moral and political issue is to take ideology, the power to control what people (both ancient and early modern) believe to be the case about Caesar and Rome, out of the play. In fact, in the construction of 'Caesar', 'the position and the idea as much as the person', which continued to be a live political issue in late Elizabethan England, the dialogic nature of the play precisely makes ideology visible as ideology.

Shakespeare's *Julius Caesar* thus not only reproduces the complexities and contradictions present in Plutarch's portrayal of Caesar, as other early modern English plays did (though these all post-date Shakespeare's and may thus be indebted to his version of the Caesar narrative as well as Plutarch's in this respect). It also calls attention to Caesar's status as an icon and the processes whereby the different, at times opposing, images were construed, as well as to their ideological underpinnings. Some of this emphasis derives from the ambiguities of Plutarch's *Caesar*, with its conflicting moral and political appraisals, and from the emphasis in this Life, as in others, on the different accounts and interpretations of various historical witnesses. But Shakespeare also took advantage of the numerous small differences in perspective on Caesar's character and the events of 44 BCE between the three Plutarchan Lives on which he based his play. While it is evidently true, in some respects, that 'welding the material [from a number of different Lives] was a very unstraightforward matter', in other ways Shakespeare's working method in *Julius Caesar* made dramatic adaptation more straightforward, as the three Lives provided a series of ready-made viewpoints that the playwright was able to use as the basis for the main characters (or groups of characters) in the play.[59] Although Plutarch's *Parallel Lives* are not written from a first-person perspective, 'the law of biographical relevance', as well as Plutarch's evident capacity for empathy with the subjects of his *Lives* and desire for his readers to identify with them, means that they reflect, to some extent at least, the outlook of his protagonists on the events recounted.[60] Above all, however, the combination of Plutarch's technique in *Caesar* and the differences in both perspective and biographical method between the different Lives directed Shakespeare's attention to the construction of the Caesar myth, which he boldly set at the very heart of his play.

Further Reading

Caesar: Pelling, *Caesar*.

---

[59] Pelling, *Caesar*, p. 68.
[60] Pelling, *Plutarch and History*, pp. 53–59; Pelling rightly points out, however, that Plutarch's biographical technique is more complex than 'simply select[ing] the items most *favourable* to each of his subjects' (p. 54).

Sources and Translation: see Introduction to North's *The Life of Demosthenes*, *The Life of Marcus Tullius Cicero*, and *The Comparison of Cicero with Demosthenes*.

Reception: *A Companion to Julius Caesar*, ed. by Griffin; Cox Jensen, *Reading the Roman Republic*; Kewes. For studies of Plutarch's influence on Shakespeare, see Further Reading in General Introduction.

Abbreviations and References

N.   North.

P.   Plutarch. Quoted from LCL, 99 (*Plutarch's 'Lives'*, VII).

A.   Amyot. Quoted from *Les Vies des hommes illustres grecs et romains*, trans. by Jacques Amyot (Lausanne: François Le Preux, 1574). Available online at <https://doi.org/10.3931/e-rara-6943>.

C.   Cruser. Quoted from *Plutarchi [...] vitae comparatae illustrium virorum, graecorum et romanorum*, trans. by Hermann Cruser (Basel: Thomas Guarin, 1573). Available online at <http://mdz-nbn-resolving.de/urn:nbn:de:bvb:12-bsb10139851-5>.

The life of Julius Caesar.

[1] At what time Sulla was made lord of all, he would have had Caesar put away his wife Cornelia, the daughter of Cinna Dictator, but when he saw he could neither with any promise nor threat bring him to it, he took her jointure° away from him.¹ The cause of Caesar's ill will unto Sulla was by means of marriage, for Marius the elder married his² father's own sister, by whom he had Marius the Younger, whereby Caesar and he were cousin-germans.³ Sulla being troubled in weighty matters, putting to death so many of his enemies, when he came to be conqueror, he made no reckoning of Caesar, and he⁴ was not contented to be hidden in safety, but came and made suit unto the people for the priesthoodship that was void when he had scant any hair on his face. Howbeit, he was repulsed by Sulla's means, that secretly was against him. Who, when he was determined to have killed him, some of his friends told him that it was to no purpose to put so young a boy as he to death.⁵ But Sulla told them again that they did not consider that there were many Marians in that young boy.⁶ Caesar, understanding that, stole out of Rome and hid himself a long time in the country of the Sabines, wandering still° from place to place. But one day being carried from house to house,⁷ he fell into the hands of Sulla's soldiers, who searched all those places and took them whom they found hidden. Caesar bribed the captain, whose name was Cornelius, with two talents which he gave him. After he had escaped them thus, he went unto the sea-side and took ship and sailed into Bithynia to go unto King Nicomedes.⁸ When he had been with him a while, he took sea again and was taken by pirates about the Isle of Pharmacusa, for those pirates kept all upon that sea-coast with a great fleet of ships and boats.⁹

[2] They asking him at the first twenty talents for his ransom, Caesar laughed

---

¹ The opening of the Life is uncharacteristically brusque, and it is unlikely that P. would have omitted description of Caesar's youth altogether, so it is suspected that some text is missing here. See Pelling, *Caesar*, 1. 1 n.
² i.e. Caesar's.
³ **Marg.** 'Caesar joined with Cinna and Marius.'
⁴ i.e. Caesar.
⁵ when he was determined to have killed him] P. 'when he was deliberating about putting him to death' (περὶ δὲ ἀναιρέσεως βουλευόμενος), but N. is closer to A. 'comme il fust entredeux de le faire davantage tuer' (when he was on the point of having him put to death moreover, p. 859). See Huguet, s.v. entredeux, 2.
⁶ Marians] i.e. persons like Marius (A. 'tels que Marius', p. 859); P. has simply 'Mariuses' (Μαρίους).
⁷ N. omits 'on account of sickness'.
⁸ **Marg.** 'Caesar took sea and went unto Nicomedes, king of Bithynia.' Bithynia is in the north of present-day Turkey.
⁹ **Marg.** 'Caesar taken of pirates.'

them to scorn, as though they knew not what a man they had taken, and of himself promised them fifty talents. Then he sent his men up and down to get him this money, so that he was left in manner alone among these thieves of the Cilicians (which° are the cruellest butchers in the world) with one of his friends and two of his slaves only, and yet he made so little reckoning of them that when he was desirous to sleep, he sent unto them to command them to make no noise. Thus was he eight and thirty days among them, not kept as prisoner, but rather waited upon by them as a prince. All this time, he would boldly exercise himself in any sport or pastime they would go to. And otherwhile also, he would write verses and make orations and call them together to say them before them, and if any of them seemed as though they had not understood him or passed° not for them, he called them blockheads and brute beasts and, laughing, threatened them that he would hang them up. But they were as merry with the matter as could be and took all in good part, thinking that this his bold speech came through the simplicity of his youth. So when his ransom was come from the city of Miletum, they being paid their money and he again set at liberty, he then presently armed and manned certain ships out of the haven of Miletum to follow those thieves, whom he found yet riding at anchor in the same island.[10] So he took the most of them and had the spoil of their goods, but for their bodies, he brought them into the city of Pergamum, and there committed them to prison, whilst he himself went to speak with Iunius, who had the government of Asia, as unto whom the execution of these pirates did belong, for that° he was praetor of that country.[11] But this praetor, having a great fancy to be fingering of the money because there was good store of it, answered that he would consider of these prisoners at better leisure. Caesar, leaving Iunius there, returned again unto Pergamum, and there hung up all these thieves openly upon a cross, as he had oftentimes promised them in the isle he would do, when they thought he did but jest.

[3] Afterwards, when Sulla's power began to decay, Caesar's friends wrote unto him to pray him to come home again. But he sailed first unto Rhodes to study there a time under Apollonius, the son of Molon, whose scholar also Cicero was, for he was a very honest man and an excellent good rhetorician. It is reported that Caesar had an excellent natural gift to speak well before the people, and besides that rare gift, he was excellently well studied, so that doubtless he was counted the second man for eloquence in his time and gave place to the first[12] because he would be the first and chiefest man of war and authority, being not yet come to the degree of perfection to speak well, which his nature could have performed in him, because he was given rather to follow wars and to

---

[10] Miletum] Miletus.
[11] **Marg.** 'Iunius, praetor of Asia.'
[12] i.e. Cicero.

manage great matters, which in the end brought him to be lord of all Rome.¹³ And therefore in a book he wrote against that which Cicero made in the praise of Cato, he prayeth the readers not to compare the style of a soldier with the eloquence of an excellent orator that had followed it the most part of his life.¹⁴

[4] When he was returned again unto Rome, he accused Dolabella for his ill behaviour in the government of his province, and he had divers cities of Greece that gave in evidence against him.¹⁵ Notwithstanding, Dolabella at the length was dismissed. Caesar, to requite the goodwill of the Grecians which they had showed him in his accusation of Dolabella, took their cause in hand when they did accuse Publius Antonius before Marcus Lucullus, praetor of Macedon, and followed° it so hard against him in their behalf that Antonius was driven to appeal before the tribunes at Rome, alleging, to colour his appeal withal,° that he could have no justice in Greece against the Grecians. Now Caesar immediately won many men's goodwills at Rome through his eloquence in pleading of their causes, and the people loved him marvellously also because of the courteous manner he had to speak to every man and to use them gently, being more ceremonious therein than was looked for in one of his years. Furthermore, he ever kept a good board and fared well at his table and was very liberal besides,¹⁶ the which indeed did advance him forward and brought him in estimation with the people.¹⁷ His enemies, judging that this favour of the common people would soon quail° when he could no longer hold out that charge and expense, suffered him to run on, till by little and little he was grown to be of great strength and power. But in fine,° when they had thus given him the bridle to grow to this greatness and that they could not then pull him back, though indeed in sight it would turn one day to the destruction of the whole state and commonwealth of Rome, too late they found that there is not so little a beginning of anything but continuance of time will soon make it strong, when through contempt there is no impediment to hinder the greatness. Thereupon, Cicero, like a wise shipmaster that feareth the calmness of the sea, was the first man that, mistrusting his manner of dealing in the commonwealth, found out his craft and malice, which he cunningly cloaked under the habit of outward courtesy and familiarity. 'And yet', said he, 'when I consider how finely he combeth his fair bush of hair and how smooth it lieth, and that I see him scratch his head with one finger only, my mind gives me then that such a kind of man should not have so wicked a thought in his head as to overthrow the state of the commonwealth.'¹⁸ But this was long time after that.

¹³ Marg. 'Caesar's eloquence.' to follow wars] to be a soldier.
¹⁴ i.e. Caesar's lost *Anticato* (45 BCE); cf. *Cicero*, line 1218.
¹⁵ In 77 BCE.
¹⁶ Marg. 'Caesar loved hospitality.'
¹⁷ Marg. 'Caesar a follower of the people.'
¹⁸ Marg. 'Cicero's judgement of Caesar.'

[5] The first show and proof of the love and goodwill which the people did bear unto Caesar was when he sued to be tribune of the soldiers (to wit, colonel of a thousand footmen), standing against Caius Pompilius,[19] at what time he was preferred and chosen before him.[20] But the second and more manifest proof than the first was at the death of his aunt Julia, the wife of Marius the Elder. For being her nephew, he made a solemn oration in the marketplace in commendation of her and at her burial did boldly venture to show forth the images of Marius, the which was the first time that they were seen after Sulla's victory, because that Marius and all his confederates had been proclaimed traitors and enemies to the commonwealth.[21] For when there were some that cried out upon Caesar for doing of it, the people on the other side kept a stir and rejoiced at it, clapping of their hands, and thanked him for that he had brought, as it were out of hell, the remembrance of Marius' honour again into Rome, which had so long time been obscured and buried. And where it had been an ancient custom of long time that the Romans used to make funeral orations in praise of old ladies and matrons when they died, but not of young women, Caesar was the first that praised his own wife with funeral oration when she was dead, the which also did increase the people's goodwills the more, seeing him of so kind and gentle nature.[22] After the burial of his wife, he was made treasurer under Antistius Vetus praetor,[23] whom he honoured ever after, so that when himself came to be praetor, he made his[24] son to be chosen treasurer. Afterwards, when he was come out of that office, he married his third wife, Pompeia, having a daughter by his first wife, Cornelia, which was married unto Pompey the Great.[25] Now, for that he was very liberal in expenses, buying (as some thought) but a vain and short glory of the favour of the people (where indeed he bought good cheap the greatest things that could be), some say that before he bore any office in the commonwealth, he was grown in debt to the sum of thirteen hundred talents. Furthermore, because he was made overseer of the work for the highway called Appius' Way, he disbursed a great sum of his own money towards the charges of the same. And, on the other side, when he was made aedilis, for that he did show the people the pastime of three hundred and twenty couple of sword players and did besides exceed all other in sumptuousness in the sports and common feasts which he made to delight them withal (and did as it were drown all the stately shows of others in the like that

---

[19] Marg. 'The love of the people in Rome unto Caesar.'
[20] Marg. 'Caesar chosen *Tribunus militum*.'
[21] Marg. 'Caesar made the funeral oration at the death of his aunt Julia.'
[22] Marg. 'Caesar the first that praised his wife in funeral oration.'
[23] Marg. 'Caesar made quaestor.' In 69 BCE.
[24] i.e. Vetus's.
[25] Marg. 'Pompeia, Caesar's third wife.'

had gone before him), he so pleased the people and won their love therewith that they devised daily to give him new offices for to requite him.²⁶

[6] At that time there were two factions in Rome, to wit, the faction of Sulla, which was very strong and of great power, and the other of Marius, which then was under foot and durst not show itself. But Caesar, because he would renew it again, even at that time when he being aedilis all the feasts and common sports were in their greatest ruff,° he secretly caused images of Marius to be made and of victories that carried triumphs, and those he set up one night within the Capitol.²⁷ The next morning, when every man saw the glistering of these golden images excellently well wrought, showing by the inscriptions that they were the victories which Marius had won upon the Cimbres, everyone marvelled much at the boldness of him that durst set them up there, knowing well enough who it was. Hereupon, it ran straight through all the city, and every man came thither to see them. Then some cried out upon Caesar and said it was a tyranny which he meant to set up by renewing of such honours as before had been trodden under foot and forgotten by common decree and open proclamation, and that it was no more but a bait to gage the people's goodwills which he had set out in the stately shows of his common plays to see if he had brought them to his lure, that they would abide such parts to be played and a new alteration of things to be made.²⁸ They of Marius' faction, on the other side, encouraging one another, showed themselves straight a great number gathered together and made the mount of the Capitol ring again with their cries and clapping of hands, insomuch as the tears ran down many of their cheeks for very joy when they saw the images of Marius, and they extolled Caesar to the skies, judging him the worthiest man of all the kindred of Marius. The senate being assembled thereupon, Catulus Luctatius, one of the greatest authority at that time in Rome, rose and vehemently inveighed against Caesar and spoke that then which ever since hath been noted much: that Caesar did not now covertly go to work, but by plain force sought to alter the state of the commonwealth. Nevertheless, Caesar at that time answered him so that the senate was satisfied. Thereupon they that had him in estimation did grow in better hope than before and persuaded him that hardily he should give place to no man and that through the goodwill of the people he should be better than all they and come to be the chiefest man of the city.

---

²⁶ Marg. 'Caesar's prodigality.' In 65 BCE.
²⁷ triumphs] P. and A. 'trophies'.
²⁸ Marg. 'Caesar accused to make a rebellion in the state.' N.'s translation obscures the point of the passage in P. and A. that it is the setting up of the images that is a test whether the people have been softened (or lured: A. 'appasté', p. 862) by his entertainments.

[7] At that time, the chief bishop Metellus died, and two of the notablest men of the city and of greatest authority (Isauricus and Catulus) contended for his room;°[29] Caesar, notwithstanding their contention, would give neither of them both place, but presented himself to the people and made suit for it as they did. The suit being equal betwixt either of them, Catulus, because he was a man of greater calling° and dignity than the other, doubting° the uncertainty of the election, sent unto Caesar a good sum of money to make him leave off his suit. But Caesar sent him word again that he would lend a greater sum than that to maintain the suit against him.[30] When the day of the election came, his mother bringing him to the door of his house, Caesar weeping kissed her and said: 'Mother, this day thou shalt see thy son chief bishop of Rome or banished from Rome.'[31] In fine, when the voices of the people were gathered together and the strife well debated,[32] Caesar won the victory and made the senate and noblemen all afraid of him for that they thought that thenceforth he would make the people do what he thought good.[33] Then Catulus and Piso fell flatly out with Cicero and condemned him for that he did not bewray° Caesar when he knew that he was of conspiracy with Catiline and had opportunity to have done it.[34] For when Catiline was bent and determined not only to overthrow the state of the commonwealth, but utterly to destroy the empire of Rome, he scaped° out of the hands of justice for lack of sufficient proof before his full treason and determination was known. Notwithstanding, he left Lentulus and Cethegus in the city, companions of his conspiracy, unto whom whether Caesar did give any secret help or comfort it is not well known. Yet this is manifest, that when they were convinced° in open senate, Cicero being at that time consul, asking every man's opinion in the senate what punishment they should have, and every one of them till it came to Caesar gave sentence they should die, Caesar then rising up to speak made an oration (penned and premeditated before) and said that it was neither lawful, nor yet their custom did bear it, to put men of such nobility to death (but in an extremity) without lawful indictment and condemnation.[35] And therefore, that if they were put in prison in some city of Italy where Cicero thought best until that Catiline were overthrown, the senate then might at their pleasure quietly take such order therein as might appear best unto their wisdoms.

---

[29] Marg. 'The death of Metellus, chief bishop of Rome.' In 63 BCE.   chief bishop] Pontifex Maximus.
[30] lend] P. and A. 'borrow' ('emprunteroit', p. 863).
[31] In P. and A. it is Caesar's mother who is crying.
[32] the strife well debated] the contest hard fought.
[33] Marg. 'Caesar made chief bishop of Rome.'
[34] Marg. 'Caesar suspected to be confederate with Catiline in his conspiracy.'
[35] Marg. 'Caesar went about to deliver the conspirators.'

[8] This opinion was thought more gentle, and withal was uttered with such a passing good grace and eloquence that not only they which were to speak after him did approve it, but such also as had spoken to the contrary before revoked their opinion and stuck to his, until it came to Cato and Catulus to speak. They both did sharply inveigh against him, but Cato chiefly, who in his oration made Caesar suspected to be of the conspiracy and stoutly spoke against him, insomuch that the offenders were put into the hands of the officers to be put to death.[36] Caesar coming out of the senate, a company of young men which guarded Cicero for the safety of his person did set upon him with their swords drawn. But some say that Curio covered Caesar with his gown and took him out of their hands. And Cicero self, when the young men looked upon him, beckoned with his head that they should not kill him, either fearing the fury of the people or else that he thought it too shameful and wicked a part. But if that were true, I marvel why Cicero did not put it into his book he wrote of his consulship. But certainly they blamed him afterwards for that he took not the opportunity offered him against Caesar, only for overmuch fear of the people, that loved him very dearly. For shortly after, when Caesar went into the senate to clear himself of certain presumptions and false accusations objected against him, and being bitterly taunted among them, the senate keeping him longer than they were wont, the people came about the council house and called out aloud for him, bidding them let him out. Cato then fearing the insurrection of the poor needy persons, which were they that put all their hope in Caesar and did also move the people to stir, did persuade the senate to make a frank° distribution of corn unto them for a month. This distribution did put the commonwealth to a new charge of five hundred and fifty myriads.° This counsel quenched a present great fear and did in happy time scatter and disperse abroad the best part of Caesar's force and power at such time as he was made praetor and that for respect of his office he was most to be feared.

[9] Yet all the time he was officer, he never sought any alteration in the commonwealth, but contrarily he himself had a great misfortune fell on his house, which was this. There was a young nobleman of the order of the patricians called Publius Clodius, who lacked neither wealth nor eloquence, but otherwise as insolent and impudent a person as any was else in Rome. He became in love with Pompeia, Caesar's wife, who misliked not withal, notwithstanding she was so straightly looked to, and Aurelia (Caesar's mother), an honest gentlewoman, had such an eye of her that these two lovers could not meet as they would without great peril and difficulty.[37] The Romans do use to honour a goddess which they call the Good Goddess, as the Grecians have her

[36] Marg. 'Cato's oration against Caesar.'
[37] Marg. 'The love of P. Clodius unto Pompeia, Caesar's wife.'

whom they call Gynaecia, to wit, the goddess of women.³⁸ Her the Phrygians do claim to be peculiar unto them, saying that she is King Midas' mother. Howbeit, the Romans hold opinion that it is a nymph of the woods, married unto the god Faunus. The Grecians, they say also that she was one of the mothers of the god Bacchus, whom they dare not name. And for proof hereof, on her feast day the women make certain tabernacles of vine twigs and leaves of vine branches, and also they make (as the tale goeth) a holy dragon for this goddess and do set it by her; besides, it is not lawful for any man to be present at their sacrifices — no, not within the house itself where they are made. Furthermore, they say that the women in these sacrifices do many things amongst themselves much like unto the ceremonies of Orpheus. Now, when the time of this feast came, the husband (whether he were praetor or consul) and all his men and the boys in the house do come out of it and leave it wholly to his wife to order the house at her pleasure, and there the sacrifices and ceremonies are done the most part of the night, and they do besides pass the night away in songs and music.

[10] Pompeia, Caesar's wife, being that year to celebrate this feast, Clodius, who had yet no hair on his face and thereby thought he should not be bewrayed, disguised himself in a singing wench's apparel, because his face was very like unto a young wench. He finding the gates open, being secretly brought in by her chambermaid that was made privy unto it, she left him and ran to Pompeia, her mistress, to tell her that he was come. The chambermaid tarried long before she came again, insomuch as Clodius, being weary waiting for her where she left him, he took his pleasure and went from one place to another in the house, which had very large rooms in it, still shunning the light, and was by chance met withal by one of Aurelia's maids, who taking him for a woman prayed her to play. Clodius refusing to play, the maid pulled him forward and asked him what he was; Clodius then answered her that he tarried for Abra, one of Pompeia's women. So, Aurelia's maid, knowing him by his voice, ran straight where the lights and ladies were and cried out that there was a man disguised in woman's apparel. The women therewith were so amazed° that Aurelia caused them presently to leave off the ceremonies of the sacrifice and to hide their secret things and, having seen the gates fast locked, went immediately up and down the house with torch-light to seek out this man, who at the last was found out in the chamber° of Pompeia's maid, with whom he hid himself. Thus Clodius being found out and known of the women, they thrust him out of the doors by the shoulders.³⁹ The same night the women told their husbands

---

³⁸ Marg. 'The Good Goddess, what she was and her sacrifices.' That is, Bona Dea, whose festival was celebrated annually in December. The following incident is described more briefly in *Cicero*, 28.
³⁹ Marg. 'Clodius taken in the sacrifices of the Good Goddess.'

of this chance as soon as they came home. The next morning there ran a great rumour through the city how Clodius had attempted a great villainy and that he deserved not only to be punished of them whom he had slandered but also of the commonwealth and the gods.⁴⁰ There was one of the tribunes of the people that did indict him and accuse him of high treason to the gods.⁴¹ Furthermore, there were also of the chiefest of the nobility and senate that came to depose against him and burdened° him with many horrible and detestable facts, and specially with incest committed with his own sister, which was married unto Lucullus. Notwithstanding, the people stoutly defended Clodius against their accusations, and this did help him much against the judges, which were amazed and afraid to stir the people. This notwithstanding, Caesar presently put his wife away, and thereupon being brought by Clodius' accuser to be a witness against him, he answered he knew nothing of that they objected against Clodius.⁴² This answer being clean contrary to their expectation that heard it, the accuser asked Caesar why then he had put away his wife; 'Because I will° not', said he, 'that my wife be so much as suspected.' And some say, that Caesar spoke truly as he thought. But others think that he did it to please the common people, who were very desirous to save Clodius. So, Clodius was discharged of this accusation, because the most part of the judges gave a confused judgement for the fear they stood one way of the danger of the common people if they condemned him, and for the ill opinion on the other side of the nobility if they did quit him.⁴³

[11] The government of the province of Spain being fallen unto Caesar for that he was praetor, his creditors came and cried out upon him and were importunate of him to be paid.⁴⁴ Caesar, being unable to satisfy them, was compelled to go unto Crassus, who was the richest man of all Rome, and that stood in need of Caesar's boldness and courage to withstand Pompey's greatness in the commonwealth. Crassus became his surety unto his greediest creditors for the sum of eight hundred and thirty talents, whereupon they suffered Caesar to depart to the government of his province.⁴⁵ In this journey it is reported that passing over the mountains of the Alps, they came through a little poor village that had not many households and yet poor cottages. There, his friends that did

---

⁴⁰ slandered] i.e. brought into disrepute (*OED*, †2; P. τοῖς ὑβρισμένοις (those whom he had insulted), translated by A. as 'ceux à qui il avoit fait cest outrage', pp. 864–65).
⁴¹ Marg. 'Clodius accused for profaning the sacrifices of the Good Goddess.'
⁴² Marg. 'Caesar putteth away his wife, Pompeia.'
⁴³ Marg. 'Clodius quit by the judges for profaning the sacrifices of the Good Goddess.'
⁴⁴ Marg. 'Caesar praetor of Spain.' As the marginal note (which does not derive from Cruser) indicates, N. has misunderstood the historical situation: Caesar became governor (proconsul) of Spain in 61–60 BCE immediately after his praetorship ended (as P. and A. write).
⁴⁵ Marg. 'Crassus surety for Caesar to his creditors.'

accompany him asked him merrily if there were any contending for offices in that town and whether there were any strife there amongst the noble men for honour. Caesar, speaking in good earnest, answered: 'I cannot tell that,' said he, 'but for my part I had rather be the chiefest man here than the second person in Rome.' Another time also, when he was in Spain, reading the history of Alexander's acts, when he had read it, he was sorrowful a good while after and then burst out in weeping. His friends seeing that marvelled what should be the cause of his sorrow. He answered them: 'Do ye not think', said he, 'that I have good cause to be heavy when King Alexander, being no older than myself is now, had in old time won so many nations and countries and that I hitherunto have done nothing worthy of myself?'.[46]

[12] Therefore, when he was come into Spain, he was very careful of his business, and had in few days joined ten new ensigns more of footmen unto the other twenty which he had before.[47] Then, marching forward against the Callaecians and Lusitanians, he conquered all and went as far as the great sea Oceanum, subduing all the people which before knew° not the Romans for their lords.[48] There, he took order for pacifying of the war and did as wisely take order for the establishing of peace. For he did reconcile the cities together and made them friends one with another, but specially he pacified all suits of law and strife betwixt the debtors and creditors which grew by reason of usury. For he ordained that the creditors should take yearly two parts of the revenue of their debtors until such time as they had paid themselves and that the debtors should have the third part themselves to live withal.[49] He, having won great estimation by this good order taken, returned from his government very rich, and his soldiers also full of rich spoils, who called him imperator, to say, sovereign captain.[50]

[13] Now, the Romans having a custom that such as demanded honour of triumph should remain a while without the city, and that they, on the other side, which sued for the consulship should of necessity be there in person, Caesar coming unhappily at that very time when the consuls were chosen, he sent to pray the senate to do him that favour that, being absent, he might by his friends sue for

---

[46] Caesar's comment on Alexander the Great takes on additional significance in the context of the pairing of the two in P.'s *Lives*.
[47] Marg. 'Caesar's acts in Spain.'
[48] the Callaecians] The Callaici, present-day Galicians.   the great sea Oceanum] Oceanus, i.e. the Atlantic, viewed as the outer end of the inhabitable world. N. (translating A. 'la grande mer Oceane', p. 865) has taken the noun to be neuter (-*um*) instead of masculine (-*us*) in Latin.
[49] Marg. 'Caesar's order betwixt the creditor and debtor.'
[50] Marg. 'Caesar's soldiers called him imperator.'

the consulship. Cato at the first did vehemently inveigh against it, vouching an express law to the contrary. But afterwards, perceiving that notwithstanding the reasons he alleged many of the senators (being won by Caesar) favoured his request, yet he cunningly sought all he could to prevent them, prolonging time in dilating his oration until night. Caesar thereupon determined rather to give over the suit of his triumph and to make suit for the consulship, and so came into the city and had such a device with him as went beyond them all, but Cato only. His device was this. Pompey and Crassus, two of the greatest personages of the city of Rome, being at jar together, Caesar made them friends, and by that means got unto himself the power of them both, for by colour of that gentle act and friendship of his he subtly (unwares° to them all) did greatly alter and change the state of the commonwealth.[51] For it was not the private discord between Pompey and Caesar, as many men thought, that caused the civil war, but rather it was their agreement together, who joined all their powers first to overthrow the state° of the senate and nobility, and afterwards they fell at jar one with another. But Cato, that then foresaw and prophesied many times what would follow, was taken but for a vain man, but afterwards they found him a wiser man than happy in his counsel.[52]

[14] Thus Caesar being brought unto the assembly of the election in the midst of these two noble persons whom he had before reconciled together, he was there chosen consul, with Calphurnius Bibulus, without gainsaying or contradiction of any man.[53] Now, when he was entered into his office, he began to put forth laws meeter for a seditious tribune of the people than for a consul,[54] because by them he preferred° the division of lands and distributing of corn to every citizen gratis to please them withal.[55] But when the noblemen of the senate were against his device, he, desiring no better occasion, began to cry out and to protest that by the over-hardness and austerity of the senate they drove him against his will to lean unto the people, and thereupon, having Crassus on the one side of him and Pompey on the other, he asked them openly in the assembly if they did give their consent unto the laws which he had put forth. They both answered, they did. Then he prayed them to stand by him against those that threatened him with force of sword to let him.[56] Crassus gave him his word he would. Pompey also did the like, and added thereunto that he would come with his sword and target° both against them that would withstand him with their swords.

[51] Marg. 'Caesar reconcileth Pompey and Crassus together.'
[52] Marg. 'Cato's foresight and prophecy.'
[53] Marg. 'Caesar's first consulship, with Calphurnius Bibulus.' P. 'Calpurnius'; N. follows A. In 59 BCE.
[54] Marg. 'Caesar's laws.'
[55] Marg. 'Lex agraria.'
[56] i.e. prevent him.

These words offended much the senate, being far unmeet for his gravity and undecent for the majesty and honour he carried, and most of all uncomely for the presence of the senate whom he should have reverenced, and were speeches fitter for a rash, light-headed youth than for his person. Howbeit, the common people on the other side, they rejoiced. Then Caesar, because he would be more assured of Pompey's power and friendship, he gave him his daughter Julia in marriage, which was made sure before unto Servilius Caepio, and promised him in exchange Pompey's daughter, the which was sure also unto Faustus, the son of Sulla.[57] And shortly after also, Caesar self did marry Calphurnia, the daughter of Piso, whom he caused to be made consul to succeed him the next year following.[58] Cato then cried out with open mouth and called the gods to witness that it was a shameful matter and not to be suffered that they should in that sort make havoc of the Empire of Rome by such horrible bawdy matches, distributing among themselves through those wicked marriages the governments of the provinces and of great armies. Calphurnius Bibulus, fellow consul with Caesar, perceiving that he did contend in vain, making all the resistance he could to withstand this law, and that oftentimes he was in danger to be slain with Cato in the marketplace and assembly, he kept close in his house all the rest of his consulship. When Pompey had married Julia, he filled all the marketplace with soldiers and by open force authorised the laws which Caesar made in the behalf of the people.[59] Furthermore, he procured that Caesar had Gaul on this side and beyond the Alps and all Illyria, with four legions granted him for five years.[60] Then Cato standing up to speak against it, Caesar bad his officers lay hold on him and carry him to prison, thinking he would have appealed unto the tribunes.[61] But Cato said never a word when he went his way. Caesar perceiving then that not only the senators and nobility were offended, but that the common people also for the reverence they bore unto Cato's virtues were ashamed and went away with silence, he himself secretly did pray one of the tribunes that he would take Cato from the officers. But after he had played this part, there were few senators that would be president of the senate under him, but left the city because they could not away° with his doings.[62] And of

[57] Marg. 'Caesar married his daughter Julia unto Pompey.'   made sure] engaged.
[58] Marg. 'Caesar married Calphurnia, the daughter of Piso.'   Calphurnia] Calpurnia (N. follows A.).
[59] Marg. 'Pompey by force of arms authorised Caesar's laws.'
[60] Gaul on this side and beyond the Alps and all Illyria] i.e. Cisalpine and Transalpine Gaul. A. has 'l'Esclavonie' (p. 867) for 'Illyria': it is unlikely that N. would have come up with his translation without reference to P.'s original Greek (τὸ Ἰλλυρικόν) or, more likely, Cruser's Latin ('Illyrico', p. 571).
[61] Marg. 'Caesar sent Cato to prison.'
[62] that would be president of the senate under him] N. is misled by A.'s phrasing: 'qui se voulussent trouver sous lui president au Senat' (p. 867: 'who wanted to be under him as president in the senate', where 'president' is construed with 'lui' (Caesar) rather than 'qui' (the senators)).

them, there was an old man called Considius, that on a time boldly told him the rest durst not come to council because they were afraid of his soldiers. Caesar answered him again: 'And why, then, doest not thou keep thee at home for the same fear?'. Considius replied: 'Because my age taketh away fear from me, for having so short a time to live, I have no care to prolong it further.' The shamefulest part that Caesar played while he was consul seemeth to be this, when he chose P. Clodius tribune of the people, that had offered his wife such dishonour and profaned the holy ancient mysteries of the women which were celebrated in his own house.[63] Clodius sued to be tribune to no other end but to destroy Cicero, and Caesar self also departed not from Rome to his army before he had set them together by the ears and driven Cicero out of Italy.[64]

[15] All these things they say he did before the wars with the Gauls. But the time of the great armies and conquests he made afterwards and of the war in the which he subdued all the Gauls (entering into another course of life far contrary unto the first) made him to be known for as valiant a soldier and as excellent a captain to lead men as those that afore him had been counted the wisest and most valiantest generals that ever were and that by their valiant deeds had achieved great honour.[65] For whosoever would compare the house of the Fabians, of the Scipios, of the Metellians — yea, those also of his own time or long before him, as Sulla, Marius, the two Lucullians, and Pompey self, 'whose fame ascendeth up unto the heavens' — it will appear that Caesar's prowess and deeds of arms did excel them all together.[66] The one, in the hard countries where he made wars; another, in enlarging the realms and countries which he joined unto the empire of Rome; another, in the multitude and power of his enemies whom he overcame; another, in the rudeness and austere nature of men with whom he had to do, whose manners afterwards he softened and made civil; another, in courtesy and clemency which he used unto them whom he had conquered; another, in great bounty and liberality bestowed upon them that served under him in those wars; and in fine, he excelled them all in the number

---

[63] when he chose P. Clodius tribune of the people] The careless phrasing implies that it was Caesar who elected Clodius to his office rather than help him get elected (as A. has: 'de faire elire Publius Clodius Tribun du peuple', p. 867).
[64] Marg. 'Caesar by Clodius drove Cicero out of Italy.'
[65] Marg. 'Caesar, a valiant soldier and a skilful captain.'
[66] Metellians [...] Lucullians] The correct forms would be Metellans (from Metellus) and Luculli or Lucullans (L. Licinius Lucullus and M. Terentius Varro Lucullus); A. has 'Metelles' and 'Luculles' (p. 867).   long] This should be 'shortly', as both P. and A. have ('ou un peu plus anciens', p. 867): the list is of Caesar's contemporaries and immediate predecessors.   'whose fame ascendeth up unto the heavens'] N. follows A. in setting this apart from the text as a verse quotation, but although the words have their source in Homer and other ancient poets, it does not scan as verse (see Turner, II, 10 n. 2, and Pelling, *Caesar*, 15. 3 n.).

of battles he had fought and in the multitude of his enemies he had slain in battle. For in less than ten years' war in Gaul, he took by force and assault above eight hundred towns; he conquered three hundred several nations; and having before him in battle thirty hundred thousand soldiers, at sundry times he slew ten hundred thousand of them and took as many more prisoners.[67]

[16] Furthermore, he was so entirely beloved of his soldiers that to do him service (where otherwise they were no more than other men in any private quarrel) if Caesar's honour were touched, they were invincible and would so desperately venture themselves, and with such fury, that no man was able to abide them.[68] And this appeareth plainly by the example of Acilius, who in a battle by sea before the city of Marseilles, boarding one of his enemies' ships, one cut off his right hand with a sword, but yet he forsook not his target, which he had in his left hand, but thrust it in his enemies' faces and made them fly, so that he won their ship from them. And Cassius Scaeva also, in a conflict before the city of Dyrrachium having one of his eyes put out with an arrow, his shoulder struck through with a dart and his thigh with another, and having received thirty arrows upon his shield, he called to his enemies and made as though he would yield unto them.[69] But when two of them came running to him, he clove one of their shoulders from his body with his sword and hurt the other in the face, so that he made him turn his back, and at the length saved himself by means of his companions that came to help him. And in Britain also, when the captains of the bands were driven into a marish (or bog full of mire and dirt) and that the enemy did fiercely assail them there, Caesar then standing to view the battle, he saw a private soldier of his thrust in among the captains and fought so valiantly in their defence that at the length he drove the barbarous people to fly and by his means saved the captains, which otherwise were in great danger to have been cast way.° Then this soldier, being the hindmost man of all the captains, marching with great pain through the mire and dirt, half swimming and half on foot, in the end got to the other side, but left his shield behind him. Caesar, wondering at his noble courage, ran to him with joy to embrace him. But the poor soldier, hanging down his head, the water standing in his eyes, fell down at Caesar's feet and besought him to pardon him for that he had left his target behind him. And in Afric also, Scipio having taken one of Caesar's ships and Granius Petronius aboard on her amongst other, not long before chosen treasurer, he put all the rest to the sword but him and said he would give him his life.[70] But Petronius answered him again that Caesar's soldiers did not use to

[67] Marg. 'Caesar's conquests in Gaul.'
[68] Marg. 'The love and respect of Caesar's soldiers unto him.'
[69] Marg. 'The wonderful valiantness of Acilius, Cassius Scaeva, and divers others of Caesar's soldiers.'   thirty] P. has 130; N. follows A.
[70] Marg. 'Granius Petronius.' Granius Petro; N. follows A.

have their lives given them but to give others their lives, and with those words he drew his sword and thrust himself through.

[17] Now Caesar's self did breed this noble courage and life in them. First, for that he gave them bountifully and did honour them also, showing thereby that he did not heap up riches in the wars to maintain his life afterwards in wantonness and pleasure, but that he did keep it in store honourably to reward their valiant service and that by so much he thought himself rich, by how much he was liberal in rewarding of them that had deserved it. Furthermore, they did not wonder so much at his valiantness in putting himself at every instant in such manifest danger and in taking so extreme pains as he did, knowing that it was his greedy desire of honour that set him on fire and pricked him forward to do it, but that he always continued all labour and hardness more than his body could bear that filled them all with admiration. For, concerning the constitution of his body, he was lean, white, and soft skinned, and often subject to headache and otherwhile to the falling sickness (the which took him the first time, as it is reported, in Corduba, a city of Spain), but yet therefore yielded not to the disease of his body, to make it a cloak to cherish him withal, but contrarily took the pains of war as a medicine to cure his sick body, fighting always with his disease, travelling continually, living soberly, and commonly lying abroad in the field.[71] For the most nights, he slept in his coach or litter, and thereby bestowed his rest to make him always able to do something,[72] and in the daytime he would travel up and down the country to see towns, castles, and strong places. He had always a secretary with him in his coach, who did still write as he went by the way, and a soldier behind him that carried his sword. He made such speed the first time he came from Rome when he had his office that in eight days he came to the river of Rhone. He was so excellent a rider of horse from his youth that, holding his hands behind him, he would gallop his horse upon the spur. In his wars in Gaul, he did further exercise himself to indite° letters as he rode by the way, and did occupy two secretaries at once with as much as they could write — and, as Oppius writeth, more than two at a time. And it is reported that Caesar was the first that devised friends might talk together by writing ciphers in letters when he had no leisure to speak with them for his urgent business and for the great distance besides from Rome.[73] How little account Caesar made of his diet,

---

[71] Marg. 'Caesar had the falling sickness.' Cf. Shakespeare, *Julius Caesar*, I. 2. 121–23.
[72] to make him always able to do something] A. 'always to do something' ('à faire tousjours quelque chose', p. 869), i.e. productively using the time he was asleep to travel.
[73] by writing ciphers in letters] P. (probably misinterpreting his own historical source) simply has 'by letters', which makes no sense; A., likely drawing on the accounts of other ancient historians (Suetonius and possibly Dio), supplies the more plausible reference to letters written in cipher ('par chiffre de letres transposees', p. 869).

this example doth prove it.⁷⁴ Caesar supping one night in Milan with his friend Valerius Leo, there was served sperage° to his board and oil of perfume put into it instead of salad oil. He simply ate it, and found no fault, blaming his friends that were offended, and told them that it had been enough for them to have abstained to eat of that they misliked, and not to shame their friend, and how that he lacked good manner that found fault with his friend.⁷⁵ Another time, as he travelled through the country, he was driven by foul weather on the sudden to take a poor man's cottage that had but one little cabin in it, and that was so narrow that one man could but scarce lie in it. Then he said to his friends that were about him: 'Greatest rooms are meetest for greatest men, and the most necessary rooms, for the sickest persons.' And thereupon he caused Oppius, that was sick, to lie there all night, and he himself with the rest of his friends lay without doors under the easing° of the house.

[18] The first war that Caesar made with the Gauls was with the Helvetians and Tigurinians, who, having set fire of all their good cities, to the number of twelve, and four hundred villages besides, came to invade that part of Gaul which was subject to the Romans, as the Cimbri and Teutons had done before,⁷⁶ unto whom for valiantness they gave no place, and they were also a great number of them, for they were three hundred thousand souls in all, whereof there were a hundred fourscore and ten thousand fighting men.⁷⁷ Of those, it was not Caesar himself that overcame the Tigurinians, but Labienus, his lieutenant,⁷⁸ that overthrew them by the river of Arax.⁷⁹ But the Helvetians themselves came suddenly with their army to set upon him as he was going towards a city of his confederates.⁸⁰ Caesar, perceiving that, made haste to get him some place of strength and there did set his men in battle-ray.° When one brought him his horse to get up on which he used in battle, he said unto them: 'When I have overcome mine enemies, I will then get up on him to follow the chase, but now let us give them charge.'⁸¹ Therewith, he marched forward on foot and gave charge, and there fought it out a long time before he could make them fly that were in battle. But the greatest trouble he had was to distress° their camp and

---

⁷⁴ Marg. 'The temperance of Caesar in his diet.'
⁷⁵ Marg. 'Caesar's civility not to blame his friend.'
⁷⁶ A. accidentally omits the Teutons, so N. must rely on the original Greek or on Cruser's Latin here.
⁷⁷ In 59 BCE. As the widespread presence of non-combatants indicates, N.'s 'invade' is misleading: the Helvetii attempted to migrate, passing through Gaul. P. and A. have 'advance through' (ἐχώρουν πρόσω διὰ; 'passer à travers', p. 869).
⁷⁸ Marg. 'The Tigurinians slain by Labienus.'
⁷⁹ Marg. 'Arax fl.' ('fluvius', river), i.e. Arar (as in both P. and A.).
⁸⁰ themselves] The reflexive personal pronoun construes with Caesar in P. and A. ('mais les Helvetiens le vindrent charger lui-mesme', p. 869).
⁸¹ Marg. 'Caesar refused his horse when he fought a battle.'

to break their strength which they had made with their carts. For there, they that before had fled from the battle did not only put themselves in force and valiantly fought it out, but their wives and children also, fighting for their lives to the death, were all slain, and the battle was scant ended at midnight.[82] Now, if the act of this victory was famous, unto that he also added another as notable or exceeding it. For of all the barbarous people that had escaped from this battle, he gathered together again above a hundred thousand of them and compelled them to return home into their country which they had forsaken and unto their towns also which they had burnt, because he feared the Germans would come over the river of Rhine and occupy that country lying void.[83]

[19] The second war he made was in defence of the Gauls against the Germans, although before he himself had caused Ariovistus, their king, to be received for a confederate of the Romans.[84] Notwithstanding, they were grown very unquiet neighbours, and it appeared plainly that having any occasion offered them to enlarge their territories, they would not content them with their own but meant to invade and possess the rest of Gaul. Caesar perceiving that some of his captains trembled for fear, but specially the young gentlemen of noble houses of Rome, who thought to have gone to the wars with him as only for their pleasure and gain, he called them to council and commanded them that were afraid that they should depart home and not put themselves in danger against their wills sith° they had such womanish faint hearts to shrink when he had need of them. And for himself, he said, he would set upon the barbarous people though he had left him but the tenth legion only, saying that the enemies were no valianter than the Cimbri had been nor that he was a captain inferior unto Marius. This oration being made, the soldiers of the tenth legion sent their lieutenants unto him to thank him for the good opinion he had of them, and the other legions also fell out with their captains, and all of them together followed him many days' journey with good will to serve him, until they came within two hundred furlongs of the camp of the enemies. Ariovistus' courage was well cooled when he saw Caesar was come and that the Romans came to seek out the Germans where they thought and made account° that they durst not have abidden them, and therefore nothing mistrusting° it would have come so to pass, he wondered much at Caesar's courage, and the more when he saw his own army in amaze° withal. But much more did their courage fall by reason of the foolish women prophesiers they had among them, which did foretell things to come, who, considering the waves and trouble of the rivers and the terrible noise they made running down the stream, did forewarn them not to

---

[82] Marg. 'The Helvetians slain by Caesar.'
[83] Marg. 'Rhenus fl.' (i.e. 'fluvius', river).
[84] Marg. 'Caesar made war with King Ariovistus.' In 58 BCE.

fight until the new moon.⁸⁵ Caesar, having intelligence thereof and perceiving that the barbarous people thereupon stirred not, thought it best then to set upon them, being discouraged with this superstitious fear, rather than, losing time, he should tarry their leisure. So he did skirmish with them even to their forts and little hills where they lay and by this means provoked them so, that with great fury they came down to fight. There he overcame them in battle and followed them in chase, with great slaughter, three hundred furlong, even unto the river of Rhine, and he filled all the fields thitherto with dead bodies and spoils.⁸⁶ Howbeit, Ariovistus, flying with speed, got over the river of Rhine and escaped with a few of his men. It is said that there were slain fourscore thousand persons at this battle.

[20] After this exploit, Caesar left his army amongst the Sequanes to winter there, and he himself in the meantime, thinking of the affairs at Rome, went over the mountains into Gaul about the river of Po, being part of his province which he had in charge.⁸⁷ For there the river called Rubico divideth the rest of Italy from Gaul on this side the Alps.⁸⁸ Caesar, lying there, did practise to make friends in Rome, because many came thither to see him, unto whom he granted their suits they demanded and sent them home also, partly with liberal rewards and partly with large promises and hope. Now, during all this conquest of the Gauls, Pompey did not consider how Caesar interchangeably did conquer the Gauls with the weapons of the Romans and won the Romans again with the money of the Gauls. Caesar being advertised that the Belgae (which were the warlikest men of all the Gauls and that occupied the third part of Gaul) were all up in arms and had raised a great power of men together, he straight made towards them with all possible speed and found them spoiling and overrunning the country of the Gauls, their neighbours and confederates of the Romans.⁸⁹ So he gave them battle, and they fighting cowardly, he overthrew the most part of them (which were in a troop together) and slew such a number of them that the Romans passed over deep rivers and lakes on foot upon their dead bodies, the rivers were so full of them.⁹⁰ After this overthrow, they that dwelt nearest

---

⁸⁵ Marg. 'The wise women of Germany, how they did foretell things to come.'   foolish] N.'s addition (just as A. has added 'superstitious' in the following sentence). See Introduction, p. 70.

⁸⁶ Marg. 'King Ariovistus overthrown by Caesar.'   three hundred] P. has 400; A. expresses the number in leagues ('dixhuit lieves', p. 870). The fact that A. had rendered P.'s 200 furlongs earlier in the paragraph as twelve leagues seems to indicate that N. relied here on A.'s numbers but converted them back to furlongs (if twelve leagues equals 200 furlongs, then eighteen leagues is 300 furlongs).

⁸⁷ Sequanes] Sequani.   Gaul] i.e. Cisalpine Gaul.

⁸⁸ Rubico] i.e. Rubicon.

⁸⁹ In 57 BCE.

⁹⁰ Marg. 'The Belgae overcome by Caesar.'

unto the sea-side and were next neighbours unto the ocean did yield themselves without any compulsion or fight, whereupon he led his army against the Nervians, the stoutest warriors of all the Belgae.[91] They, dwelling in the wood country, had conveyed their wives, children, and goods into a marvellous great forest, as far from their enemies as they could, and being about the number of sixscore thousand fighting men and more, they came one day and set upon Caesar when his army was out of order and fortifying of his camp, little looking to have fought that day.[92] At the first charge, they broke the horsemen of the Romans, and compassing in the twelfth and seventh legion, they slew all the centurions and captains of the bands. And had not Caesar self taken his shield on his arm and, flying in amongst the barbarous people, made a lane through them that fought before him, and the tenth legion also, seeing him in danger, run unto him from the top of the hill where they stood in battle and broken the ranks of their enemies, there had not a Roman escaped alive that day. But taking example of Caesar's valiantness, they fought desperately beyond their power,[93] and yet could not make the Nervians fly, but they fought it out to the death, till they were all in manner slain in the field.[94] It is written that of threescore thousand fighting men, there escaped only but five hundred, and of four hundred gentlemen and councillors of the Romans, but three saved.[95]

[21] The senate understanding it at Rome ordained that they should do sacrifice unto the gods and keep feasts and solemn processions fifteen days together without intermission, having never made the like ordinance at Rome for any victory that ever was obtained. Because they saw the danger had been marvellous great, so many nations rising as they did in arms together against him, and further the love of the people unto him made his victory much more famous. For when Caesar had set his affairs at a stay in Gaul on the other side of the Alps, he always used to lie about the river of Po in the winter-time, to give direction for the establishing of things at Rome at his pleasure. For not only they that made suit for offices at Rome were chosen magistrates by means of Caesar's money which he gave them (with the which, bribing the people, they bought their voices and, when they were in office, did all that they could to increase Caesar's power and greatness), but the greatest and chiefest men also of the nobility went unto Luke unto him.[96] As Pompey, Crassus, Appius

---

[91] Marg. 'Nervii, the stoutest warriors of all the Belgae.'

[92] sixscore thousand] P. and A. have 60,000; N. gives the correct number (threescore thousand) a few lines down.

[93] N. omits P.'s 'as the saying is' (τὴν λεγομένην), translated by A. as 'ainsi qu'on dit en commun langage' (as is said in everyday speech, p. 871). See Introduction, p. 63.

[94] Marg. 'The Nervii slain by Caesar.' Cf. Shakespeare, *Julius Caesar*, III. 2. 168–71.

[95] of the Romans] N.'s addition. This should refer to the Nervii.

[96] Marg. 'The great lords of Rome came to Luca to Caesar.'   Luke] i.e. Luca (modern-

(praetor of Sardinia), and Nepos (proconsul in Spain). Insomuch that there were at one time sixscore sergeants carrying rods and axes before the magistrates and above two hundred senators besides. There they fell in consultation, and determined that Pompey and Crassus should again be chosen consuls the next year following.[97] Furthermore, they did appoint° that Caesar should have money again delivered him to pay his army, and besides did prorogue the time of his government five years further. This was thought a very strange and an unreasonable matter unto wise men. For they themselves that had taken so much money of Caesar persuaded the senate to let him have money of the common treasure, as though he had had none before — yea, to speak more plainly, they compelled the senate unto it, sighing and lamenting to see the decrees they passed. Cato was not there then, for they had purposely sent him before into Cyprus. Howbeit, Faonius, that followed Cato's steps, when he saw that he could not prevail nor withstand them, he went out of the senate in choler and cried out amongst the people that it was a horrible shame.[98] But no man did hearken to him, some for the reverence they bore unto Pompey and Crassus, and others, favouring Caesar's proceedings, did put all their hope and trust in him and therefore did quiet themselves and stirred not.

[22] Then Caesar, returning into Gaul beyond the Alps unto his army, found there a great war in the country.[99] For two great nations of Germany had not long before passed over the river of Rhine to conquer new lands, and the one of these people were called Ipes and the other, Tenterides.[100] Now, touching the battle which Caesar fought with them, he himself doth describe it in his *Commentaries* in this sort. That the barbarous people, having sent ambassadors unto him to require° peace for a certain time, they notwithstanding, against law of arms, came and set upon him as he travelled by the way, insomuch as eight hundred of their men of arms overthrew five thousand of his horsemen, who nothing at all mistrusted their coming.[101] Again, that they sent him other ambassadors to mock[102] him once more, but that he kept them and therewith caused his whole army to march against them, thinking it a folly and madness to keep faith with such traitorous, barbarous breakers of leagues. Canutius writeth that the senate appointing again to do new sacrifice, processions, and feasts

day Lucca), as in the marginal note.
[97] The conference of Luca took place in April 56 BCE.
[98] Faonius] A. (and hence N.) follow the Greek spelling of this name; the more common Roman form is Favonius.
[99] In 55 BCE.
[100] **Marg.** 'Ipes and Tenterides, people of Germany.' P. calls the tribes the Usipes (Usipi or Usipetes in Latin) and Tenteritae (Tencteri). N. follows A., who translates the corrupt manuscript reading 'Ipes' (οὖσ ἴπας for Οὐσίπας).
[101] **Marg.** 'Caesar's horsemen put to flight.'
[102] Deceive (without the modern connotation of ridicule).

to give thanks to the gods for this victory, Cato was of contrary opinion that Caesar should be delivered into the hands of the barbarous people, for to purge their city and commonwealth of this breach of faith and to turn the curse upon him that was the author of it.[103] Of these barbarous people which came over the Rhine (being about the number of four hundred thousand persons), they were all in manner slain,[104] saving a very few of them, that flying from the battle got over the river of Rhine again, who were received by the Sicambrians, another people of the Germans.[105] Caesar taking this occasion against them, lacking no goodwill of himself besides to have the honour to be counted the first Roman that ever passed over the river of Rhine with an army, he built a bridge over it.[106] This river is marvellous broad and runneth with great fury. And in that place specially where he built his bridge, for there it is of a great breadth from one side to the other, and it hath so strong and swift a stream besides that men casting down great bodies of trees into the river (which the stream bringeth down with it) did with the great blows and force thereof marvellously shake the posts of the bridge he had set up. But to prevent the blows of those trees, and also to break the fury of the stream, he made a pile of great wood above the bridge a good way and did forcibly ram them into the bottom of the river, so that in ten days' space he had set up and finished his bridge of the goodliest carpenters' work and most excellent invention to see to that could be possibly thought or devised.

[23] Then, passing over his army upon it, he found none that durst any more fight with him. For the Swevians, which were the warlikest people of all Germany, had gotten themselves with their goods into wonderful great valleys and bogs, full of woods and forests.[107] Now when he had burnt all the country of his enemies and confirmed the league with the confederates of the Romans, he returned back again into Gaul, after he had tarried eighteen days at the most in Germany on the other side of the Rhine. The journey he made also into England was a noble enterprise and very commendable.[108] For he was the first that sailed the West Ocean with an army by sea and that passed through the Sea Atlanticum with his army to make war in that so great and famous island (which many ancient writers would not believe that it was so indeed and did make them vary° about it, saying it was but a fable and a lie) and was the first that enlarged the Roman Empire beyond the earth inhabitable.[109] For twice he

---

[103] Canutius] P. 'Tanusius'; N. follows A. ('Canusius', p. 872), with 's' changed (by N. or the compositor) to 't'.
[104] Marg. 'The Ipes and Tenterides slain by Caesar.'
[105] Marg. 'Sicambri, a people of the Germans.' P. 'Sugambri'; N. follows A.
[106] Marg. 'Caesar made a bridge over the river of Rhine.'
[107] Swevians] Suebi.
[108] Marg. 'Caesar's journey into England.'
[109] The journey [...] inhabitable] N. makes significant changes to P. and A. here for

passed over the narrow sea against° the firm land of Gaul and, fighting many battles there, did hurt his enemies more than enrich his own men, because of men hardly brought up and poor there was nothing to be gotten. Whereupon his war had not such success° as he looked for, and therefore, taking pledges only of the king and imposing a yearly tribute upon him to be paid unto the people of Rome, he returned again into Gaul. There he was no sooner landed, but he found letters ready to be sent over the sea unto him, in the which he was advertised from Rome of the death of his daughter, that she was dead with child by Pompey.[110] For the which, Pompey and Caesar both were marvellous sorrowful, and their friends mourned also, thinking that this alliance which maintained the commonwealth (that otherwise was very tickle)° in good peace and concord was now severed and broken asunder, and the rather likely because the child lived not long after the mother. So the common people at Rome took the corpse of Julia, in despite of the tribunes, and buried it in the field of Mars.

[24] Now Caesar being driven to divide his army (that was very great) into sundry garrisons for the winter time and returning again into Italy as he was wont, all Gaul rebelled again and had raised great armies in every quarter to set upon the Romans and to assay if they could distress their forts where they lay in garrison.[111] The greatest number and most warlike men of these Gauls that entered into action of rebellion were led by one Ambiorix and first did set upon the garrisons of Cotta and Titurius, whom they slew and all the soldiers they had about them.[112] Then they went with threescore thousand fighting men to besiege the garrison which Quintus Cicero had in his charge, and had almost taken them by force, because all the soldiers were every man of them hurt, but they were so valiant and courageous that they did more than men (as they say) in defending of themselves. These news being come to Caesar, who was far from thence at that time, he returned with all possible speed and, levying seven thousand soldiers, made haste to help Cicero, that was in such distress. The Gauls that did besiege Cicero, understanding of Caesar's coming, raised their siege incontinently° to go and meet him, making account that he was but a handful in their hands, they were so few. Caesar, to deceive them, still° drew back and made as though he fled from them, lodging in places meet for a captain that had but a few to fight with a great number of his enemies, and commanded his men in no wise to stir out to skirmish with them, but compelled them to raise up the rampires° of his camp and to fortify the gates, as men that were afraid, because the enemies should the less esteem of them,

---

patriotic reasons. See Introduction, p. 70.
[110] Marg. 'The death of Julia, Caesar's daughter.'
[111] Marg. 'The rebellion of the Gauls.'
[112] Marg. 'Cotta and Titurius with their army slain.' In 54 BCE.

until that at length he took opportunity by their disorderly coming to assail the trenches of his camp (they were grown to such a presumptuous boldness and bravery), and then sallying out upon them, he put them all to flight with slaughter of a great number of them.[113]

[25] This did suppress all the rebellions of the Gauls in those parts, and furthermore he himself in person went in the midst of winter thither where he heard they did rebel, for that° there was come a new supply out of Italy of three whole legions in their room which he had lost, of the which two of them Pompey lent him and the other legion he himself had levied in Gaul about the river of Po. During these stirs broke forth the beginning of the greatest and most dangerous war that he had in all Gaul, the which had been secretly practised of long time by the chiefest and most warlike people of that country, who had levied a wonderful great power. For everywhere they levied multitudes of men and great riches besides to fortify their strongholds. Furthermore, the country where they rose was very ill to come unto, and specially at that time being winter, when the rivers were frozen, the woods and forests covered with snow, the meadows drowned with floods, and the fields so deep of snow that no ways were to be found, neither the marishes nor rivers to be discerned, all was so overflown and drowned with water — all which troubles together were enough (as they thought) to keep Caesar from setting upon the rebels.[114] Many nations of the Gauls were of this conspiracy, but two of the chiefest were the Arvernians and Carnutes, who had chosen Vercingentorix for their lieutenant general, whose father the Gauls before had put to death because they thought he aspired to make himself king.[115]

[26] This Vercingentorix, dividing his army into divers parts and appointing divers captains over them, had gotten to take his part all the people and countries thereabouts, even as far as they that dwell towards the Sea Adriatic,[116] having further determined (understanding that Rome did conspire against Caesar) to make all Gaul rise in arms against him. So that if he had but tarried a little longer, until Caesar had entered in his civil wars, he had put all Italy in as great fear and danger as it was when the Cimbri did come and invade it. But Caesar, that was valiant in all assays° and dangers of war and that was very skilful to take time and opportunity, so soon as he understood the news of the

---

[113] Marg. 'Caesar slew the Gauls led by Ambiorix.'
[114] Marg. 'The second rebellion of the Gauls against Caesar.'
[115] Marg. 'Vercingentorix, captain of the rebels against Caesar.'   Arvernians] Arverni. Vercingentorix] Vercingetorix.
[116] Marg. '* Some say, that in this place [i.e. instead of 'towards the Sea Adriatic'] is to be read in the Greek πρὸς τὸν Ἄραριν, which is "to the river of Saone".' The reading in A.'s note is the one adopted in modern editions of P. (though in the form Ἄραρα).

rebellion he departed with speed and returned back the selfsame way which he had gone, making the barbarous people know that they should deal with an army invincible, and which they could not possibly withstand, considering the great speed he had made with the same in so sharp and hard a winter. For where they would not possibly have believed that a post or courier could have come in so short a time from the place where he was unto them, they wondered when they saw him burning and destroying the country, the towns, and strong forts where he came with his army, taking all to mercy that yielded unto him, until such times as the Hedui took arms against him, who before were wont to be called the brethren of the Romans and were greatly honoured of them.[117] Wherefore Caesar's men, when they understood that they had joined with the rebels, they were marvellous sorry and half discouraged. Thereupon, Caesar, departing from those parts, went through the country of the Lingones to enter the country of the Burgonians,[118] who were confederates of the Romans and the nearest unto Italy on that side in respect of all the rest of Gaul. Thither the enemies came to set upon him and to environ him of all sides with an infinite number of thousands of fighting men. Caesar, on the other side, tarried their coming, and fighting with them a long time, he made them so afraid of him that at length he overcame the barbarous people.[119] But at the first it seemeth notwithstanding that he had received some overthrow, for the Arvernians showed a sword hung up in one of their temples which they said they had won from Caesar. Insomuch as Caesar self, coming that way by occasion, saw it and fell a-laughing at it. But some of his friends going about to take it away, he would not suffer them but bad them let it alone and touch it not for it was a holy thing.

[27] Notwithstanding, such as at the first had saved themselves by flying, the most of them were gotten with their king into the city of Alexia, the which Caesar went and besieged, although it seemed inexpungible, both for the height of the walls as also for the multitude of soldiers they had to defend it.[120] But now during this siege, he fell into a marvellous great danger without, almost

---

[117] Marg. 'The Hedui rebel against the Romans.' Hedui] Aedui.
[118] Marg. '* Sequani.' P., A. (p. 874), and Cruser (p. 575) all refer to the Sequani, without a marginal note indicating that they were the Burgundians (of which N.'s 'Burgonian' is a variant spelling according to OED). The only other place where I have found the two together is John Higgins's revised edition of Huloet's Latin dictionary, which frequently includes French alongside the Latin and English and has the entry: 'Burgonians people in Fraunce. Hedui, orum. Sequani et Sequanici dicti sunt.' (John Higgins, *Huloets dictionarie, newelye corrected, amended, set in order and enlarged* (1572), sig. F6r, credited to Calepinus's Latin dictionary (1502)). Huloet's dictionary may thus have been one of the reference works drawn on by N.
[119] Marg. 'Vercingentorix overthrown by Caesar.'
[120] Marg. 'The siege of Alexia.'   Alexia] Alesia.

incredible.[121] For an army of three hundred thousand fighting men of the best men that were among all the nations of the Gauls came against him, being at the siege of Alexia, besides them that were within the city, which amounted to the number of threescore and ten thousand fighting men at the least, so that perceiving he was shut in betwixt two so great armies, he was driven to fortify himself with two walls, the one against them of the city and the other against them without.[122] For if those two armies had joined together, Caesar had been utterly undone. And therefore this siege of Alexia, and the battle he won before it, did deservedly win him more honour and fame than any other.[123] For there, in that instant and extreme danger, he showed more valiantness and wisdom than he did in any battle he fought before. But what a wonderful thing was this, that they of the city never heard anything of them that came to aid them until Caesar had overcome them, and furthermore that the Romans themselves which kept watch upon the wall that was built against the city knew also no more of it than they until it was done and that they heard the cries and lamentations of men and women in Alexia when they perceived on the other side of the city such a number of glistering shields of gold and silver, such store of bloody corselets and armours, such a deal of plate and moveables, and such a number of tents and pavilions after the fashion of the Gauls which the Romans had gotten of their spoils in their camp? Thus suddenly was this great army vanished, as a dream or vision, where the most part of them were slain that day in battle. Furthermore, after that they within the city of Alexia had done great hurt to Caesar and themselves also, in the end they all yielded themselves.[124] And Vercingentorix (he that was their king and captain in all this war) went out of the gates excellently well armed, and his horse furnished with rich caparison accordingly, and rode round about Caesar, who sat in his chair of estate. Then, lighting from his horse, he took off his caparison and furniture° and unarmed himself and laid all on the ground and went and sat down at Caesar's feet and said never a word. So Caesar at length committed him as a prisoner taken in the wars to lead him afterwards in his triumph at Rome.

[28] Now Caesar had of long time determined to destroy Pompey, and Pompey him also. For Crassus being killed amongst the Parthians, who only did see that one of them two must needs fall, nothing kept Caesar from being the greatest person, but because he destroyed not Pompey that was the greater;[125]

---

[121] Marg. 'Caesar's danger and wise policy.'
[122] threescore and ten thousand] P. has 170,000; N. follows A.
[123] Marg. 'Caesar's great victory at Alexia.'
[124] Marg. 'Alexia yielded up to Caesar.'
[125] who only did see that one of them two must needs fall] P. writes 'who was ἔφεδρος to them both', referring to the third competitor in contests, who waits to take on the winner. A. paraphrases 'qui seul pouvoit espier, que l'un d'eux deux donnast en terre' (who alone could

neither did anything let Pompey to withstand that it should not come to pass, but because he did not first overcome Caesar, whom only he feared.[126] For till then, Pompey had not long feared him,[127] but always before set light by° him, thinking it an easy matter for him to put him down when he would, sith he had brought him to that greatness he was come unto. But Caesar contrarily, having had that drift in his head from the beginning, like a wrestler that studieth for tricks to overthrow his adversary, he went far from Rome to exercise himself in the wars of Gaul, where he did train his army and presently by his valiant deeds did increase his fame and honour.[128] By these means became Caesar as famous as Pompey in his doings and lacked no more to put his enterprise in execution but some occasions of colour,° which Pompey partly gave him and partly also the time delivered him, but chiefly the hard fortune and ill government at that time of the commonwealth at Rome. For they that made suit for honour and offices bought the voices of the people with ready money, which they gave out openly to usury, without shame or fear.[129] Thereupon, the common people that had sold their voices for money came to the marketplace at the day of election to fight for him that had hired them, not with their voices but with their bows, slings, and swords. So that the assembly seldom-time broke up but that the pulpit° for orations was defiled and sprinkled with the blood of them that were slain in the marketplace, the city remaining all that time without government of magistrate, like a ship left without a pilot. Insomuch as men of deep judgement and discretion, seeing such fury and madness of the people, thought themselves happy if the commonwealth were no worse troubled than with the absolute state of a monarchy and sovereign lord to govern them. Furthermore, there were many that were not afraid to speak it openly that there was no other help to remedy the troubles of the commonwealth but by the authority of one man only that should command them all and that this medicine must be ministered by the hands of him that was the gentlest physician, meaning covertly Pompey. Now Pompey used many fine speeches, making semblance as though he would

watch for one of the two of them to crash on the rocks, p. 875). Crassus died in 53 BCE.
[126] Marg. 'The discord betwixt Caesar and Pompey and the cause of the civil wars.' neither did anything let Pompey to withstand that it should not come to pass] N.'s second negative (which derives from A.'s French, 'ny à Pompeius pour obvier à ce que cela ne lui advinst' (p. 875), where 'ne' is required following a verb of denial) confuses the sense: the only way for Pompey to stop Caesar becoming the most powerful man in Rome was to destroy him.
[127] i.e. it was only recently that Pompey had begun to fear him.
[128] Marg. 'Caesar's craftiness.'
[129] Marg. 'The people's voices bought at Rome for money.' 'P. merely says, "they set up (money-)tables in public, and bribed the common people", i.e. they established regular shops at which electors could apply for bribes. A. translates, "they bought the votes of the people for ready cash, which they handed over publicly at the bank". N. then takes *à la banque* in the sense of "to the bank"' (Turner, II, 19 n. 3).

none of it, and yet cunningly underhand did lay all the irons in the fire he could to bring it to pass that he might be chosen dictator. Cato finding the mark he shot at and fearing lest in the end the people should be compelled to make him dictator, he persuaded the senate rather to make him sole consul, that° contenting himself with that more just and lawful government, he should not covet the other unlawful.[130] The senate following his counsel did not only make him consul, but further did prorogue his government of the provinces he had. For he had two provinces, all Spain and Afric, the which he governed by his lieutenants, and further he received yearly of the common treasure to pay his soldiers a thousand talents.[131]

[29] Hereupon Caesar took occasion also to send his men to make suit in his name for the consulship and also to have the government of his provinces prorogued.[132] Pompey at the first held his peace. But Marcellus and Lentulus (that otherwise hated Caesar) withstood them, and to shame and dishonour him had much needless speech in matters of weight.[133] Furthermore, they took away the freedom from the colonies which Caesar had lately brought unto the city of Novum Comum in Gaul towards Italy, where Caesar not long before had lodged them.[134] And moreover, when Marcellus was consul, he made one of the senators in that city to be whipped with rods who came to Rome about those matters, and said he gave him those marks that he should know he was no Roman citizen, and bad him go his way and tell Caesar of it. After Marcellus' consulship, Caesar, setting open his coffers of the treasure he had gotten among the Gauls, did frankly° give it out amongst the magistrates at Rome, without restraint or spare.[135] First, he set Curio, the tribune, clear out of debt and gave also unto Paul, the consul, a thousand five hundred talents, with which money he built that notable palace by the marketplace called Paul's Basilic° in the place of Fulvius' Basilic. Then Pompey, being afraid of this practice, began openly to procure, both by himself and his friends, that they should send Caesar a successor and, moreover, he sent unto Caesar for his two legions of men of war which he had lent him for the conquest of Gaul. Caesar sent him them again and gave every private soldier two hundred and fifty silver drachmas. Now, they that brought these two legions back from Caesar gave out ill and seditious

---

[130] In 52 BCE.
[131] Marg. 'Pompey governed Spain and Afric.'
[132] Marg. 'Caesar sueth the second time to be consul and to have his government prorogued.' In 51 BCE.
[133] had much needless speech in matters of weight] A very loose rendering of A.'s 'en adjoustant, à ce qui estoit necessaire à dire ou à faire, d'autres choses, qui ne l'estoient pas' (adding to that which was necessary to say or to do other things that were not, p. 876).
[134] the freedom] i.e. the privilege of Roman citizenship.
[135] Marg. 'Caesar bribeth the magistrates at Rome.'

words against him among the people and did also abuse° Pompey with false persuasions and vain hopes, informing him that he was marvellously desired and wished for in Caesar's camp, and though in Rome for the malice and secret spite which the governors there did bear him he could hardly° obtain that he desired, yet in Gaul he might assure himself that all the army was at his commandment.[136] They added further also that if the soldiers there did once return over the mountains again into Italy, they would all straight come to him, they did so hate Caesar, because he wearied them with too much labour and continual fight and, withal, for that they suspected he aspired to be king. These words, breeding security in Pompey and a vain conceit of himself, made him negligent in his doings, so that he made no preparation for war, as though he had no occasion to be afraid, but only studied to thwart Caesar in speech and to cross the suits he made.[137] Howbeit, Caesar passed° not of all this. For the report went that one of Caesar's captains which was sent to Rome to prosecute his suit being at the senate door and hearing that they denied to prorogue Caesar's time of government, which he sued for, clapping his hand upon his sword, he said: 'Sith you will not grant it him, this shall give it him.'

[30] Notwithstanding, the requests that Caesar propounded carried great semblance of reason with them.[138] For he said that he was contented to lay down arms, so that Pompey did the like,[139] and that both of them as private persons should come and make suit of their citizens to obtain honourable recompense, declaring unto them that taking arms from him and granting them unto Pompey, they did wrongfully accuse him in going about to make himself a tyrant and, in the meantime, to grant the other means to be a tyrant. Curio making these offers and persuasions openly before the people in the name of Caesar, he was heard with great rejoicing and clapping of hands, and there were some that cast flowers and nosegays upon him when he went his way, as they commonly use to do unto any man when he hath obtained victory and won any games.[140] Then Antonius, one of the tribunes, brought a letter sent from Caesar and made it openly to be read, in despite of the consuls. But Scipio, in the senate, Pompey's father-in-law, made this motion: that if Caesar did not dismiss his army by a certain day appointed him, the Romans should proclaim him an enemy unto Rome. Then the consuls openly asked, in the presence of the senators, if they thought it good that Pompey should dismiss his army, but few agreed to that demand. After that again they asked if they liked that Caesar

---

[136] Marg. 'Pompey abused by flatterers.'
[137] N. omits 'thinking that he opposed him well by saying "I am of the opinion that this or that"' ('cuidant bien le combatre pour dire, Je suis d'advis de ceci ou de cela', p. 877).
[138] Marg. 'Caesar's requests unto the senate.'
[139] i.e. provided that...
[140] Cf. Shakespeare, *Julius Caesar*, I. 1. 48–51.

should dismiss his army, thereto they all in manner answered: 'yea, yea'. But when Antonius requested again that both of them should lay down arms, then they were all indifferently° of his mind. Notwithstanding, because Scipio did insolently behave himself, and Marcellus also, who cried that they must use force of arms and not men's opinions against a thief, the senate rose straight upon it without further determination, and men changed apparel through the city because of this dissention, as they use to do in a common calamity.[141]

[31] After that, there came other letters from Caesar, which seemed much more reasonable, in the which he requested that they would grant him Gaul that lieth between the mountains of the Alps and Italy and Illyria, with two legions only, and then that he would request nothing else until he made suit for the second consulship. Cicero, the orator, that was newly come from the government of Cilicia, travelled to reconcile them together and pacified Pompey the best he could, who told him he would yield to anything he would have him so he did let him alone with his army. So Cicero persuaded Caesar's friends to be contented to take those two provinces and six thousand men only, that they might be friends and at peace together. Pompey very willingly yielded unto it and granted them. But Lentulus, the consul, would not agree to it, but shamefully drove Curio and Antonius out of the senate, whereby they themselves gave Caesar a happy occasion and colour as could be, stirring up his soldiers the more against them when he showed them these two notable men and tribunes of the people that were driven to fly, disguised like slaves in a carrier's cart. For they were driven for fear to steal out of Rome, disguised in that manner.[142]

[32] Now at that time, Caesar had not in all about him above five thousand footmen and three thousand horsemen, for the rest of his army he left on the other side of the mountains to be brought after him by his lieutenants.[143] So, considering that for the execution of his enterprise he should not need so many men of war at the first, but rather suddenly stealing upon them to make them afraid with his valiantness, taking benefit of the opportunity of time, because he should more easily make his enemies afraid of him, coming so suddenly when they looked not for him, than he should otherwise distress them, assailing them with his whole army, in giving them leisure to provide° further for him, he commanded his captains and lieutenants to go before, without any other armour than their swords, to take the city of Ariminum (a great city of Gaul, being the first city men come to when they come out of Gaul) with as little

---

[141] Marcellus] P. has Lentulus, but N. follows A.
[142] **Marg.** 'Antonius and Curio, tribunes of the people, fly from Rome to Caesar.'
[143] three thousand horsemen] P. and A. 'three hundred'.

bloodshed and tumult as they could possible.¹⁴⁴ Then, committing that force and army he had with him unto Hortensius, one of his friends, he remained a whole day together openly in the sight of every man to see the sword-players handle their weapons before him. At night he went into his lodging and, bathing his body a little, came afterwards into the hall amongst them and made merry with them a while whom he had bidden to supper. Then, when it was well forward night and very dark, he rose from the table and prayed his company to be merry and no man to stir, for he would straight come to them again; howbeit, he had secretly before commanded a few of his trustiest friends to follow him, not altogether,° but some one way and some another way. He himself in the meantime took a coach he had hired and made as though he would have gone some other way at the first, but suddenly he turned back again towards the city of Ariminum. When he was come unto the little river of Rubicon, which divideth Gaul on this side the Alps from Italy, he stayed° upon a sudden. For, the nearer he came to execute his purpose, the more remorse he had in his conscience to think what an enterprise he took in hand, and his thoughts also fell out more doubtful when he entered into consideration of the desperateness of his attempt.¹⁴⁵ So he fell into many thoughts with himself and spoke never a word, waving sometime° one way, sometime another way, and oftentimes changed his determination contrary to himself. So did he talk much also with his friends he had with him, amongst whom was Asinius Pollio, telling them what mischiefs the beginning of this passage over that river would breed in the world and how much their posterity and them that lived after them would speak of it in time to come. But at length, casting from him with a noble courage all those perilous thoughts to come and speaking these words which valiant men commonly say that attempt dangerous and desperate enterprises, 'A man can be but once undone, come on!',¹⁴⁶ he passed over the river, and when he was come over, he ran with his coach and never stayed, so that before daylight he was within the city of Ariminum and took it.¹⁴⁷ It is said that the night before he passed over this river he dreamed a damnable dream, that he carnally knew his mother.¹⁴⁸

[33] The city of Ariminum being taken and the rumour thereof dispersed

---

¹⁴⁴ a great city of Gaul] 'of Gaul' is N.'s incongruous addition.
¹⁴⁵ Marg. 'Caesar's doubtful thoughts at the river of Rubicon.'
¹⁴⁶ Marg. 'The Greek useth this phrase of speech: "cast the die".' This famous phrase (best known in its Latin form, 'alea iacta est') is proverbially translated by A. as 'A tout perdre n'y a qu'un coup perilleux, poussons' (p. 878). N. replaces his straightforward translation in the first edition ('A desperate man feareth no danger, come on!') with this idiomatic-sounding jingle in the third edition (1603).
¹⁴⁷ Marg. 'Caesar took the city of Ariminum.'
¹⁴⁸ Marg. 'Caesar's damnable dream.'

through all Italy, even as if it had been open war both by sea and land and as if all the laws of Rome together with the extreme bounds and confines° of the same had been broken up, a man would have said that not only the men and women for fear, as experience proved at other times, but whole cities themselves, leaving their habitations, fled from one place to another through all Italy. And Rome itself also was immediately filled with the flowing repair° of all the people their neighbours thereabouts, which came thither from all parts like droves of cattle, that there was neither officer nor magistrate that could any more command them by authority, neither by any persuasion of reason bridle such a confused and disorderly multitude, so that Rome had in manner destroyed itself for lack of rule and order.[149] For in all places men were of contrary opinions, and there were dangerous stirs and tumults everywhere, because they that were glad of this trouble could keep in no certain place, but running up and down the city, when they met with others in divers places that seemed either to be afraid or angry with this tumult (as otherwise is it impossible in so great a city), they flatly fell out with them and boldly threatened them with that that was to come. Pompey himself, who at that time was not a little amazed,° was yet much more troubled with the ill words some gave him on the one side, and some on the other. For some of them reproved him and said that he had done wisely and had paid for his folly because he had made Caesar so great and strong against him and the commonwealth.[150] And other again did blame him because he had refused the honest offers and reasonable conditions of peace which Caesar had offered him, suffering Lentulus the consul to abuse him too much. On the other side, Faonius spoke unto him and bad him stamp on the ground with his foot; for Pompey, being one day in a bravery in the senate, said openly, let no man take thought for preparation of war, for when he listed, with one stamp of his foot on the ground he would fill all Italy with soldiers. This notwithstanding, Pompey at that time had a greater number of soldiers than Caesar, but they would never let him follow his own determination. For they brought him so many lies and put so many examples of fear before him, as if Caesar had been already at their heels and had won all, so that in the end he yielded unto them and gave place to their fury and madness,[151] determining (seeing all things in such tumult and garboil)° that there was no way but to forsake the city, and thereupon commanded the senate to follow him and not a man to tarry there unless he loved tyranny more than his own liberty and the commonwealth.[152]

[149] Marg. 'Rome in uproar with Caesar's coming.'
[150] he had done wisely] N.'s literal rendering of A.'s idiomatic 'c'estoit bien employé' (it was well-deserved, p. 879; see Huguet, s.v. employer).
[151] and gave place to their fury and madness] A. 'et se laissa emporter à la foule des autres' (and let himself be carried away in the throng of the others, p. 879). It seems that N. has confused 'foule' (throng) with 'folie' (madness).
[152] Marg. 'Pompey flyeth from Rome.'

[34] Thus the consuls themselves, before they had done their common sacrifices accustomed at their going out of the city, fled every man of them. So did likewise the most part of the senators, taking their own things in haste, such as came first to hand, as if by stealth they had taken them from another. And there were some of them also that always loved Caesar, whose wits were then so troubled and besides themselves with the fear they had conceived that they also fled and followed the stream of this tumult without manifest cause or necessity. But above all things, it was a lamentable sight to see the city itself, that in this fear and trouble was left at all adventure, as a ship tossed in storm of sea, forsaken of her pilots and despairing of her safety.[153] This their departure being thus miserable, yet men esteemed their banishment (for the love they bore unto Pompey) to be their natural country and reckoned Rome no better than Caesar's camp. At that time also Labienus, who was one of Caesar's greatest friends and had been always used as his lieutenant in the wars of Gaul and had valiantly fought in his cause, he likewise forsook him then and fled unto Pompey.[154] But Caesar sent his money and carriage° after him, and then went and encamped before the city of Corfinium, the which Domitius kept, with thirty cohorts or ensigns. When Domitius saw he was besieged, he straight thought himself but undone, and despairing of his success he bad a physician, a slave of his, give him poison. The physician gave him a drink, which he drank, thinking to have died. But shortly after, Domitius, hearing them report what clemency and wonderful courtesy Caesar used unto them he took, repented him then that he had drunk this drink and began to lament and bewail his desperate resolution taken to die. The physician did comfort him again and told him that he had taken a drink only to make him sleep but not to destroy him. Then Domitius rejoiced, and went straight and yielded himself unto Caesar, who gave him his life, but he notwithstanding stole away immediately and fled unto Pompey.[155] When these news were brought to Rome, they did marvellously rejoice and comfort them that still remained there, and moreover there were of them that had forsaken Rome which returned thither again.

[35] In the meantime, Caesar did put all Domitius' men in pay, and he did the like through all the cities where he had taken any captains that levied men for Pompey. Now Caesar, having assembled a great and dreadful power together, went straight where he thought to find Pompey himself. But Pompey tarried not his coming, but fled into the city of Brundusium, from whence he had sent the two consuls before with that army he had unto Dyrrachium, and he himself also went thither afterwards when he understood that Caesar was come, as

---

[153] at all adventure] at the mercy of fortune.
[154] Marg. 'Labienus forsook Caesar and fled to Pompey.'
[155] Marg. 'Domitius escaped from Caesar and fled to Pompey.'

you shall hear more amply hereafter in his life.¹⁵⁶ Caesar lacked no goodwill to follow him, but wanting ships to take the seas, he returned forthwith to Rome, so that in less than threescore days he was lord of all Italy, without any bloodshed. Who when he was come to Rome and found it much quieter than he looked for and many senators there also, he courteously entreated them and prayed them to send unto Pompey to pacify all matters between them upon reasonable conditions. But no man did attempt it, either because they feared Pompey for that they had forsaken him or else for that they thought Caesar meant not as he spoke but that they were words of course to colour his purpose withal.¹⁵⁷ And when Metellus also, one of the tribunes, would not suffer him to take any of the common treasure out of the temple of Saturn, but told him that it was against the law: 'Tush,' said he, 'time of war and law are two things.'¹⁵⁸ 'If this that I do', quoth he, 'do offend thee, then get thee hence for this time; for war cannot abide this frank and bold speech. But when wars are done and that we are all quiet again, then thou shalt speak in the pulpit what thou wilt, and yet I do tell thee this of favour, impairing so much my right, for thou art mine, both thou and all them that have risen against me and whom I have in my hands.' When he had spoken thus unto Metellus, he went to the temple door where the treasure lay, and finding no keys there, he caused smiths to be sent for and made them break open the locks.¹⁵⁹ Metellus thereupon began again to withstand him, and certain men that stood by praised him in his doing, but Caesar at length, speaking bigly to him, threatened him he would kill him presently if he troubled him any more, and told him furthermore: 'Young man,' quoth he, 'thou knowest it is harder for me to tell it thee than to do it.' That word made Metellus quake for fear, that he got him away roundly,° and ever after that Caesar had all at his commandment for the wars.

[36] From thence he went into Spain to make war with Petreius and Varro, Pompey's lieutenants, first to get their armies and provinces into his hands which they governed, that afterwards he might follow Pompey the better, leaving never an enemy behind him.¹⁶⁰ In this journey, he was oftentimes himself in danger through the ambushes that were laid for him in divers strange sorts° and places, and likely also to have lost all his army for lack of victuals. All this

---

¹⁵⁶ Marg. 'Pompey flyeth into Epirus.'
¹⁵⁷ they were words of course to colour his purpose withal] they were conventional expressions with which to conceal his intention.
¹⁵⁸ Marg. 'Silent leges inter arma' (The laws are mute in the presence of arms), quoted from Cruser, p. 578.   the temple of Saturn] Mentioned by neither P. nor A., so N. must be following Cruser (ibid.), who refers to the temple of Saturn both in the text and in a marginal note (translated by N. below).
¹⁵⁹ Marg. 'Caesar taketh money out of the temple of Saturn.'
¹⁶⁰ Marg. 'Caesar's journey into Spain against Pompey's lieutenants.'   Petreius] P. 'Afranius'; N. follows A.

notwithstanding, he never left following of Pompey's lieutenants, provoking them to battle and entrenching them in until he had gotten their camp and armies into his hands, albeit that the lieutenants themselves fled unto Pompey.

[37] When Caesar returned again to Rome, Piso his father-in-law gave him counsel to send ambassadors unto Pompey to treat for peace.[161] But Isauricus, to flatter Caesar, was against it. Caesar, being then created dictator by the senate, called home again all the banished men, and restored their children to honour whose fathers before had been slain in Sulla's time, and did somewhat cut off the usuries that did oppress them, and besides did make some such other ordinances as those, but very few.[162] For he was dictator but eleven days only, and then did yield it up of himself and made himself consul with Servilius Isauricus, and after that determined to follow the wars.[163] All the rest of his army he left coming on the way behind him, and went himself before with six hundred horse and five legions only of footmen in the winter quarter, about the month of January, which after the Athenians is called Posideon. Then, having passed over the Sea Ionium and landed his men, he won the cities of Oricum and Apollonia.[164] Then he sent his ships back again unto Brundusium to transport the rest of his soldiers, that could not come with that speed he did. They, as they came by the way, like men whose strength of body and lusty youth was decayed, being wearied with so many sundry battles as they had fought with their enemies, complained of Caesar in this sort: 'To what end and purpose doth this man hale° us after him, up and down the world, using us like slaves and drudges? It is not our armour but our bodies that bear the blows away, and, what, shall we never be without our harness on our backs and our shields on our arms? Should not Caesar think at the least when he seeth our blood and wounds that we are all mortal men and that we feel the misery and pains that other men do feel? And now, even in the dead of winter, he putteth us unto the mercy of the sea and tempest, yea, which the gods themselves cannot withstand, as if he fled before his enemies and pursued them not.'[165] Thus, spending time with this talk, the soldiers, still marching on, by small journeys came at length unto the city of Brundusium. But when they were come and found that Caesar had already passed over the sea, then they straight changed their complaints and minds. For they blamed themselves, and took on also with their captains because they had not made them make more haste in marching, and sitting upon the rocks and cliffs of the sea, they looked over the main sea towards the realm of Epirus to see if they could discern the ships returning back to transport them over.

[161] In 49 BCE.
[162] Marg. 'Caesar dictator.'
[163] Marg. 'Caesar and Isauricus consuls.'
[164] Marg. 'Caesar goeth into the kingdom of Epirus.'
[165] Marg. 'Complaints of the old soldiers against Caesar.'

[38] Caesar in the meantime being in the city of Apollonia, having but a small army to fight with Pompey, it grieved him for that the rest of his army was so long a-coming, not knowing what way to take. In the end, he followed a dangerous determination, to embark unknown in a little pinnace° of twelve oars only to pass over the sea again unto Brundusium, the which he could not do without great danger, considering that all that sea was full of Pompey's ships and armies.[166] So he took ship in the night, apparelled like a slave, and went aboard upon this little pinnace and said never a word, as if he had been some poor man of mean condition. The pinnace lay in the mouth of the river of Anius, the which commonly was wont to be very calm and quiet by reason of a little wind that came from the shore, which every morning drove back the waves far into the main sea.[167] But that night, by ill fortune there came a great wind from the sea that overcame the land wind, insomuch as the force and strength of the river fighting against the violence of the rage and waves of the sea, the encounter was marvellous dangerous, the water of the river being driven back and rebounding upward with great noise and danger in turning of the water. Thereupon the master of the pinnace, seeing he could not possibly get out of the mouth of this river, bad the mariners to cast about again and to return against the stream. Caesar, hearing that, straight discovered° himself unto the master of the pinnace, who at the first was amazed when he saw him, but Caesar then, taking him by the hand, said unto him: 'Good fellow, be of good cheer and forwards hardily; fear not, for thou hast Caesar and his fortune with thee.' Then the mariners, forgetting the danger of the storm they were in, laid on load with oars and laboured for life what they could against the wind to get out of the mouth of this river.[168] But at length perceiving they laboured in vain, and that the pinnace took in abundance of water and was ready to sink, Caesar then to his great grief was driven to return back again. Who when he was returned unto his camp, his soldiers came in great companies unto him and were very sorry that he mistrusted he was not able with them alone to overcome his enemies but would put his person in danger to go fetch them that were absent, putting no trust in them that were present.[169]

[39] In the meantime, Antonius arrived and brought with him the rest of his army from Brundusium. Then Caesar, finding himself strong enough, went and offered Pompey battle, who was passingly well lodged for victualing of his camp both by sea and land. Caesar, on the other side, who had no great plenty of victuals at the first, was in a very hard case, insomuch as his men gathered roots and mingled them with milk and ate them. Furthermore, they did make

---

[166] Marg. 'A great adventure of Caesar.'
[167] Marg. 'Anius fl.' (i.e. 'fluvius', river). Modern editions of P. emend to Aous, but A. (and thus N.) follows the manuscripts.
[168] laid on load] struck with repeated blows.
[169] Marg. 'Caesar's dangers and troubles in the realm of Epirus.'

bread of it also, and sometime when they skirmished with the enemies and came alongst° by them that watched and warded, they cast of their bread into their trenches and said that as long as the earth brought forth such fruits they would never leave besieging of Pompey. But Pompey straightly commanded them that they should neither carry those words nor bread into their camp, fearing lest his men's hearts would fail them and that they would be afraid when they should think of their enemies' hardness with whom they had to fight, sith they were weary with no pains, no more than brute beasts. Caesar's men did daily skirmish hard to the trenches of Pompey's camp, in the which Caesar had ever the better, saving once only, at what time his men fled with such fear that all his camp that day was in great hazard to have been cast away.[170] For Pompey came on with his battle upon them, and they were not able to abide it, but were fought with and driven into their camp, and their trenches were filled with dead bodies, which were slain within the very gate and bulwarks of their camp, they were so valiantly pursued. Caesar stood before them that fled to make them to turn head again, but he could not prevail. For when he would have taken the ensigns to have stayed them, the ensign-bearers threw them down on the ground, so that the enemies took two and thirty of them, and Caesar's self also escaped hardly with life. For striking a great big soldier that fled by him, commanding him to stay and turn his face to his enemy, the soldier, being afraid, lift up his sword to strike at Caesar. But one of Caesar's pages, preventing° him, gave him such a blow with his sword that he struck off his shoulder. Caesar that day was brought unto so great extremity that (if Pompey had not either for fear or spiteful fortune left off to follow his victory and retired into his camp, being contented to have driven his enemies into their camp)[171] returning to his camp with his friends, he said unto them: 'The victory this day had been our enemies' if they had had a captain that could have told how to have overcome.'[172] So, when he was come to his lodging, he went to bed, and that night troubled him more than any night that ever he had. For still his mind ran with great sorrow of the foul fault he had committed in leading of his army, of self-will to remain there so long by the sea-side, his enemies being the stronger by sea, considering that he had before him a goodly country, rich and plentiful of all things, and goodly cities of Macedon and Thessaly, and had not the wit to bring the war from thence but to lose his time in a place where he was rather besieged of his enemies for lack of victuals than that he did besiege them by force of arms.[173] Thus, fretting and chafing to see himself so straited°

[170] Marg. 'Caesar's army fled from Pompey.'
[171] (if [...] not ...)] N.'s translation of A.'s 'quand' (when, p. 882), which anticipates the thought of Caesar's statement ('if Pompey had not retreated, he would have won the war') but makes no sense in the context of the rest of the sentence.
[172] Marg. 'Caesar's words of Pompey's victory.'
[173] Marg. 'Caesar troubled in mind after his loss.'

with victuals and to think of his ill luck, he raised his camp, intending to go set upon Scipio, making account° that either he should draw Pompey to battle against his will when he had not the sea at his back to furnish him with plenty of victuals or else that he should easily overcome Scipio, finding him alone, unless he were aided.

[40] This remove of Caesar's camp did much encourage Pompey's army and his captains, who would needs in any case have followed after him, as though he had been overcome and had fled. But for Pompey himself, he would in no respect hazard battle, which was a matter of so great importance.[174] For, finding himself so well provided of all things necessary to tarry time, he thought it better to draw this war out in length by tract of time, the rather to consume this little strength that remained in Caesar's army, of the which the best men were marvellous well-trained and good soldiers and for valiantness at one day's battle were incomparable. But on the other side again, to remove here and there so oft, and to fortify their camp where they came, and to besiege any wall or to keep watch all night in their armour, the most part of them could not do it by reason of their age, being then unable to away with that pains, so that the weakness of their bodies did also take away° the life and courage of their hearts. Furthermore, there fell a pestilent disease among them that came by ill meats hunger drove them to eat, yet was not this the worst. For besides, he had no store of money, neither could tell how to come by victuals, so that it seemed in all likelihood that in very short time he would come to nothing.

[41] For these respects° Pompey would in no case fight, and yet had he but Cato only of his mind in that, who stuck° in it the rather because he would avoid shedding of his countrymen's blood.[175] For when Cato had viewed the dead bodies slain in the camp of his enemies at the last skirmish that was between them, the which were no less than a thousand persons, he covered his face and went away weeping. All other but he contrarily fell out with him and blamed him because he so long refrained from battle,[176] and some pricked him forward and called him Agamemnon and king of kings, saying that he delayed this war in this sort because he would not leave his authority to command them all and that he was glad always to see many captains round about him which came to his lodging to honour him and wait upon him.[177] And Faonius also, a hare-

---

[174] Marg. 'Pompey's determination for the war.'
[175] had he [...] blood] i.e. Cato alone agreed with him on this matter, and that because he wanted to avoid shedding his fellow Romans' blood.
[176] he [...] him [...] him [...] he] Cato, Pompey, Pompey, Pompey.
[177] Marg. 'Pompey called Agamemnon and king of kings.' Agamemnon is the commander-in-chief of the Greek army besieging Troy in Homer's *Iliad*, where he is frequently called 'lord of men', though not 'king of kings'. He nearly brings the Greek campaign to a

brained fellow, franticly counterfeiting the round and plain speech of Cato, made as though he was marvellous angry and said: 'Is it not great pity that we shall not eat this year of Tusculum figs and all for Pompey's ambitious mind to reign alone?'. And Afranius, who not long before was but lately come out of Spain (where, because he had but ill success, he was accused of treason, that for money he had sold his army unto Caesar), he went busily asking why they fought not with that merchant unto whom they said he had sold the province of Spain. So that Pompey with these kind of speeches against his will was driven to follow Caesar to fight with him. Then was Caesar at the first marvellously perplexed and troubled by the way, because he found none that would give him any victuals, being despised of every man for the late loss and overthrow he had received. But after that he had taken the city of Gomphes in Thessaly, he did not only meet with plenty of victuals to relieve his army with, but he strangely also did rid them of their disease.[178] For the soldiers, meeting with plenty of wine, drinking hard and making merry, drove away the infection of the pestilence. For they disposed themselves unto dancing, masking, and playing the Baccherians by the way, insomuch that drinking° drunk they overcame their disease and made their bodies new again.[179]

[42] When they both came into the country of Pharsalia and both camps lay before each other, Pompey returned again to his former determination, and the rather because he had ill signs and tokens of misfortune in his sleep.[180] For he thought in his sleep that when he entered into the theatre, all the Romans received him with great clapping of hands.[181] Whereupon, they that were about him grew to such boldness and security, assuring themselves of victory, that Domitius, Spinther, and Scipio in a bravery contended between themselves for the chief bishopric which Caesar had.[182] Furthermore, there were divers that sent unto Rome to hire the nearest houses unto the marketplace, as being the fittest places for praetors and consuls, making their account already that those

catastrophic end when, after ten years of fighting, he decides to assert his authority by taking the concubine of one of his generals, Achilles.
[178] Marg. 'The city of Gomphes in Thessaly.' Gomphes is Gomphi; N. follows A.'s French version of the name, even in the marginal note taken from Cruser (who has 'Gomphi', p. 580).
[179] playing the Baccherians] Bacchanals (as in P. and A.), i.e. indulging in debauchery.
[180] Marg. 'Pompey's dream in Pharsalia.' The battle took place in 48 BCE.
[181] There is usually thought to be a lacuna here in the Greek text because it does not explain why the dream is an evil omen, as A. notes in a marginal comment not reproduced by N. (p. 883). In *Pompey*, 68 (p. 655), to which A.'s note refers, P. explains that Pompey further dreamed that he decorated the temple of Venus Victrix with spoils, which was a bad sign as Caesar claimed descent from Venus. The apparently favourable character of the dream in the text here prompts N. to start the next sentence with 'Whereupon' rather than with 'But' as in P. and A.
[182] Marg. 'The security of the Pompeians.'

offices could not scape them incontinently after the wars. But besides those, the young gentlemen and Roman knights were marvellous desirous to fight, that were bravely mounted and armed with glistering gilt armours, their horses fat and very finely kept, and themselves goodly young men to the number of seven thousand, where the gentlemen of Caesar's side were but one thousand only. The number of his footmen also were much after the same reckoning. For he had five and forty thousand against two and twenty thousand.[183]

[43] Wherefore Caesar called his soldiers together and told them how Cornificius was at hand, who brought two whole legions, and that he had fifteen ensigns led by Calenus, the which he made to stay about Megara and Athens. Then he asked them if they would tarry for that aid or not, or whether they would rather themselves alone venture battle. The soldiers cried out to him and prayed him not to defer battle but rather to devise some fetch to make the enemy fight as soon as he could. Then, as he sacrificed unto the gods for the purifying of his army, the first beast was no sooner sacrificed but his soothsayer assured him that he should fight within three days. Caesar asked him again if he saw in the sacrifices any lucky sign or token of good luck. The soothsayer answered: 'For that thou shalt answer thyself better than I can do, for the gods do promise us a marvellous great change and alteration of things that are now unto another clean contrary. For if thou beest well now, doest thou think to have worse fortune hereafter?[184] And if thou be ill, assure thyself thou shalt have better.' The night before the battle, as he went about midnight to visit the watch, men saw a great firebrand in the element,° all of alight fire, that came over Caesar's camp and fell down in Pompey's.[185] In the morning also, when they relieved the watch, they heard a false alarm in the enemies' camp, without any apparent cause, which they commonly call a sudden fear that makes men besides themselves.[186] This notwithstanding, Caesar thought not to fight that day but was determined to have raised his camp from thence and to have gone towards the city of Scotusa, [44] and his tents in his camp were already overthrown° when his scouts came in with great speed to bring him news that his enemies were preparing themselves to fight.[187] Then he was very glad, and

---

[183] **Marg.** 'Pompey's army as great again as Caesar's.'
[184] doest [...] hereafter?] An imperative instead of a question in A. and P.
[185] **Marg.** 'A wonder seen in the element before the battle in Pharsalia.'
[186] a false alarm [...] themselves] P. simply has 'a panic confusion among the enemy' (πανικὸν τάραχον [...] παρὰ τοῖς πολεμίοις). A. incorporates a gloss to the recent term *panique*, derived (as its capitalization in A. highlights) from the god Pan, said to be responsible for spreading sudden and groundless fear in the enemy: 'une fausse alarme, sans cause apparente, qu'on appelle communement terreur Panique' (a false alarm, without apparent cause, which is commonly referred to as 'Panic' fear, p. 884). N. paraphrases as the word *panic* was not yet part of the English language.
[187] Scotusa] Scotussa.

after he had made his prayers unto the gods to help him that day, he set his men in battle-ray and divided them into three squadrons, giving the middle battle° unto Domitius Calvinus and the left wing unto Antonius, and placed himself in the right wing, choosing his place to fight in the tenth legion.¹⁸⁸ But seeing that against that his enemies had set all their horsemen, he was half afraid when he saw the great number of them, and so brave besides.¹⁸⁹ Wherefore he closely° made six ensigns to come from the rearward of his battle, whom he had laid as an ambush behind his right wing, having first appointed his soldiers what they should do when the horsemen of the enemies came to give them charge.¹⁹⁰ On the other side, Pompey placed himself in the right wing of his battle, gave the left wing unto Domitius, and the middle battle unto Scipio, his father-in-law.¹⁹¹ Now all the Roman knights (as we have told you before) were placed in the left wing, of purpose to environ Caesar's right wing behind and to give their hottest charge there where the general of their enemies was, making their account that there was no squadron of footmen how thick soever they were that could receive the charge of so great a troop of horsemen, and that at the first onset they should overthrow them all and march upon their bellies.¹⁹² When the trumpets on either side did sound the alarm° to the battle, Pompey commanded his footmen that they should stand still without stirring, to receive the charge of their enemies, until they came to throwing of their darts. Wherefore Caesar afterwards said that Pompey had committed a foul fault, not to consider that the charge which is given running with fury, besides that it giveth the more strength also unto their blows, doth set men's hearts also on fire, for the common hurling of all the soldiers that run together is unto them as a box on the ear that sets men on fire.¹⁹³ Then Caesar, making his battle-march forward to give the onset, saw one of his captains (a valiant man and very skilful in war, in whom he had also great confidence) speaking to his soldiers that he had under his charge, encouraging them to fight like men that day. So he called him aloud by his name and said unto him: 'Well, Caius Crassinius, what hope shall we have today? How are we determined to fight it out manfully?' Then Crassinius, casting up his hand, answered him aloud: 'This day, O Caesar, we shall have a noble victory, and I promise thee ere night thou shalt praise me alive or dead.'¹⁹⁴ When he had told him so, he was himself

[188] Marg. 'Caesar's army and his order of battle in the fields of Pharsalia.'
[189] brave] The French ('en si brave equippage', p. 884) indicates that the predominant meaning is 'splendid'.
[190] had laid] A. 'laid' ('mit', p. 884).
[191] Marg. 'Pompey's army and his order of battle.'
[192] march upon their bellies] N.'s literal translation of A.'s idiomatic 'leur passeroient par dessus le ventre' (to overthrow, p. 884).
[193] Marg. 'An ill counsel and foul fault of Pompey.'   a box on the ear] A. 'soufflet' (p. 884), which can mean a slap but here carries its alternative meaning: 'bellows'.
[194] Marg. 'The battle in the fields of Pharsalia.'

the foremost man that gave charge upon his enemies, with his band following of him being about sixscore men, and making a lane through the foremost ranks, with great slaughter he entered far into the battle of his enemies, until that valiantly fighting in this sort he was thrust in at length in the mouth with a sword, that the point of it came out again at his neck.

[45] Now the footmen of both battles being come to the sword, the horsemen of the left wing of Pompey did march as fiercely also, spreading out their troops to compass in the right wing of Caesar's battle. But before they began to give charge, the six ensigns of footmen which Caesar had laid in ambush behind him, they began to run full upon them, not throwing away their darts far off as they were wont to do, neither striking their enemies on the thighs nor on the legs, but to seek to hit them full in the eyes and to hurt them in the face, as Caesar had taught them.[195] For he hoped that these lusty young gentlemen that had not been often in the wars nor were used to see themselves hurt and the which, being in the prime of their youth and beauty, would be afraid of those hurts, as well for the fear of the present danger to be slain as also for that their faces should not forever be deformed.[196] As indeed it came to pass, for they could never abide that they should come so near their faces with the points of their darts, but hung down their heads for fear to be hit with them in their eyes and turned their backs, covering their face because they should not be hurt. Then, breaking off themselves, they began at length cowardly to fly and were occasion also of the loss of all the rest of Pompey's army. For they that had broken them ran immediately to set upon the squadron of the footmen behind and slew them. Then Pompey, seeing his horsemen from the other wing of his battle so scattered and dispersed flying away, forgot that he was any more Pompey the Great, which he had been before, but rather was like a man whose wits the gods had taken from him, being afraid and amazed with the slaughter sent from above, and so retired into his tent speaking never a word and sat there to see the end of this battle.[197] Until at length all his army being overthrown and put to flight, the enemies came and got up upon the rampires° and defence of his camp and fought hand to hand with them that stood to defend the same. Then, as a man come to himself again, he spoke but this only word: 'What, even into our camp?'. So, in haste casting off his coat-armour° and apparel of a general, he shifted him and put on such as became his miserable fortune, and so

---

[195] Marg. 'Caesar's stratagem.'
[196] The sentence is grammatically incomplete as a result of N.'s decision to turn the verb in the clause 'being in the prime of their youth and beauty' from an indicative ('estoient', i.e. 'were', p. 885) into a present participle ('being'), so that the remainder of the sentence becomes a subordinate instead of a main clause.
[197] Marg. 'Caesar overcometh Pompey.'

stole out of his camp.[198] Furthermore, what he did after this overthrow, and how he had put himself into the hands of the Egyptians, by whom he was miserably slain, we have set it forth at large in his Life.

[46] Then Caesar, entering into Pompey's camp and seeing the bodies laid on the ground that were slain, and others also that were a-killing, said, fetching a great sigh: 'It was their own doing, and against my will.'[199] For Caius Caesar, after he had won so many famous conquests and overcome so many great battles, had been utterly condemned notwithstanding if he had departed from his army.[200] Asinius Pollio writeth that he spoke these words then in Latin, which he afterwards wrote in Greek, and saith furthermore that the most part of them which were put to the sword in the camp were slaves and bondmen and that there were not slain in all at this battle above six thousand soldiers. As for them that were taken prisoners, Caesar did put many of them amongst his legions and did pardon also many men of estimation, among whom Brutus was one, that afterwards slew Caesar himself; and it is reported that Caesar was very sorry for him when he could not immediately be found after the battle and that he rejoiced again when he knew he was alive and that he came to yield himself unto him.[201]

[47] Caesar had many signs and tokens of victory before this battle, but the notablest of all other that happened to him was in the city of Tralles.[202] For, in the temple of victory within the same city, there was an image of Caesar, and the earth all about it very hard of itself and was paved besides with hard stone, and yet some say that there sprang up a palm hard by the base of the same image. In the city of Padua, Caius Cornelius, an excellent soothsayer (a countryman and friend of Titus Livius, the historiographer) was by chance at that time set to behold the flying of birds.[203] He (as Livy reporteth) knew the very time when the battle began, and told them that were present: 'Even now they give the onset on both sides, and both armies do meet at this instant.' Then, sitting down again to consider of the birds, after he had bethought him of the signs, he suddenly rose up on his feet and cried out as a man possessed with some spirit: 'O Caesar, the victory is thine!'. Every man wondering to see him, he took the crown he had on his head and made an oath that he would never put it on again till the event of his prediction had proved his art true. Livy testifieth that it came so to pass.

[198] Marg. 'Pompey's flight.'
[199] a-killing] Should be 'being killed', as in P. and A. ('d'autres qu'on tuoit encore', p. 885).
[200] i.e. Caesar claimed that if he had disbanded his armies, he would have been (unfairly) prosecuted and convicted by his enemies in the courts at Rome.
[201] Marg. 'Brutus, that slew Caesar, taken prisoner at the battle of Pharsalia.'
[202] Marg. 'Signs and tokens of Caesar's victory.'
[203] Marg. 'A strange tale of Cornelius, an excellent prognosticator.'

[48] Caesar afterwards giving freedom unto the Thessalians in respect of the victory which he won in their country, he followed after Pompey. When he came into Asia, he gave freedom also unto the Guidians for Theopompus' sake, who had gathered the fables together.[204] He did release Asia also the third part of the tribute which the inhabitants paid unto the Romans. Then he came into Alexandria, after Pompey was slain, and detested Theodotus, that presented him Pompey's head, and turned his head aside because he would not see it. Notwithstanding, he took his seal and, beholding it, wept. Furthermore, he courteously used all Pompey's friends and familiars, who wandering up and down the country were taken of the king of Egypt, and won them all to be at his commandment.[205] Continuing these courtesies, he wrote unto his friends at Rome that the greatest pleasure he took of his victory was that he daily saved the lives of some of his countrymen that bore arms against him. And for the war he made in Alexandria,[206] some say he needed not have done it, but that he willingly did it for the love of Cleopatra, wherein he won little honour and besides did put his person in great danger.[207] Others do lay the fault upon the king of Egypt's ministers,° but specially on Pothinus the eunuch, who, bearing the greatest sway of all the king's servants, after he had caused Pompey to be slain and driven Cleopatra from the court, secretly laid° wait all the ways he could how he might likewise kill Caesar.[208] Wherefore Caesar, hearing an inkling of it, began thenceforth to spend all the night long in feasting and banqueting, that his person might be in the better safety. But besides all this, Pothinus the eunuch spoke many things openly not to be borne, only to shame Caesar and to stir up the people to envy him. For he made his soldiers have the worst and oldest wheat that could be gotten; then, if they did complain of it, he told them they must be contented, seeing they ate at another man's cost. And he would serve them also at the table in treen° and earthen dishes, saying that Caesar had away all their gold and silver for a debt that the king's father (that then reigned) did owe unto him, which was a thousand seven hundred and fifty myriads,° whereof Caesar had before forgiven seven hundred and fifty thousand unto his children. Howbeit, then he asked a million to pay his soldiers withal. Thereto Pothinus answered him that at that time he should do better to follow his other causes of greater importance and afterwards that he should at more leisure recover his debt with the king's goodwill and favour. Caesar replied unto him and said that he would not ask counsel of the Egyptians for his affairs but would be paid, and thereupon secretly sent for Cleopatra, which was in the country, to come unto him.

[204] Guidians] Gnidians (or Cnidians); 'u' for 'n' is a common misprint, but this is not corrected in the later editions.
[205] Marg. 'Caesar's clemency in victory.'
[206] In Egypt, where Alexandria is located, rather. P. simply has αὐτόθι (right there); N. follows A.
[207] Marg. 'The cause of Caesar's war in Alexandria.'
[208] Marg. 'Pothinus the eunuch caused Pompey to be slain.'

[49] She, only taking Apollodorus Sicilian of all her friends, took a little boat and went away with him in it in the night, and came and landed hard by the foot of the castle.[209] Then, having no other mean to come into the court without being known, she laid herself down upon a mattress or flock-bed, which Apollodorus, her friend, tied and bound up together like a bundle with a great leather thong, and so took her up on his back, and brought her thus hampered in this fardel unto Caesar in at the castle-gate.[210] This was the first occasion (as it is reported) that made Caesar to love her,[211] but afterwards when he saw her sweet conversation° and pleasant entertainment, he fell then in further liking with her, and did reconcile her again unto her brother the king, with condition that they two jointly should reign together. Upon this new reconciliation a great feast being prepared, a slave of Caesar's that was his barber, the fearfulest wretch that lived, still° busily prying and listening abroad in every corner, being mistrustful by nature, found that Pothinus and Achillas did lie in wait to kill his master Caesar. This being proved unto Caesar, he did set such sure watch about the hall where the feast was made that in fine° he slew the eunuch Pothinus himself. Achillas, on the other side, saved himself and fled unto the king's camp, where he raised a marvellous dangerous and difficult war for Caesar, because he having then but a few men about him as he had, he was to fight against a great and strong city. The first danger he fell into was for lack of water he had, for that° his enemies had stopped the mouth of the pipes the which conveyed the water unto the castle. The second danger he had was that seeing his enemies came to take his ships from him, he was driven to repulse that danger with fire, the which burnt the arsenal where the ships lay and that notable library of Alexandria withal.[212] The third danger was in the battle by sea that was fought by the tower of Phar, where meaning to help his men that fought by sea, he leapt from the pier into a boat.[213] Then the Egyptians made towards him with their oars on every side, but he, leaping into the sea, with great hazard saved himself by swimming. It is said that then holding divers books in his hand, he did never let them go, but kept them always upon his head above water and swam with the other hand, notwithstanding that they shot marvellously at him, and was driven sometime to duck into the water; howbeit, the boat was drowned presently.[214] In fine, the king coming to his men that made war with Caesar, he went against him and gave him battle and won it

---

[209] **Marg.** 'Cleopatra came to Caesar.'
[210] **Marg.** 'Cleopatra trussed up in a mattress and so brought to Caesar upon Apollodorus' back.' Cf. Shakespeare, *Antony and Cleopatra*, II. 6. 70–72.
[211] N. omits: 'pource que ceste ruse lui fit appercevoir qu'elle estoit femme de gentil esprit' (because this ruse made him see that she was a woman of noble spirit, p. 887).
[212] **Marg.** 'The great library of Alexandria burnt.'
[213] Phar] i.e. Pharos, an island off Alexandria.
[214] **Marg.** 'Caesar's swimming with books in his hand.'

with great slaughter and effusion of blood. But for the king, no man could ever tell what became of him after. Thereupon Caesar made Cleopatra, his sister, queen of Egypt,[215] who, being great with child by him, was shortly brought to bed of a son, whom the Alexandrians named Caesarion.[216] From thence he went into Syria, [50] and so going into Asia, there it was told him that Domitius was overthrown in battle by Pharnaces, the son of King Mithridates, and was fled out of the realm of Pont with a few men with him and that this King Pharnaces, greedily following his victory, was not contented with the winning of Bithynia and Cappadocia but further would needs attempt to win Armenia the Less, procuring all those kings, princes, and governors of the provinces thereabouts to rebel against the Romans. Thereupon Caesar went thither straight with three legions and fought a great battle with King Pharnaces by the city of Zela, where he slew his army and drove him out of all the realm of Pont.[217] And because he would advertise one of his friends of the suddenness of this victory, he only wrote three words unto Anitius at Rome: 'veni, vidi, vici', to wit, 'I came, I saw, I overcame.'[218] These three words, ending all with like sound and letter in the Latin, have a certain short grace more pleasant to the ear than can be well expressed in any other tongue.

[51] After this, he returned again into Italy and came to Rome, ending his year for the which he was made dictator the second time, which office before was never granted for one whole year but unto him.[219] Then was he chosen consul for the year following. Afterwards he was very ill spoken of, for that his soldiers in a mutiny having slain two praetors, Cosconius and Galba, he gave them no other punishment for it but instead of calling them soldiers he named them citizens, and gave unto every one of them a thousand drachmas a man and great possessions in Italy. He was much misliked also for the desperate parts and madness of Dolabella; for the covetousness of Anitius; for the drunkenness of Antonius and Cornificius, which made Pompey's house be pulled down and built up again as a thing not big enough for him, wherewith the Romans were marvellously offended.[220] Caesar knew all this well enough, and would have been contented to have redressed them, but to bring his matters to pass he

---

[215] Marg. 'Caesar made Cleopatra queen of Egypt.'
[216] Marg. 'Caesarion, Caesar's son, begotten of Cleopatra.'
[217] Marg. 'Caesar's victory of King Pharnaces.' Zela is present-day Zile, in northern Turkey.
[218] Marg. 'Caesar writeth three words to certify his victory.' Anitius] The manuscripts have conflicting and probably incorrect readings; modern editions tend to emend to 'Matius'. N. follows A.
[219] Caesar returned to Italy in 47 BCE.
[220] Cornificius] A.'s emendation of the manuscript reading 'Corfinius'; modern editions tend to omit the name and make what follows apply to Antony too.

pretended, he was driven to serve his turn by such instruments.²²¹

[52] After the battle of Pharsalia, Cato and Scipio being fled into Afric, King Juba joined with them and levied a great puissant army. Wherefore Caesar determined to make war with them, and in the midst of winter he took his journey into Sicily.²²² There, because he would take all hope from his captains and soldiers to make any long abode there, he went and lodged upon the very sands by the sea-side, and with the next gale of wind that came he took the sea with three thousand footmen and a few horsemen. Then, having put them aland,° unwares° to them, he hoised° sail again to go fetch the rest of his army, being afraid lest they should meet with some danger in passing over, and meeting them midway, he brought them all into his camp. Where, when it was told him that his enemies trusted in an ancient oracle which said that it was predestined unto the family of the Scipios to be conquerors in Afric, either of purpose to mock Scipio the general of his enemies or otherwise in good earnest to take the benefit of this name (given by the oracle) unto himself, in all the skirmishes and battles fought he gave the charge of his army unto a man of mean quality and account called Scipio Salutius, who came of the race of Scipio African, and made him always his general when he fought.²²³ For he was eftsoons° compelled to weary and harry his enemies, for that neither his men in his camp had corn enough nor his beasts forage,²²⁴ but the soldiers were driven to take seaweeds called alga and (washing away the brackishness thereof with fresh water, putting° to it a little herb called dog's tooth) to cast it so to their horse to eat.²²⁵ For the Numidians (which are light horsemen and very ready of service), being a great number together, would be on a sudden in every place

---

²²¹ pretended] The meaning must be *intend* (*OED*, pretend, v., †10; cf. line 1823 below), as the French makes clear: 'pour parvenir aux fins où il pretendoit' (p. 888). N.'s translation is ambiguous due to his omission of the relative present in A. ('où'), but the punctuation in early editions of the text (followed here) confirms that it belongs with the preceding clause. Modern editions have tended to put the comma before 'he pretended' and taken the verb with the following clause (in its usual meaning of 'profess'). As Pelling, *Caesar*, 51. 4 n., notes, the phrase translated by N. as 'to bring his matters to pass he pretended' is, in fact, ambiguous in the original Greek (διὰ τὴν ὑπόθεσιν τῆς πολιτείας), and can mean either 'due to the needs of the state' or 'due to the principles on which [Caesar] was basing his own political programme', with A. preferring the latter, more sceptical, interpretation of Caesar's motives.
²²² Marg. 'Caesar's journey into Afric against Cato and Scipio.'
²²³ Salutius] The name is disputed, although the ending should be -o rather than -us. A. Frenchifies the reading of the manuscripts to 'Sallution' (p. 888); Teubner (followed by Pelling, *Caesar*, 52. 5 and n.) emends to 'Salvito'. The single 'l' in the third edition of 1603 is likely to be a misprint, but it may just reflect acquaintance with the text of other ancient historians (Dio and Suetonius), which have 'Salutio' in the manuscripts.
²²⁴ Marg. 'Caesar's troubles in Afric.'
²²⁵ Marg. 'Alga and dog's tooth given to the horse to eat.'

and spread all the fields over thereabout, so that no man durst peep out of the camp to go for forage.²²⁶ And one day, as the men of arms were staying° to behold an African doing notable things in dancing and playing with the flute, they being set down quietly to take their pleasure of the view thereof, having in the meantime given their slaves their horses to hold, the enemies, stealing suddenly upon them, compassed them in round about and slew a number of them in the field and, chasing the other also that fled, followed them pell-mell° into their camp. Furthermore, had not Caesar himself in person, and Asinius Pollio with him, gone out of the camp to the rescue and stayed them that fled, the war that day had been ended. There was also another skirmish where his enemies had the upper hand, in the which it is reported that Caesar, taking the ensign-bearer by the collar that carried the eagle in his hand, stayed him by force and, turning his face, told him: 'See, there be thy enemies.'

[53] These advantages did lift up Scipio's heart aloft and gave him courage to hazard battle, and leaving Afranius on the one hand of him and King Juba on the other hand, both their camps lying near to other,° he did fortify himself by the city of Thapsacus, above the lake, to be a safe refuge for them all in this battle. But whilst he was busy entrenching of himself, Caesar having marvellous speedily passed through a great country full of wood by bypaths which men would never have mistrusted,° he stole upon some behind and suddenly assailed the other before, so that he overthrew them all and made them fly. Then, following this first good hap he had, he went forthwith to set upon the camp of Afranius, the which he took at the first onset, and the camp of the Numidians also, King Juba being fled. Thus, in a little piece of the day only, he took three camps and slew fifty thousand of his enemies, and lost but fifty of his soldiers.²²⁷ In this sort is set down the effect° of this battle by some writers. Yet others do write also that Caesar self was not there in person at the execution of this battle. For as he did set his men in battle-ray, the falling sickness took him, whereunto he was given, and therefore feeling it coming, before he was overcome withal, he was carried into a castle not far from thence where the battle was fought and there took his rest till the extremity of his disease had left him.²²⁸ Now, for the praetors and consuls that scaped° from this battle, many of them being taken prisoners did kill themselves, and others also Caesar did put to death, [54] but he being specially desirous of all men else to have Cato alive in his hands, he went with all possible speed unto the city of Utica, whereof Cato was governor, by means whereof he was not at the battle. Notwithstanding, being certified by the way that Cato had slain himself with his own hands,

---

²²⁶ Marg. 'Caesar's dangers in Afric.'
²²⁷ Marg. 'Caesar's great victory and small loss.'
²²⁸ Marg. 'Caesar troubled with the falling sickness.'

he then made open show that he was very sorry for it, but why or wherefore no man could tell.²²⁹ But this is true, that Caesar said at that present time: 'O Cato, I envy thy death because thou didst envy° my glory to save thy life.' This notwithstanding, the book that he wrote afterwards against Cato, being dead, did show no very great affection nor pitiful heart towards him.²³⁰ For how could he have pardoned him if, living, he had had him in his hands that, being dead, did speak so vehemently against him? Notwithstanding, men suppose he would have pardoned him if he had taken him alive by the clemency he showed unto Cicero, Brutus, and divers others that had borne arms against him. Some report that he wrote that book not so much for any private malice he had to his death as for civil ambition, upon this occasion. Cicero had written a book in praise of Cato, which he intituled *Cato*.²³¹ This book in likelihood was very well liked of by reason of the eloquence of the orator that made it and of the excellent subject thereof. Caesar therewith was marvellously offended, thinking that to praise him of whose death he was author was even as much as to accuse himself, and therefore he wrote a letter against him, and heaped up a number of accusations against Cato, and intituled the book *Anti-Caton*.²³² Both these books have favourers unto this day, some defending the one for the love they bore to Caesar and others allowing° the other for Cato's sake.

[55] Caesar, being now returned out of Afric, first of all made an oration to the people, wherein he greatly praised and commended this his last victory, declaring unto them that he had conquered so many countries unto the empire of Rome that he could furnish the commonwealth yearly with two hundred thousand bushels of wheat and twenty hundred thousand pound weight of oil.²³³ Then he made three triumphs: the one for Egypt; the other for the kingdom of Pont; and the third for Afric, not because he had overcome Scipio there but King Juba. Whose son, being likewise called Juba, being then a young boy, was led captive in the show of this triumph. But this his imprisonment fell out happily for him, for where he was but a barbarous Numidian, by the study he fell unto when he was prisoner he came afterwards to be reckoned one of the wisest historiographers of the Grecians.²³⁴ After these three triumphs ended, he very liberally rewarded his soldiers, and to curry favour with the people he made great feasts and common sports. For he feasted all the Romans at one time at two and twenty thousand tables and gave them the pleasure to see divers

²²⁹ Marg. 'Caesar was sorry for the death of Cato.'
²³⁰ Marg. 'Caesar wrote against Cato, being dead.'
²³¹ Marg. 'Cicero wrote a book in praise of Cato, being dead.'
²³² In his translation of *Cicero* (lines 1217–18), North anglicizes to *Anti-Cato*, but Ἀντικάτων is the Greek as well as the French form.
²³³ In 46 BCE.
²³⁴ Marg. 'Juba, the son of King Juba, a famous historiographer.'

sword players to fight at the sharp and battles also by sea, for the remembrance of his daughter Julia, which was dead long before.[235] Then, after all these sports, he made the people (as the manner was) to be mustered, and where there were at the last musters before three hundred and twenty thousand citizens, at this muster only there were but a hundred and fifty thousand.[236] Such misery and destruction had this civil war brought unto the commonwealth of Rome and had consumed such a number of Romans, not speaking at all of the mischiefs and calamities it had brought unto all the rest of Italy and to the other provinces pertaining to Rome.

[56] After all these things were ended, he was chosen consul the fourth time and went into Spain to make war with the sons of Pompey, who were yet but very young but had notwithstanding raised a marvellous great army together and showed to have had manhood and courage worthy to command such an army, insomuch as they put Caesar himself in great danger of his life.[237] The greatest battle that was fought between them in all this war was by the city of Munda.[238] For then, Caesar seeing his men sorely distressed and having their hands full of their enemies, he ran into the press° among his men that fought and cried out unto them: 'What, are ye not ashamed to be beaten and taken prisoners, yielding yourselves with your own hands to these young boys?'.[239] And so, with all the force he could make, having with much ado put his enemies to flight, he slew above thirty thousand of them in the field and lost of his own men a thousand of the best he had.[240] After this battle, he went into his tent and told his friends that he had often before fought for victory, but this last time now that he had fought for the safety of his own life. He won this battle on the very feast-day of the Bacchanalians, in the which men say that Pompey the Great went out of Rome about four years before to begin this civil war.[241] For his sons, the younger scaped from the battle, but within few days after Diddius brought the head of the elder.[242] This was the last war that Caesar made. But the triumph he made into Rome for the same did as much offend the Romans, and more, than anything that ever he had done before, because he had not overcome captains that were strangers nor barbarous kings, but had destroyed the sons

---

[235] Marg. 'Caesar's feasting of the Romans.'
[236] Marg. 'The muster taken of the Romans.'
[237] Marg. 'Caesar consul the fourth time.'
[238] Marg. 'Battle fought betwixt Caesar and the young Pompeys by the city of Munda.' In 45 BCE, near Córdoba in southern Spain.
[239] The point of Caesar's rebuke in P. and A. is that the soldiers are handing him (not themselves) over by fighting in a cowardly manner.
[240] Marg. 'Caesar's victory of the sons of Pompey.'
[241] Bacchanalians] i.e. Bacchanals.
[242] Diddius] Didius (as in P. and A.).

of the noblest man in Rome, whom fortune had overthrown.²⁴³ And because he had plucked up his race by the roots, men did not think it meet for him to triumph so for the calamities of his country, rejoicing at a thing for the which he had but one excuse to allege in his defence unto the gods and men, that he was compelled to do that he did.²⁴⁴ And the rather they thought it not meet because he had never before sent letters nor messengers unto the commonwealth at Rome for any victory that he had ever won in all the civil wars but did always for shame refuse the glory of it.

[57] This notwithstanding, the Romans inclining to Caesar's prosperity and taking the bit in the mouth,²⁴⁵ supposing that to be ruled by one man alone, it would be a good mean for them to take breath a little after so many troubles and miseries as they had abidden in these civil wars, they chose him perpetual dictator.²⁴⁶ This was a plain tyranny, for to this absolute power of dictator they added this, never to be afraid to be deposed. Cicero propounded before the senate that they should give him such honours as were meet for a man, howbeit others afterwards added too honours beyond all reason. For men striving who should most honour him, they made him hateful and troublesome to themselves that most favoured him, by reason of the unmeasurable greatness and honours which they gave him. Thereupon, it is reported that even they that most hated him were no less favourers and furtherers of his honours than they that most flattered him, because they might have greater occasions to rise, and that it might appear they had just cause and colour to attempt that they did against him. And now for himself, after he had ended his civil wars, he did so honourably behave himself that there was no fault to be found in him, and therefore methinks amongst other honours they gave him he rightly deserved this, that they should build him a temple of clemency to thank him for his courtesy he had used unto them in his victory.²⁴⁷ For he pardoned many of them that had borne arms against him and, furthermore, did prefer some of them to honour and office in the commonwealth, as, amongst others, Cassius and Brutus, both the which were made praetors.²⁴⁸ And where Pompey's images had been thrown down, he caused them to be set up again, whereupon Cicero said then that Caesar setting up Pompey's images again, he made his own to stand the surer. And when some of his friends did counsel him to have a guard for the safety of his person, and some also did offer themselves to serve him, he would never consent to it, but said it was better to die once than always to

---

²⁴³ Marg. 'Caesar's triumph of Pompey's sons.'
²⁴⁴ Cf. Shakespeare, *Julius Caesar*, I. 1. 30–51.
²⁴⁵ i.e. accepting the yoke.
²⁴⁶ Marg. 'Caesar dictator perpetual.' In 44 BCE.
²⁴⁷ Marg. 'The temple of clemency dedicated unto Caesar for his courtesy.'
²⁴⁸ Marg. 'Cassius and Brutus praetors.'

be afraid of death.²⁴⁹ But to win himself the love and goodwill of the people, as the honourablest guard and best safety he could have, he made common feasts again and general distributions of corn.²⁵⁰ Furthermore, to gratify the soldiers also, he replenished many cities again with inhabitants which before had been destroyed and placed them there that had no place to repair unto, of the which the noblest and chiefest cities were these two, Carthage and Corinth, and it chanced also that like as aforetime they had been both taken and destroyed together, even so were they both set afoot again and replenished with people at one self° time.

[58] And as for great personages, he won them also, promising some of them to make them praetors and consuls in time to come, and unto others honours and preferments, but to all men generally good hope, seeking all the ways he could to make every man contented with his reign. Insomuch as one of the consuls, called Maximus, chancing to die a day before his consulship ended, he declared Caninius Rebilius consul only for the day that remained.²⁵¹ So, divers going to his house (as the manner was) to salute him and to congratulate with him of his calling° and preferment, being newly chosen officer, Cicero pleasantly said: 'Come, let us make haste and be gone thither before his consulship come out.°' Furthermore, Caesar being born to attempt all great enterprises and having an ambitious desire besides to covet great honours, the prosperous good success he had of his former conquests bred no desire in him quietly to enjoy the fruits of his labours but rather gave him the hope of things to come, still kindling more and more in him thoughts of greater enterprises and desire of new glory, as if that which he had present were stale and nothing worth. This humour of his was no other but an emulation with himself as with another man and a certain contention to overcome° the things he prepared to attempt.²⁵² For he was determined and made preparation also to make war with the Persians.²⁵³ Then, when he had overcome them, to pass through Hyrcania (compassing in the Sea Caspium and Mount Caucasus) into the realm of Pontus and so to invade Scythia, and overrunning all the countries and people adjoining unto high Germany and Germany itself, at length to return by Gaul into Italy, and so to enlarge the Roman Empire round that it might be every way compassed

---

²⁴⁹ Marg. 'Caesar's saying of death.' Cf. Shakespeare, *Julius Caesar*, II. 2. 32–33.
²⁵⁰ Marg. 'Goodwill of subjects, the best guard and safety for princes.'
²⁵¹ Marg. 'Caninius Rebilius, consul for one day.' Rebilius] Rebilus.
²⁵² a certain contention to overcome the things he prepared to attempt] P. 'a sort of rivalry between what he had done and what he purposed to do'; A. adds substantial rhetorical amplification but retains the same basic meaning ('une obstination de se vouloir tousjours vaincre soi-mesme, combatant tousjours en lui l'esperance de l'advenir avec la gloire du passé, et l'ambition de ce qu'il desiroit faire avec ce qu'il avoit desja fait', p. 891), which is however lost in N.'s translation.
²⁵³ Persians] P. and A. 'Parthians'.

in with the great sea Oceanum.²⁵⁴ But whilst he was preparing for this voyage, he attempted to cut the bar of the strait of Peloponnesus in the place where the city of Corinth standeth. Then, he was minded to bring the rivers of Anienes and Tiber straight from Rome unto the city of Circees with a deep channel and high banks cast up on either side, and so to fall into the sea at Terracina, for the better safety and commodity of the merchants that came to Rome to traffic there.²⁵⁵ Furthermore, he determined to drain and sew° all the water of the marishes betwixt the cities of Nomentum and Setium to make it firm land for the benefit of many thousands of people, and on the sea coast next unto Rome to cast great high banks, and to cleanse all the haven about Ostia of rocks and stones hidden under the water and to take away all other impediments that made the harbour dangerous for ships, and to make new havens and arsenals meet to harbour such ships as did continually traffic thither.²⁵⁶ All these things were purposed to be done, but took no effect.

[59] But the ordinance° of the calendar and reformation of the year to take away all confusion of time, being exactly calculated by the mathematicians and brought to perfection, was a great commodity unto all men.²⁵⁷ For the Romans, using then the ancient computation of the year,²⁵⁸ had not only such

---

²⁵⁴ Sea Caspium] i.e. the Caspian Sea.
²⁵⁵ **Marg.** 'Anienes. Tiber. flu.' (i.e. 'fluvii', rivers).   the rivers of Anienes and Tiber] The Greek text is corrupt. A. has 'des rivieres de Teveron et du Tibre' (p. 891), but N. follows Cruser: 'Hinc Anienem in animo habebat Tiberimque statim ab urbe alta exceptos fossa atque ad Circeum deflexos in mare ad Tarracinam deducere' (After this, he had in mind to draw a deep canal out of the Anienes and the Tiber immediately below the city and divert them to Circeum before leading them into the sea by Tarracina, p. 584; possibly recalling Livy, *Ab urbe condita*, XXVI. 10, which refers to Hannibal crossing 'Anienem fluvium'). Modern editions take Anienus to be a person, and relate him to the previous clause: 'During this expedition, moreover, he [Caesar] intended to dig through the isthmus of Corinth, and had already put Anienus in charge of this work; he intended also to divert the Tiber just below the city into a deep channel, give it a bend towards Circeium, and make it empty into the sea at Terracina'.
²⁵⁶ Nomentum] Modern editions emend to 'Pomentinum', but N. translates A., who follows the manuscripts.
²⁵⁷ **Marg.** 'Caesar reformed the inequality of the year.' N. appears to have struggled with, or lacked interest in, the scientific subject matter of this paragraph, of which his translation is unusually loose; the most significant deviations from his source are noted below. It appears that N. relied on Cruser in a number of places here. His 'calculated by the mathematicians' may pick up on Cruser's formulation 'ratione mathematica' (by means of mathematical calculation, p. 584); in P. and A. ('par lui', p. 892), it is Caesar who studied and reformed the calendar. The unexpected use of 'ordinance' earlier in the sentence appears to echo Cruser's 'ordinatio' (A. has 'composition'), just as the expression 'Annus Solaris' may derive from the reference to the circular motion of the sun ('anfractus [...] solaris') in Cruser, and the phrase 'mensis intercalaris' that N. added to Cruser's marginal note (below) is probably taken from his main text (ibid.).
²⁵⁸ using then the ancient computation of the year] P. and A. 'in very ancient times' ('dans

The Life of Julius Caesar

incertainty° and alteration of the month and times that the sacrifices and yearly feasts came by little and little to seasons contrary for the purpose they were ordained, but also in the revolution of the sun (which is called Annus Solaris) no other nation agreed with them in account, and of the Romans themselves only the priests understood it.[259] And therefore when they listed, they suddenly (no man being able to control them) did thrust in a month above their ordinary number, which they called in old time Mercedonius.[260] Some say that Numa Pompilius was the first that devised this way to put a month between, but it was a weak remedy and did little help the correction of the errors that were made in the account of the year, to frame them to perfection. But Caesar, committing this matter unto the philosophers and best expert mathematicians at that time, did set forth an excellent and perfect calendar, more exactly calculated than any other that was before, the which the Romans do use until this present day and do nothing err as others in the difference of time.[261] But his enemies, notwithstanding, that envied his greatness, did not stick to find fault withal. As Cicero the orator, when one said 'Tomorrow the star Lyra will rise', 'Yea,' said he, 'at the commandment of Caesar', as if men were compelled so to say and think by Caesar's edict.

[60] But the chiefest cause that made him mortally hated was the covetous desire he had to be called king, which first gave the people just cause and next his secret enemies honest colour to bear him ill will.[262] This notwithstanding, they that procured° him this honour and dignity gave it out among the people that it was written in the Sibylline prophecies how the Romans might overcome the Parthians if they made war with them and were led by a king, but otherwise that they were unconquerable. And furthermore they were so bold besides that Caesar returning to Rome from the city of Alba, when they came to salute him, they called him king. But the people being offended, and Caesar also angry, he said he was not called king, but Caesar. Then every man keeping silence, he went his way heavy and sorrowful. When they had decreed divers honours

---

les plus anciens temps', p. 892).

[259] but [...] account] P. and A. 'but also at this time people generally had no way of computing the actual solar year' ('mais encore lors le peuple ne scavoit en façon quelconque, combien montoit le cours de la revolution du Soleil', p. 892).

[260] **Marg.** '* Mercedonius, mensis intercalaris' (intercalary month, i.e. additional month to make up for the fact that the Roman calendar was ahead of the solar year.)

[261] in the difference of time] A. 'en la reduction de ceste inegalité des mois aux ans' (in the reduction of this disparity between months and years, p. 892). Caesar lengthened the year to 365 days (a lunar year, i.e. twelve lunar months, is about 354 days) and corrected for the fact that this is just short of a solar year (i.e. the time it takes the earth to orbit the sun) through the insertion of a leap year every fourth year, in order that the seasons remained in sync from year to year.

[262] **Marg.** 'Why Caesar was hated.'

for him in the senate, the consuls and praetors, accompanied with the whole assembly of the senate, went unto him in the marketplace, where he was set° by the pulpit for orations, to tell him what honours they had decreed for him in his absence.²⁶³ But he, sitting still in his majesty, disdaining to rise up unto them when they came in, as if they had been private men, answered them that his honours had more need to be cut off than enlarged. This did not only offend the senate, but the common people also, to see that he should so lightly esteem of the magistrates of the commonwealth, insomuch as every man that might lawfully go his way departed thence very sorrowfully. Thereupon also Caesar rising departed home to his house, and tearing open his doublet collar, making his neck bare, he cried out aloud to his friends that his throat was ready to offer to any man that would come and cut it.²⁶⁴ Notwithstanding, it is reported that afterwards to excuse this folly he imputed it to his disease, saying that their wits are not perfect which have this disease of the falling evil, when standing on their feet they speak to the common people, but are soon troubled with a trembling of their body and a sudden dimness and giddiness.²⁶⁵ But that was not true. For he would have risen up to the senate, but Cornelius Balbus, one of his friends (or rather a flatterer), would not let him, saying: 'What, do you not remember that you are Caesar, and will you not let them reverence you and do their duties?'.²⁶⁶

[61] Besides these occasions and offences, there followed also his shame and reproach abusing the tribunes of the people in this sort. At that time, the feast Lupercalia was celebrated, the which in old time men say was the feast of shepherds or herdmen, and is much like unto the feast of the Lycaeians in Arcadia.²⁶⁷ But howsoever it is, that day there are divers noblemen's sons, young men (and some of them magistrates themselves that govern then), which run naked through the city, striking in sport them they meet in their way with leather thongs, hair and all on, to make them give place. And many noblewomen, and gentlewomen also, go of purpose to stand in their way and do put forth their hands to be stricken, as scholars hold them out to their schoolmaster to be stricken with the ferula,° persuading themselves that, being with child, they shall have good delivery and also, being barren, that it will make

---

²⁶³ When they had decreed divers honours for him in the senate] P. describes these honours as ὑπερφυεῖς (extravagant), which A. translates as 'transcendans toute hautesse humaine' (exceeding all human greatness, p. 892).
²⁶⁴ rising] A. (following P.) has 's'en appercevant' (realising [his mistake], p. 893).
²⁶⁵ Cf. Shakespeare, *Julius Caesar*, I. 2. 251–71.
²⁶⁶ P. devoted a whole essay to 'Friends and Flatterers' in the *Moralia*.
²⁶⁷ **Marg.** 'The feast Lupercalia.'   the feast of the Lycaeians] The feast of Lycaea, a religious festival in honour of Zeus.

them to conceive with child.²⁶⁸ Caesar sat to behold that sport upon the pulpit for orations in a chair of gold, apparelled in triumphant manner. Antonius, who was consul at that time, was one of them that ran this holy course.²⁶⁹ So when he came into the marketplace, the people made a lane for him to run at liberty, and he came to Caesar and presented him a diadem wreathed about with laurel.²⁷⁰ Whereupon, there rose a certain cry of rejoicing, not very great, done only by a few appointed for the purpose. But when Caesar refused the diadem, then all the people together made an outcry of joy. Then, Antonius offering it him again, there was a second shout of joy, but yet of a few. But when Caesar refused it again the second time, then all the whole people shouted. Caesar, having made this proof, found that the people did not like of it and thereupon rose out of his chair and commanded the crown to be carried unto Jupiter in the Capitol.²⁷¹ After that, there were set up images of Caesar in the city with diadems upon their heads like kings. Those the two tribunes, Flavius and Marullus, went and pulled down, and furthermore meeting with them that first saluted Caesar as king, they committed them to prison.²⁷² The people followed them, rejoicing at it, and called them 'Brutes' because of Brutus, who had in old time driven the kings out of Rome, and that brought the kingdom of one person unto the government of the senate and people.²⁷³ Caesar was so offended withal that he deprived Marullus and Flavius of their tribuneships, and accusing them, he spoke also against the people and called them 'Bruti' and 'Cumani', to wit, beasts and fools.²⁷⁴

[62] Hereupon the people went straight unto Marcus Brutus, who from his father came of the first Brutus and by his mother of the house of the Servilians, a noble house as any was in Rome, and was also nephew and son-in-law of Marcus Cato. Notwithstanding, the great honours and favour Caesar showed unto him kept him back, that of himself alone he did not conspire nor consent to depose him of his kingdom.²⁷⁵ For Caesar did not only save his life after the battle of Pharsalia when Pompey fled, and did at his request also save many moᵒ of his friends besides, but furthermore he put a marvellous confidence in him.²⁷⁶ For he had already preferred him to the praetorship for that year,

---

²⁶⁸ Cf. Shakespeare, *Julius Caesar*, I. 2. 5–11.
²⁶⁹ **Marg.** 'Antonius, being consul, was one of the Lupercalians.'
²⁷⁰ **Marg.** 'Antonius presented the diadem to Caesar.'
²⁷¹ Cf. Shakespeare, *Julius Caesar*, I. 2. 236–48.
²⁷² Cf. Shakespeare, *Julius Caesar*, I. 1. 64–69.
²⁷³ Brutes] i.e. Brutuses or Bruti, the Latin form used below; 'Brutes' is A.'s French form (p. 893).
²⁷⁴ Cumani] Cumaeans. Cf. Shakespeare, *Julius Caesar*, I. 2. 285–86.
²⁷⁵ kingdom] In the obsolete sense of 'supreme rule', although N.'s word choice (translating A. 'Monarchie' (p. 894), i.e. sole rule) is confusing in the context.
²⁷⁶ **Marg.** 'Caesar saved Marcus Brutus' life after the battle of Pharsalia.'

and furthermore was appointed to be consul the fourth year after that, having through Caesar's friendship obtained it before Cassius, who likewise made suit for the same, and Caesar also, as it is reported, said in this contention: 'Indeed Cassius hath alleged best reason, but yet shall he not be chosen before Brutus.' Some one day accusing Brutus while he practised this conspiracy, Caesar would not hear of it but, clapping his hand on his body, told them 'Brutus will look for this skin', meaning thereby that Brutus, for his virtue, deserved to rule after him but yet that, for ambition's sake, he would not show himself unthankful or dishonourable.[277] Now, they that desired change and wished Brutus only their prince and governor above all other, they durst not come to him themselves to tell him what they would have him to do, but in the night did cast sundry papers into the praetor's seat where he gave audience, and the most of them to this effect: 'Thou sleepest, Brutus, and art not Brutus indeed.'[278] Cassius, finding Brutus' ambition stirred up the more by these seditious bills,° did prick him forward and egg him on the more for a private quarrel he had conceived against Caesar, the circumstance whereof we have set down more at large in Brutus' Life.[279] Caesar also had Cassius in great jealousy° and suspected him much, whereupon he said on a time to his friends: 'What will Cassius do, think ye? I like not his pale looks.' Another time, when Caesar's friends complained unto him of Antonius and Dolabella, that they pretended° some mischief towards him, he answered them again: 'As for those fat men and smooth combed heads,' quoth he, 'I never reckon of them, but these pale-visaged and carrion-lean people, I fear them most', meaning Brutus and Cassius.[280]

[63] Certainly, destiny may easier be foreseen than avoided, considering the strange and wonderful signs that were said to be seen before Caesar's death.[281] For, touching the fires in the element° and spirits running up and down in the night and also the solitary birds to be seen at noondays° sitting in the great marketplace, are not all these signs perhaps worth the noting in such a wonderful chance as happened?[282] But Strabo the philosopher writeth that divers men were seen going up and down in fire and, furthermore, that there was a slave of the soldiers that did cast a marvellous burning flame out of his hand, insomuch as they that saw it thought he had been burnt, but when the fire

---

[277] In P. and A., Caesar says that Brutus will 'wait for' his skin ('Brutus attendra ceste peau', p. 894), i.e. until he had died of natural causes.   **Marg.** 'Brutus conspireth against Caesar.'
[278] Cf. Shakespeare, *Julius Caesar*, I. 2. 315–20; I. 3. 142–44; II. 1. 46–48.
[279] *Brutus*, 8.   **Marg.** 'Cassius stirreth up Brutus against Caesar.'
[280] Cf. Shakespeare, *Julius Caesar*, I. 2. 193–202.
[281] **Marg.** 'Predictions and foreshows of Caesar's death.'
[282] Cf. Shakespeare, *Julius Caesar*, I. 3. 9–32, 62–71; II. 2. 24–27.

was out, it was found he had no hurt.²⁸³ Caesar self also, doing sacrifice unto the gods, found that one of the beasts which was sacrificed had no heart, and that was a strange thing in nature, how a beast could live without a heart.²⁸⁴ Furthermore, there was a certain soothsayer that had given Caesar warning long time afore to take heed of the day of the Ides of March (which is the fifteenth of the month), for on that day he should be in great danger.²⁸⁵ That day being come, Caesar, going unto the senate-house and speaking merrily unto the soothsayer, told him: 'The Ides of March be come.' 'So they be,' softly answered the Soothsayer, 'but yet are they not past.'²⁸⁶ And the very day before, Caesar, supping with Marcus Lepidus, sealed certain letters, as he was wont to do at the board; so talk falling out amongst them reasoning what death was best, he, preventing° their opinions, cried out aloud: 'Death unlooked for.' Then, going to bed the same night as his manner was and lying with his wife Calpurnia, all the windows and doors of his chamber° flying open, the noise awoke him and made him afraid when he saw such light,²⁸⁷ but more when he heard his wife Calpurnia, being fast asleep, weep and sigh and put forth many fumbling lamentable speeches. For she dreamed that Caesar was slain and that she had him in her arms.²⁸⁸ Others also do deny that she had any such dream, as amongst other Titus Livius writeth that it was in this sort. The senate having set upon the top of Caesar's house for an ornament and setting forth of the same a certain pinnacle, Calpurnia dreamed that she saw it broken down and that she thought she lamented and wept for it. Insomuch that Caesar rising in the morning, she prayed him if it were possible not to go out of the doors that day, but to adjourn the session of the senate until another day. And if that he made no reckoning of her dream, yet that he would search further of the soothsayers by their sacrifices to know what should happen him that day. Thereby it seemed that Caesar likewise did fear and suspect somewhat, because his wife Calpurnia until that time was never given to any fear or superstition, and that then he saw her so troubled in mind with this dream she had. But much more afterwards, when the soothsayers, having sacrificed many beasts one after another, told him that none did like° them; then he determined to send Antonius to adjourn the session of the senate.²⁸⁹

[64] But in the meantime came Decius Brutus, surnamed Albinus, in whom Caesar put such confidence that in his last will and testament he had appointed

---

283 Cf. Shakespeare, *Julius Caesar*, I. 3. 15–25.
284 Cf. Shakespeare, *Julius Caesar*, II. 2. 37–40.
285 Marg. 'Caesar's day of his death prognosticated by a soothsayer.' In 44 BCE.
286 Cf. Shakespeare, *Julius Caesar*, I. 2. 20–25; III. 1. 1–2.
287 From the moon, as P. and A. explain.
288 Marg. 'The dream of Calpurnia, Caesar's wife.'
289 Cf. Shakespeare, *Julius Caesar*, II. 2. 1–56, 75–82.

him to be his next heir and yet was of the conspiracy with Cassius and Brutus;²⁹⁰ he, fearing that if Caesar did adjourn the session that day the conspiracy would be betrayed, laughed at the soothsayers and reproved Caesar, saying that he gave the senate occasion to mislike with him and that they might think he mocked them, considering that by his commandment they were assembled, and that they were ready willingly to grant him all things and to proclaim him king of all the provinces of the Empire of Rome out of Italy, and that he should wear his diadem in all other places, both by sea and land.²⁹¹ And, furthermore, that if any man should tell them from him they should depart for that present time and return again when Calpurnia should have better dreams, what would his enemies and ill-willers say, and how could they like of his friends' words?²⁹² And who could persuade them otherwise, but that they would think his dominion a slavery unto them and tyrannical in himself? 'And yet, if it be so', said he, 'that you utterly mislike of this day, it is better that you go yourself in person, and saluting the senate to dismiss them till another time.' Therewithal, he took Caesar by the hand and brought him out of his house.²⁹³ Caesar was not gone far from his house, but a bondman, a stranger, did what he could to speak with him, and when he saw he was put back by the great press and multitude of people that followed him, he went straight into his house and put himself into Calpurnia's hands to be kept till Caesar came back again, telling her that he had greater matters to impart unto him.²⁹⁴

[65] And one Artemidorus also, born in the Isle of Gnidos, a doctor of rhetoric in the Greek tongue, who by means of his profession was very familiar with certain of Brutus' confederates and therefore knew the most part of all their practices against Caesar, came and brought him a little bill written with his own hand of all that he meant to tell him. He, marking how Caesar received all the supplications that were offered him and that he gave them straight to his men that were about him, pressed nearer to him and said: 'Caesar, read this memorial to yourself, and that quickly, for they be matters of great weight and touch you nearly.'° Caesar took it off him but could never read it, though he many times attempted it, for the number of people that did salute him, but, holding it still in his hand, keeping it to himself, went on withal into the senate-house.²⁹⁵ Howbeit, other are of opinion that it was some man else that gave him

---

²⁹⁰ Decius] Decimus. See Introduction, pp. 57–58.   next heir] P. and A. 'second heir' ('son second heritier', p. 895), i.e. he would inherit only if the first heirs renounced their share (see Pelling, *Caesar*, 64. 1 n.).
²⁹¹ Marg. 'Decius Brutus Albinus' persuasion to Caesar.'
²⁹² Cf. Shakespeare, *Julius Caesar*, I. 3. 84–87; II. 1. 202–10; II. 2. 57–59, 92–101.
²⁹³ Marg. 'Decius Brutus brought Caesar into the senate-house.'
²⁹⁴ Marg. 'The tokens of the conspiracy against Caesar.'
²⁹⁵ Cf. Shakespeare, *Julius Caesar*, II. 3; III. 1. 3–9.

that memorial, and not Artemidorus, who did what he could all the way as he went to give it Caesar, but he was always repulsed by the people.

[66] For these things, they may seem to come by chance, but the place where the murder was prepared, and where the senate were assembled, and where also there stood up an image of Pompey, dedicated by himself amongst other ornaments which he gave unto the theatre — all these were manifest proofs that it was the ordinance of some god that made this treason to be executed specially in that very place.[296] It is also reported that Cassius (though otherwise he did favour the doctrine of Epicurus) beholding the image of Pompey before they entered into the action of their traitorous enterprise, he did softly call upon it to aid him.[297] But the instant danger of the present time, taking away his former reason, did suddenly put him into a furious passion and made him like a man half besides himself. Now Antonius, that was a faithful friend to Caesar and a valiant man besides of his hands, him Decius Brutus Albinus entertained out of the senate-house, having begun a long tale of set purpose.[298] So Caesar coming into the house, all the senate stood up on their feet to do him honour. Then, part of Brutus' company and confederates stood round about Caesar's chair, and part of them also came towards him, as though they made suit with Metellus Cimber to call home his brother again from banishment, and thus prosecuting still their suit, they followed Caesar till he was set in his chair.[299] Who, denying their petitions and being offended with them one after another, because the more they were denied, the more they pressed upon him and were the earnester with him, Metellus at length, taking his gown with both his hands, pulled it over his neck, which was the sign given the confederates to set upon him.[300] Then Casca behind him struck him in the neck with his sword.[301] Howbeit, the wound was not great nor mortal, because, it seemed, the fear of such a devilish attempt did amaze° him and take his strength from him, that he killed him not at the first blow.[302] But Caesar, turning straight unto him, caught hold of his sword and held it hard, and they both cried out: Caesar, in Latin, 'O vile traitor Casca, what doest thou?', and Casca, in Greek, to his brother, 'Brother,

---

[296] **Marg.** 'The place where Caesar was slain.'
[297] Epicurus did not believe in an afterlife, or in divine or spiritual influences. Cf. Shakespeare, *Julius Caesar*, v. 1. 76–78.
[298] **Marg.** 'Antonius, Caesar's faithful friend.'
[299] Metellus] Modern editions emend to 'Tillius'; N. follows A., who translates the reading of the manuscripts.
[300] pulled it over his neck] This should be 'pulled it down from his neck' as in P. and A. ('la lui avalla d'alentour du col', p. 896).
[301] **Marg.** 'Casca, the first that struck at Caesar.' Cf. Shakespeare, *Julius Caesar*, III. 1. 27–76.
[302] such a devilish attempt] N. uses more negative lexis than P. and A. to describe Caesar's assassination throughout this paragraph. See Introduction, p. 159.

help me.' At the beginning of this stir, they that were present, not knowing of the conspiracy, were so amazed with the horrible sight they saw, they had no power to fly, neither to help him, nor so much as once to make an outcry. They, on the other side, that had conspired his death compassed him in on every side with their swords drawn in their hands, that Caesar turned him nowhere but he was struck at by some, and still had naked swords in his face, and was hacked and mangled among them as a wild beast taken of hunters.[303] For it was agreed among them that every man should give him a wound, because all their parts should be in this murder, and then Brutus himself gave him one wound about his privities.° Men report also that Caesar did still defend himself against the rest, running every way with his body, but when he saw Brutus with his sword drawn in his hand, then he pulled his gown over his head and made no more resistance, and was driven, either casually or purposely by the counsel of the conspirators, against the base whereupon Pompey's image stood, which ran all of a gore blood till he was slain.[304] Thus it seemed that the image took just revenge of Pompey's enemy, being thrown down on the ground at his feet and yielding up his ghost there for the number of wounds he had upon him. For it is reported that he had three and twenty wounds upon his body and divers of the conspirators did hurt themselves, striking one body with so many blows.[305]

[67] When Caesar was slain, the senate (though Brutus stood in the midst amongst them as though he would have said something touching this fact) presently ran out of the house and flying filled all the city with marvellous fear and tumult. Insomuch as some did shut to their doors, others forsook their shops and warehouses, and others ran to the place to see what the matter was, and others also that had seen it ran home to their houses again. But Antonius and Lepidus, which were two of Caesar's chiefest friends, secretly conveying themselves away, fled into other men's houses and forsook their own.[306] Brutus and his confederates, on the other side, being yet hot with this murder they had committed, having their swords drawn in their hands, came all in a troop together out of the senate and went into the marketplace, not as men that made countenance° to fly, but otherwise boldly holding up their heads like men of courage, and called to the people to defend their liberty, and stayed to speak with every great personage whom they met in their way.[307] Of them, some

[303] Cf. Shakespeare, *Julius Caesar*, III. 1. 205–11.
[304] all of a gore blood] all covered with blood. Cf. Shakespeare, *Julius Caesar*, III. 2. 172–87.
[305] Marg. 'Caesar slain and had twenty-three wounds upon him.'
[306] Cf. Shakespeare, *Julius Caesar*, III. 1. 81–99.
[307] Marg. 'The murderers of Caesar do go to the Capitol.' North's reliance on two different sources here leads to a contradiction between the main text (translated from A.), in which the conspirators march to the Forum ('la place', p. 897), and the marginal note (translated from Cruser, p. 587), which correctly translates P.'s τὸ Καπιτώλιον. Cf. Shakespeare, *Julius*

followed this troop and went amongst them as if they had been of the conspiracy and falsely challenged part of the honour with them; amongst them was Caius Octavius and Lentulus Spinther. But both of them were afterwards put to death for their vain covetousness of honour by Antonius and Octavius Caesar the Younger, and yet had no part of that honour for the which they were both put to death, neither did any man believe that they were any of the confederates or of counsel with them. For they that did put them to death took revenge rather of the will they had to offend than of any fact they had committed. The next morning, Brutus and his confederates came into the marketplace to speak unto the people, who gave them such audience that it seemed they neither greatly reproved nor allowed the fact, for by their great silence they showed that they were sorry for Caesar's death and also that they did reverence Brutus. Now, the senate granted general pardon for all that was past, and to pacify every man ordained besides that Caesar's funerals° should be honoured as a god and established all things that he had done, and gave certain provinces also and convenient° honours unto Brutus and his confederates, whereby every man thought all things were brought to good peace and quietness again.[308]

[68] But when they had opened Caesar's testament and found a liberal legacy of money bequeathed unto every citizen of Rome, and that they saw his body (which was brought into the marketplace) all bemangled with gashes of swords, then there was no order[309] to keep the multitude and common people quiet, but they plucked up forms,° tables, and stools, and laid them all about the body, and setting them afire burnt the corpse. Then, when the fire was well kindled, they took the firebrands and went unto their houses that had slain Caesar, to set them afire. Other also ran up and down the city to see if they could meet with any of them, to cut them in pieces; howbeit, they could meet with never a man of them, because they had locked themselves up safely in their houses.[310] There was one of Caesar's friends called Cinna, that had a marvellous strange and terrible dream the night before.[311] He dreamed that Caesar bad him to supper, and that he refused and would not go; then, that Caesar took him by the hand and led him against his will. Now, Cinna hearing at that time that they burnt Caesar's body in the marketplace, notwithstanding that he feared his dream and had an ague° on him besides, he went into the marketplace to honour his funerals. When he came thither, one of the mean sort asked him what his name was. He was straight called by his name. The first man told it to another, and

---

Caesar, III. 1. 77–80, 109–11, 120–22.
[308] Marg. 'Caesar's funerals.'
[309] There was no way; N.'s literal translation of A.'s idiomatic 'n'y il eut plus d'ordre' (p. 897).
[310] Cf. Shakespeare, *Julius Caesar*, III. 2. 129–61, 193–252.
[311] Marg. 'Cinna's dream of Caesar.'

that other unto another, so that it ran straight through them all that he was one of them that murdered Caesar (for indeed one of the traitors to Caesar was also called Cinna as himself), wherefore taking him for Cinna the murderer, they fell upon him with such fury that they presently dispatched him in the marketplace.³¹² This stir and fury made Brutus and Cassius more afraid than of all that was past, and therefore within few days after they departed out of Rome, and touching their doings afterwards and what calamity they suffered till their deaths, we have written it at large in *The Life of Brutus*.

[69] Caesar died at six and fifty years of age, and Pompey also lived not passing four years more than he.³¹³ So he reaped no other fruit of all his reign and dominion, which he had so vehemently desired all his life and pursued with such extreme danger, but a vain name only and a superficial glory that procured him the envy and hatred of his country. But his great prosperity and good fortune, that favoured him all his lifetime, did continue afterwards in the revenge of his death, pursuing the murderers both by sea and land till they had not left a man more to be executed of all them that were actors or counsellors in the conspiracy of his death.³¹⁴ Furthermore, of all the chances that happen unto men upon the earth, that which came to Cassius above all other is most to be wondered at.³¹⁵ For he, being overcome in battle at the journey° of Philippes, slew himself with the same sword with the which he struck Caesar.³¹⁶ Again, of signs in the element,³¹⁷ the great comet which seven nights together was seen very bright after Caesar's death the eighth night after was never seen more.³¹⁸ Also, the brightness of the sun was darkened, the which all that year through rose very pale and shined not out, whereby it gave but small heat; therefore, the

---

³¹² Marg. 'The murder of Cinna.' Cf. Shakespeare, *Julius Caesar*, III. 3.
³¹³ Marg. 'Caesar fifty-six year old at his death.'   Pompey [...] than he] P. and A. 'he had survived Pompey not much more than four years' ('Caesar [...] ne survescut Pompeius gueres plus de quatre ans', p. 898). N. confuses subject and object, possibly (as Brooke, I, 205, suggests) because A. uses the Latin form of Pompey's name in the nominative case.
³¹⁴ Marg. 'The revenge of Caesar's death.'   his great prosperity and good fortune] P. ὁ [...] μέγας αὐτοῦ δαίμων (his great guardian spirit, trans. in Pelling, *Caesar*). The Greek term *daimōn* has a wide range of meanings, 'god, goddess, divine power, destiny, fortune, good or evil genius, tutelary divinity, lesser god, or evil spirit' (Miola, p. 29; see further Pelling, *Caesar*, 69. 2 n.), but N. follows A. 'celle grande fortune et faveur du ciel' (p. 898) in highlighting the effect instead of the agent that caused it.
³¹⁵ The distinction that P. (followed by A.) makes between the most remarkable human and divine (below: 'Again, of signs in the element [...]. Also, the brightness of the sun ...') events that followed Caesar's death is lost in N.'s translation.
³¹⁶ Marg. 'Cassius, being overthrown at the battle of Philippes, slew himself with the selfsame sword wherewith he struck Caesar.' The Battle of Philippi (N.'s 'Philippes') took place in 42 BCE. Cf. Shakespeare, *Julius Caesar*, V. 3. 40-45.
³¹⁷ Marg. 'Wonders seen in the element after Caesar's death.'
³¹⁸ Marg. 'A great comet.' Cf. Shakespeare, *Julius Caesar*, II. 2. 30-31.

air being very cloudy and dark by the weakness of the heat that could not come forth did cause the earth to bring forth but raw and unripe fruit, which rotted before it could ripe. But above all, the ghost that appeared unto Brutus showed plainly that the gods were offended with the murder of Caesar.[319] The vision was thus.[320] Brutus, being ready to pass over his army from the city of Abydos to the other coast lying directly against° it, slept every night (as his manner was) in his tent, and being yet awake, thinking of his affairs (for by report he was as careful a captain and lived with as little sleep as ever man did), he thought he heard a noise at his tent-door, and looking towards the light of the lamp that waxed very dim, he saw a horrible vision of a man of a wonderful greatness and dreadful look, which at the first made him marvellously afraid.[321] But when he saw that it did him no hurt but stood by his bedside and said nothing, at length he asked him what he was. The image answered him: 'I am thy ill angel, Brutus, and thou shalt see me by the city of Philippes.'[322] Then Brutus replied again and said: 'Well, I shall see thee then.' Therewithal, the spirit presently vanished from him.[323] After that time, Brutus being in battle near unto the city of Philippes against Antonius and Octavius Caesar, at the first battle he won the victory, and overthrowing all them that withstood him, he drove them into young Caesar's camp, which he took. The second battle being at hand, this spirit appeared again unto him, but spoke never a word.[324] Thereupon Brutus, knowing that he should die, did put himself to all hazard in battle, but yet fighting could not be slain.[325] So, seeing his men put to flight and overthrown, he ran unto a little rock not far off, and there setting his sword's point to his breast, fell upon it and slew himself, but yet, as it is reported, with the help of his friend that dispatched him.[326]

---

[319] ghost] P. φάσμα (apparition, phantom), translated by A. as 'vision' (p. 898). N.'s translation is the immediate source of the ghost in Shakespeare's play, though the word had a much wider semantic range in the sixteenth century (including apparition and spirit, good or evil) than today, when one sense ('the soul of a deceased person, spoken of as appearing in a visible form [...] to the living') has become dominant (*OED*, ghost, *n*.).

[320] Marg. 'Brutus' vision.'

[321] Marg. 'A spirit appeared unto Brutus.'

[322] thy ill angel] i.e. evil. A.'s rendering of P. ὁ σός [...] δαίμων κακός (your evil spirit, trans. in Pelling, *Caesar*) as 'ton mauvais ange et esprit' (p. 898) that N. translates here brings the reference into the orbit of Christianity and obscures the relationship with the reference to Caesar's *daimōn* (N. 'his great prosperity and good fortune') earlier in the paragraph. On the relationship between Caesar's and Brutus's *daimones* in Plutarch and in Shakespeare, see Pelling, *Caesar*, 69. 2 n.

[323] Cf. Shakespeare, *Julius Caesar*, IV. 2. 326–38.

[324] Marg. 'The second appearing of the spirit unto Brutus.'

[325] Cf. Shakespeare, *Julius Caesar*, V. 5. 17–20.

[326] The third edition of North's *Lives*, published in 1603, introduces Simon Goulart's comparison of Alexander and Caesar here.

TEXTUAL NOTES

Thomas Wyatt, *The Quiet of Mind* (1528)

Wyatt's *The Quiet of Mind* went through a single edition, of which a sole copy survives. Printed by Richard Pynson in London, the edition is undated, but the date of the letter of dedication (31 December 1527) makes it likely that it was published in 1528. The volume is generally well printed with few errors, although there is evidence that the type was inadequately inked in places, making *n* and *u* in particular difficult to distinguish in places. There are two modern editions of *The Quiet of Mind* (listed below), whose readings are recorded in the notes where relevant. All textual variants from the first edition have been recorded in the Textual Notes, but errors in the transcription of Muir and Thomson have not been included because they are available in Powell. Powell also helpfully records information about the contemporary underlining and marks in the margin of the sole surviving copy of the first edition.

Copy-Text

1528   ℂ *Tho. wyatis translatyon | of Plutarckes boke / of | the Quyete of | mynde.|*
∴ STC, 20058.5. Copy used: Huntington, 88834.

Other Editions Cited

M&T   Muir and Thomson.
Powell   *The Complete Works of Sir Thomas Wyatt the Elder*, 1: *Prose*, ed. by Jason E. Powell (Oxford: Oxford University Press, 2016).

Textual Variants

158 noughty] this edn; nouhhty *1528*, M&T, Powell
200 miserable] this edn; mesurable *1528*, M&T, Powell
228 we are] M&T, Powell; wear *1528*
238 boxings] *1528*; boringes M&T, Powell
286 men, in] M&T, Powell; menlin *1528*
301 pease] this edn; pees Powell; pecs *1528*, M&T
358 passed] M&T, Powell; [.]assed *1528*
541 glittering] M&T, Powell; glytteriug *1528*
545 a part] Powell; aparte *1528*, M&T
576 born] M&T, Powell; borue *1528*

592 Anytus] M&T, Powell; Auitus *1528*
593 Anytus] M&T, Powell; Auytus *1528*
605 helpeth] Powell; helph *1528*, M&T
623 man never] Powell; mann euer M&T; manneuer *1528*

TEXTUAL NOTES   243

Thomas Elyot, *The Education or Bringing up of Children* (1528–1530)

As noted in the Introduction, the undated first edition of *The Education or Bringing up of Children* was in all probability published during the eighteen-month period between the end of 1528 and the early months of 1530. The similarly undated second edition is assigned a date of around 1532 by *STC* on the basis of typographical evidence. No further editions survive; two facsimiles of the second edition were published in the 1960s.[1] There are few differences between the texts of the first and the second editions. Apart from the change in Elyot's title on the title page (discussed in the Introduction), the second edition adds a table of contents on the verso of the title page and corrects a small number of errors in the first, though it introduces a roughly equal amount of new ones. In a very few instances, it makes minute changes to the wording in ways that are unnecessary and consistent with the involvement of a typesetter or corrector instead of the author (e.g. 'myxe' for the rare verb 'mixte', with the second occurrence of 'myxte' unchanged).[2] As there is no evidence of authorial involvement in the second edition, this edition takes the first as its copy-text.

Copy-Text

1530?   The Educacion or | bringinge vp of chil|dren / translated out of | Plutarche by Tho=|mas Eliot esq*uier* / | one of y^e kingis | most hono=|rable | Counsayle. *STC*, 20056.7. Copy used: Chicago, Newberry Library, Vault Case 3A 619.

Other Editions Cited

1532?   ☙ The Education or brin|ginge vp of children / tran-|slated oute of Plu-|tarche by syr | Thomas | Eliot | knyght. *STC*, 20057. Copy used: Huntington, 62925.

Textual Variants

Dedication. 4 body,] *1532?*; body. *1530?*
Dedication. 14 learning,] *1532?*; lerninge. *1530?*

5 expedient] *1530?*; exediente *1532?*
29 Athens,] *1532?*; Athenes) *1530?*
47 procreation] *1532?*; procreacon *1530?*

---

[1] *Four Tudor Books on Education*, ed. by Robert David Pepper (Gainesville: Scholars' Facsimiles & Reprints, 1966); *The education or bringinge up of children, translated oute of Plutarche*, trans. by Thomas Elyot (Amsterdam: Theatrum Orbis Terrarum, 1969).
[2] *1530?*, sigs D2r, F3v; *1532?*, sigs D2r, F3v.

86 set by] *1532?*; setby *1530?*
101 or] this edn; of *1530?*, *1532?*
111 purported] *1532?*; p[..]ported (letters obscured by stain in sole surviving copy) *1530?*
152 depraved] *1530?*; depryued *1532?*
277 difficile] *1530?*; diffificile *1532?*
277 also (second occurrence)] *1530?*; om. *1532?*
280 is it] *1530?*; it is *1532?*
325–26 (the most cunning painter that ever was) *1530?*; the moste counnyng peinter that euer was *1532?*
375 honour] *1532?*; hououre *1530?*
387 mixt] *1530?*; myxe *1532?*
459 sweetness] *1532?* s wetnes *1530?*
510 of] *1532?*; of of *1530?*
518 victory.)] this edn; victory. *1530?*, *1532?*
532 displeasantly] *1530?*; dsiplesantly *1532?*
554 hands)] this edn; handes *1530?*, *1532?*
566 but that *1530?*; but it that *1532?*
573 philosopher] *1530?*; philsopher *1532?*
576 indignation] *1532?*; indignacon *1530?*
587 (But *1530?*; But *1532?*
619 drowned in] *1532?*; drowned ['in' as catchword, but not in text] *1530?*
632 desiring] *1530?*; desired *1532?*
639 him.)] this edn; hym. *1530?*, *1532?*

Thomas Blundeville, *The Learned Prince* (1561)

The text of Blundeville's poem survives in three sixteenth-century versions: an undated manuscript presented to Queen Elizabeth (BL, MS Royal 18.A.43); the first item in *Three Moral Treatises*, a collection of three translations of essays from Plutarch's *Moralia* published by William Seres in 1561; and in the second edition of the volume printed by Henry Denham in 1580. *The Learned Prince* has to date after *The Fruits of Foes*, the second item in *Three Moral Treatises*, to which it refers in the dedication. Steven W. May and Heather Wolfe claim in passing that the manuscript of *The Learned Prince* was copied from the first printed edition of 1561, but it is more likely to have been the other way around.[1] In addition to the intrinsic likelihood that the manuscript was presented to the queen before the poem was printed, and the close connection between the two verse translations in *Three Moral Treatises* (discussed in the Introduction), the textual variants point to the priority of the manuscript version. Thus, it is more probable that a compositor would have changed the manuscript reading 'falling evil' (line 381), the latter word monosyllabic as throughout and rhyming with 'still' (line 383), to 'falling ill' (*1561*) than vice-versa. Similarly, it is more plausible that 'pretend' in the sense of 'To profess or claim to have (an authority, power, right, title, etc.)' (*OED*, *v.*, 4. a) in 'The prince God's likeness doth pretend' (line 147) was changed to the less apposite verb 'portend' due to the potentially negative connotations of 'pretend' than conversely.

Whether or not it is an autograph, Blundeville is likely to have supervised the production of the presentation manuscript, which is in a neat and formal secretary hand, with the title and subscription in italic and a few flourishes, and presents few textual problems. The text in *Three Moral Treatises*, which was entered to Seres in the Stationers' Register on 11 May 1561 and has a colophon dated 7 June of the same year, closely follows the manuscript, although it makes frequent changes to accidentals (spelling, punctuation, capitalization, etc.).[2] The small number of substantive variants (e.g. 'or' for 'and' and minor variations in word order) are consistent with the involvement of an editor or compositor instead of the author. The second edition, printed in 1580 by Henry Denham, was evidently based on the first and retains the changes it made to the manuscript. It modernises spelling (e.g. 'Caesar' for 'Cezar' (line 241) and 'close' for 'closse' (line 256)) and word choice (e.g. 'adultery' for 'advowtry' (line 347) and 'no' for 'nis' (line 349)) and makes changes to the metre to reflect changes

---

[1] Steven W. May and Heather Wolfe, 'Manuscripts in Tudor England', in *A Companion to Tudor Literature*, ed. by Kent Cartwright (Chichester: Wiley-Blackwell, 2010), pp. 123–39 (pp. 135–36), referring to Carlo M. Bajetta, 'The Manuscripts of Verse Presented to Elizabeth I: A Preliminary Investigation', *Ben Jonson Journal*, 8 (2001), 147–205, who in fact states more cautiously that the poem was presented to Elizabeth 'probably in the late 1550s or early 1560s' (p. 162).
[2] Arber, I, 96.

in pronunciation (e.g. 'ill' for 'evil' (line 334) and 'Thus in desire and in good will' for 'Thus in desire and good will' (line 343), where 'desire' is trisyllabic), which are similarly unlikely to be authorial. There are no modern editions or facsimiles of the text, but a transcription of the first printed edition is available on Literature Online <https://search.proquest.com/lion/>.

The copy-text for this edition is BL, MS Royal 18.A.43, which the evidence presented suggests is both the earliest and most authoritative text of the poem. Variants in the 1561 and 1580 editions are recorded in the Textual Notes. As a poem, *The Learned Prince* presents some special challenges in terms of modernisation and annotation, which are discussed in the Editorial Principles at the start of Volume 1.

Copy-Text

MS BL, MS Royal 18.A.43.

Other Editions Cited

1561 ☙ Three [morall] | Treatises, no lesse pleasau[nt] | than necessary for all men to read[e,] | wherof the one is called the Learned Prince, | the other the Fruites of Foes, the thyrde | the Porte of rest. | ∴ | ☙ Imprynted at London by | Wyllyam Seres, dwellynge at | the west ende of Poules at | the signe of the Hedg=|hogge. | *Cum priuilegio ad imprimendum* | *solum*. STC, 20063.5. Copy used: Huntington, 51793.[3]

1580 THREE | MORALL TREA-|tises, no lesse pleasant | *than neceßarie for all* | men to reade, | *VVhereof the first is called*, The | Learned Prince: *The second*, The | Fruites of Foes: *The third*, | The Port of Rest | *Set foorth by* Tho. Blundeuille | Gentleman. | Imprinted at London by | Henrie Denham, dwelling | in Pater noster row at | *the signe of the Starre.* | 1580. *Cum priuilegio ad imprimendum solum*. STC, 20064. Copy used: BL, C.71.a.16.

Textual Variants

Dedication. o Plutarchi commentarium In principe requiri doctrinam] MS; The

---

[3] Part of the title-page of the sole complete surviving copy of this edition (in the Huntington) is missing and the text in square brackets is conjectural. In addition to the copy in the Huntington, the only item recorded in ESTC, an imperfect copy of the first edition is listed in the library catalogue of Princeton University Library (Rare Books, Robert H. Taylor Collection, shelfmark 16th-6).

Textual Notes

Learned Prince *1561, 1580*
Dedication. 17 she] MS, *1561*; he *1580*

1 *1580* includes the heading 'The first morall Treatise intituled, The learned Prince.'
37 rigour] *1580*; riguor MS, *1561*
60 and] MS; or *1561, 1580*
125 do] MS, *1561*; doth *1580*
126 goodly] MS; godly *1561, 1580*
129 the ample] MS, *1561*; th'ample *1580*
130 do] MS, *1561*; doth *1580*
141 goodly] MS; godly *1561, 1580*
143 also] MS, *1561*; likewise *1580*
147 pretend] MS; portend *1561, 1580*
226–27 to him that lest | Unwares] MS; Vnwares that lest | to hym *1561, 1580*
255 How] MS, *1561*; Who *1580*
257 t'Aristodem *1580*; Taristodeme MS, *1561*
261 concubine MS, *1580*; concupyne *1561*
302 Diogenes] MS, *1561*; D ogenes *1580*
307 would fain] MS, *1561*; faine would *1580*
309 t'apply] MS, *1580*; tapply? *1561*
311 envy] MS, *1580*; enuy? *1561*
317 and good] MS, *1561*; and in good *1580*
334 Evil] MS, *1561*; Ill *1580*
347 advowtry] MS, *1561*; adultery *1580*
349 nis] MS, *1561*; no *1580*
362 th'accusèd] MS, *1561*; accusd they *1580*
365 nought] MS, *1561*; not *1580*
381 falling evil] MS; fallyng yll *1561, 1580*
395 Let fill] MS, *1561*; Fill vp *1580*
400 anger] *1561, 1580*; anguer MS
401 be said] MS, *1580*; besayde *1561*
407 also] MS, *1561*; likewise *1580*
436 *1561* includes 'Finis.' after this line.

Philemon Holland, 'How a Young Man Ought to Hear Poets and How He May Take Profit By Reading Poems' and 'Of Intemperate Speech or Garrulity' from *The Morals* (1603)

Holland's *The Morals* was first printed by Arnold Hatfield in 1603 in a large folio edition running to well over a thousand pages, including a detailed glossary and index and three pages of errata at the end of the volume. A second edition was published by Sarah Griffin for a variety of different booksellers in 1657.[1] The title page advertises the edition as 'Newly Revised and Corrected', but apart from incorporating the errata from the first edition in the text (with some omissions), there are few changes, and those all minor: alterations to verb tenses and word order, omissions of articles, modernisation of word forms and spellings, and so on. Although it corrects a few misprints, moreover, the second edition is overall printed less carefully than the first and introduces numerous errors not present in the earlier version. There is no evidence of the involvement of the author, who had died at the age of 84 two decades earlier. Reprints of Holland's versions of the 'Roman Questions' and 'Consolation to my Wife' appeared in 1892 and 1905, respectively, followed by a reprint of twenty essays from the 1603 edition of Holland's translation in the Everyman Library in 1911.[2]

The copy-text for this edition is the first edition of 1603, and substantial variants in the 1657 edition are recorded in the Textual Notes. The edition incorporates the errata listed at the end of the first edition, with the original readings in the Textual Notes. The errata were apparently supplied by the printer and not by the translator (as the former asks to be exonerated from the remaining errors 'considering the farre absence of our Author'); they mostly appear to reflect misreadings of the manuscript: 'marke' for 'mocke', for example, or 'Patrochus' for 'Patroclus'.[3]

Copy-Text

1603   THE PHILOSOPHIE, | commonlie called, | THE | MORALS | WRITTEN BY | the learned Philosopher | PLUTARCH | of *Chæronea*. | Translated out of Greeke into English, and conferred | *with the Latine translations and the French,* | by Philemon Holland of | Coventrie, Doctor in | *Physicke.* | *VVhereunto are annexed the Summaries*

---

[1] Wing, P2654, P2255, P2255A, P2256.
[2] *Plutarch's 'Romane Questions'. Translated A.D. 1603 by Philemon Holland, M.A., Fellow of Trinity College, Cambridge*, ed. by Frank Byron Jevons (London: David Nutt, 1892); *A Consolatorie Letter or Discourse Sent by Plutarch of Chaeronea unto his Owne Wife As Touching the Death of her and his Daughter*, ed. by anon. (Boston: Houghton Mifflin, 1905); *Plutarch's 'Moralia': Twenty Essays, Translated by Philemon Holland*, ed. by E. H. Blakeney (London: Dent, [1911]).
[3] *1603*, sig. 6F5v.

necessary to be | read before every Treatise. | At London | Printed by *Arnold Hatfield*. | 1603. STC, 20063. Copy used: Newberry Library, Chicago, Case Y 642. P6411.

Other Editions Cited

1603 Errata	*1603*, sigs 6F5v–6v.
1657	THE | PHILOSOPHY | COMMONLY CALLED, | THE | MORALS | WRITTEN | By the Learned Philosopher | PLUTARCH | OF | *CHÆRONEA*. | Translated out of Greek into English, and conferred | with the Latine Translations and the French, | By *PHILEMON HOLLAND*, | Doctor of Physick. | Whereunto are annexed the Summaries necessary | to be read before every Treatise. | Newly Revised and Corrected. | *LONDON*. | Printed by *S.G.* and are to be sold by *George Sawbridge*, at the Sign of | the Bible on *Ludgate-Hill*, 1657. Wing, P2654. Copy used: Rylands, Methodist Printed Collections (Richmond College) M0000123.

Textual Variants

'How a Young Man Ought to Hear Poets and How He May Take Profit by Reading Poems'

Summary. 39 testimonies] *1603*; testimony *1657*

27 haply] *1603*; happily *1657*
80 outrageous] *1603*; ouragious *1657*
105 beginning] *1657*; be ginning *1603*
119 haply] *1603*; happily *1657*
126–27 as in a picture drawn to the life] *1603* Errata, *1657*; as a picture drawen to the like *1603*
142 *Theriaca*] *1603* Errata, *1657*; *Thersara 1603*
161 with Apollo for] *1603* Errata, *1657*; with for *Apollo 1603*
185 peis'd] *1603*; pois'd *1657*
188 souls] *1603*; Soule *1657*
191 is (second occurrence)] *1657*; it *1603*
216 cliffs] *1603*; clifts *1657*
228 loss of] *1657*; losseof *1603*
269 the] *1603*; its *1657*
277 rage] *1603* Errata, *1657*; race *1603*
289 cartwheel or pulley] *1603* Errata, *1657*; cart wheele *1603*

299 maidens] this edn; maiden 1603, 1657
299 Betrochus] 1603; Petrochus 1657
314 the] 1603; thy 1657
319 my] 1657; may 1603
324 Nay, sleep] 1603 Errata, 1657; Nay sleepe 1603
337 unto] 1603; to 1657
385 choler. He] 1603 Errata, 1657; choler, he 1603
390 Patroclus] 1603 Errata, 1657; Patrochus 1603
397 him] 1657; him him 1603
419 *hyponoeae*] this edn; *Hypponaeae* 1603, 1657
420 would] 1603; wou d 1657
445 showeth] 1603; shewed 1657
463 heavily] 1603 Errata; levelly 1603, 1657
485 Should I for God's cause die?] 1603 Errata, 1657; should I die? For Gods cause die? 1603
543 for poor] 1603; far more 1657
554 have] 1603; hath 1657
577 worse] 1603 Errata, 1657; woorst 1603
581 haply] 1603; happily 1657
615 presently cried] 1657; presently cried presently 1603
655 i.] 1603; i.e. 1657
659 i.] 1603; i.e. 1657
660 i.] 1603; i.e. 1657
664 ὑψόροφον] this edn; ὑψύροφον 1603, 1657
666 i.] 1603; i.e. 1657
672 Envying] 1657; enyving 1603
678 when] 1603; om. 1657
679 ἡ δ'] this edn; ἡδ'1603, 1657
679 ἀπεβήσετο] this edn; ἀπεβήσατο 1603, 1657
683 ἀλήτην] this edn; ἀλείτην 1603, 1657
689 of] 1603; o' 1657
692 ἕδρας] this edn; εἴδρας 1603, 1657
692 τάσδε μοι] this edn; τάσ δὲμοι 1603; τάσ δὲ μοι 1657
693 ἐξεστεμμένοι] this edn; ἐξεστεμμένοις 1603, 1657
703 i.] 1603; i.e. 1657
705 i.] 1603; i.e. 1657
705 i.] 1603; i.e. 1657
717 κλῦθ'] this edn; κλῦθι 1603, 1657
724 wanted] 1603; want 1657
748 Ἴδηθεν] 1603; Ἴδηθην 1657
761 i.] 1603; i.e. 1657

761 will] *1603* Errata, *1657*; wit *1603*
783 he meaneth] *1603* Errata, *1657*; meaneth *1603*
835 i.] *1603*; i.e. *1657*
839 i.] *1603*; i.e. *1657*
855 in] *1603*; im *1657*
870 otherwhile] *1603*; otherwhiles *1657*
879 world] *1603*; worldly *1657*
897 i.] *1603*; i.e. *1657*
916 Euripides] *1657*; Euripdes *1603*
973 deeds or words] *1603*; words or deeds *1657*
978 buncht-back] *1603*; bunch-backt *1657*
1017 had] *1603*; hath *1657*
1057 perceived] *1603*; percei- *1657*
1062 [court] her] *1603*; here *1657*
1064 rejoice] *1603*; rejoyces *1657*
1077 hope] *1603*; hopes *1657*
1088 goods] this edn; gods *1603, 1657*
1118 Phaedra] this edn; Phœdra *1603, 1657*
1224 profitable] *1603*; unprofitable *1657*
1266 mark] this edn; worke *1603, 1657*
1266 wise] *1603*; wife *1657*
1287 The party] *1657*; Thepartie *1603*
1297 speaketh] *1603*; spake *1657*
1319 seeketh] *1603* Errata, *1657*; searcheth *1603*
1365 perfection] *1657*; perfections *1603*
1387–88 For fear lest when he saw his son, | so mangled and berayed,] this edn; For feare least when he saw | his sonne, so mangled and beraid *1603, 1657*
1393–94 Without regard of Jupiter, | his hests, his will, and word.] this edn; Without regard of Iupiter, his hests, | his will and word. *1603, 1657*
1429 μεδέων] *1603* Errata, *1657*; με δέων *1603*
1431 ὑφ' ἕν] this edn; ἰφὲν *1603*, ὑφὲν *1657*
1456 Behold, one father] *1603* Errata, *1657*; Beholde one father *1603*
1471 What Glaucus, you] *1603* Errata; You *1603, 1657*
1476 Pandarus] *1603* Errata; he *1603, 1657*
1486 Clytemnestra] *1657*; Clytemnestro *1603*
1532 Aetha, which] *1603* Errata, *1657*; Aetha *1603*
1545 Semblably] *1657*; Semblaby *1603*
1550 that] *1603*; then *1657*
1567 weal] *1603*; weales *1657*
1573 τί δ'] this edn; Τὶδ' *1603, 1657*
1573 δοκῆ] *1603*; δοκῆ *1657*

1592 ἐμπορεύεται] this edn; εἰ πορεύεται *1603, 1657*
1593 κείνου 'στὶ] this edn; κείν οὐστὶ *1603, 1657*
1610 συμφέρει] this edn; συμφέρον *1603, 1657*
1617 Atreus] *1603* Errata, *1657*; Athens *1603*
1621 Atreus] *1603* Errata; Athens *1603, 1657*
1638 where] *1603*; when *1657*
1653 fearful] *1603* Errata, *1657*; too fearefull *1603*
1672 not at all] *1603* Errata, *1657*; not all *1603*
1716 quails] *1603* Errata; quoites *1603*; quoiles *1657*
1760 illiberal] *1603*; illiberable *1657*
1803 derideth] *1603* Errata; *1657*; devideth *1603*
1821 provoked him] *1603* Errata, *1657*; provoked *1603*
1849 so] *1603* Errata, *1657*; to *1603*
1850 love] *1603*; loves *1657*
1854 overmatchèd] *1603* Errata, *1657*; unmatched *1603*
1855 i.] *1603*; i.e. *1657*
1864 than] *1657*; that *1603*
1889 but] *1603*; om. *1657*
1920 decisions] *1603* Errata, *1657*; divisions *1603*
1922 endure] *1603* Errata, *1657*; reduce *1603*

Of Intemperate Speech or Garrulity

Summary. 7 moderation] *1603*; modera ion *1657*

24 is] *1603*; in *1657*
30 of] *1603*; f *1657*
37 void] *1603*; avoid *1657*
44 good] *1603*; om. *1657*
53 For] *1603*; or *1657*
59 are either] *1603*; either are *1657*
65 a] *1603*; om. *1657*
79 prittle-prattle] *1657*; pritlte prattle *1603*
92 rampire] *1603*; rampart *1657*
101 run] *1603*; to run *1657*
107 be it] *1603*; it be *1657*
128–29 be that] *1657*; bethat *1603*
136 mock] *1603* Errata, *1657*; marke *1603*
200 chatterers] *1603*; charterers *1657*
201 thing] *1603*; things *1657*
210 cause it] *1603*; caused *1657*

213 made] *1603*; make *1657*
213 he] *1603*; he be *1657*
227 privities] *1603*; privies *1657*
235 harried] *1603 Errata, 1657*; harmed *1603*
276 constraint] *1603*; straint *1657*
287 hers] *1603*; her *1657*
291 endured] *1603*; endures *1657*
297 undaunted] *1657*; undanuted *1603*
299 making] *1603*; taking *1657*
319 the] *1603*; om. *1657*
330 log] *1603*; lodg *1657*
351 next] *1603*; next to *1657*
378 very] *1603*; very good *1657*
426 waiting-maidens] *1603*; waiting-maids *1657*
428 woe's] *1603*; woe is *1657*
447 flying] *1603*; om. *1657*
474 charged] *1603 Errata, 1657*; there *1603*
476 declare] *1603*; declared *1657*
493 with all] *1657*; with-all *1603*
531 dissembling] *1603*; in dissembling *1657*
557 by] *1603*; hy *1657*
568 whiles] *1603 Errata, 1657*; and whiles *1603*
625 might] *1603*; om. *1657*
647 the [means]] *1603*; om. *1657*
654 rampire] *1603*; rampart *1657*
655 evermore be] *1603*; be evermore *1657*
664 by] *1603 Errata, 1657*; for *1603*
666 Macedony] *1603*; Macedonia *1657*
674 judicial] *1657*; ju iciall *1603*
676 beholden] *1603*; beholding *1657*
698 inconveniences] *1603*; inconveniencies *1657*
712 immediately] *1657*; immedialy *1603*
724 were] *1603*; was *1657*
732 unto] *1603*; om. *1657*
739 *Odyssey* or *Ilias*] *1603*; Odysses or Iliads *1657*
783 were] *1603 Errata, 1657*; now *1603*
789 master] *1603*; make master *1657*
817 put] *1603*; pnt *1657*
864 demandé] *1603*; demané *1657*
865 up] *1603*; upon *1657*
873 the] *1603*; om. *1657*

894 or] *1603*; and *1657*
895 be] *1603*; om. *1657*
914 now] this edn; not *1603*, *1657*
925 place] *1603*; places *1657*
928 me] *1603* Errata, *1657*; men *1603*
949 Agrypnia] *1603* Errata; Agryppina *1603*, *1657*
965 Bacchis] *1603* Errata, *1657*; Bacchus *1603*
971 himself] *1603* Errata, *1657*; him els *1603*
1013 refuted] *1603* Errata, *1657*; refused *1603*
1025 themselves] There is a small hole in the page in the Newberry Library copy, with the result that the first two letters are illegible, but they are clearly visible in the Huntington Library copy on EEBO.
1028 advisement] *1603*; advice *1657*
1040 worldly] *1603*; wordly *1657*

Henry Parker, Lord Morley, *The Story of Paullus Aemilius* (1542–46/7)

The sole witness of the text of Morley's translation of *Aemilius Paullus* is Laud MS misc. 684 in the Bodleian Library in Oxford, the original presentation manuscript.[1] It is written in a fine court hand with many secretary features, by the same scribe as Morley's translation of *Theseus*, and embellished with flourishes and decorated initials.[2] There are few corrections but some scribal errors (recorded in the Textual Variants). The green velvet binding is original, though folios 5 and 6 have been bound in inverse order. The manuscript carries ownership marks of the antiquarian Robert Hare (dated 1559) and William Laud, Archbishop of Canterbury (dated 1633), who donated his manuscripts to the Bodleian Library.[3] Morley's translation has not been previously published, except for the prologue to Henry VIII, which is included in Wright's edition of Morley's translation of Boccaccio's *De claris mulieribus*.[4]

Copy-Text

MS   Oxford, Bodleian Library, MS Laud misc. 684.

Textual Variants

Prologue. 11 Caesar] this edn; Ceasar MS
Prologue. 30 dignity] this edn; dingnite MS

5 *haemulia*] this edn; Emiliay MS
6 Pythagoras] this edn; Pictagoras MS
9 Cannae] this edn; Cannas MS
24 aedile] this edn; Edilite MS
43 Antiochus] this edn; Antiocus MS
44 Hesperia] this edn; Esperia MS
47 commonly] Following 'com-' (fol. 4v), leaves 5 and 6 are bound in the wrong order.
48 dignity] this edn; dingnite MS
57 Maso] this edn; NAsonis MS
91 Gauls] this edn; galles MS
91 Iberians] this edn; Iberis MS
132 Gonatas] this edn; Gonnatus MS
139 Doson] this edn; doso MS

---

[1] There is a detailed description of the manuscript in Carley, 'Writings of Morley', p. 32.
[2] Ibid., p. 45.
[3] See further ibid., p. 48.
[4] Morley, *Forty-Six Lives*, ed. by Wright, pp. 164–65.

142 overcome] this edn; overc[.]m MS
162 legitime] this edn; legytme MS
184 Aemilius] this edn; Emilus MS
232 thought] this edn; though MS
252 Galatians] this edn; Galathiens MS
261 Olympus] this edn; Olimpius MS
270 charge] this edn; charde MS
281 denies] this edn; demis MS
305 Heracleum] this edn; heraclius MS
309 Pithium] this edn; Pithius MS
310 Olympus] this edn; Olimpius MS
310 furlongs] this edn; furlandes MS
311 Olympus] this edn; Olimpius MS
312 Xenagoras] this edn; zemagoras MS
316 Xenagoras] this edn; Zemagoras MS
323 Milo] this edn; Mylon MS
332 Pydna] this edn; Pidnam MS
342 Aeson] this edn; Eson MS
348 Nasica] this edn; Anassica MS
390 Thrace] this edn; Trase MS
463 Pydna] this edn; Pydnam MS
477 overrun] this edn; overrum MS
482 Archedamus] this edn; Archedam MS
483 Boeotia] this edn; Boecia MS
486 Amphipolis] this edn; Amphiolum MS
514 Sagra] this edn; Sagar MS
515 Peloponnesus] this edn; Peleponeso MS
536 Samothrace] this edn; Samatracia MS
540 Oroandes] this edn; Orander MS
542 Oroandes] this edn; Orander MS
544 Oroandes] this edn; Orander MS
595 Delphi] this edn; delphyus MS
598 Macedons] this edn; Masidones MS
623 Epirus] this edn; Epious MS
637 Servius] this edn; Sergius MS
652 the] this edn; the the MS
683 Antigonus] this edn; Antigonius MS
684 Thericles] this edn; Theryades MS
703 cities] this edn; Cyte MS
710 and some of them] this edn; And sum of them And sum of them MS
730 presence] this edn; presns MS

736 Brundisium] this edn; Brondusyon MS
736 Delphi] this edn; delphis MS
754 overcome] this edn; overcunne MS
771 Hirtius] this edn; Hirsius MS
771 Pansa] this edn; pansas MS

Thomas North, *The Life of Demosthenes*, *The Life of Marcus Tullius Cicero*, *The Comparison of Cicero with Demosthenes*, and *The Life of Julius Caesar*, from *The Lives* (1579)

Three editions of North's *Lives* were published during his lifetime, in 1579, 1595, and 1603. Modern editions have generally based their texts on the first edition of 1579 or the second edition of 1595. This makes sense where the main interest is the influence of Plutarch on Shakespeare (as has often been the case), as Shakespeare must have used one of these editions as the basis for *Julius Caesar* (1599, i.e. before the publication of the third edition of North's translation in 1603) and likely his other plays. It ignores, however, the substantial revisions that North made to the text in the final edition published during his lifetime (1603), which forms the basis of this edition.

The first edition of North's *Lives*, a large folio of well over 1000 pages, was published by Thomas Vautrollier in 1579. The second edition, published by Richard Field for Bonham Norton in 1595, generally follows the first very closely, to the extent that from time to time the two editions have breaks in exactly the same places in the text for many pages.[1] The 1595 edition does, however, make a considerable number of minor alterations to the text of the first edition of 1579.[2] Almost all variants affect single words, and many are simply alternative forms of the same word ('my' for 'mine', 'the other' for 'thother', 'unto' for 'to', 'amongst' for 'among', etc.). The second edition also emends a few classical names, but only where the correct form is found elsewhere in the text or the fault is obvious, and it also introduces a number of new errors in the spelling of names (which are generally retained in the following edition). On occasion, this edition adds or omit words too, and at times it inverts the word order, but it makes no substantial changes to the meaning. All of these facts point to editorial rather than authorial involvement.

The situation is quite different in the third edition of 1603, once more printed by Richard Field though this time for Thomas Wight. Previous editors have noted the third edition's correction of a number of major errors in the two previous editions. Notoriously, the edition emends 'the highway going unto Appius' to 'the highway called Appius' Way', as it corrects 'Pompey's wife' to 'Pompey's daughter' and the origin of Cicero's name from 'riche pease' to 'cich pease' (i.e. chickpea), for instance.[3] There are a large number of smaller improvements

---

[1] E.g. North, *Lives* (1579), pp. 766–78; North, *Lives* (1595), pp. 762–73.

[2] See also Brooke, I, p. xx, although his observations on the text should be treated with caution (as Law points out). Brooke does not explicitly comment on North's contribution to the edition of 1603, but some of his notes appear to reject authorial involvement as they contrast the readings of the third edition with what 'North probably wrote' (II, 223, n. on p. 142, l. 7; II, 226, n. on p. 174, l. 16).

[3] *Cicero*, lines 10, 12, 20; *Caesar*, lines 129, 380; North, *Lives* (1579), pp. 765, 769, 912–13; North, *Lives* (1595), pp. 760, 764, 911–12; North, *Lives* (1603), pp. 714, 718, 859.

too, such as 'Aegina' for 'Aegines', 'Ascalon' for 'Ascalona', and 'Atreus' for 'Atrius'.[4] While it is just about conceivable that these corrections could have been made by an editor with a sound knowledge of classical antiquity, others indicate that the author of the revisions had recourse to the source text, at least in a few instances. For example, 'the Corcyriaeians' is changed to 'those of Corfu', following Amyot's 'ceux de Corfou'.[5] Likewise, when Plutarch elaborates on the knowledge of languages at the start of *Demosthenes*, North originally translates what 'a marvellous pleasant and sweet thing' it is 'to understand the signification, translations, and fine joining of the simple words one with another, which do beautify and set forth the tongue', but changes 'signification' to 'figures' (i.e. the figures of rhetoric) in 1603. Given that 'signification' makes perfect sense in this context, it is difficult to see how the alteration could have been arrived at other than by recourse to Amyot, who has 'figures'.[6] That is not to say that the third edition of 1603 systematically attempts to bring the translation closer to the source text: comparison with Amyot appears to have been intermittent and prompted by specific issues.

Authorial involvement in the edition of 1603 is further supported by evidence that North revised his other translations for later editions. A 1582 copy of *The Dial for Princes* now in Cambridge University Library includes corrections and printer's symbols by North, evidently with the purpose of serving as printer's copy for a subsequent edition.[7] The changes are similar in nature to those in the third edition of the *Lives*: in the main, substitutions of individual words (to improve style and content as well as simple modernisations), with some changes to word order and corrections of ancient Greek and Roman names. The copy also demonstrates North's interest in incidentals such as spelling and punctuation and in marginal notes, which are added throughout. It appears that North made his corrections to the *Lives* in a copy of the earlier printed edition of 1595 (instead of to his manuscript), as he did with *The Dial for Princes*, for the third edition of 1603 follows the readings of the second rather than the first edition in many cases, even when the edition is evidently in error (e.g. 'Myrrhenian' for 'Myrrinaeian' and 'Androcion' for 'Androtion').[8]

---

[4] *Demosthenes*, line 823; *Cicero*, lines 83, 138; North, *Lives* (1579), pp. 910, 914, 915; North, *Lives* (1595), pp. 909, 913, 914; North, *Lives* (1603), pp. 857, 860, 861. Not all changes were improvements, however. In *Caesar*, lines 46 and 52, North, *Lives* (1603), p. 713, hypercorrects 'Pergamum' to 'Pergamus', presumably on the assumption that the word is masculine and therefore the *-um* ending is an accusative which should be normalised to the nominative *-us* ending, when in fact the word is neuter and thus ends *-um* in the nominative.

[5] *Demosthenes*, line 477; North, *Lives* (1579), p. 904; North, *Lives* (1595), p. 904; North, *Lives* (1603), p. 851; Amyot, *Vies* (1574), p. 1026.

[6] *Demosthenes*, lines 42–45; North, *Lives* (1579), p. 898; North, *Lives* (1595), p. 887; North, *Lives* (1603), p. 845 (mis-signed 445); Amyot, *Vies* (1574), p. 1018.

[7] Cambridge University Library, Adv.d.14.4; see Quinn.

[8] *Demosthenes*, lines 236, 423; North, *Lives* (1595), pp. 900, 903; North, *Lives* (1603), pp.

Finally, North's continued involvement in the project of the *Lives* around the time of the publication of the third edition is witnessed by his publication of fifteen additional *Lives* (not by Plutarch) in 1602, translated from the enlarged edition of Amyot's *Vies* prepared by Simon Goulart and re-issued with the edition of 1603. As well as the new *Lives*, the third edition included a comparison between Alexander the Great and Caesar, written by Goulart and printed in the editions from which North translated the additional *Lives*, which leaves little room for doubt that it too was translated by North.[9] His connection with the edition of 1603 and revisions to his other translations, combined with the nature and extent of the corrections in this third edition, make it virtually certain that the changes were authorial and provide a strong argument for using the final edition published during his lifetime as the copy-text for this edition.

There are numerous modern reprints of selections of North's *Lives*, notably by T. J. B. Spencer (1964) and Judith Mossman (1998), most of which are based on the first edition of 1579. The sole previous critical edition of North's *Lives* is the two-volume selection *Shakespeare's Plutarch* by C. F. Tucker Brooke in 1909. Brooke's edition is based on the first edition and claims 'All variants in the edition of 1595 which are not purely typographical are recorded in the notes, together with all important alterations in the editions 1603–1631'.[10] However, it has been demonstrated that Brooke worked from the older Tudor Translations edition instead of a copy of the first edition, which has led to several inaccuracies;[11] nor did Brooke note all significant variants in the editions of 1595 and 1603 as he claimed. I have not, therefore, taken Brooke's edition into account in editing the text, though I have drawn on his valuable notes on North's use of Amyot and the relation of North's text to Shakespeare's plays. I have also profited from the annotations in the 1963 edition of a wide selection of North's *Lives* by Paul Turner (whose edition claims to be based on the first edition but silently includes variants from the third edition of 1603).

Copy-Text

1603   THE LIVES | OF THE NOBLE GRE-|CIANS AND ROMAINES, COMPARED | TOGETHER BY THAT GRAVE LEARNED | PHILOSOPHER AND HISTORIOGRAPHER, | *Plutarke of Chæronea.* | Translated out of Greeke into French by Iames Amiot, Ab-|*bot of*

848, 851. This is confirmed by the coincidences in spelling between the editions of 1595 and 1603, but not the first edition of 1579: see the table in Law, pp. 199–200.

[9]   The second edition adds 'A table of the principallest things conteined in this volume' (North, Lives (1595), sigs 5F2v–5H4v) based on the marginal notes, retained in the third edition of 1603 and subsequent editions, but such indexes were commonly put in by printers or editors.

[10]   Brooke, I, p. xxii.

[11]   Law.

Bellozane, Bishop of Auxerre, one of the Kings priuie Counsell, | and great Amner of France. VVith the liues of Hannibal and of Scipio | African: translated out of Latine into French by Charles | de l'Esclvse, and out of French into English, | *By Sir Thomas North Knight.* | *Hereunto are also added the liues of* Epaminondas, *of* Philip *of Macedon, of* Dionysius *the elder,* | *tyrant of Sicilia, of* Augustus Cæsar, *of* Plutarke, *and of* Seneca: *with the liues of nine other* | *excellent Chiefetaines of warre : collected out of Æmylius Probus, by* | *S.G.S. and Englished by the aforesaid Translator.* | Imprinted at London by Richard Field | for Thomas VVight. | 1603. STC, 20068. Copy used: BL, 10605.i.2.

Other Editions Cited

1579   THE LIVES | OF THE NOBLE GRE-|CIANS AND ROMANES, COMPARED | *together by that graue learned Philosopher and Historiogra-|pher, Plutarke of Chæronea*: Translated out of Greeke into French by Iames Amyot, Abbot of Bellozane, | Bishop of Auxerre, one of the Kings priuy counsel, and great Amner | of Fraunce, and out of French into Englishe, by | *Thomas North.* | Imprinted at London by Thomas Vautroullier dvvelling | in the Black Friers by Ludgate. | 1579. STC, 20065. Copies used: Rylands, SC9404D for *Demosthenes and Cicero*; Huntington, 62967 for *Caesar*.

1595   THE LIVES | OF THE NOBLE GRE-| CIANS AND ROMANES, COMPARED | TOGETHER BY THAT GRAVE LEARNED | PHILOSOPHER AND HISTORIOGRAPHER, | *Plutarke of Chæronea*: | Translated out of Greeke into French by Iames Amiot, Abbot of Bello-|zane, Bishop of Auxerre, one of the Kings priuie counsell, and great | Amner of France, and out of French into English, by | *Thomas North.* | Imprinted at London by Richard Field for | Bonham Norton. | 1595. STC, 20067. Copy used: Rylands, R76168 (lacking title page, taken from Harvard University Library copy on EEBO).

Textual Variants

The Life of Demosthenes

14 comedians] *1603*; Comediants *1579, 1595*
25 but] *1579, 1603*; and *1595*
26 to be gathered] *1603*; are to be gathered *1579, 1595*
38–39 Latin books in hand] *1603*; my Latine bookes in my hand *1579, 1595*
43 figures] *1603*; signification *1579, 1595*

53 were] *1595, 1603*; was *1579*
63 ambitious] *1579, 1603*; ambitions *1595*
77 Machaeropoeus] *1579, 1595*; Machaeropaeus *1603*
83 but] *1603*; om. *1579, 1595*
84 years] *1603*; yeare *1579, 1595*
85 **Marg.** of] *1595, 1603*; left *1579*
105 Callistratus] *1595, 1603*; Calistratus *1579*
113 their] *1595, 1603*; his *1579*
114 hear and see] *1595, 1603*; see and heare *1579*
127 fine and subtle] *1595, 1603*; finer, & sutler *1579*
152 as] *1603*; as if *1579, 1595*
155 ventured to] *1579, 1603*; ventredto *1595*
175 Demosthenes] *1595, 1603*; *Domosthenes 1579*
180 the other] *1595, 1603*; thother *1579*
227 up on] *1603*; vpon *1579, 1595*
229 the other] *1595, 1603*; thother *1579*
236 Myrrinaeian] *1579*; Myrrhenian *1595, 1603*
275 at] *1595, 1603*; of *1579*
287 twinkling] *1579, 1595*; twickling *1603*
287 the head] *1603*; his head *1579, 1595*
292 touching] *1579, 1603*; touchiug *1595*
308 credit] *1603*; beleeue *1579, 1595*
311 amongst] *1595, 1603*; amonge *1579*
317 otherwhiles] *1595, 1603*; otherwhile *1579*
325 therefore, my lords] *1603*; therefore, you, my Lords *1579, 1595*
328 pleasant and witty] *1595, 1603*; wittie and pleasant *1579*
336 years] *1603*; yeare *1579, 1595*
348–49 he behaved] *1603*; wherein he handled *1579, 1595*
358 But] *1603*; For *1579, 1595*
362 **Marg.** Demosthenes against] *1595, 1603*; Demosthenes defended against] *1579*
365 **Marg.** evasion] *1579, 1603*; inuasion *1595*
366 Callistratus] *1579, 1603*; Challistratus *1595*
366 many times stopped] *1595, 1603*; stopped many times *1579*
368 my] *1595, 1603*; mine *1579*
371 afterwards] *1579, 1603*; afterward *1595*
390 the other] *1595, 1603*; thother *1579*
392 by] *1603*; with *1579, 1595*
397 unto] *1595, 1603*; to *1579*
403 you] *1595, 1603*; ye *1579*
410 and] *1595, 1603*; ahd *1579*
410 for] *1603*; vpon *1579, 1595*

418 so a naughty man] *1579, 1603*; so naughty a man *1595*
419 to] *1595, 1603*; vnto *1579*
423 Androtion] *1579*; Androcion *1595, 1603*
426 years] *1603*; yeare *1579, 1595*
427 Chabrias] *1595, 1603*; *Cabrias 1579*
430 Magnesian] *1603*; Magnesius *1579, 1595*
432–33 was recited] *1595, 1603*; was euer recited *1579*
449 all things] *1595, 1603*; all those things *1579*
455 orations, the] *1603*; orations. Whereupon, the *1579, 1595*
459 to (second occurrence)] *1595, 1603*; vnto *1579*
469 also] *1595, 1603*; om. *1579*
475 united] *1603*; vnite *1579, 1595*
477 those of Corfu] *1603*; the Corcyriaeians *1579, 1595*
480 Greece] *1579, 1595*; Crece *1603*
495 unto] *1579, 1603*; into *1595*
497 Thrasydaeus] *1579*; *Thracydaeus 1595, 1603*
515 revolution] *1579, 1595*; rouolution *1603*
518 amongst] *1595, 1603*; amonge *1579*
526 which] *1595, 1603*; the which *1579*
536 hurt] *1603*; hart *1579, 1595*
543 buzz] *1595, 1603*; buffe *1579*
543 such] *1595, 1603*; those *1579*
544 furthermore] *1579, 1595*; furrhermore *1603*
559 proclaimed] *1579, 1595*; ploclaimed *1603*
597 had] *1595, 1603*; had had *1579*
599 and] *1603*; that *1579, 1595*
610 unto] *1595, 1603*; to *1579*
614 while he lived and] *1603*; and while he liued *1579, 1595*
616 bounds] *1603*; bondes *1579, 1595*
639 unto] *1595, 1603*; to *1579*
657 Cithaeron] *1595, 1603*; Cytheron *1579*
666 people] *1603*; contrie *1579, 1595*
667 called] *1603*; calling *1579, 1595*
667 Moreover] *1603*; And so forth *1579, 1595*
670 shall] *1603*; will *1579, 1595*
671 Cassandria] *1603*; CASSANDRA *1579, 1595*
674 ambassage] *1595, 1603*; Ambassade *1579*
678 Alexander, whom he so handled] *1603*; him, and so handled *Alexander 1579, 1595*
688 till ten years after, when] *1603*; but ten yeres after that *1579, 1595*
695 on his side] *1603*; in his behalfe *1579, 1595*

695 the] *1603*; om. *1579, 1595*
701 **Marg.** monied] *1603*; money *1579, 1595*
708 inventory] *1595, 1603*; inuentoty *1579*
713 bring] *1603*; wey *1579, 1595*
720 people] *1595, 1603*; poople *1579*
724 squinance] *1603*; sinanche *1579, 1595*
725 money] *1603*; argentsynanche *1579, 1595*
729 and] *1603*; that *1579, 1595*
730 **Marg.** κηλεῖν] this edn; κυλειν *1579, 1595, 1603*
735 by no means have searched] *1603*; haue searched by no meanes *1579, 1595*
737 in no fault] *1603*; in fault *1579, 1595*
772 valour] *1595, 1603*; valure *1579*
784 whither] *1595, 1603*; whether *1579*
793 him to] *1595, 1603*; himto *1579*
821 **Marg.** banished men] *1595, 1603*; banishedmen *1579*
823 Aegina] *1603*; AEGINES *1579, 1595*
824 place] *1603*; recite *1579, 1595*
833 with] *1603*; and *1579, 1595*
836 thought] *1579, 1603*; though *1595*
841 and] *1603*; who *1579, 1595*
855 laughed] *1603*; laughing *1579, 1595*
856 calling] *1603*; called *1579, 1595*
866 altar] *1595, 1603*; author *1579*
876 examined] *1603*; examined by *Archias 1579, 1595*
881 friend said), who said] *1603*; frende) sayd *1579*; friend said *1595*

The Life of Marcus Tullius Cicero

10 chickpea] *1603*; riche pease *1579, 1595*
12 chickpea] *1603*; riche pease *1579, 1595*
15 of] *1595, 1603*; of the *1579*
20 chickpea] *1603*; riche pease *1579, 1595*
21 to bed] *1595, 1603*; a bedde *1579*
34 midst] *1603*; middest *1579, 1595*
51 Mucius] *1603*; Mutius *1579, 1603*
68 shrank back] *1603*; shronke colour *1579, 1595*
83 Ascalon] *1603*; Ascalona *1579, 1595*
85 Antiochus] *1579, 1603*; Antiocbus *1595*
95 affairs of] *1603*; orators in *1579, 1595*
118 honours] *1603*; honor *1579, 1595*
137 comedian] *1603*; commediant *1579, 1595*

Textual Notes

265

137 **Marg.** Aesop] *1603*; Aesopus *1579, 1595*
138 Atreus'] *1603*; Atrius *1579, 1595*
143 great] *1603*; so great *1579, 1595*
146 on foot] *1603*; a foote *1579, 1595*
150 when] *1579, 1603*; where *1595*
159 was] *1595, 1603*; om. *1579*
168 vanished] *1603*; vanquished *1579, 1595*
173 these] *1603*; those *1579, 1595*
189 took] *1595, 1603*; had *1579*
196 time] *1603*; day light *1579*; anie light *1595*
208 boar] *1603*; swine *1579, 1595*
211 effeminate] *1603*; womanly *1579, 1595*
211 Thy] *1603*; his *1579, 1595*
219 threescore and fifteen] *1603*; seuentie fiue *1579, 1595*
226 he had also] *1603*; also he had *1579, 1595*
235 also] *1595, 1603*; alwayes *1579*
243 the increase] *1595, 1603*; thincrease *1579*
252 pronounced] *1603*; proceeded *1579, 1595*
275 unto] *1595, 1603*; to *1579*
300 resist] *1603*; oppresse *1579, 1595*
301 Catiline] *1603*; Catilina *1579, 1595*
318 the [mean men]] *1595, 1603*; om. *1579*
361 And] *1603*; But *1579, 1595*
372 commonweal] *1595, 1603*; comman weale *1579*
402 home] *1595, 1603*; hand *1579*
410 no] *1595, 1603*; not *1579*
438 the (second occurrence)] *1595, 1603*; his *1579*
439 made a great slaughter in Rome] *1603*; a great slaughter in Rome made *1579, 1595*
449 is] *1595, 1603*; was *1579*
453 the end] *1595, 1603*; thend *1579*
462 longer] *1595, 1603*; lenger *1579*
469 and] *1595, 1603*; but *1579*
470 the end] *1595, 1603*; thend *1579*
472 as (second occurrence)] *1603*; a *1579, 1595*
484 **Marg.** departed] *1595, 1603*; departed Rome *1579*
494 **Marg.** was] *1595, 1603*; why *1579*
511 through] *1595, 1603*; thorow *1579*
518 plot] *1595, 1603*; plat *1579*
520 they] *1579, 1603*; tthey *1595*
537 through] *1595, 1603*; thorow *1579*

548 say that] 1603; say 1579, 1595
580 being] 1603; that was 1579, 1595
582 rinds] 1603; ryend 1579, 1595
586 flame] 1579, 1595; flamel 1603
632 ear] 1579, 1603; eate 1595
649 [thinking] they [were]] 1579, 1595; thy 1603
663 riches and spoils] 1603; riches, spoyles 1579, 1595
707 Catiline] 1603; *Catulus* 1579, 1595
710 him] 1603; them 1579, 1595
723 **Marg.** orations] 1579, 1595; Oratious 1603
730 Peripatetic] 1579, 1603; Peripaticke 1595
758 had] 1603; that 1579, 1595
758 threescore] 1603; lx. 1579, 1595
761 thou] 1603; om. 1579, 1595
769 **Marg.** Κράσσου] 1579, 1603; Κράστου 1595
776 Vatinius] 1595, 1603; *Vitinius* 1579
797 Cotta] 1603; *Scotta* 1579, 1595
806 turned] 1603; returned 1579, 1595
808 seeing] 1603; finding 1579, 1595
813 to perform nothing of all that] 1603; that thou hast performed none of all these 1579, 1595
819 following his suit] 1603; beeing there 1579, 1595
820 election] 1603; the election 1579, 1595
829 at] 1595, 1603; of 1579
894 Notwithstanding] 1579, 1603; Notwithstandig 1595
897 dishonesty] 1579, 1603; dishonestly 1595
939 the other] 1595, 1603; thother 1579
958 the other] 1595, 1603; thother 1579
978 Luke] 1579, 1595; Lvne 1603
997 they] 1579, 1603; the 1595
1042 Italy] 1579, 1603; Italia 1595
1053 liked of] 1595, 1603; liked any of 1579
1091 Publius] 1603; P. 1579, 1595
1093-4 two thousand and five hundred] 1603; two thowsand fiue hundred 1579, 1595
1113 restored] 1595, 1603; restored them 1579
1114 did] 1595, 1603; did he 1579
1139 longer] 1595, 1603; lenger 1579
1154 presently] 1603; immediatly 1579, 1595
1159 the other] 1595, 1603; thother 1579
1206 [news] was] 1603; being 1579, 1595

1217 Theramenes] *1579, 1595*; Theramines *1603*
1225 colour often] *1603*; diuers colours *1579, 1595*
1227 the end] *1595, 1603*; thend *1579*
1279 the end] *1595, 1603*; thend *1579*
1337 nothing] *1595, 1603*; no thing *1579*
1353 and] *1603*; om. *1579, 1595*
1371 away] *1603*; om. *1579, 1595*
1373 **Marg.** adopted son] *1595, 1603*; the adopted son *1579*
1377 he] *1579*; they *1595, 1603*
1391 flatter] *1579, 1595*; flattter *1603*
1442 Q.] *1595, 1603*; Quintus *1579*
1465 an] *1603*; a *1579, 1595*
1465 furlongs] *1603*; furlong *1579, 1595*
1473 **Marg.** Caieta] Caiete *1579*
1504 the other] *1595, 1603*; thother *1579*
1510 **Marg.** Cicero] *1595, 1603*; Ciccro *1579*

The Comparison of Cicero with Demosthenes

18 not only smelleth] *1603*; smelleth not *1579, 1595*
18 Pytheas] *1579, 1595*; Pythias *1603*
33 my lords!] this edn; my lords? *1579–1603*
35 the other] *1595, 1603*; thother *1579*
47 Yet] *1603*; Yea *1579, 1595*
58 auditory] *1579, 1595*; auditority *1603*
72 the other] *1595, 1603*; thother *1579*
89 reports] *1595, 1603*; reporters *1579*
108 into] *1595, 1603*; vnto *1579*
116 being] *1603*; and being *1579, 1595*

The Life of Julius Caesar

6 the elder] *1595, 1603*; thelder *1579*
9 and] *1603*; but *1579, 1595*
43 manned] *1603*; manned out *1579, 1595*
46 Pergamum] *1579, 1595*; Pergamvs *1603*
52 Pergamum] *1579, 1595*; Pergamvs *1603*
65 the end] *1595, 1603*; thende *1579*
97 scratch] *1595, 1603*; scrat *1579*
103 Pompilius] *1579, 1595*; Pompilins *1603*
111 the other] *1595, 1603*; thother *1579*

129 called Appius' way] *1603*; going vnto Appius *1579, 1595*
136 **Marg.** prodigality] *1579, 1595*; prodigility *1603*
139 under] *1579, 1595*; vndeer *1603*
154 the other] *1595, 1603*; thother *1579*
177 the election] *1595, 1603*; thelection *1579*
200 appear best] *1603*; best appeare *1579, 1595*
220 longer] *1595, 1603*; lenger *1579*
231–32 on his house] *1603*; in his owne house *1579, 1595*
236 and] *1603*; and that *1579, 1595*
238 **Marg.** Caesar's wife] *1595, 1603*; Caesars, wife *1579*
242 the woods] *1603*; wodde *1579, 1595*
242 the [god]] *1603*; om. *1579, 1595*
296 on the other] *1603*; of thother *1579*; of the other *1595*
305 this] *1603*; his *1579, 1595*
330 themselves] *1603*; to them selues *1579, 1595*
335 the other] *1595, 1603*; thother *1579*
340 to] *1603*; forbidding *1579, 1595*
343 in] *1603*; om. *1579, 1595*
356 **Marg.** prophecy] *1579, 1595*; proph cy *1603*
366 the one] *1595, 1603*; thone *1579*
367 the other] *1595, 1603*; thother *1579*
367 the assembly] *1595, 1603*; thassemblie *1579*
377 the other] *1595, 1603*; thother *1579*
380 daughter] *1603*; wife *1579, 1595*
396 on] *1595, 1603*; of *1579*
408 for] *1579, 1595*; far *1603*
443 Marseilles] *1603*; Marselles *1579, 1595*
455 enemy] *1603*; enemies *1579, 1595*
459 way] *1603*; away *1579, 1595*
461 on foot] *1603*; a foote *1579, 1595*
464 left] *1579, 1603*; lef *1595*
472 did] *1579, 1595*; hid *1603*
479 on fire] *1603*; a fire *1579, 1595*
493 he] *1579, 1595*; the *1603*
498 And] *1579, 1595*; As *1603*
529 on foot] *1603*; a foote *1579, 1595*
565 courage] *1603*; corages *1579, 1595*
581 the affairs] *1595, 1603*; thaffayres *1579*
588 Gauls,] *1579*; Gauls. *1595, 1603*
597 on foot] *1603*; a foote *1579, 1595*
631 nobility] *1595, 1603*; noblitie *1579*

676 the other] *1595, 1603*; thother *1579*
690 the other] *1595, 1603*; thother *1579*
695 saying] *1603*; saying that *1579, 1595*
737 parts] *1603*; parties *1579, 1595*
754 Arvernians] *1579, 1595*; Avernians *1603*
759 thereabouts] *1603*; thereabout *1579, 1595*
759 **Marg.** to the river of Saone] *1603*; the riuer Saone *1579, 1595*
762 longer] *1595, 1603*; lenger *1579*
762 in (first occurrence)] *1603*; into *1579, 1595*
764 valiant] *1595, 1603*; very valiant *1579*
768 invincible] *1603*; vnuincible *1579, 1595*
774 times] *1603*; time *1579, 1595*
778 parts] *1603*; parties *1579, 1595*
782 the other] *1595, 1603*; thother *1579*
787 way] *1579, 1603*; away *1595*
790 flying] *1595, 1603*; fleeing *1579*
809 until] *1603*; but when *1579, 1595*
810 the other] *1595, 1603*; thother *1579*
824 Rome] *1579, 1603*; Roωe *1595*
830 **Marg.** cause] *1579, 1595*; canse *1603*
892 and [though]] *1603*; and that *1579, 1595*
902 cross] *1579, 1595*; cr osse *1603*
905 he] *1579, 1595*; see *1603*
936 the [government]] *1603*; his *1579, 1595*
949–50 the other] *1595, 1603*; thother *1579*
951 the execution] *1595, 1603*; thexecution *1579*
958 Ariminum] *1595, 1603*; Ariminvn *1579*
985–86 A man can be but once undone] *1603*; A desperat man feareth no daunger *1579, 1595*
993 the extreme] *1595, 1603*; thextreme *1579*
998 parts] *1603*; parties *1579, 1595*
1006 is it] *1603*; it is *1579, 1595*
1014 the other] *1595, 1603*; thother *1579*
1015 Faonius] this edn; Phaonius *1579–1603*
1019 a] *1595, 1603*; om. *1579*
1100 for] *1603*; of *1579, 1595*
1118 on] *1595, 1603*; of *1579*
1167 the other] *1595, 1603*; thother *1579*
1188 escaped] *1603*; scaped *1579, 1595*
1215 so [well]] *1603*; om. *1579, 1595*
1219 the other] *1595, 1603*; thother *1579*

1236 king] *1579, 1595*; kings *1603*
1237 many] *1595, 1603*; so many *1579*
1258 each other] *1603*; thother *1579*; the other *1595*
1307 the other] *1595, 1603*; thother *1579*
1319 running] *1579, 1595*; rnnning *1603*
1321 on fire] *1603*; a fire *1579, 1595*
1322 on [the ear]] *1595, 1603*; of *1579*
1322 on fire] *1603*; a fire *1579, 1595*
1334 thrust] *1579, 1603*; trust *1595*
1392 give] *1595, 1603*; gaue *1579*
1397 it] *1579, 1595*; in *1603*
1398 came so] *1603*; so came *1579, 1595*
1405 aside] *1603*; at toe side *1579, 1595*
1424 another] *1595, 1603*; anothers *1579*
1452 the other] *1595, 1603*; thother *1579*
1455 lack] *1603*; the lacke *1579, 1595*
1485 letter] *1603*; letters *1579, 1595*
1490 was he] *1603*; he was *1579, 1595*
1516 fought] *1595, 1603*; he fought *1579*
1517 Salutius] *1595, 1603*; Sallutius *1579*
1532 Asinius] *1595, 1603*; Afinius *1579*
1550 the effect] *1595, 1603*; theffect *1579*
1551 the execution] *1595, 1603*; thexecution *1579*
1555 the extremity] *1595, 1603*; thextremity *1579*
1556 praetors] *1579*; Praetor *1595, 1603*
1572 civil ambition] *1595, 1603*; a ciuil ambition *1579*
1597 before] *1595, 1603*; afore *1579*
1642 too] *1603*; to *1579, 1595*
1666 repair] *1595, 1603*; repaiɹ *1579*
1668 also] *1595, 1603*; so *1579*
1683 the] *1603*; om. *1579, 1595*
1695 place] *1579, 1595*; market place *1603*
1718 **Marg.** intercalaris] this edn; intercularis *1579–1603*
1734 Sibylline] *1579*; Sybiline *1595, 1603*
1754 this] *1603*; his *1579, 1595*
1755 on] *1595, 1603*; of *1579*
1758 or] *1603*; but *1579, 1595*
1774 triumphant] *1603*; triumphing *1579, 1595*
1778 rejoicing] *1579, 1595*; reoycing *1603*
1811 or] *1595, 1603*; nor *1579*
1830 the [solitary birds]] *1595, 1603*; these *1579*

1842 being] *1595, 1603*; beng *1579*
1843 unto] *1595, 1603*; to *1579*
1843 they be] *1603*; be they *1579, 1595*
1863 and that then] *1603*; and then, for that *1579, 1595*
1872 be betrayed] *1603*; out *1579, 1595*
1872 at the soothsayers] *1603*; the Soothsayers to scorne *1579, 1595*
1888 into [his house]] *1595, 1603*; vnto *1579*
1890 greater] *1603*; great *1579, 1595*
1934 they] *1595, 1603*; that they *1579*
1935 nor] *1603*; not *1579, 1595*
1935 an] *1603*; any *1579, 1595*
1936 the other] *1595, 1603*; thother *1579*
1947 image] *1595, 1603*; image. *1579*
1953 something] *1603*; somwhat *1579, 1595*
1960 the other] *1595, 1603*; thother *1579*
1967 amongst] *1595, 1603*; among *1579*
1970 were both put] *1603*; were put *1579, 1595*
1999 him] *1595, 1603*; om. *1579*
2014 lifetime] *1595, 1603*; lfe time *1579*
2029 Abydos] *1579, 1595*; Arydos *1603*
2044 that] *1603*; om. *1579, 1595*
2049 *1603* introduces Simon Goulart's comparison of Alexander and Caesar at this point; *1579* and *1595* have 'The end of Caesars life.'

GLOSSARY

abate destroy, flatten
abject cast out, reject as inferior
ability strength
abuse deceive
abusion misapplication
acception sense, meaning
according fitting, correspondingly
accumber oppress
adapt fit
address turn to a purpose, send
adminiculate support
adulterate stained by adultery
adventure risk
advertisement instruction, warning
advisement deliberation
advowtry adultery (variant spelling)
affection state of mind, feeling, passion, lust
affectionate inclined
again against, in preparation for
against before, adjoining, opposite
a-good heartily
ague fever
aland on dry land
alarm call to battle
alate lately
alienate estranged
allege quote
allow approve, commend
allowance approval
alongst along
altogether all together
alway always
amate daunt
amaze (n.) amazement
amaze (v.) stun, terrify
amazed stunned, terrified
amove remove
angerly angrily

apophthegmatical pithy
appassionate influenced by passion
appellative naming
appliable well-disposed
apply devote oneself to
appoint agree, decree
assay attempt, trial
assist attend
assoil resolve
assure secure
astone stun, astound
athirst thirsty
attach arrest
attain discover
attend look after, await
atwite taunt, reproach
author instigator
avaunt (yourself) speak proudly of, boast
avoid depart
await ambush
away (with) endure

bailiff steward
bain bath
barbarous foreign
bark strip the bark off a tree
barrator quarreller
bash to be abashed
basilic basilica (palace)
basin 'Hollow metal dishes clashed together to produce sound; ? cymbals' (*OED*, *n*., 4)
battle battalion
battle-ray order of troops arranged for battle
bear (one) in hand lead (one) to believe
beclip seize
become go
beech-mast fruit of the beech
behove have need of
belive 'With little semantic content' (*OED*)
beray disfigure
bereavable removable by violence
betime early

bewray expose
bib drink
bill note, list
board (dining-)table
botch ulcer
bottom a deep place
bourd jest
brave worthy
brief outline
brigantine body armour
brothel prostitute
buncht-back hump-backed
burden charge with
by and by straightaway

calling rank
can know, know how to
caple horse
captivate captivated
carriage luggage
carver sculptor
cas case
cast device
cast up vomit
catch capture
certes certainly
chamber bedroom
chanceable happening by chance, subject to chance
changeling an inconstant person
chare chariot
charge load
chargeable costly
chaste (adj.) restrained
chaste (v.) chasten
check taunt, rebuke
cheer (n.) food
cheer (v.) welcome, offer hospitality
chevance wealth
christen Christian
clemence clemency
clerk scholar

clip clasp
closely secretly
coat-armour armour
cockney pamper
colour pretext
colourable plausible
colt fool
comedian writer of comedies
come out come to an end
commodious beneficial
commodity benefit
communication conversation
compass ingenuity, cunning
competent reasonable
conceive understand
confines territory, borderlands
conject conjecture
contain retain
con thank(s) give thanks
contrary (v.) oppose
control censure
convenable suitable
convenience appropriateness
convenient appropriate, proper
conversant 'passing much of one's time' (*OED*, A. 1)
conversation conduct, social interaction, living
converse (in) to be engaged (in)
convince convict, confute
coptank 'a high peaked head' (*OED*)
corroborate strengthen [a faculty, as opposed to an argument]
cottier cottager
countenance bearing, appearance, conduct, estimation, show of intention
covetous covetousness
crazy ailing
cresset vessel containing fuel, used for lighting
crump-shouldered crooked
cumber (n.) distress
cumber (v.) trouble
cunning knowledge, learning
cup-shotten drunk
cure effort, pains

curiosity fastidiousness
curiously fastidiously, finely

dade support
dam mother
damnify harm
daze to be stupified
dead flat, vapid
debate strife
declaration interpretation, exposition
decline turn
default lack, fault
default of for want of
defeature defeat
delicate delectable, indulgent, indolent
delices voluptuousness
demand question, request
demandé one who is asked a question
demander one who asks a question
deny denial, refusal
deprave disparage
deprehend seize
derive impart
derogate diminish
descry reveal
despiteous cruel, full of ill-will
detect inform against
device chatter
devise converse
difficile difficult
dight (past participle *dight*) array
disallow reject, reprove
discomfiture defeat in battle
discover reveal, expose to view
discretion understanding, discernment
discuss examine
dishonest dishonour
displeasantly in an irritated manner
dissemble pretend not to notice
distract insane
distress overcome in battle

doctrine learning
doubt fear, suspect
doubtful suspect
dram drachma (Greek coin)
drink drunk drink to inebriation
duke general, ruler
dure last

eager pungent
easing eaves
effect sum and substance
eftsoons again, repeatedly
egall equal
eke also
element sky
embraid upbraid
enchafe make hot
endamage harm
enfarce stuff
engender produce offspring, bring into existence
ensample example
ensearch pry into
ensue follow
entail endow
entertain sustain, 'to retain as an advocate' (*OED*, †5. b)
entreat treat
envy begrudge
erne eagle
err stray
erst earlier
espy spy
esteem assess
execrable fearful
expect await
expedition prompt supply
exploit execute, accomplish
exquisite exact, careful
exquisitely carefully, minutely

factor mercantile agent
fain glad, gladly

faith trustworthiness
fame common report
farthermore furthermore
fashion shape, appearance
fastidious wearisome
fatigate tire
favour indulgence
fear cause fear in
feign form
fere companion, husband or wife
ferula cane
field battle, order of troops for battle
finder discoverer
flagitious criminal, wicked
fleer mock
flesh (n.) meat
flesh (v.) 'To inflame the ardour, rage, or cupidity of (a person) by a foretaste of success or gratification' (*OED*)
foison abundance
follow 'To pursue (an affair) to its conclusion or accomplishment' (*OED*, 6. †b)
fondly foolishly
for in preference to
forbear bear up
fordo undo, remove
foreign external
foresee take care in advance
forlet omit, cease to do
form bench
for that because
fortrust be (over-)confident
fountain fount, source
franchise immunity, exemption
frank free
frankly freely, generously
frapling arguing
freedom immunity, exemption
fro from
froward obstinate, unruly, awkward
frump (n.) jeer
frump (v.) mock
frustrate of deprived of

fulfil fill to the full
full very
fulsome wearisome
funerals funeral
furnish equip
furniture dress, equipment, provisions, embellishment

gan began (past tense of *gin*, aphetic form of *begin*)
garboil disturbance
generation reproduction
Genoways Genoese
gere 'A sudden fit of passion, feeling, transient fancy, or the like' (*OED*)
gin device
gird (n.) gibe
gird (v.) assail with jest
give back retreat
glad take joy, make glad
glass mirror
glozing specious talk
graff graft
Greekish Greek
grief disease
grutching complaint
guard trimming
guarded trimmed
guise habit
gyve shackle

habit bodily condition
hale haul
halt lame
handsome seemly, convenient
handsomely skilfully
hardily quickly
hardiness audacity
haunt habitually practise
head silver tax paid per head
heaviness sadness
hent (past tense *hent*) lift
hest behest
hicket hiccup

hind agricultural labourer
hoise raise
housewife disreputable woman
husband husbandman, farmer
husbandry cultivate

i. i.e., that is
ill (adj.) wicked
ill (n.) sickness
ill-apaid ill-pleased
impostume abscess
impression push, assault
incertainty uncertainty
incontinent immediately
incontinently immediately
indifferently equally
indiscreet lacking judgement
indite dictate, compose
inditing literary composition
in fine in the end, at last
inflate inflated
infortunity misfortune
inleaguer 'To encamp with a besieging or beleaguering force' (*OED*)
innocency innocence
instant importunate
instantly persistently
instruct educated
insurge arise
intach imbue
intend direct one's course
inter put in the ground
interline 'to mark with lines, esp. of various colours' (*OED*)
interlude play
interpreter translator, commentator
inward internal part, inner character
iwis certainly

jangling noisy or excessive talking
jealousy mistrust
jointure dowry
journey battle

joy enjoy

kern peasant
kim-kam awry
kind innate, appropriate
kitling young animal
knap snap
knitch bundle
knot obligation
know acknowledge

Lacedaemon, Lacedaemonian Spartan
Laconize to imitate the Spartans (Lacedaemonians)
largely liberally
late recently
lay for lie in wait for
lay wait carefully watch
learning lesson, branch of learning
leeful lawful
leese lose
left-handed inept
lere learn
lewd wicked, worthless
lewdly badly
lewdness ignorance, wickedness
lie along lie outstretched
light alight
like please
likelihood likeness
link torch
lob lout
lodesman steersman
losel scoundrel
lusk idler
lyam leash for hounds

maffle mumble
maistrice deed of might or skill
make account expect, reckon
mean of middling degree
measurable moderate

meat food
meddle associate (with), have sex (with), mix, contend
merely entirely
mickle much
mids middle
minish diminish
minister servant, attendant
mistrust suspect
mixt mix
mo more
monstruous monstrous
mould soil
mutilate imperfect
mutine mutiny
myriad ten thousand of a currency

naughtly wickedly
naughty wicked
ne neither, nor, not
nearly particularly, closely
nice particular, rigorous
nill be unwilling
nip taunt
nis is not
noint anoint
noondays noon
nother neither; other (following a negative)
(no) notherwise (not) otherwise
nothing in no way
nourish nurture, breastfeed
nouther neither

oblivion amnesty
occupation use
occupy make use of
occurrent event
odible hateful
open held in public
opinion estimation, reputation
opportunity timeliness
or at a former time

ordinance arrangement
other either, others
otherwhiles from time to time, at other times
ought owed
ounce lynx (or other medium-sized member of cat family)
outcept unless
outher either
out of without
overcome exceed
overseen rash, betrayed into error
overthrow demolish
overthwart oppose, hinder
overthwartly adversely

pap breast
palisado fence made of pales or stakes
pardie by God!
pareil equal
pass care, omit
pass forth go out
pathetical producing an emotional response
peise to weigh, 'To estimate or assess the weight of by lifting or holding in the hand' (*OED*, *v.*, 1. b)
pelf wealth
pell-mell mixed up in confusion
pelting insignificant
peradventure perhaps
Perse Persia
persecute chase
pick dress up
picked refined
pinnace small boat
pistle epistle
pitch plant
plain lament
plainingly complainingly
plump band, group
point point out
poise weight
ponder 'To estimate or reckon the worth, value, or amount of' (*OED*, v., 1. a)
port status

practice scheme
practise persuade
prefer submit for consideration
prejudicate prejudiced
preoccupate prevent
press thick of the fight
pretend intend, profess
prevent anticipate, act in advance
prey (n.) booty
prey (v.) plunder
priestress priestess
pristinate pristine
private 'Peculiar to a particular person, community, etc.' (*OED*, *adj.*^{1}, A. 3. b)
privily secretly
privities genitals
privity familiarity, knowledge, consent
procure make every effort to, seek to get
prone easy
property characteristic quality
propice advantageous
proscript someone who is proscribed
provide prepare
provided prepared
pulpit rostrum, i.e. a stage for public speeches
put add
put by bar, dissuade

quail die out
quaint ingenious, curious
qualify mitigate
quean prostitute
quick lively, having a sharp taste
quietous quiet
quit (past participle *quit*) acquit

ramp 'to trample upon in triumph' (*OED*, *v.*^{1}, 6)
rampire rampart
ravener glutton
read teach by reading aloud
rear up bring about
reasonable reasonably

reboundable moving back and forth, echoing
receipt receptacle, remedy
rede advise
refel refute
reject dismiss from one's mind
rejournment adjournment
religion religious observation
remission release from work
remove (n.) 'A signal for a military force to depart' (*OED*, 3. b)
remove (v.) depart
repair 'The gathering or assembling of people at a place' (*OED*, *n.*^{1}, 1. a)
repugnance contradiction
repugnant contradictory
require beseech, seek, demand
resort company
respect reason
rest in have confidence in
revoke bring back
rivality rivalry
roll bandage
room office
round whisper
roundly swiftly
rout company
rudeness lack of learning
ruff 'an exalted or elated state' (*OED*, *n.*^{2}, 1. a)
ruinate ruin

sacrify sacrifice
sad serious
sadly seriously
salve vindicate
savourly wisely
saw decree
scape (n. and v.) escape
schoolmaster tutor
science knowledge
scrip 'a small bag, wallet, or satchel, *esp.* one carried by a pilgrim, a shepherd, or a beggar' (*OED*, *n.* 1)
self same
semblably similarly, likewise

sentence saying, aphorism, sense
set sit, to be seated (passive)
set light by despise, account of low value
sew drain
ship-boat skiff
shove impel
shrewd naughty, malicious
silly unfortunate
sith since
skill make a difference
slake loosen
slipper slippery
smatch taste
so that provided that
sometime sometimes
sometimes sometime
soil region
sophister sophist, teacher of rhetoric
sort manner
sort with go in the company of
spear soldier armed with a spear
spent yield, produce
sperage asparagus
spill bring to ruin
squinance tonsillitis
stable to make stable
stablish establish, render stable
state power
stay stop, prevent, wait, hold up
stepped in years advanced in age
stick (in) persist (in)
stick with 'to side persistently with' (*OED*)
still always, continually
story history, work of history
strait to bring into straits
strake streak
strange foreign, alien, not affable
strength stronghold
stripe blow with a weapon
sturdy harsh
stut stutter

subtle-witted devious, sly
success result
suffer endure, bear
suit succession
sure safe
surely safely
swallow whirlpool

table tablet, picture
take give
take up settle, be content, restrain oneself, mend one's ways
target small round shield
tarry remain (in)
temper 'The due or proportionate mixture or combination of elements or qualities' (*OED*)
terrene earthy
that so that, in order that, that which
thorough through
throughly thoroughly
tickle uncertain
tissue 'A band or girdle of rich stuff' (*OED*)
to in addition to
tone the one (of two)
tother the other (of two)
touch relate
towardness willingness to learn
train course
travail (n.) toil
travail (v.) exert oneself
traverse 'A curtain or screen placed crosswise, or drawn across a room, hall, or theatre' (*OED*)
treasure treasury
treatable tractable
treen wooden
trim adorn, prepare
troth truth
trow believe
trunk 'A pipe used as a speaking-tube or ear-trumpet' (*OED*)
turn change
twit taunt

uncunning ignorant
undelayed undiluted
uneath hardly
ungracious wicked, unfavourable
unhandsome inconvenient
unhappily wretchedly
unkept unguarded
unkindness ingratitude
unknit untie
unleeful illicit
unreverently irreverently
unslipper not slippery
untempted unattempted
unthriftily dissolutely
untilthy untillable
unware without knowing it
unwares unexpectedly, unknowingly
unweened unexpected
unwittily unwisely
unwrest untighten
use habit
utter outward

vanquer vanquisher
vary disagree, quarrel
venereal sexual
venge avenge
vengeable characterized by vengeance
vie challenge
villain low-born rustic
virtue efficacy, force, magical power
vocable word
voice word, speech
void remove

wait lie in wait for
ward custody
ware aware, watchful
watch (n.) wakefulness
watch (v.) remain awake, be on the look-out
waw wave

way (adv.) away
way (v.) 'To *Way a Horse*, is to teach him to travel in the Ways' (quoted in OED, v., 2)
wealfulness happiness
wealth well-being, happiness
ween think
weezle windpipe
weigh balance, counterpoise
well to be a source of
welladay alas
well-apaid well-pleased
wench female servant, wanton woman
whereas where, seeing that
wherewithal wherewith
which who
whitlow 'A suppurative inflammatory sore or swelling in a finger or thumb, usually in the terminal joint' (*OED*)
whole healed
wight person, being
will want, ought to
wist knew
without outside
witty wise
wonder look or regard with wonder
wonders wondrous
wondersly wondrously
wood mad
word saying
workmaster creator
world region
world goods worldly possessions
worship condition of deserving esteem, honour
wrest twist, 'To screw or turn (the pin or pins of a musical instrument) so as to tighten or tune the strings' (*OED*)
writhe divert

yclad clothed
yesk the hiccups
yet even

NEOLOGISMS

This list includes words for which the translations collected in these volumes provide either the first citation or which antedate the relevant entry in OED (i.e. in the meaning in which they are used in the translation, not necessarily the word in general). It is not comprehensive, but aims to provide a sense of the linguistic innovation of Renaissance translators of Plutarch. For the meaning of the words in this list, please refer to the Glossary above.

Thomas Wyatt, *The Quiet of Mind* (1528)

affection (antedates first citation in OED, $n.^1$, †5)
appassionate (antedates first citation in OED)
appearance (antedates first citation in OED, n., 6)
bereavable (not in OED)
chanceable (antedates first citation in OED)
check (antedates first citation in OED, int. and $n.^1$, B. 3)
commentary (antedates first citation in OED, n., †1)
contain (antedates first citation in OED, v., †13. a)
dead (antedates first citation in OED, adj., n., and adv., A. 12. a)
done (antedates first citation in OED, $adj.^1$ and n., A. 2)
exquisite (antedates first citation in OED, adj. and n., A. †2. a)
fortrust (not in OED)
handsome (antedates first citation in OED, adj., adv., and n., A. †1. b)
interline (antedates first citation in OED, $v.^1$, †5)
over-suffer (not in OED)
plainingly (not in OED)
prospect (antedates first citation in OED, n., 3. a)
quietous (first citation in OED)
reboundable (antedates first citation in OED, rebound, v.)
rivality (first citation in OED)
ship-boat (not in OED)
sport (first citation in OED, v., 2. c)
unhandsome (antedates first citation in OED, adj. (and adv.), †2)
unvincible (antedates first citation in OED)
weigh (antedates first citation in OED, $v.^1$, 16. †c.; cf. 16. †f)
whirlpool (antedates first citation in OED, n.2)
wonder (antedates first citation in OED, v., †3. a)

Thomas Elyot, *The Education or Bringing up of Children* (1528–1530)

according (not in *OED* in this sense)
adminiculate (first citation in *OED*)
adulterate (antedates first citation in *OED*, *adj.*, 2)
bark (antedates first citation in *OED*, *v.*², 3)
bounteously (antedates first citation in *OED*)
cockney (antedates first citation in *OED*, *v.*)
corroborate (antedates first citation in *OED*, *v.*, 3)
dastard (antedates first citation in *OED*, *n.* and *adj.*, B)
depraved (antedates first citation in *OED*)
deprehend (antedates first citation in *OED*, *v.*, 1)
device (antedates first citation in *OED*, *n.*, 10)
displeasantly (antedates first citation in *OED*)
enfarce (antedates first citation in *OED*, *v.*, 2)
epigram (antedates first citation in *OED*, *n.*, †1)
exact (antedates first citation in *OED*, *v.*, 2)
fastidious (antedates first citation in *OED*, *adj.*, †1)
fatigate (antedates first citation in *OED*, *v.*)
frankly (antedates first citation in *OED*)
fore-study (antedates first citation in *OED*)
habit (antedates first citation in *OED*, *n.*, 5)
husbandry (first citation in *OED*, *v.*)
in favour of (antedates first citation in *OED*, favour, *n.*)
ingurgitation (antedates first citation in *OED*)
intach (not in *OED*)
kicker (antedates first citation in *OED*)
pristinate (antedates first citation in *OED*)
recreation (not in *OED* in this sense)
qualify (antedates first citation in *OED*, *v.*, II, specifically 9. a)
spent (n.) (not in *OED*, but cf. spend, *v.*¹, 16. b)
untilthy (not in *OED*)
unwrest (not in *OED* in this sense)
world (antedates first citation in *OED*, 9)

Philemon Holland, 'Of Intemperate Speech or Garrulity', from *The Morals* (1603)

demandé (sole citation in *OED*)
inleaguer (sole citation in *OED*)
kim-kam (first citation in *OED*, *adv.*)

Laconize (first citation in *OED*, *v.*)
sea-needle (first citation in *OED*)

Henry Parker, Lord Morley, *The Story of Paullus Aemilius* (1542–1546/7)

contrariways (antedates first citation in *OED*)
Cretical (not in *OED*)
thereunto (antedates first citation in *OED*, *adv.*, 2)
untempted (antedates first citation in *OED*, *adj.*, 2)
vanquer (antedates first citation in *OED*)

Thomas North, *The Life of Demosthenes*, from *The Lives* (1579)

attend (antedates first citation in *OED*, *v.*, 13. c)
buzz (antedates first citation in *OED*, *v.^{1}*, 5 or possibly 2. a)
corn-master (first citation in *OED*)
people-pleaser (first citation in *OED*)
ramp (first citation in *OED*, *v.^{1}*, 6)

Thomas North, *The Life of Marcus Tullius Cicero*, from *The Lives* (1579)

ashore (antedates first citation in *OED*, *adv.^{2}*)
broach (not in *OED* in this sense)
colt (first citation in *OED*, *v.*)
envy (antedates first citation in *OED*, *v.^{1}*, †3. a.)
myriad (antedates first citation in *OED*, A. 1. †b)
put by (antedates first citation in *OED*, 1. c)
rejournment (first citation in *OED*)
shoal (first citation in *OED*, *n.^{2}*, 2)
stayer (first citation in *OED*, *n.^{2}*)

Thomas North, *The Life of Julius Caesar*, from *The Lives* (1579)

basilic (antedates first citation in *OED*, *n.*)
battle-ray (antedates first citation in *OED*)
caparison (antedates first citation in *OED*, *n.*)
coat-armour (antedates first citation in *OED*, *n.*, 5)
ferula (first citation in *OED*, *n.*, 2)
inexpungible (antedates first citation in *OED*)
over-hardness (antedates first citation in *OED*)

pell-mell (first citation in *OED*, *adv.*, *adj.*, and *n.*, 1. b)
priesthoodship (not in *OED*)
prorogue (first citation in *OED*, *v.* 1. b)
troop (antedates first citation in *OED*, *n.* 1. b.)
underhand (antedates first citation in *OED*, *adj.* and *n.*, 2. a)

BIBLIOGRAPHY

Early modern translations of Plutarch are listed under their translators, with the exception of collections with multiple translators. The place of publication of early modern books is London unless otherwise indicated.

AFFORTUNATI, MONICA, and BARBARA SCARDIGLI, 'La vita "plutarchea" di Annibale: Un'imitazione di Donato Acciaiuoli', *Atene e Roma*, n.s. 37 (1992), 88–105

AKKERMAN, F., and others, eds, *Opera omnia Desiderii Erasmi Roterodami* (Amsterdam: North-Holland, 1969–)

ALEXANDER, GAVIN, ed., *Sidney's 'The Defence of Poesy' and Selected Renaissance Literary Criticism* (London: Penguin, 2004)

[ALEXANDER, SIR WILLIAM, EARL OF STIRLING], *The Poetical Works of Sir William Alexander Earl of Stirling*, ed. by L. E. Kastner and H. B. Charlton, 2 vols (Manchester: Manchester University Press, 1921–1929)

ALLEN, DON CAMERON, 'The Classical Scholarship of Francis Meres', *PMLA*, 48 (1933), 418–25

ALLEN, P. S., ed., *Opus epistolarum Des. Erasmi Roterodami*, 12 vols (Oxford: Clarendon Press, 1906–1958)

AMYOT, JACQUES, trans., *Les Œuvres morales et meslees de Plutarque* (Paris: Michel de Vascosan, 1572), USTC, 20878

——— trans., *Les Vies des hommes illustres grecs et romains*, ed. by Simon Goulart (Lausanne: François Le Preux, 1574), USTC, 47642

——— trans., *Les Œuvres morales et meslees de Plutarque*, ed. by Simon Goulart, 2 vols (Geneva: François Estienne, 1581–1582), USTC, 83256

——— trans., *Les Vies des hommes illustres grecs et romains*, ed. by Simon Goulart (Geneva: Jérémie des Planches, 1583), USTC, 83256

——— trans., *Les Œuvres morales de Plutarque*, ed. by Simon Goulart, 2 vols (Paris: Sébastien Molin, 1587), USTC, 1784

——— trans., *Les Œuvres morales de Plutarque*, ed. by Simon Goulart, 2 vols (Lyon: for Paul Frellon and Abraham Cloquemin, 1594), USTC, 24671

ANGLO, SYDNEY, *Machiavelli – The First Century: Studies in Enthusiasm, Hostility, and Irrelevance* (Oxford: Oxford University Press, 2005)

APHTHONIUS, *Progymnasmata*, trans. by Rudolph Agricola and Giovanni Maria Cataneo, ed. by Reinhard Lorich (1572), STC, 700

[APPIAN], *Shakespeare's Appian: A Selection from the Tudor Translation of Appian's 'Civil Wars'*, ed. by Ernest Schanzer (Liverpool: Liverpool University Press, 1956)

ARBER, EDWARD, ed., *A Transcript of the Registers of the Company of Stationers of London; 1554–1640, A.D.*, 5 vols (London: privately printed, 1875–1894)

[ARIOSTO, LUDOVICO], *Ludovico Ariosto's 'Orlando Furioso': Translated into English Heroical Verse by Sir John Harington (1591)*, ed. by Robert McNulty (Oxford: Clarendon Press, 1972)

ASCHAM, ROGER, *The scholemaster* (1570), STC, 832

AULOTTE, ROBERT, *Amyot et Plutarque: la tradition des 'Moralia' au XVIe siècle* (Geneva: Droz, 1965)
AXTON, MARIE, 'Lord Morley's Tryumphes of Fraunces Petrarcke: Reading Spectacles' in *'Triumphs of English'*, ed. by Axton and Carley, pp. 171–200
AXTON, MARIE, and JAMES P. CARLEY, eds, *'Triumphs of English': Henry Parker, Lord Morley: Translator to the Tudor Court: New Essays in Interpretation* (London: The British Library, 2000)
BACON, FRANCIS, *The Essayes or Counsels, Civill and Morall*, ed. by Michael Kiernan (Oxford: Clarendon Press, 1985, repr. 2000)
—— *The Advancement of Learning*, ed. by Michael Kiernan (Oxford: Oxford University Press, 2012)
BAJETTA, CARLO M., 'The Manuscripts of Verse Presented to Elizabeth I: A Preliminary Investigation', *Ben Jonson Journal*, 8 (2001), 147–205
BALARD, MICHEL, ed., *Fortunes de Jacques Amyot: actes du colloque international (Melun, 18–20 avril 1985)* ([Paris]: A.-G. Nizet, 1986)
BALDWIN, T. W., *William Shakspere's Small Latine & Lesse Greeke*, 2 vols (Urbana: University of Illinois Press, 1944)
BALDWIN, WILLIAM, *A treatise of morall philosophie* (1547), STC, 1253
BALDWIN, WILLIAM, and others, *The mirour for magistrates* (1587), STC, 13445
BARBOUR, REID, and CLAIRE PRESTON, 'Discursive and Speculative Writing', in *Oxford History of Classical Reception*, II: *1558–1660*, ed. by Cheney and Hardie, pp. 461–83
BASKERVILL, CHARLES READ, 'Taverner's *Garden of Wisdom* and the *Apophthegmata* of Erasmus', *Studies in Philology*, 29 (1932), 149–59
BEARDSLEE, WILLIAM A., 'De Garrulitate', in *Plutarch's Ethical Writings*, ed. by Betz, pp. 264–88
[BEAUMONT, FRANCIS, AND JOHN FLETCHER], *The Dramatic Works in the Beaumont and Fletcher Canon*, ed. by Fredson Bowers, 10 vols (Cambridge: Cambridge University Press, 1966–1996)
BECK, MARK, 'Plutarch to Trajan: The Dedicatory Letter and the *Apophthegmata* Collection', in *Sage and Emperor*, ed. by Stadter and Van der Stockt, pp. 163–74
—— ed., *A Companion to Plutarch* (Chichester: Wiley Blackwell, 2014)
BELLE, MARIE-ALICE, and LINE COTTEGNIES, eds, *Robert Garnier in Elizabethan England: Mary Sidney Herbert's 'Antonius' and Thomas Kyd's 'Cornelia'*, MHRA Tudor & Stuart Translations, 16 (Cambridge: Modern Humanities Research Association, 2017)
BENEKER, JEFFREY, 'Plutarch and Saint Basil as Readers of Greek Literature', *Syllecta Classica*, 22 (2011), 95–111
BERGK, THEODOR, ed., *Poetae lyrici graeci*, 5th edn, 3 vols (Leipzig: Teubner, 1914–1923)
BERGUA CAVERO, JORGE, *Estudios sobre la tradición de Plutarco en España (siglos XIII–XVII)* ([Zaragoza]: Departamento de Ciencias de la Antigüedad, Universidad de Zaragoza, 1995)
BERS, GÜNTER, *Die Schriften des niederländischen Humanisten Dr. Hermann Cruser* (Nieuwkoop: De Graaf, 1971)
BETZ, HANS DIETER, ed., *Plutarch's Theological Writings and Early Christian Literature* (Leiden: Brill, 1975)

—— ed., *Plutarch's Ethical Writings and Early Christian Literature* (Leiden: Brill, 1978)
—— 'De tranquillitate animi (*Moralia* 464E–477F)', in *Plutarch's Ethical Writings*, ed. by Betz, pp. 198–230
BIETENHOLZ, PETER G., and others, eds, *Collected Works of Erasmus* (Toronto: University of Toronto Press, 1974–)
BISHOP, MORRIS, *Petrarch and his World* (Bloomington: Indiana University Press, 1963)
BJORK, ROBERT E., ed., *The Oxford Dictionary of the Middle Ages*, 4 vols (Oxford: Oxford University Press, 2010)
BLACK, SCOTT, *Of Essays and Reading in Early Modern Britain* (Basingstoke: Palgrave Macmillan, 2006)
BLAKENEY, E. H., ed., *Plutarch's 'Moralia': Twenty Essays, Translated by Philemon Holland* (London: Dent, [1911])
BLAMIRES, ALCUIN, with KAREN PRATT and C. W. MARX, eds, *Women Defamed and Women Defended: An Anthology of Medieval Texts* (Oxford: Clarendon Press, 1992)
BLANSHARD, ALASTAIR J. L., and TRACEY A. SOWERBY, 'Thomas Wilson's Demosthenes and the Politics of Tudor Translation', *International Journal of the Classical Tradition*, 12 (2005), 46–80
BLENERHASSET, THOMAS, *The seconde part of the mirrour for magistrates, conteining the falles of the infortunate princes of this lande. From the conquest of Caesar, unto the comming of Duke William the Conquerour* (1578), STC, 3131
BLOOMER, W. MARTIN, *The School of Rome: Latin Studies and the Origins of Liberal Education* (Berkeley: University of California Press, 2011)
BLOUNT, THOMAS, *Glossographia: or a dictionary interpreting all such hard words, whether Hebrew, Greek, Latin, Italian, Spanish, French, Teutonick, Belgick, British or Saxon, as are now used in our refined English tongue* (1656), Wing, B3334
BLUNDEVILLE, THOMAS, *Three [morall] treatises* (1561), STC, 20063.5
BOAISTUAU, PIERRE, *Theatrum mundi, the theator or rule of the world*, trans. by John Alday (1566?), STC, 3168
—— *Le théâtre du monde*, ed. by Michel Simonin (Geneva: Droz, 1981)
BOTLEY, PAUL, *Latin Translation in the Renaissance: The Theory and Practice of Leonardo Bruni, Giannozzo Manetti and Desiderius Erasmus* (Cambridge: Cambridge University Press, 2004)
BOULET, BERNARD, 'The Philosopher-King', in *Companion to Plutarch*, ed. by Beck, pp. 449–62
BOUTCHER, WARREN, *The School of Montaigne in Early Modern Europe*, 2 vols (Oxford: Oxford University Press, 2017)
BOWIE, EWEN, 'Poetry and Education', in *Companion to Plutarch*, ed. by Beck, pp. 177–90
BRADEN, GORDON, *Renaissance Tragedy and the Senecan Tradition: Anger's Privilege* (New Haven: Yale University Press, 1985)
—— 'Plutarch, Shakespeare, and the Alpha Males', in *Shakespeare and the Classics*, ed. by Charles Martindale and A. B. Taylor (Cambridge: Cambridge University Press, 2004), pp. 188–206
—— 'Classical Translation', in *The Oxford Handbook of English Prose, 1500–1640*,

ed. by Andrew Hadfield (Oxford: Oxford University Press, 2013), pp. 106–20
BRAMMALL, SHELDON, *The English Aeneid: Translations of Virgil 1555–1646* (Edinburgh: Edinburgh University Press, 2015)
BRANDON, SAMUEL, *The tragicomoedi of the vertuous Octavia* (1598), STC, 3544
BRATHWAITE, RICHARD, *The schollers medley* (1614), STC, 3583
—— *The honest ghost, or a voice from the vault* (1658), Wing, B4267
BRAUNMULLER, A. R., 'Chapman's Use of Plutarch's *De Fortuna Romanorum* in *The Tragedy of Charles, Duke of Byron*', *Review of English Studies*, 23 (1972), 178–79
BRIGDEN, SUSAN, *Thomas Wyatt: The Heart's Forest* (London: Faber and Faber, 2012)
BRILLIANT, A. N., 'The Style of Wyatt's the *Quyete of Mynde*', *Essays and Studies*, 24 (1971), 1–21
BROOKE, C. F. TUCKER, ed., *Shakespeare's Plutarch*, 2 vols (London: Chatto & Windus, 1909)
BRUCE, YVONNE, '"That Which Marreth All": Constancy and Gender in *The Virtuous Octavia*', *Medieval and Renaissance Drama in England*, 22 (2009), 42–59
BRUTO, GIOVANNI MICHELE, *The necessarie, fit, and convenient education of a yong gentlewoman*, trans. by William Phiston (1598), STC, 3947
BUDRA, PAUL, *'A Mirror for Magistrates' and the De casibus Tradition* (Toronto: University of Toronto Press, 2000)
BURKE, VICTORIA E., 'Contexts for Women's Manuscript Miscellanies: The Case of Elizabeth Lyttelton and Sir Thomas Browne', *Yearbook of English Studies*, 33 (2003), 316–28
BURROW, COLIN, *Shakespeare and Classical Antiquity* (Oxford: Oxford University Press, 2013)
BURTON, ROBERT, *The Anatomy of Melancholy*, ed. by Thomas C. Faulkner and others, 6 vols (Oxford: Clarendon Press, 1989–2000)
BUSH, DOUGLAS, 'The Petite Pallace of Pettie His Pleasure', *Journal of English and Germanic Philology*, 27 (1928), 162–69
CAMDEN, WILLIAM, *Remaines of a greater worke, concerning Britaine* (1605), STC, 4521
CARABIN, DENISE, 'Comment Goulart indexe-t-il le Plutarque d'Amyot?', *Bibliothèque d'Humanisme et Renaissance*, 65 (2003), 331–45
CARLEY, JAMES P., 'The Writings of Henry Parker, Lord Morley: A Bibliographical Survey', in *'Triumphs of English'*, ed. by Axton and Carley, pp. 27–68
CASTIGLIONE, BALDASSARE, *Il libro del Cortegiano*, ed. by Walter Barberis (Turin: Einaudi, 1998)
—— *The Courtier*, trans. by George Bull (London: Penguin, 1967, repr. 2003)
CAVENDISH, MARGARET, Duchess of Newcastle upon Tyne, *CCXI sociable letters* (1664), Wing, N872
—— *'The Blazing World' and Other Writings*, ed. by Kate Lilley (London: Penguin, 1992, repr. 2004)
CAZES, HÉLÈNE, 'Genèse et renaissance des *Apophthegmes*: aventures humanistes', in *'Moralia' et 'Œuvres morales'*, ed. by Guerrier, pp. 15–35
CHAPMAN, GEORGE, *The warres of Pompey and Caesar* (1631), STC, 4992
—— *The Plays and Poems of George Chapman*, ed. by Thomas Marc Parrott, 2 vols (London: Routledge, 1910–1914)

—— *Bussy D'Ambois*, ed. by Nicholas Brooke (Manchester: Manchester University Press, 1964, repr. 1999)

CHENEY, PATRICK, and PHILIP R. HARDIE, eds, *The Oxford History of Classical Reception in English Literature*, II: *1558–1660* (Oxford: Oxford University Press, 2015)

[CICERO], *The thre bookes of Tullies offices*, trans. by Robert Whittington (1534), STC, 5278

CLAPHAM, JOHN, trans., *A philosophicall treatise concerning the quietnes of the mind. Taken out of the morall workes written in Greeke, by the most famous philosopher, and historiographer, Plutarch of Cherronea, counsellor to Trajan the emperor.* (1589), STC, 20059

CLELAND, JAMES, Ἡρω-παιδεια, *or the institution of a young noble man* (Oxford, 1607), STC, 5393

A Consolatorie Letter or Discourse Sent by Plutarch of Chaeronea unto his Owne Wife As Touching the Death of her and his Daughter (Boston: Houghton Mifflin, 1905)

COOGAN, ROBERT, 'Petrarch's Latin Prose and the English Renaissance', *Studies in Philology*, 68 (1971), 270–91

[CORNWALLIS, SIR WILLIAM], *Essayes by Sir William Cornwallis, the Younger*, ed. by Don Cameron Allen (Baltimore: Johns Hopkins Press, 1946)

COUZINET, DOMINIQUE, 'Les *Essais* de Montaigne et les *miscellanées*', in *Ouvrages miscellanées & théories de la connaissance à la Renaissance: Actes de la journée d'études organisée par l'École nationale des chartes (Paris, 5 et 6 avril 2002)*, ed. by Dominique de Courcelles (Paris: École des chartes, 2003), pp. 153–69

COX JENSEN, FREYJA, 'After Peter Burke: The Popularity of Ancient Historians, 1450–1600', *The Historical Journal*, 61 (2018), 561–95

—— *Reading the Roman Republic in Early Modern England* (Leiden: Brill, 2012)

CRANE, RONALD S., 'The Relation of Bacon's *Essays* to his Program for the Advancement of Learning', in *Essential Articles for the Study of Francis Bacon*, ed. by Brian Vickers (London: Sidgwick & Jackson, 1972), pp. 272–92

CRANE, WILLIAM G., *Wit and Rhetoric in the Renaissance: The Formal Basis of Elizabethan Prose Style* (New York: Columbia University Press, 1937)

CRUSER, HERMANN, trans., *Plutarchi [...] vitae comparatae illustrium virorum, graecorum et romanorum* (Basel: Thomas Guarin, 1564), USTC, 684403

—— trans., *Plutarchi [...] vitae comparatae illustrium virorum, graecorum et romanorum* (Basel: Thomas Guarin, 1573), USTC, 684404

CULHANE, PETER, 'Philemon Holland's Livy: Peritexts and Contexts', *Translation and Literature*, 13 (2004), 268–86

CUMMINGS, ROBERT, 'Classical Moralists and Philosophers', in *The Oxford History of Literary Translation in English, Vol. 2: 1550–1660*, ed. by Gordon Braden, Robert Cummings, and Stuart Gillespie (Oxford: Oxford University Press, 2010), pp. 371–89

—— 'Versifying Philosophy: Thomas Blundeville's Plutarch', in *Renaissance Cultural Crossroads: Translation, Print and Culture in Britain, 1473–1640*, ed. by Brenda M. Hosington and S. K. Barker (Leiden: Brill, 2013), pp. 103–20

CUMMINGS, ROBERT, and Stuart Gillespie, 'Translations from Greek and Latin Classics 1550–1700: A Revised Bibliography', *Translation and Literature*, 18 (2009), 1–42

CURRAN, JOHN E., 'Fletcher, Massinger, and Roman Imperial Character', *Comparative Drama*, 43 (2009), 317–54

CURTIS, CATHY, 'Richard Pace's *De Fructu* and Early Tudor Pedagogy', in *Reassessing Tudor Humanism*, ed. by Jonathan Woolfson (Basingstoke: Palgrave Macmillan, 2002), pp. 43–77

CUST, RICHARD, 'Reading for Magistracy: The Mental World of Sir John Newdigate', in *The Monarchical Republic of Early Modern England: Essays in Response to Patrick Collinson*, ed. by John F. McDiarmid (Aldershot: Ashgate, 2007), pp. 181–99

CUVIGNY, MARCEL, ed., Plutarch, *Œuvres morales* (Paris: Belles Lettres, 1971–), XI. 1: *Le philosophe doit surtout s'entretenir avec les grands; A un chef mal éduqué; Si la politique est l'affaire des vieillards* (1984)

DAVIES OF HEREFORD, JOHN, *Wittes pilgrimage* (1605), STC, 6344

DAVIS, HAROLD H., 'The Military Career of Thomas North', *Huntington Library Quarterly*, 12 (1948–1949), 315–21

DENT, R. W., *Shakespeare's Proverbial Language: An Index* (Berkeley: University of California Press, 1981)

—— *Proverbial Language in English Drama Exclusive of Shakespeare, 1495–1616: An Index* (Berkeley: University of California Press, 1984)

DENTON, JOHN, 'Wearing a Gown in the Market Place or a Toga in the Forum: Coriolanus from Plutarch to Shakespeare via Renaissance Translation', in *Shakespeare e la sua eredità*, ed. by Grazia Caliumi (Parma: Zara, 1993), pp. 97–109

—— 'Plutarch, Shakespeare, Roman Politics and Renaissance Translation', *Poetica*, 48 (1997), 187–209

—— 'Renaissance Translation Strategies and the Manipulation of a Classical Text: Plutarch from Jacques Amyot to Thomas North', in *Europe et traduction*, ed. by Michel Ballard (Arras: Artois Presses Université, 1998), pp. 67–78

—— *Translation and Manipulation in Renaissance England*, Quaderni di JEMS, 1 (Florence: Firenze University Press, 2016) <https://doi.org/10.13128/JEMS-2279-7149-19761>

DESIDERI, SAVERIO, ed., *La 'Institutio Traiani'* (Genoa: Istituto di Filologia Classica, 1958)

DEVEREUX, E. J., 'Richard Taverner's Translations of Erasmus', *The Library*, 5th series, 19 (1964), 212–14

DIEHL, ERNST, ed., *Anthologia lyrica Graeca*, 3 vols (Leipzig: Teubner, 1949–1952)

DIELS, HERMANN, ed., *Die Fragmente der Vorsokratiker: griechisch und deutsch* (Berlin: Weidmann, 1903)

DIELS, HERMANN, and W. KRANZ, eds, *Die Fragmente der Vorsokratiker*, 3 vols (Berlin: Weidmannsche Verlagsbuchhandlung, 1960)

DODDS, LARA, 'Reading and Writing in Sociable Letters; or, How Margaret Cavendish Read her Plutarch', *English Literary Renaissance*, 41 (2011), 189–218

DOWLING, MARIA, *Humanism in the Age of Henry VIII* (London: Croom Helm, 1986)

DRAYTON, MICHAEL, *Peirs Gaveston Earle of Cornwall. His life, death, and fortune* (1594?), STC, 7214

DUFF, TIMOTHY E., *Plutarch's Lives: Exploring Virtue and Vice* (Oxford: Oxford University Press, 1999, repr. 2005)

DURKAN, JOHN, 'Henry Scrimgeour, Renaissance Bookman', *Edinburgh Bibliographical Society Transactions*, 5 (1978), 1–31
DUST, PHILIP, 'Philemon Holland's Translation of Suetonius's Lives of Julius and Augustus', *Babel*, 21 (1975), 109–22
EARLE, JOHN, *Micro-cosmographie. Or, a peece of the world discovered in essayes and characters* (1628), STC, 7439
EDMONDS, J. M., ed., *Elegy and Iambus*, 2 vols, LCL, 258–259 (Cambridge, MA: Harvard University Press, 1931–1982)
ELIZABETH I, *Translations, 1592–1598*, ed. by Janel Mueller and Joshua Scodel (Chicago: University of Chicago Press, 2009)
ELLIOTT, JOHN R., JR, 'Queen Elizabeth at Oxford: New Light on the Royal Plays of 1566', *English Literary Renaissance*, 18 (1988), 218–29
ELSMANN, THOMAS, *Untersuchungen zur Rezeption der 'Institutio Traiani'* (Stuttgart: Teubner, 1994)
ELYOT, THOMAS, *The educacion or bringinge up of children* (1530), STC, 20056.7
—— *The boke named the governour* (1531), STC, 7635
—— *The dictionary* (1538), STC, 7659
—— *The bankette of sapience* (1539), STC, 7630
—— *The image of governance* (1541), STC, 7664
—— *Bibliotheca Eliotae* (1542), STC, 7659.5
—— trans., *The education or bringinge up of children, translated oute of Plutarche* (Amsterdam: Theatrum Orbis Terrarum, 1969)
Erasmus, Desiderius, *Les apophthegmes*, trans. by Antoine Macault (Paris: widow of Claude Chevallon, 1539), USTC, 13021
—— *Apophthegmes*, trans. by Nicholas Udall (1542), STC, 10443
—— *Declamatio de pueris statim ac liberaliter instituendis*, ed. by Jean-Claude Margolin (Geneva: Librarie Droz, 1966)
ERBSE, HARTMUT, 'Die Bedeutung der Synkrisis in den Parallelbiographien Plutarchs', *Hermes*, 84 (1956), 398–424
FELLHEIMER, JEANNETTE, 'Hellowes' and Fenton's Translations of Guevara's *Epistolas Familiares*', *Studies in Philology*, 44 (1947), 140–56
FIDOE, JOHN, THOMAS JEANES, and WILLIAM SHAWE, *The Parliament justified in their late proceedings against Charls [sic] Stuart, or a brief discourse concerning the nature and rise of government, together with the abuse of it in tyranny, and the peoples reserve* (1649), Wing, P502
FLACELIÈRE, ROBERT, 'État présent des études sur Plutarque', in *Association Guillaume Budé: actes du VIIIe congrès (Paris, 5–10 avril 1968)* (Paris: Les Belles Lettres, 1969), pp. 483–506
FLEMING, RUDD, 'Plutarch in the English Renaissance' (unpublished doctoral thesis, Cornell University, 1935)
FLORBY, GUNILLA, *The Painful Passage to Virtue: A Study of George Chapman's 'The Tragedy of Bussy D'Ambois' and 'The Revenge of Bussy D'Ambois'* (Lund: Gleerup, 1982)
FOX, ALISTAIR, 'Thomas Elyot', in *Sixteenth-Century British Nondramatic Writers: Second Series*, ed. by David A. Richardson (Detroit: Gale, 1994), pp. 94–106
FULLER, THOMAS, *The history of the worthies of England* (1662), Wing, F2440
GARROD, H. W., 'Erasmus and His English Patrons', *The Library*, 5th series, 4 (1949–1950), 1–13

GENTILI, VANNA, 'Thomas Lodge's *Wounds of Civil War*: An Assessment of Context, Sources and Structure', *REAL: The Yearbook of Research in English and American Literature*, 2 (1984), 119–64

—— *La Roma antica degli elisabettiani* (Bologna: Il Mulino, 1991)

GILL, CHRISTOPHER, 'Peace of Mind and Being Yourself: Panaetius to Plutarch', *Aufstieg und Niedergang der römischen Welt*, ii. 36 (1994), 4599–4640

GOODWIN, WILLIAM W., trans., *Plutarch's 'Morals'* (Boston: Little, Brown, and Company, 1874)

GORDON, D. J., 'Name and Fame: Shakespeare's *Coriolanus*', in *Papers Mainly Shakespearian*, ed. by G. I. Duthie (Edinburgh: Oliver and Boyd, 1964), pp. 40–57

GRANT, EDWARD, trans., *A president for parentes, teaching the vertuous training up of children and holesome information of yongmen* (1571), STC, 20057.5

GRAY, HANNA H., 'Renaissance Humanism: The Pursuit of Eloquence', *Journal of the History of Ideas*, 24 (1963), 497–514

GRIFFIN, JULIA, 'Shakespeare's *Julius Caesar* and the Dramatic Tradition', in *A Companion to Julius Caesar*, ed. by Griffin, pp. 371–98

GRIFFIN, MIRIAM T., ed., *A Companion to Julius Caesar* (Oxford: Wiley-Blackwell, 2009)

GUAL, CARLOS GARCÍA, 'El Plutarco de Fray Antonio de Guevara', in *L'eredità culturale di Plutarco dall'antichità al Rinascimento: atti del VII Convegno plutarcheo, Milano-Gargnano, 28–30 maggio 1997*, ed. by Italo Gallo (Naples: D'Auria, 1998), pp. 367–75

GUERRIER, OLIVIER, ed., *'Moralia' et 'Œuvres morales' à la Renaissance: Actes du colloque international de Toulouse (19–21 mai 2005)* (Paris: Champion, 2008)

—— 'L'Ordre du discours: sur les sommaires et manchettes des "contrefaçons" Goulart des *Œuvres morales et meslées*', in *Plutarque: éditions, traductions, paratextes*, ed. by Françoise Frazier and Olivier Guerrier (Coimbra: Imprensa da Universidade de Coimbra, 2017), pp. 201–17

GUERRINI, ROBERTO, and MADDALENA SANFILIPPO, 'Plutarch, Poussin, Carracci, and Baroque Art', in *The Afterlife of Plutarch*, ed. by North and Mack, pp. 85–98

GUEVARA, ANTONIO DE, *The diall of princes*, trans. by Thomas North (1557), STC, 12427

—— *Golden epistles*, trans. by Geoffrey Fenton (1575), STC, 10794

—— *The Diall of Princes: by Don Anthony of Guevara, Translated by Sir Thomas North*, ed. by K. N. Colvile (London: Philip Allan, 1919)

—— *Libro primero de las epístolas familiares*, ed. by José María de Cossío, 2 vols (Madrid: Aldus, 1950–1952)

HADDON, WALTER, *Lucubrationes* (1567), STC, 12596

HADFIELD, ANDREW, *Shakespeare and Republicanism* (Cambridge: Cambridge University Press, 2005)

HALES, JOHN, *The preceptes of the excellent clerke and grave philosopher Plutarche for the preservacion of good healthe* (1543), STC, 20062

HAMLIN, WILLIAM M., *Montaigne's English Journey: Reading the 'Essays' in Shakespeare's Day* (Oxford: Oxford University Press, 2013)

HAMPTON, TIMOTHY, *Writing from History: The Rhetoric of Exemplarity in Renaissance Literature* (Ithaca, NY: Cornell University Press, 1990)

HAMRICK, STEPHEN, 'The "Bardi Brytannorum": Lodowick Lloyd and Welsh Identities in the Atlantic Archipelago Region', in *Religion and English Renaissance*

Literature, ed. by David Coleman (Farnham: Ashgate, 2013), pp. 45–65

HANKINS, JAMES, 'Translation Practice in the Renaissance: The Case of Leonardo Bruni', in *Méthodologie de la traduction: de l'antiquité à la Renaissance: théorie et praxis*, ed. by C. M. Ternes and M. Mund-Dopchie (Luxembourg: Actes des 3es rencontres scientifiques de Luxembourg, 1994), pp. 154–75, repr. in *Humanism and Platonism in the Italian Renaissance*, 2 vols (Rome: Edizioni di storia e letteratura, 2003–2004), I, 177–92

HARRIS, OLIVER D., 'William Camden, Philemon Holland and the 1610 Translation of *Britannia*', *The Antiquaries Journal*, 95 (2015), 279–303

HAYNE, WILLIAM, *Certaine epistles of Tully verbally translated* (1611), STC, 5304

HECK, ADRIANO VAN, 'Plutarco e l'educazione nell'umanesimo', in *L'educazione e la formazione intellettuale nell'età dell'Umanesimo: atti del II convegno internazionale – 1990*, ed. by Luisa Rotondi Secchi Tarugi (Milan: Guerini, 1992), pp. 99–108

HIERONYMUS, FRANK, *Griechischer Geist aus Basler Pressen: Katalog der frühen griechischen Drucke aus Basel in Text und Bild*, ed. by Christoph Schneider und Benedikt Vögeli (Universitätsbibliothek Basel, 2003) <http://www.ub.unibas.ch/cmsdata/spezialkataloge/gg/> [accessed 7 March 2017]

HIGGINS, JOHN, *Huloets dictionarie, newelye corrected, amended, set in order and enlarged* (1572), STC, 13941

HOBGOOD, ALLISON P., 'Caesar Hath the Falling Sickness: The Legibility of Early Modern Disability in Shakespearean Drama', *Disability Studies Quarterly*, 29 (2009) <http://dx.doi.org/10.18061/dsq.v29i4.993>

HOGREFE, PEARL, *The Life and Times of Sir Thomas Elyot Englishman* (Ames: Iowa State University Press, 1967)

HOLINSHED, RAPHAEL, and others, *The first and second volumes of Chronicles* (1587), STC, 13569

HOLLAND, PHILEMON, trans., *The philosophie, commonlie called, the Morals* (1603), STC, 20063

HOLLAND, PHILEMON, trans., *The philosophy commonly called, the Morals* (1657), Wing, P2654

HORKAN, VINCENT JOSEPH, *Educational Theories and Principles of Maffeo Vegio* (Washington, DC: Catholic University of America Press, 1953)

HOSINGTON, BRENDA, and others, *The Renaissance Cultural Crossroads Catalogue* <https://www.dhi.ac.uk/rcc/> [accessed 2 June 2020]

HOWARD, MARTHA WALLING, *The Influence of Plutarch in the Major European Literatures of the Eighteenth Century* (Chapel Hill: University of North Carolina Press, 1970)

HOWATSON, M. C., ed., *The Oxford Companion to Classical Literature*, 2nd edn (Oxford: Oxford University Press, 1989, repr. 1997)

HUDSON, WINTHROP S., *The Cambridge Connection and the Elizabethan Settlement of 1559* (Durham, NC: Duke University Press, 1980)

HUGUET, EDMOND, ed., *Dictionnaire de la langue française du seizième siècle*, 7 vols (Paris: Champion; Didier, 1925–1973)

HUNTER, RICHARD, and DONALD RUSSELL, eds, *Plutarch: 'How to Study Poetry' (De Audiendis Poetis)* (Cambridge: Cambridge University Press, 2011)

HURAULT, JACQUES, *Politicke, moral, and martial discourses*, trans. by Arthur Golding (1595), STC, 14000

IDE, RICHARD S., 'Chapman's *Caesar and Pompey* and the Uses of History', *Modern Philology*, 82 (1985), 255-68
INGENKAMP, HEINZ GERD, *Plutarchs Schriften über die Heilung der Seele* (Göttingen: Vandenhoeck & Ruprecht, 1971)
JARDINE, LISA, and ANTHONY GRAFTON, '"Studied for Action": How Gabriel Harvey Read his Livy', *Past and Present*, 129 (1990), 30-78
JEVONS, FRANK BYRON, ed., *Plutarch's 'Romane Questions'. Translated A.D. 1603 by Philemon Holland, M.A., Fellow of Trinity College, Cambridge* (London: David Nutt, 1892)
[JOHN OF SALISBURY], *Ioannis Saresberiensis Episcopi Carnotensis Policratici, sive, De nugis curialium et vestigiis philosophorum, libri VIII*, ed. by Clemens C. I. Webb, 2 vols (Oxford: Clarendon Press, 1909)
—— *Policraticus*, ed. and trans. by Cary J. Nederman (Cambridge: Cambridge University Press, 1990)
JONES, HOWARD, *Master Tully: Cicero in Tudor England* (Nieuwkoop: De Graaf, 1998)
JONES, JOSEPH R., *Antonio de Guevara* (Boston: Twayne, 1975)
JONES, LEONARD Chester, *Simon Goulart, 1543-1628: étude biographique et bibliographique* (Genève: Georg, 1917)
JONES, TOM, 'Pope and Translations of Plutarch's *Moralia*', *Translation and Literature*, 12 (2003), 263-73
[JONSON, BEN], *The Cambridge Edition of the Works of Ben Jonson Online*, ed. by Martin Butler and others (Cambridge: Cambridge University Press, 2014) <http://universitypublishingonline.org/cambridge/benjonson/> [accessed 15 January 2020]
JUHÁSZ-ORMSBY, ÁGNES, 'Erasmus' *Apophthegmata* in Henrician England', *Erasmus Studies*, 37 (2017), 45-67
KAHN, COPPÉLIA, *Roman Shakespeare: Warriors, Wounds, and Women* (London: Routledge, 1997)
KAIBEL, GEORG, *Comicorum graecorum fragmenta* (Berlin: Weidman, 1899)
KALLENDORF, CRAIG W., ed. and trans., *Humanist Educational Treatises* (Cambridge, MA: Harvard University Press, 2002)
KEMPE, WILLIAM, *The education of children in learning* (1588), STC, 14926
KER, JAMES, and JESSICA WINSTON, eds, *Elizabethan Seneca: Three Tragedies*, MHRA Tudor & Stuart Translations, 8 (London: Modern Humanities Research Association, 2012)
KEWES, PAULINA, 'Julius Caesar in Jacobean England', *The Seventeenth Century*, 17 (2002), 155-86
KINNEY, ARTHUR F., *Markets of Bawdrie: The Dramatic Criticism of Stephen Gosson* (Salzburg: Institut für Englische Sprache und Literatur, Universität Salzburg, 1974)
KIRKHAM, VICTORIA, and ARMANDO MAGGI, eds, *Petrarch: A Critical Guide to the Complete Works* (Chicago: University of Chicago Press, 2009)
KLOFT, HANS, and MAXIMILIAN KERNER, eds, *Die 'Institutio Traiani': ein pseudoplutarchischer Text im Mittelalter: Text, Kommentar, zeitgenössischer Hintergrund* (Stuttgart: Teubner, 1992)
KOCK, THEODOR, ed., *Comicorum atticorum fragmenta*, 3 vols (Leipzig: Teubner, 1880-1888)

KONSTANTINOVIC, ISABELLE, *Montaigne et Plutarque* (Geneva: Droz, 1989)
KÖRTE, ALFRED, ed., *Metrodori Epicurei fragmenta* (Leipzig: Teubner, 1890)
KRAUS, MANFRED, 'Progymnasmata, Gymnasmata', in *Historisches Wörterbuch der Rhetorik*, ed. by Gert Ueding, 10 vols (Tübingen: Niemeyer, 1992–2011), VII, 159–91
KRISTELLER, PAUL OSKAR, *Renaissance Thought and its Sources* (New York: Columbia University Press, 1979)
LATHROP, HENRY BURROWES, 'Some Rogueries of Robert Wyer', *The Library*, 3rd series, 5 (1914), 349–64
—— *Translations from the Classics into English from Caxton to Chapman 1477–1620* (Madison: University of Wisconsin Press, 1933, repr. New York: Octagon Books, 1967)
LAW, ROBERT ADGER, 'The Text of *Shakespeare's Plutarch*', *Huntington Library Quarterly*, 6 (1943), 197–203
LEAVENWORTH, RUSSELL E., *Daniel's 'Cleopatra': A Critical Study* (Salzburg: Institut für Englische Sprache und Literatur, Universität Salzburg, 1974)
LEGRAND, MARIE-DOMINIQUE, 'Simon Goulart éditeur de Plutarque: exploration de ses notes et de ses commentaires à la traduction de Jacques Amyot', in *Simon Goulart: un pasteur aux intérêts vastes comme le monde*, ed. by Olivier Pot (Genève: Droz, 2013), pp. 111–24
LEHMBERG, STANFORD E., *Sir Thomas Elyot: Tudor Humanist* (Austin: University of Texas Press, 1960)
LEWIS, CHARLTON T., and CHARLES SHORT, eds, *A Latin Dictionary* (Oxford: Clarendon Press, 1879)
LIDDELL, HENRY GEORGE, and ROBERT SCOTT, eds, *A Greek-English Lexicon*, rev. edn (Oxford: Clarendon Press, 1940)
LIEBESCHÜTZ, H., 'John of Salisbury and Pseudo-Plutarch', *Journal of the Warburg and Courtauld Institutes*, 6 (1943), 33–39
LIEDMEIER, CHRISTIANA, ed., *Plutarchus' Biographie van Aemilius Paulus: Historische Commentaar* (Utrecht: Dekker & Van de Vegt, 1935)
LINTOTT, ANDREW, ed., *Plutarch: 'Demosthenes and Cicero'* (Oxford: Oxford University Press, 2013)
LLOYD, LODOWICK, *The pilgrimage of princes* (1573?), STC, 16624
LODGE, THOMAS, [*A defence of poetry*] (1579), STC, 16663
—— *Scillaes metamorphosis* (1589), STC, 16674
LOVASCIO, DOMENICO, 'The Roman Civil Wars in the Anonymous *Caesar's Revenge*', in *Proceedings of the 'Shakespeare and his Contemporaries' Graduate Conference 2012 and 2013*, ed. by Mark Roberts (Florence: British Institute of Florence, 2014), pp. 23–33
—— '"All Our Lives Upon Ones Lippes Depend": Caesar as a Tyrant in William Alexander's *Julius Caesar*', *Medieval and Renaissance Drama in England*, 29 (2016), 68–102
—— '"Of Higher State | Than Monarch, King or World's Great Potentate": The Name of Caesar in Early Modern English Drama', *Early Modern Literary Studies*, Special Issue 24: *Rome and Home: The Cultural Uses of Rome in Early Modern English Literature*, ed. by Daniel Cadman, Andrew Duxfield, and Lisa Hopkins (2016) <https://extra.shu.ac.uk/emls/journal/index.php/emls/article/view/134> [accessed 17 September 2020]

LYCOSTHENES, KONRAD, *Apophthegmatum* [...] *Parabolarum item seu similitudinum, loci communes* (1579), *STC*, 17003.3

[LYLY, JOHN], *The Complete Works of John Lyly*, ed. by R. Warwick Bond, 3 vols (Oxford: Clarendon Press, 1902)

MACCALLUM, M. W., *Shakespeare's Roman Plays and their Background* (London: Macmillan, 1910, repr. 1925)

MACDONALD, ALASDAIR A., 'Florentius Volusenus and Tranquillity of Mind: Some Applications of an Ancient Ideal', in *Christian Humanism: Essays in Honour of Arjo Vanderjagt*, ed. by MacDonald, Zweder R. W. M. von Martels, and Jan R. Veenstra (Leiden: Brill, 2009), pp. 119-38

MACDONALD, KATHERINE M., 'The Presence of Plutarch in the Preface to the Reader of Cruserius' Latin Translation of the *Lives* (1561)', *Bibliothèque d'Humanisme et Renaissance*, 62 (2000), 129-34

MACK, PETER, *Elizabethan Rhetoric: Theory and Practice* (Cambridge: Cambridge University Press, 2002)

MACPHAIL, ERIC M., *Dancing around the Well: The Circulation of Commonplaces in Renaissance Humanism* (Leiden: Brill, 2014)

MAEHLER, HERWIG, and BRUNO SNELL, eds, *Pindari carmina cum fragmentis*, 2 vols (Leipzig: Teubner, 1989-), II: *Fragmenta. Indices* (1989)

MAJOR, JOHN M., *Sir Thomas Elyot and Renaissance Humanism* (Lincoln, NE: University of Nebraska Press, 1964)

MANN, NICHOLAS, 'Dal moralista al poeta: appunti per la fortuna del Petrarca in Inghilterra', in *Atti dei convegni lincei 10: convegno internazionale Francesco Petrarca* (Rome: Accademia Nazionale dei Lincei, 1976), pp. 59-69

—— *Petrarch* (Oxford: Oxford University Press, 1984)

MAPSTONE, SALLY, 'Drunkenness and Ambition in Early Seventeenth-Century Scottish Literature', *Studies in Scottish Literature*, 35-36 (2007), 131-55

MARCELLINE, GEORGE, *The triumphs of King James the First, of Great Brittaine, France, and Ireland, King; Defender of the Faith* (1610), *STC*, 17309

MARION, OLGA VAN, 'The Reception of Plutarch in the Netherlands: Octavia and Cleopatra in the Heroic Epistles of J. B. Wellekens (1710)', in *Recreating Ancient History: Episodes from the Greek and Roman Past in the Arts and Literature of the Early Modern Period*, ed. by Karl A. Enenkel, Jan L. de Jong, and Jeanine de Landtsheer (Leiden: Brill, 2002), pp. 213-34

MARTIN, JANET, 'Uses of Tradition: Gellius, Petronius, and John of Salisbury', *Viator*, 10 (1979), 57-76

MARTIN, JESSICA, *Walton's Lives: Conformist Commemorations and the Rise of Biography* (Oxford: Oxford University Press, 2001)

MATTHIESSEN, F. O., *Translation: An Elizabethan Art* (Cambridge, MA: Harvard University Press, 1931)

MAULE, JEREMY, 'What Did Morley Give When He Gave a "Plutarch" Life?', in *'Triumphs of English'*, ed. by Axton and Carley, pp. 107-30

MAY, STEVEN W., 'George Puttenham's Lewd and Illicit Career', *Texas Studies in Literature and Language*, 50 (2008), 143-76

MAY, STEVEN W., and HEATHER WOLFE, 'Manuscripts in Tudor England', in *A Companion to Tudor Literature*, ed. by Kent Cartwright (Chichester: Wiley-Blackwell, 2010), pp. 123-39

MAY, STEVEN W., and WILLIAM A. RINGLER, JR, eds, *Elizabethan Poetry: A*

Bibliography and First-Line Index of English Verse, 1559–1603 (London: Thoemmes Continuum, 2004)

Mazzio, Carla, 'Sins of the Tongue in Early Modern England', *Modern Language Studies*, 28 (1998), 95–124 (first publ. in *The Body in Parts: Fantasies of Corporeality in Early Modern Europe*, ed. by David Hillman and Mazzio (New York: Routledge, 1997), pp. 53–79)

McCarthy, Dennis, 'Thomas North Was the "T. N." Who Prefaced Belleforest's *Tragicall Hystories*', *Notes and Queries*, 54 (2007), 244–48

McConica, James, 'Elizabethan Oxford: The Collegiate Society', in *History of the University of Oxford*, III: *The Collegiate University*, ed. by McConica, pp. 645–732

—— ed., *The History of the University of Oxford*, ed. by T. H. Aston, 8 vols (Oxford: Oxford University Press, 1984–2000), III: *The Collegiate University* (1986)

McDiarmid, John F., 'John Cheke's Preface to *De Superstitione*', *Journal of Ecclesiastical History*, 48 (1997), 100–20

McGrath, Elizabeth, *Rubens: Subjects from History*, 2 vols (London: Harvey Miller, 1997)

McKerrow, R. B., *A Dictionary of Printers and Booksellers in England, Scotland and Ireland, and of Foreign Printers of English Books 1557–1640* (London: Printed for the Bibliographical Society by Blades, East & Blades, 1910)

Medine, Peter E., *Thomas Wilson* (Boston: Twayne, 1986)

Meer, Tineke ter, 'A True Mirror of the Mind: Some Observations on the *Apophthegmata* of Erasmus', *Erasmus of Rotterdam Society Yearbook*, 23 (2003), 67–93

Merkelbach, R., and M. L. West, eds, *Fragmenta Hesiodea* (Oxford: Clarendon Press, 1967)

Meres, Francis, *Palladis tamia* (1598), STC, 17834

Miert, Dirk van, *Hadrianus Junius (1511–1575): Een humanist uit Hoorn* (Hoorn: Bas Baltus, 2011)

Miles, Geoffrey, *Shakespeare and the Constant Romans* (Oxford: Clarendon Press, 1996)

Miller, Anthony, *Roman Triumphs and Early Modern English Culture* (Basingstoke: Palgrave, 2001)

Milne, Kirsty, 'The Forgotten Greek Books of Elizabethan England', *Literature Compass*, 4 (2007), 677–87

Milton, John, *Of education* (1644), Wing, M2132

Miola, Robert S., 'Remembering Greece in Shakespeare's Rome', *Memoria di Shakespeare*, 4 (2017), 20–34

Moles, J. L., ed., *Plutarch: The Life of Cicero* (Warminster: Aris and Phillips, 1988, repr. 2007)

—— *A Commentary on Plutarch's 'Brutus'*, ed. by Christopher Pelling, Histos Supplement, 7 (Newcastle upon Tyne: Histos, 2017) <https://research.ncl.ac.uk/histos/documents/SV07.MolesBrutus.pdf> [accessed 2 June 2020]

Monsarrat, Gilles D., *Light from the Porch: Stoicism and English Renaissance Literature* (Paris: Didier-Érudition, 1984)

Montaigne, Michel de, *The essayes or morall, politike and millitarie discourses*, trans. by John Florio (1603), STC, 18041

—— *Les Essais*, ed. by Jean Balsamo, Michel Magnien, and Catherine Magnien-Simonin (Paris: Gallimard, 2007)

—— *The Complete Essays of Montaigne*, trans. by Donald M. Frame (Stanford: Stanford University Press, 1958)
—— *The Complete Essays*, trans. by M. A. Screech (Harmondsworth: Penguin, 1987, repr. 1991)
MOORE, HELEN, 'Of Marriage, Morals and Civility', in *Early Modern Civil Discourses*, ed. by Jennifer Richards (Houndmills: Palgrave Macmillan, 2003), pp. 35–50
MORALES ORTIZ, ALICIA, 'Traductions et traducteurs de Plutarque en Espagne', in *'Moralia' et 'Œuvres morales'*, ed. by Guerrier, pp. 37–54
—— *Plutarco en España: Traducciones de Moralia en el siglo XVI* (Murcia: University of Murcia, 2000)
MORE, THOMAS, *Utopia: Latin Text and English Translation*, ed. by George M. Logan, Robert M. Adams, and Clarence H. Miller (Cambridge: Cambridge University Press, 1995, repr. 2006)
MORGAN, MATTHEW, and others, trans., *Plutarch's Morals*, 5 vols (1684–1686), Wing, P2642
MORGAN, TERESA, *Literate Education in the Hellenistic and Roman Worlds* (Cambridge: Cambridge University Press, 1998)
MORINI, MASSIMILIANO, *Tudor Translation in Theory and Practice* (Aldershot: Ashgate, 2006)
MORLEY, HENRY PARKER, LORD, *Forty-Six Lives: Translated from Boccaccio's 'De claris mulieribus' by Henry Parker, Lord Morley*, ed. by Herbert G. Wright, Early English Text Society, Original Series no. 214 (London: Published for the Early English Text Society by Oxford University Press, 1943)
MOSS, ANN, *Printed Commonplace-Books and the Structuring of Renaissance Thought* (Oxford: Clarendon Press, 1996)
MÜHLFELD, WILHELM, *'The Tragedie of Cæsar and Pompey or Cæsars Reuenge': Ein Beitrag zur Geschichte der englischen Caesardramen zur Zeit Shakespeares* (Weimar: Wagner, 1912)
MUIR, KENNETH, *Life and Letters of Sir Thomas Wyatt* (Liverpool: Liverpool University Press, 1963)
MUIR, KENNETH, and PATRICIA THOMSON, eds, *Collected Poems of Sir Thomas Wyatt* (Liverpool: Liverpool University Press, 1969)
NAOGEORGUS, THOMAS, *Satyrarum libri quinque priores [...]. His sunt adiuncti, de animi tranquillitate duo libelli: unus Plutarchi, latinus ab eodem factus: alter Senecae: cum annotationibus in utrumque* (Basel: Johann Oporinus, 1555), USTC, 692124
[NASHE, THOMAS], *The Works of Thomas Nashe*, ed. by R. B. McKerrow, 5 vols (London: Sidgwick & Jackson, 1910)
NAUCK, AUGUST, *Tragicorum Graecorum Fragmenta*, 2nd edn (Leipzig: Teubner, 1889)
NEVALAINEN, TERTTU, 'Early Modern English Lexis and Semantics', in *The Cambridge History of the English Language*, 6 vols (Cambridge: Cambridge University Press, 2000), III: *1476–1776*, ed. by Roger Lass (2000), pp. 332–458
NIKOLAIDIS, ANASTASIOS G., ed., *The Unity of Plutarch's Work* (Berlin: De Gruyter, 2008)
—— 'Plutarch's "Minor" Ethics: Some Remarks on *De garrulitate*, *De curiositate*, and *De vitioso pudore*', in *Virtues for the People: Aspects of Plutarchan Ethics*,

ed. by Geert Roskam and Luc Van der Stockt (Leuven: Leuven University Press, 2011), pp. 205–22

NORTH, JOHN, and PETER MACK, eds, *The Afterlife of Plutarch*, Bulletin of the Institute of Classical Studies Supplement, 137 (London: Institute of Classical Studies, University of London, 2018)

NORTH, THOMAS, trans., *The lives of the noble Grecians and Romanes, compared together by that grave learned philosopher and historiographer, Plutarke of Chaeronea* (1579), STC, 20065

—— trans., *The lives of the noble Grecians and Romanes, compared together by that grave learned philosopher and historiographer, Plutarke of Chaeronea* (1595), STC, 20067

—— trans., *The Lives of Epaminondas, of Philip of Macedon, of Dionysius the Elder, and of Octavius Caesar Augustus: collected out of good authors. Also the lives of nine excellent chieftaines of warre, taken out of Latine from Emilius Probus, by S. G. S. By whom also are added the lives of Plutarch and of Seneca* (1602), STC, 20071

—— trans., *The lives of the noble Grecians and Romaines, compared together by that grave learned philosopher and historiographer, Plutarke of Chaeronea* (1603), STC, 20068

O'BRIEN, JOHN, 'Montaigne, Sir Ralph Bankes and other English Readers of the *Essais*', *Renaissance Studies*, 28 (2014), 377–91

ONG, WALTER J., *Rhetoric, Romance, and Technology: Studies in the Interaction of Expression and Culture* (Ithaca, NY: Cornell University Press, 1971)

PADE, MARIANNE, 'Hermann Crusers Plutarchübersetzungen', in *Erudition and Eloquence: The Use of Latin in the Countries of the Baltic Sea (1500–1800)*, ed. by Outi Merisalo and Raija Sarasti-Wilenius ([Helsinki]: Academia Scientarium Fennica, 2003), pp. 9–32

—— *The Reception of Plutarch's 'Lives' in Fifteenth-Century Italy*, 2 vols (Copenhagen: Museum Tusculanum Press, University of Copenhagen, 2007)

—— 'The Reception of Plutarch from Antiquity to the Italian Renaissance', in *Companion to Plutarch*, ed. by Beck, pp. 529–43

—— ed., *Plutarchi Chaeronensis Vita Dionis et Comparatio et de Bruto ac Dione iudicium Guarino Veronensi interprete* (Florence: SISMEL – Edizioni del Galluzzo, 2013)

—— '"I Give You Back Plutarch in Latin": Guarino Veronese's Version of Plutarch's *Dion* (1414) and Early Humanist Translation', *Canadian Review of Comparative Literature / Revue Canadienne de Littérature Comparée*, 41 (2014), 354–68

PAINTER, WILLIAM, *The second tome of the palace of pleasure* (1567), STC, 19124

PALEIT, EDWARD, *War, Liberty, and Caesar: Responses to Lucan's 'Bellum Ciuile', ca. 1580–1650* (Oxford: Oxford University Press, 2013)

PANICHI, NICOLA, '"Jouer à la paume": La présence de Plutarque chez les théoriciens italiens de la *civil conversazione*', in *'Moralia' et 'Œuvres morales'*, ed. by Guerrier, pp. 217–36

PARKER, PATRICIA, 'On the Tongue: Cross Gendering, Effeminacy, and the Art of Words', *Style*, 23 (1989), 445–65

PASTER, GAIL KERN, '"In the Spirit of Men There Is No Blood": Blood as Trope of Gender in *Julius Caesar*', *Shakespeare Quarterly*, 40 (1989), 284–98

PATCH, H. R., *The Goddess Fortuna in Medieval Literature* (Cambridge, MA: Harvard University Press, 1927)

PEACHAM, HENRY, *The compleat gentleman* (1622), STC, 19502
PELLING, C. B. R., ed., *Plutarch: 'Life of Antony'* (Cambridge: Cambridge University Press, 1988, repr. 1999)
—— *Plutarch and History* (Swansea: Classical Press of Wales, 2002, repr. 2011)
PEPPER, ROBERT DAVID, 'The Education of Children in Learning (1588) by William Kempe of Plymouth: A Critical Edition' (unpublished doctoral dissertation, Stanford University, 1963)
—— ed., *Four Tudor Books on Education* (Gainesville: Scholars' Facsimiles & Reprints, 1966)
[PETRARCA, FRANCESCO], *Physicke against fortune, aswell prosperous, as adverse*, trans. by Thomas Twyne (1579), STC, 19809
—— *Petrarch's Remedies for Fortune Fair and Foul: A Modern English Translation of 'De remediis utriusque fortune', with a Commentary*, ed. by Conrad H. Rawski, 5 vols (Bloomington: Indiana University Press, 1991)
PETRINA, ALESSANDRA, ed., *Petrarch's 'Triumphi' in the British Isles*, MHRA Tudor & Stuart Translations (Cambridge: Modern Humanities Research Association, 2020)
PHILO, JOHN-MARK, '"An Ocean Untouched and Untried": Translating Livy in the Sixteenth Century' (unpublished doctoral thesis, University of Oxford, 2015)
PINEAUX, JACQUES, 'Un continuateur des *Vies Parallèles*: Simon Goulart de Senlis (S.G.S.)', in *Fortunes de Jacques Amyot*, ed. by Balard, pp. 331–42
PLINY THE ELDER, *The historie of the world. Commonly called, the naturall historie*, trans. by Philemon Holland (1601), STC, 20029
PLUTARCH, *De liberis educandis* (Verona: Paulus Butzbach and Georgius de Augusta, c. 1471–1472), ISTC, ip00821000
—— *Vitae illustrium virorum* (Venice: Nicolaus Jenson, 1478), ISTC, ip00832000
—— *Opuscula tria* (Paris: for Olivier Senant, 1505?)
—— *Moralia* (Venice: Bernardino Vitali, 1505?), USTC, 849973
—— *De tranquillitate et securitate animi. Lib. I. De fortuna romanorum ex Plutarcho. Lib. I. De fortuna vel virtute Alexandri. Lib. II. Basilii magni epistola de vita per solitudinem transigenda* (Rome: Giacomo Mazzocchi, 1510), USTC, 849948
—— *Opuscula* (Paris: Josse Bade, 1514), USTC, 144320
—— *Vitae* (Paris: Josse Bade and Jean Petit, 1514), USTC, 181498
—— *Opuscula* (Paris: Josse Bade, 1521), USTC, 145440
—— *Opuscula* (Paris: Josse Bade, 1526), USTC, 184603
—— *Vitae graecorum romanorumque illustrium* (Basel: Johannes Bebel, 1531), USTC, 701520
—— *Moralium opusculorum tomus tertius continens ea, quae post superiorem nostram editionem a viris doctis e graeco in latinum sunt conversa* (Lyon: Sébastien Gryphe, 1551), USTC, 150929
—— *Moralia opuscula, quotquot reperire licuit latio donata*, 3 vols (Paris: Guillaume Guillard and Thomas Belot, 1566), USTC, 158154
—— *Quae extant opera, cum latina interpretatione*, 13 vols (Geneva: Henri II Estienne, 1572), USTC, 450618
—— *Varia scripta, quae Moralia vulgo dicuntur* (Basel: Eusebius Episcopius, 1574), USTC, 684250
—— *Quae exstant omnia* ([Geneva]: [Paul Estienne], 1599), USTC, 684243

—— *Les Vies des hommes illustres*, trans. by Jacques Amyot, ed. by Gérard Walter, 2 vols (Paris: Nouvelle revue française, 1937)
—— *Essays*, trans. by Robin Waterfield, ed. by Ian Kidd (London: Penguin, 1992)
—— *Selected Essays and Dialogues*, trans. by Donald Russell (Oxford: Oxford University Press, 1993)
—— *The Lives of the Noble Grecians and Romans, Translated by Thomas North*, ed. by Judith Mossman (Ware: Wordsworth, 1998)
—— *Roman Lives*, trans. by Robin Waterfield, ed. by Philip A. Stadter (Oxford: Oxford University Press, 2008)
POLLARD, A. W., and G. R. REDGRAVE, eds, *A Short-Title Catalogue of Books Printed in England, Scotland, & Ireland and of English Books Printed Abroad, 1475–1640*, 2nd edn, rev. by Katharine F. Pantzer, 3 vols (London: Bibliographical Society, 1976–1991)
POLLARD, TANYA, ed., *Shakespeare's Theater: A Sourcebook* (Oxford: Blackwell, 2004)
POLYBIUS, *The Histories*, trans. by Robin Waterfield, ed. by Brian McGing (Oxford: Oxford University Press, 2010)
POST, JONATHAN F. S., *Henry Vaughan: The Unfolding Vision* (Princeton: Princeton University Press 1982)
POUTIAINEN, HANNU, 'Autoapotropaics: "Daimon and Psuché" between Plutarch and Shakespeare', *Oxford Literary Review*, 34 (2012), 51–70
POWELL, JASON E., ed., *The Complete Works of Sir Thomas Wyatt the Elder*, I: *Prose* (Oxford: Oxford University Press, 2016)
PREMINGER, ALEX, and T. V. F. BROGAN, eds, *The New Princeton Encyclopedia of Poetry and Poetics* (Princeton: Princeton University Press, 1993)
PRESCOTT, ANNE LAKE, 'Pierre de la Primaudaye's *French Academy*: Growing Encyclopaedic', in *The Renaissance Computer: Knowledge Technology in the First Age of Print*, ed. by Neil Rhodes and Jonathan Sawday (London: Routledge, 2000), pp. 157–69
PRIMAUDAYE, PIERRE DE LA, *The French academie*, trans. by Thomas Bowes (1586), STC, 15233
QUINN, KELLY A., 'Sir Thomas North's Marginalia in his *Dial of Princes*', *Publications of the Bibliographical Society of America*, 94 (2000), 283–87
RADT, SEFAN, ed., *Tragicorum graecorum fragmenta*, ed. by Bruno Snell and others, 5 vols (Göttingen: Vandenhoeck & Ruprecht: 1971–2004), IV: *Sophocles*, 2nd edn (1999)
RAINOLDS, JOHN, *Th'overthrow of stage-playes* ([Middelburg], 1599), STC, 20616
—— *Orationes duodecim* (Oxford, 1614), STC, 20613
—— *John Rainolds's Oxford Lectures on Aristotle's 'Rhetoric'*, ed. and trans. by Lawrence D. Green (Newark: University of Delaware Press, 1986)
RALEGH, SIR WALTER, *The history of the world* (1614), STC, 20637
READ, CONYERS, *Mr. Secretary Walsingham and the Policy of Queen Elizabeth*, 3 vols (Oxford: Clarendon Press, 1925)
Remedies against discontentment, drawn into severall discourses, from the writings of aunciate philosophers (1596), STC, 20869
RENOUARD, PHILIPPE, *Imprimeurs & libraires parisiens du XVIe siècle* (Paris: Service des travaux historiques de la ville de Paris, 1964–)

REX, RICHARD, 'Morley and the Papacy: Rome, Regime, and Religion', in *'Triumphs of English'*, ed. by Axton and Carley, pp. 87–105

RHODES, NEIL, *The Power of Eloquence and English Renaissance Literature* (Basingstoke: Palgrave Macmillan, 1992)

RICHARDS, JENNIFER, 'Commonplacing and Prose Writing: William Baldwin and Robert Burton', in *The Oxford Handbook of English Prose 1500–1640*, ed. by Andrew Hadfield (Oxford: Oxford University Press, 2013), pp. 43–58

ROJAS, FERNANDO DE, *The Spanish bawd*, trans. by James Mabbe (1631), STC, 4911

ROSE, VALENTIN, ed., *Aristotelis qui ferebantur librorum fragmenta* (Leipzig: Teubner, 1886)

ROSKAM, GEERT, 'A Παιδεία for the Ruler: Plutarch's Dream of Collaboration between Philosopher and Ruler', in *Sage and Emperor*, ed. by Stadter and Van der Stockt, pp. 175–89

—— ed., *Plutarch's 'Maxime Cum Principibus Philosopho Esse Disserendum': An Interpretation with Commentary* (Leuven: Leuven University Press, 2009)

ROWLAND, RICHARD, *Killing Hercules: Deianira and the Politics of Domestic Violence, from Sophocles to the War on Terror* (Abingdon: Routledge, 2017)

RUMMEL, ERIKA, *Erasmus as a Translator of the Classics* (Toronto: University of Toronto Press, 1985)

—— 'The Reception of Erasmus' *Adages* in Sixteenth-Century England', *Renaissance and Reformation / Renaissance et Réforme*, 18 (1994), 19–30

RUNDLE, DAVID, '"Not So Much Praise as Precept": Erasmus, Panegyric, and the Renaissance Art of Teaching Princes', in *Pedagogy and Power: Rhetorics of Classical Learning*, ed. by Yun Lee Too and Niall Livingstone (Cambridge: Cambridge University Press, 1998), pp. 148–69

RUSSELL, D. A., *Plutarch* (London: Duckworth, 1973)

RUSSELL, D. A., and Michael Winterbottom, eds, *Classical Literary Criticism* (Oxford: Oxford University Press, 1972)

SABBADINI, REMIGIO, *La scuola e gli studi di Guarino Guarini Veronese (con 44 documenti)* (Catania: Francesco Galati, 1896)

SALTER, THOMAS, *A mirrhor mete for all mothers, matrones, and maidens, intituled the mirrhor of modestie* (1579), STC, 21634

SANCHI, LUIGI-ALBERTO, 'Budé et Plutarque: des traductions de 1505 aux *Commentaires de la langue grecque*', in *'Moralia' et 'Œuvres morales'*, ed. by Guerrier, pp. 91–108

SANDROCK, KIRSTEN, 'Ancient Empires and Early Modern Colonialism in William Alexander's *Monarchicke Tragedies* (1603–07)', *Renaissance Studies*, 31 (2016), 346–64

SCARDIGLI, BARBARA, ed., *Essays on Plutarch's 'Lives'* (Oxford: Clarendon Press, 1995)

SCHANZER, ERNEST, ed., *Shakespeare's Appian: A Selection from the Tudor Translation of Appian's 'Civil Wars'* (Liverpool: Liverpool University Press, 1956)

SCHETTINO, MARIA T., 'Trajan's Rescript *De bonis relegatorum* and Plutarch's Ideal Ruler', in *Sage and Emperor*, ed. by Stadter and Van der Stockt, pp. 201–12

SCHOELL, FRANCK L., *Études sur l'humanisme continental en angleterre: à la fin de la Renaissance: M. Ficinus, L. Gyraldus, N. Comes, D. Erasmus, G. Xylander, H. Wolfius, H. Stephanus, J. Spondanus* (Paris: Champion, 1926)

SCHURINK, FRED, 'An Elizabethan Grammar School Exercise Book', *Bodleian Library Record*, 18 (2003), 174–96
—— 'Education and Reading in Elizabethan and Jacobean England' (unpublished doctoral thesis, University of Oxford, 2004)
—— 'Print, Patronage, and Occasion: Translations of Plutarch's *Moralia* in Tudor England', *Yearbook of English Studies*, 38 (2008), 86–101
—— 'The Intimacy of Manuscript and the Pleasure of Print: Literary Culture from *The Schoolmaster* to *Euphues*', in *The Oxford Handbook of Tudor Literature, 1485–1603*, ed. by Mike Pincombe and Cathy Shrank (Oxford: Oxford University Press, 2009), pp. 671–86
—— 'Manuscript Commonplace Books, Literature, and Reading in Early Modern England', *Huntington Library Quarterly*, 73 (2010), 453–69
—— 'Lives and Letters: Three Early Seventeenth-Century Manuscripts with Extracts from Sidney's *Arcadia*', *English Manuscript Studies 1100–1700*, 16 (2011), 170–96
SCODEL, JOSHUA, 'The Early English Essay', in *A Companion to British Literature*, ed. by Robert DeMaria Jr, Heesok Chang, and Samantha Zacher, 4 vols (Chichester: Wiley Blackwell, 2014), II, 213–30
SCOTT, WILLIAM, *The Model of Poesy*, ed. by Gavin Alexander (Cambridge: Cambridge University Press, 2013)
SCOTT-WARREN, JASON, 'Commonplacing and Originality: Reading Francis Meres', *Review of English Studies*, 68 (2017), 902–23
SENECA, *Thyestes*, trans. by Jasper Heywood (1560), STC, 22226
SHACKFORD, MARTHA HALE, *Plutarch in Renaissance England* (n.p.: n. pub., 1929)
SHAKESPEARE, WILLIAM, *The Tragedy of Anthony and Cleopatra*, ed. by Michael Neill (Oxford: Oxford University Press, 1994, repr. 2008)
—— *The Tragedy of Coriolanus*, ed. by R. B. Parker (Oxford: Oxford University Press, 1994, repr. 2008)
—— *Julius Caesar*, ed. by David Daniell, The Arden Shakespeare, Third Series (Walton-on-Thames: Nelson, 1998, repr. London: Bloomsbury, 2017)
—— *The Oxford Shakespeare: The Complete Works*, ed. by Stanley Wells, Gary Taylor, John Jowett, and William Montgomery, 2nd edn (Oxford: Oxford University Press, 2005)
—— *The Complete Poems of Shakespeare*, ed. by Cathy Shrank and Raphael Lyne (London: Routledge, 2018)
SHAPIRO, JAMES S., *A Year in the Life of William Shakespeare: 1599* (New York: HarperCollins, 2005)
SHARPE, KEVIN, *Reading Revolutions: The Politics of Reading in Early Modern England* (New Haven: Yale University Press, 2000)
SHRANK, CATHY, 'Civility and the City in *Coriolanus*', *Shakespeare Quarterly*, 54 (2003), 406–23
—— 'Sir Thomas Elyot and the Bonds of Community', in *The Oxford Handbook of Tudor Literature 1485–1603*, ed. by Mike Pincombe and Shrank (Oxford: Oxford University Press, 2009), pp. 154–69
[SIDNEY, SIR PHILIP], *Miscellaneous Prose of Sir Philip Sidney*, ed. by Katherine Duncan-Jones and Jan van Dorsten (Oxford: Oxford University Press, 1973)
—— *An Apology for Poetry; or, The Defence of Poesy*, ed. by Geoffrey Shepherd and

R. W. Maslen, 3rd edn (Manchester: Manchester University Press, 2002)

—— *The Correspondence of Sir Philip Sidney*, ed. by Roger Kuin (Oxford: Oxford University Press, 2012)

SIMPSON, JAMES, 'The Sacrifice of Lady Rochford: Henry Parker, Lord Morley's Translation of *De claris mulieribus*', in *'Triumphs of English'*, ed. by Axton and Carley, pp. 153–69

SIRINELLI, JEAN, and others, eds, Plutarch, *Œuvres morales* (Paris: Belles Lettres, 1971–), I. 1: *Introduction générale. De l'éducation des enfants. Comment lire les poètes* (1987)

SKINNER, QUENTIN, *The Foundations of Modern Political Thought*, 2 vols (Cambridge: Cambridge University Press, 1978)

—— *Reason and Rhetoric in the Philosophy of Hobbes* (Cambridge: Cambridge University Press, 1996)

—— 'Political Philosophy', in *The Cambridge History of Renaissance Philosophy*, ed. by Charles B. Schmitt and others (Cambridge: Cambridge University Press, 1988), pp. 389–452

SMITH, DENZELL S., *'The Tragoedy of Cleopatra, Queene of Aegypt' by Thomas May: A Critical Edition* (New York: Garland, 1979)

SMITH, PAUL J., *Dispositio: Problematic Ordering in French Renaissance Literature* (Leiden: Brill, 2007)

SMYTH, ADAM, *Autobiography in Early Modern England* (Cambridge: Cambridge University Press, 2010)

SOARES, NAIR DE NAZARÉ CASTRO, *O príncipe ideal no século XVI e a obra de D. Jerónimo Osório* (Coimbra: Instituto Nacional de Investigação Científica, 1994)

SOWERBY, ROBIN, 'Ancient History', in *The Oxford History of Literary Translation in English, Vol. 2: 1550–1660*, ed. by Gordon Braden, Robert Cummings, and Stuart Gillespie (Oxford: Oxford University Press, 2010), pp. 301–11

SPARGO, JOHN WEBSTER, *Juridical Folklore in England: Illustrated by the Cucking-Stool* (Durham, NC: Duke University Press, 1944)

SPEED, JOHN, *The history of Great Britaine* (1611), STC, 23045

SPENCER, T. J. B., ed., *Shakespeare's Plutarch* (Harmondsworth: Penguin, 1964)

STADTER, PHILIP A., 'Introduction: Setting Plutarch in his Context', in *Sage and Emperor*, ed. by Stadter and Van der Stockt, pp. 1–26

—— 'Plutarch's Compositional Technique: The Anecdote Collections and the Parallel Lives', *Greek, Roman, and Byzantine Studies*, 54 (2014), 665–86

—— *Plutarch and his Roman Readers* (Oxford: Oxford University Press, 2014)

STADTER, PHILIP A., and L. VAN DER STOCKT, eds, *Sage and Emperor: Plutarch, Greek Intellectuals, and Roman Power in the Time of Trajan, 98–117 A.D.* (Leuven: Leuven University Press, 2002)

STALLYBRASS, PETER, 'Patriarchal Territories: The Body Enclosed', in *Rewriting the Renaissance: The Discourses of Sexual Difference in Early Modern Europe*, ed. by Margaret W. Ferguson, Maureen Quilligan, and Nancy Vickers (Chicago: University of Chicago Press, 1986), pp. 123–42

STALLYBRASS, PETER, and others, 'Hamlet's Tables and the Technologies of Writing in Renaissance England', *Shakespeare Quarterly*, 55 (2004), 379–419

STARKEY, DAVID, 'An Attendant Lord? Henry Parker, Lord Morley', in *'Triumphs of English'*, ed. by Axton and Carley, pp. 1–25

STEVENSON, JANE, 'Women Writers and the Classics', in *Oxford History of Classical Reception*, II: *1558–1660*, ed. by Cheney and Hardie, pp. 129–46

STUREL, RENÉ, *Jacques Amyot: traducteur des 'Vies parallèles' de Plutarque* (Paris: Champion, 1908)

SULLIVAN, GARRETT, and ALAN STEWART, eds, *The Blackwell Encyclopedia of English Renaissance Literature*, 3 vols (Chichester: Wiley-Blackwell, 2012)

SWAIN, SIMON, 'Plutarch: Chance, Providence, and History', *American Journal of Philology*, 110 (1989), 272–302

—— 'Plutarch's Aemilius and Timoleon', *Historia: Zeitschrift für Alte Geschichte*, 38 (1989), 314–34

TANGA, FABIO, 'Il *De fraterno amore* di Plutarco tra Thomas Naogeorgus, Ludovicus Russardus e Stephanus Niger', in *Plutarque: éditions, traductions, paratextes*, ed. by Françoise Frazier and Olivier Guerrier (Coimbra: Imprensa da Universidade de Coimbra, 2017), pp. 19–39

TAVERNER, RICHARD, *The garden of wisdom* (1539), STC, 23711a

—— *The second booke of the garden of wisdome* (1539), STC, 23712.5

TAYLOR, ANDREW W., '"Ad omne virtutum genus?" Mary between Piety, Pedagogy and Praise in Early Tudor Humanism', in *Mary Tudor: Old and New Perspectives*, ed. by Susan Doran and Thomas S. Freeman (Houndmills: Palgrave Macmillan, 2011), pp. 103–22

—— 'How to Hold Your Tongue: John Christopherson's Plutarch and the Mid-Tudor Politics of Catholic Humanism', *Canadian Review of Comparative Literature / Revue Canadienne de Littérature Comparée*, 41 (2014), 411–31

TAYLOR, JEREMY, Ἐνιαυτός *A course of sermons for all the Sundayes of the year* (1653), Wing, T329

TELES, *Reliquiae*, ed. by Otto Hense, 2nd edn (Tübingen: Mohr Siebeck, 1909)

TEMPESTA, STEFANO MARTINELLI, 'Guillaume Budé traduttore di Plutarco: il caso del *De tranquillitate animi*', in *Plutarco nelle traduzioni latine di età umanistica: Seminario di studi, Fisciano, 12–13 luglio 2007*, ed. by Paola Volpe Cacciatore (Naples: D'Auria, 2009), pp. 87–123

THOMSON, PATRICIA, *Sir Thomas Wyatt and his Background* (Stanford: Stanford University Press, 1964)

TILLEY, MORRIS PALMER, *A Dictionary of the Proverbs in England in the Sixteenth and Seventeenth Centuries* (Ann Arbor: University of Michigan Press, 1950)

TILNEY, EDMUND, *'The Flower of Friendship': A Renaissance Dialogue Contesting Marriage* (Ithaca, NY: Cornell University Press, 1992)

TODD, MARGO, *Christian Humanism and the Puritan Social Order* (Cambridge: Cambridge University Press, 1987)

Trésor de la langue française informatisé <http://atilf.atilf.fr/> [accessed 14 August 2019]

A true and plaine declaration of the horrible treasons, practised by William Parry the traitor, against the Queenes Majestie (1585), STC, 19342

TUBB, AMOS, 'Printing the Regicide of Charles I', *History*, 89 (2004), 500–24

TURNBULL, G. H., 'John Hall's Letters to Samuel Hartlib', *Review of English Studies*, 4 (1953), 221–33

TURNER, PAUL, ed., *Selected Lives from 'The Lives of the Noble Grecians and Romans'*, 2 vols (Fontwell: Centaur Press, 1963)

TUVILL, DANIEL, *Asylum Veneris, or a sanctuary for ladies* (1616), STC, 24393
—— *'Essays politic and moral' and 'Essays moral and theological'*, ed. by John L. Lievsay (Charlottesville: University Press of Virginia for the Folger Shakespeare Library, 1971)
TYACKE, NICHOLAS, ed., *The History of the University of Oxford*, ed. by T. H. Aston, 8 vols (Oxford: Oxford University Press, 1984–2000), IV: *Seventeenth-Century Oxford* (1997)
UHLIG, CLAUS, *Hofkritik im England des Mittelalters und der Renaissance: Studien zu einem Gemeinplatz der europäischen Moralistik* (Berlin: de Gruyter, 1973)
USENER, HERMANN, ed., *Epicurea* (Leipzig: Teubner, 1887)
VAN DER STOCKT, LUC, 'A Plutarchan Hypomnema on Self-Love', *American Journal of Philology*, 120 (1999), 575–99
VAN HOOF, LIEVE, *Plutarch's Practical Ethics: The Social Dynamics of Philosophy* (Oxford: Oxford University Press, 2010)
VENUTI, LAWRENCE, *The Translator's Invisibility: A History of Translation* (London: Routledge, 1995)
VERBEKE, DEMMY, 'Cato in England: Translating Latin Sayings for Moral and Linguistic Instruction', in *Renaissance Cultural Crossroads: Translation, Print and Culture in Britain, 1473–1640*, ed. by Brenda M. Hosington and S. K. Barker (Leiden: Brill, 2013), pp. 139–55
VICKERS, BRIAN, *In Defence of Rhetoric* (Oxford: Clarendon Press, 1988)
—— ed., *English Renaissance Literary Criticism* (Oxford: Clarendon Press, 1999)
VIENNE-GUERRIN, NATHALIE, ed., *The Unruly Tongue in Early Modern England: Three Treatises* (Madison: Fairleigh Dickinson University Press, 2012)
[VIVES, JUAN LUÍS], *Vives: On Education: A Translation of the 'De tradendis disciplinis' of Juan Luis Vives*, ed. and trans. by Foster Watson (Cambridge: Cambridge University Press, 1913)
—— *The Instruction of a Christen Woman*, trans. by Richard Hyrde, ed. by Virginia Walcott Beauchamp, Elizabeth H. Hageman, and Margaret Mikesell (Urbana: University of Illinois Press, 2001)
VOCHT, HENRY DE, *De invloed van Erasmus op de Engelsche tooneelliteratuur der XVIe en XVIIe eeuwen* (Gent: Siffer, 1908)
VOLPE, PAOLA, 'Riflessioni sulla traduzione del *De liberis educandis* di Guarino Guarini', in *El amor en Plutarco*, ed. by Jesús-María Nieto Ibáñez and Raúl López López (Leon: Universidad de León, 2007), pp. 699–708
VON LEUTSCH, E L. and F. G. SCHNEIDEWIN, eds, *Corpus paroemiographorum graecorum*, 2 vols (Göttingen: Vanderhoeck & Ruprecht, 1839–1851)
WAITH, EUGENE M., *The Herculean Hero in Marlowe, Chapman, Shakespeare and Dryden* (New York: Columbia University Press, 1962)
WALKER, GREG, *Writing under Tyranny: English Literature and the Henrician Reformation* (Oxford: Oxford University Press, 2005)
WARD, RICHARD, *Two very usefull and compendious theological treatises* (1673), Wing, W807
WARDMAN, ALAN, *Plutarch's 'Lives'* (London: Paul Elek, 1974)
WIGGINS, MARTIN, and CATHERINE RICHARDSON, eds, *British Drama 1533–1642: A Catalogue* (Oxford: Oxford University Press, 2011–)
WILSON, K. J., ed., *The Letters of Sir Thomas Elyot* (= *Studies in Philology*, 73. 5 (1976))

WILSON, THOMAS, *The three orations of Demosthenes* (1570), STC, 6578
—— *A discourse uppon usurie* (1572), STC, 25807
WING, DONALD, ed., *Short-Title Catalogue of Books Printed in England, Scotland, Ireland, Wales, and British America, and of English Books Printed in Other Countries, 1641–1700*, rev. edn, 4 vols (New York: Modern Language Association of America, 1982–1998)
WINSTON, JESSICA, *Lawyers at Play: Literature, Law, and Politics at the Early Modern Inns of Court, 1558–1581* (Oxford: Oxford University Press, 2016)
WITHINGTON, PHIL, *Society in Early Modern England* (Cambridge: Polity, 2010)
WORTH, VALERIE, 'Les fortunes de Jacques Amyot en Angleterre: une traduction de Sir Thomas North', in *Fortunes de Jacques Amyot*, ed. by Balard, pp. 285–95
WORTHAM, JAMES, 'Sir Thomas Elyot and the Translation of Prose', *Huntington Library Quarterly*, 11 (1948), 219–40
WYATT, SIR THOMAS, trans., *Tho. wyatis translation of Plutarckes boke / of the quiete of mynde* (1528?), STC, 20058.5
—— *The Complete Poems*, ed. by R. A. Rebholz, rev. edn (Harmondsworth: Penguin, 1997)
XENOPHONTOS, SOPHIA, *Ethical Education in Plutarch: Moralising Agents and Contexts* (Berlin: de Gruyter, 2016)
XENOPHONTOS, SOPHIA, and KATERINA OIKONOMOPOULOU, eds, *Brill's Companion to the Reception of Plutarch* (Leiden: Brill, 2019)
XYLANDER, WILHELM, trans. (Latin), *Plutarchi [...] opus, quod parallela et vitas appellant: in quo vitae illustrissimorum virorum, graecorum ac romanorum [...] exponuntur* (Heidelberg: Ludwig Lucius aus der Wetterau, 1561), USTC, 684437
—— trans. (Latin), *Plutarchi Chaeronensis Moralia* (Basel: Thomas Guarin, 1570), USTC, 684409
ZADOROJNYI, ALEXEY, 'Safe Drugs for the Good Boys: Platonism and Pedagogy in Plutarch's *De Audiendis Poetis*', in *Sage and Emperor*, ed. by Stadter and Van der Stockt, pp. 297–314
ZAJKO, VANDA, and HELENA HOYLE, eds, *A Handbook to the Reception of Classical Mythology* (Malden: Wiley, 2017)
ZECCHINI, GIUSEPPE, 'Plutarch as Political Theorist and Trajan: Some Reflections', in *Sage and Emperor*, ed. by Stadter and Van der Stockt, pp. 191–200
ZIEGLER, KONRAT, *Plutarchos von Chaironeia*, rev. edn (Stuttgart: Alfred Druckenmüller, 1964)
ZUCCHELLI, BRUNO, 'Petrarca, Plutarco e l'*Institutio Traiani*', in *L'eredità culturale di Plutarco dall'antichità al Rinascimento: atti del VII Convegno plutarcheo, Milano-Gargnano, 28–30 maggio 1997*, ed. by Italo Gallo (Naples: D'Auria, 1998), pp. 203–27

INDEX

Names cover both the edited texts and the editorial material; subject headings, editorial matter alone. Gods and mythological figures are listed under their Roman names (normally used by English Renaissance translators), but where both appear in the edition I have included the Greek version of the name with a cross-reference to the Latin one. The indexes in the relevant Loeb volumes of Plutarch's *Moralia* and *Lives* usefully provide further information about historical and mythological figures listed here.

Academy I: 132, 226, 318, II: 106, 151
Acciaiuoli, Donato I: 58, 97, II: 5, 57
Achillas II: 220
Achilles I: 91, 128, 129, 140, 163, 182, 276, 277, 283, 301, 302, 303, 307, 308, 310, 311, 312, 313, 317, 322, 324, II: 41, 84, 214
Acrasia I: 333
Acropolis of Athens I: 353, II: 98
Acropolis of Sparta I: 362
Actium, battle of I: 74
Adrastus (king of Argos) II: 129
Adrastus (Trojan killed by Agamemnon) I: 311
Adrastus (uncle of Alcmaeon) I: 326
Aeacus, temple of II: 62, 100
Aelian (Claudius Aelianus) I: 28, 42, 338
Aemilius Paullus, Lucius I: 58, II: 1-44
Aeneas I: 80, 266
Aeschines (Athenian orator) II: 51, 76, 81, 85, 87-88, 93, 94, 96
   Against Ctesiphon II: 76, 88, 96
Aeschylus I: 149, 263, 276, 277, 309, 316, 327, II: 152
Aesop (actor Aesopus) II: 108
Aesop (author of the *Fables*) I: 265, 272, 276
Afranius, Lucius II: 209, 214, 223
Agamemnon I: 130, 277, 283, 301-02, 307-08, 309, 317, 319-20, II: 213
Agis II, king of Sparta I: 133
Agis III, king of Sparta II: 95
agnomina *see* names and naming
Agrippa (Marcus Vipsanius Agrippa) II: 153
Ahura Mazda *see* Oromasdes
Ajax I: 297, 309, 310, 325, 348, II: 62, 100
Alcibiades I: 133, 370, II: 66, 74, 99, 154
Alcidamas II: 78
Alcmaeon I: 326
Alday, John I: 44
Alexander the Great I: 75, 91-92, 130, 140, 141, 142, 196, 208, 214, 215, 218, 228-29, 233, II: 2, 20-21, 25, 33, 37, 39, 46, 48, 52, 58, 81, 92, 94-98, 160, 186, 239, 260

Index

Alexander, Sir William, first earl of Stirling I: 63-64
    The Alexandrean Tragedy I: 61, 64
    Croesus I: 64
    Darius I: 61, 64
    Julius Caesar I: 61, 64, II: 164-65
Alexis I: 289
Allington Castle I: 110, 111, 126
Amasis I: 337
ambassadors I: 111, 113, 114-15, 159, 336, II: 53, 54
ambition I: 56, 64, 68, 80, 333, II: 49-50, 156, 158-59, 163, 164-65, 168
Ammianus Marcellinus I: 243, 246
Ammonius I: 6
Amyot, Jacques:
    life I: 19, 246, II: 54, 57
    works:
        Les Œuvres morales et meslees I: 1, 8, 10-11, 12, 19, 23, 34, 43-44, 45-47, 50, 93, 96, 97, 120, 169, 178, 219, 246-62, 269, 270-330 (commentary on Philemon Holland, 'How a Young Man Ought to Hear Poets and How He May Take Profit by Reading Poems'), 335, 341-42, 343-74 (commentary on Philemon Holland, 'Of Intemperate Speech or Garrulity')
        Les Vies des hommes illustres grecs et romains I: 10-11, 12, 15-16, 17, 20, 43-44, 60, 62, 65, 66, 76, 78, 79, 83, 84, 86, 88, 97, 98, 253, II: 50, 51, 53, 54, 55-70, 74-154 (commentary on *The Life of Demosthenes, The Life of Marcus Tullius Cicero, The Comparison of Cicero with Demosthenes*), 158-59, 160, 167, 170, 177-239 (commentary on *The Life of Julius Caesar*), 259, 260
Anacharsis I: 350
Anaxagoras I: 145
Anaxarchus I: 130, 228-29
Anaximenes II: 100, 152
ancestors I: 68-70, 73-78, II: 86
Angeli, Iacopo I: 8
Anicius Gallus, Lucius II: 26
Antigonus Doson II: 21
Antigonus Gonatas II: 21
Antigonus Monophthalmos I: 196, 198, 354, II: 20-21, 103
Antimachus (Trojan) I: 311
Antimachus of Colophon I: 370
Antiochus of Ascalon II: 106-07
Antiochus the Great II: 17, 20
Antipater (Macedonian statesman) I: 142, II: 98-99, 100-01, 103, 154
Antipater of Tarsus (Stoic philosopher) I: 135, 136, 373
Antiphanes II: 56, 77, 82
Antisthenes I: 318
Antoninus Pius, emperor of Rome II: 6, 14-15
Antonius, Publius *see* Antonius Hybrida, Gaius
Antonius Hybrida, Gaius II: 114-15, 119, 124, 179
Antonius Saturninus, Lucius II: 35
Antony, Mark (Marcus Antonius) I: 55, 61, 62-63, 65-67, 71, 72, 73, 74-81, II: 43, 47-48, 50, 68,

71, 126, 142, 143-44, 145-47, 149-50, 164, 167, 169, 170, 173, 204-05, 211, 216, 221, 231, 232, 233, 235, 236, 237, 239
Anytus I: 148
Apelles I: 140, 187
Aphrodite *see* Venus
Aphthonius II: 72
Apollo I: 6, 141, 276-77, 283, 365, II: 28, 148, 171
    see also Delphic oracle (temple of Apollo)
Apollonius Molon II: 107, 178
Appian of Alexandria I: 61, 98
Appius *see* Claudius Pulcher, Appius
Archedemus of Aetolia II: 33
Archelaus I: 261, 360
Archias II: 47, 100-01
Archidamus II I: 168, 177
Archilochus I: 137, 293, 318, 346
Archytas I: 190, 195
Ares *see* Mars
Ariosto, Ludovico I: 42
    Orlando furioso I: 263, 267-68
Aristarchus of Samothrace I: 303
Aristippus of Cyrene I: 135, 183
Aristobulus of Cassandreia II: 95
Aristodemus, king of Argos I: 216, 231
Aristogiton (orator) II: 87-88
Aristogiton (tyrannicide) I: 252, 352
Ariston of Ceos I: 272
Ariston of Chios II: 82
Aristophanes I: 195, 311
Aristophon (Athenian politician) II: 96
Aristophon (Greek painter) I: 280
Aristotle I: 34, 42, 142, 263, 265, 272, 301, 317, 333, 346, II: 49, 126
Armada, Spanish II: 1
Arsinoë II Philadelphus I: 167, 196
Artemidorus of Cnidus I: 72, II: 234-35
Ascham, Roger I: 116, 210
    The Schoolmaster I: 40, 171, 172, 212-13
    Toxophilus I: 39
Aspasia I: 90, 93
Astley, John I: 210
Athena *see* Juno; Minerva
Atreus I: 130, 283, 308, 319-20, II: 108
Attia II: 62, 145
Aubry, Johann I: 11
Audley, Thomas I: 25
Aufidius I: 86-87, 88-89
Augustus Caesar, emperor of Rome I: 65, 73, 75, 76, 77-78, 80, 339, 357-58, II: 43, 47, 50, 144, 145-47, 148, 150, 153, 154, 157, 167, 173, 237, 239

Aulus Gellius I: 37, 356
Aurispa, Giovanni I: 21

B., W. (William Barker?) I: 98
Bacchis I: 372
Bacchus I: 74-75, 152, 274, II: 184
Bacchylides I: 328
Bachet, Claude-Gaspar II: 57
Bacon, Francis I: 91-92, II: 7
    The Advancement of Learning I: 33-34, 47-49
    Essays I: 47-49, 50, 51
Bacon, Sir Nicholas I: 208
Badius Ascensius, Jodocus (Josse Bade) I: 8, 9, 15, 114-15, 162, 212, II: 8-9
Balbus, Lucius Cornelius II: 230
Baldwin, William I: 16-17, 38
barbarism I: 158, 332, II: 70
Barbaro, Francesco I: 9, 169-70
Barbour, Reid I: 52
Barlaeus (Caspar van Baerle) II: 12
Basil, St:
    Address to Young Men on How to Read Greek Literature I: 262-63, 267
    Letter 2 (to St Gregory on the solitary life) I: 114
Batrachus I: 281
Beard, Thomas I: 264
Beaufort, Lady Margaret II: 4
Bebel, Johannes II: 8
Beck, Mark I: 16
Belcamp, Jan van, I: 2
Belle, Marie-Alice I: 62
Bellerophon I: 315
Belot, Thomas I: 9, 15
Berners, John Bourchier, Lord, I: 121
Bestia, Lucius Calpurnius II: 125
Bias I: 162, 189, 327, 347
Bible I: 1, 17, 47, 68, 116, 337, II: 61
Bibulus, Lucius Calpurnius II: 187, 188
Bion I: 162, 189, 290
Blenerhasset, Thomas II: 12
Blundeville, Thomas:
    life I: 208-10
    works:
        Three Moral Treatises I: 96, 117, 120, 208-210, 212, 215, 261
        The Fruits of Foes I: 22, 96, 209, 212, 215
        The Learned Prince I: 22, 25, 96, 103, 205-38, 246-47, II: 245-46
        The Port of Rest I: 96, 108, 113, 116, 117-20, 134, 140, 148, 210, 212
Boaistuau, Pierre I: 44
Boccaccio, Giovanni:
    De casibus virorum illustrium II: 3

INDEX

De claris mulieribus II: 5, 255
Bochetel, Guillaume I: 335
Bodenham, John I: 38
body politic I: 78, II: 174
Boedromion II: 100
Boethius I: 212, II: 3, 68
Boleyn, Anne I: 110-11
Bona Dea II: 121, 129, 183-85
Book of Common Prayer II: 61
Botzheim, Johann von I: 1
Braden, Gordon I: 57, 101, II: 61
Brandon, Samuel I: 62-63
Brathwaite, Richard I: 29
Briareus I: 138
Brigden, Susan I: 113
Briseis I: 302, 317
Brooke, C. F. Tucker II: 57, 58, 59, 238, 258, 260
Brooke, Elizabeth I: 110
Brooke, Thomas, Lord Cobham I: 110
Browne, Thomas I: 52, 94
Bruni, Leonardo I: 8-9
    Cicero novus II: 72
    translation (Latin) of *Aemilius Paullus* I: 97, II: 3, 7-10, 14-44 (commentary on Henry Parker, Lord Morley, *The Story of Paullus Aemilius*)
Brutus, Lucius Iunius (ouster of Tarquinius Superbus) I: 68-70
Brutus, Lucius Iunius (tribune of the people) I: 83
Brutus, Marcus Iunius I: 61, 64, 65-74, II: 65, 69, 143, 146, 147, 154, 158, 159, 161, 164, 165, 169-70, 171, 172-73, 174, 218, 224, 226, 231-32, 234, 235-37, 238, 239
Brutus Albinus, Decimus Iunius II: 57, 233-34, 235
Budé, Guillaume I: 9
    Commentarii linguae graecae I: 116
    De tranquillitate et securitate animi I: 95, 96, 108, 113-20, 122, 123, 125-53 (commentary on Thomas Wyatt, *The Quiet of Mind*), 211, 212
Burghley, William Cecil, Lord II: 55, 71
Burke, Kenneth I: 87
Burrow, Colin I: 66, 69, 83, 84
Burton, Robert I: 52-53

Cadmus I: 167, 194
Cadwaladr II: 12
Caecilius II: 75, 110
Caelius Rufus, Marcus II: 138, 151
Caepio, Quintus Servilius II: 188
Caesar, Gaius Iulius I: 42, 57, 61, 63, 64, 65-74, 78, 89, 91, 92, 210, 230, II: 14, 46, 47, 50, 57, 58, 62, 65, 69, 70, 122-23, 125, 126, 128, 129-30, 131-32, 133, 138-41, 142, 143, 145, 156-239
    assassination I: 61, 64, 67-68, 69, 71-72, 73, 88, 247, II: 143, 235-36
    ghost I: 64, II: 158, 164, 169-70, 239
    works:

Anti-Cato II: 140, 224
Commentaries II: 161, 196
Caesar, Lucius Iulius II: 147
Calchas I: 308
Calenus, Quintus Fufius II: 215
Callias II: 78
Callisthenes II: 95
Callistratus of Aphidna II: 49, 77, 85
Calphurnius, Ioannes I: 114
Calpurnia II: 158, 169, 188, 233-34
Calvin, Jean II: 55
Cambridge, University of I: 2, 41, 110, 219, 243, 336, 340, II: 52, 71
Camden, William I: 31, 243, 246
Camma I: 41, 92
Campano, Giovanni Antonio I: 9, II: 8
Cannae, battle of II: 16
Carneades I: 146, 151, 370, 373, II: 106
Carracci, Ludovico, Agostino, and Annibale I: 2
Casaubon, Isaac II: 162, 165
Casaubon, Meric I: 17
Casca Longus, Publius Servilius I: 71, II: 170, 174, 235
de casibus see fall of princes
Cassander II: 85, 103
Cassius Longinus, Gaius I: 61, 67-73, II: 69, 143, 159, 164-65, 169, 170, 171-72, 174, 226, 232, 234, 235, 238
Castelvetro, Ludovico I: 263
Castiglione, Baldassare I: 41, 216, 219
Catiline (Lucius Sergius Catilina) II: 47, 49, 50, 69, 113-24, 125, 130, 132, 153, 161, 182
Cato, Marcus Porcius (the elder) I: 272, 309, II: 18, 31, 161, 165-66
Cato, Marcus Porcius (the younger) I: 63, 69, 89, 210, 230-31, 305, II: 72, 123, 125, 136, 139, 140, 151-52, 166, 179, 183, 187, 188, 196, 197, 203, 213-14, 222, 223-24, 231
Cato, Marcus Porcius Licinianus II: 18, 31
Catuli II: 104
Catullus I: 264
Catulus, Quintus Lutatius II: 123, 131, 181, 182, 183
Cavendish, Margaret, duchess of Newcastle upon Tyne I: 89-91, 93, 94
Cebes I: 121, 172
cento *see* patchwork (image)
Ceres I: 290, II: 56, 102
Chaerephanes I: 280
Chapman, George I: 10, 63, 124
   Bussy D'Ambois I: 216-18
   Caesar and Pompey I: 61, 63, II: 165-66
   The Revenge of Bussy D'Ambois I: 217
   The Tears of Peace I: 123
   translation of Homer's *Iliad* I: 217
Chares II: 153
Charles I, king of England I: 219, II: 12

Charles V, Emperor I: 21, 110, 112, 159, 215
Charles IX, king of France I: 19, II: 54
Charmides I: 368
Charybdis I: 115, 149
Chaucer, Geoffrey II: 68
Cheke, John, *De Superstitione* I: 98
Chilon I: 327
Cholmondeley, Randolph I: 28
Christianity I: 7, 59-60, 67, 78, 116, 124, 152, 183, 232, 248, 262-63, 336, II: 3-4, 56, 66, 68, 159-60, 165, 170, 239
   see also religious controversy
Christopherson, John I: 98, 335, 336
Chrysippus I: 242, 314, 321
Chrysoloras, Manuel I: 8, 163
Church Fathers I: 7, 262, 268, 336, 337
Cicero, Marcus Tullius I: 31, 32, 33, 39, 46, 92, 108, 163, II: 11, 23, 161, 174, 178, 179, 182-83, 189, 205, 224, 226, 227, 229
Cicero, Quintus Tullius II: 198
Ciceronians and Ciceronianism I: 3, 32, 33, 34, 46, 116
Cimon I: 216, 237, II: 86
Cinesias I: 290
Cinna, Gaius Helvius II: 237-38
Cinna, Lucius Cornelius (conspirator) II: 238
Cinna, Lucius Cornelius (dictator) II: 119, 177
Clapham, John I: 15, 96, 120
Claudius Pulcher, Appius II: 128, 195
Cleander I: 272, 273
Cleanthes I: 314, 318
Clearchus (king of Heraclea) I: 216, 231
Clearchus (Macedonian) II: 90
Cleitus I: 228
clemency I: 207, 209, II: 159-60, 163, 166
Clement VII, Pope I: 115
Cleopatra I: 62-63, 75-77, 79-80, II: 71, 166-67, 168, 219-21
Cleophantus I: 177
Clifford, Lady Anne I: 2, 94
Clitomachus II: 105, 106
Clodius Pulcher, Publius I: 366, II: 50, 129-36, 183-85, 189
Cloquemin, Abraham I: 248
Clytemnestra I: 300, 315
Collinson, Patrick I: 27
colossus *see* statues
Colossus of Rhodes II: 171-72
Colville, Elizabeth II: 53
Cominius I: 83, 87
commentaries I: 11, II: 60
commonplace-books and commonplacing I: 4, 5, 26-27, 29, 31, 32, 35-39, 40, 41, 43, 44-45, 48, 51-52, 53, 94, 268, II: 162, 163

see also hypomnēmata
comparison *see* synkrisis
constancy I: 38, 69, 72, 88, 89, 108, II: 50-51
Constantinople, fall of I: 8
Corbinelli, Angelo I: 163
Corinna I: 93
Coriolanus, Gnaeus Marcius I: 81-89
Cornificius, Quintus II: 215, 221
Cornwallis, William I: 49-50, 51, 124
Cottegnies, Line I: 62
counsel I: 4, 13-27, 33, 38, 58-60, 102, 113, 159-60, 207, 210, 211, 215-16, 246, 336, II: 71, 165
courts I: 22-23, 40, 59, 110-13, 123, 124, 216-18, II: 4-5, 16, 53, 54, 165, 166
Crane, Ronald S. I: 48
Craterus I: 251, 354, II: 100
Crates of Thebes I: 130, 183
Cratippus II: 126
Creon I: 361, II: 101
Crison I: 140
Cromwell, Thomas I: 58, 111, 159, II: 4, 5
Cronos *see* Saturn
Cruser, Hermann I: 8, 10-11, 60, 84, 98, 219, 250, 335, II: 51, 55, 58-60, 82, 87, 92, 100, 111, 141, 149, 185, 188, 192, 200, 209, 214, 228, 236
Ctesibius II: 78
Cummings, Robert I: 212, 214, 232, 250
Curio, Gaius Scribonius (the elder) II: 183
Curio, Gaius Scribonius (the younger) II: 203, 204, 205
Curran, John II: 166-67, 171
Cust, Richard I: 27
Cyclops I: 167, 197-98, 256, 353
Cynics I: 133, 233
Cyrus the Great I: 266, 313, 372

daimones II: 68, 169-70, 238, 239
Damonidas I: 281
Daniel, Samuel I: 61, 62
Darrell, Elizabeth I: 110
Davies of Hereford, John I: 29
Decembrio, Pier Candido II: 8
dedications I: 14, 16, 18, 19, 20, 21, 22, 23, 24, 30, 31, 34, 42, 45, 47, 48, 49, 51, 58, 95, 108, 111-12, 113, 115, 118-19, 160-61, 164, 167, 208-10, 211, 212, 215, 217, 245-46, 247, 336, II: 3, 4, 5, 6, 7, 9, 53, 54, 71, 241, 245
Deianira I: 76-77
Delamere, Alice I: 158
Delphic oracle (temple of Apollo) I: 6, 141, 249, 365, 369, II: 76, 90, 108
  see also Apollo
demagogues *see* popular politics
Demetrius (son of Philip V) II: 22
Demetrius I (Poliorcetes) I: 55, 75, 79, 147, 185, 365, II: 21, 85

Demetrius II (son of Antigonus Gonatas) II: 21
Demetrius of Magnesia II: 87, 99
Demetrius of Phalerum II: 81, 83, 86, 100
Democritus I: 109, 141, 194
Demosthenes I: 102, 186, 187, 363, II: 46-103, 108, 126, 151-54
Denham, Henry I: 215, II: 245
Denny, Edward I: 265
Denton, John II: 57, 69
Denys *see* Dionysius
Desmond, Gerald Fitzgerald, 14th earl of II: 53
Diana I: 290
Dicta Catonis I: 212
Dido I: 80
Dio Chrysostom I: 207
Dio, Cassius II: 191, 222
Diogenes Laertius I: 42, 327, 330
Diogenes the Cynic I: 54, 130, 132, 152, 177, 184, 213, 214, 215, 218, 233, 289-90
Diomedes I: 307-08, 309, 311
Dion I: 71, 190
Dionysius I I: 140, 234
Dionysius II I: 132, 160, 207, 234, 360, 365
Dionysius of Magnesia II: 107
Dionysus *see* Bacchus
Diopithes II: 153
Diotima I: 93
Dodds, Lara I: 90
Dolabella, Gnaeus Cornelius II: 179
Dolabella, Publius Cornelius II: 143, 144, 221, 232
Dolon I: 309
Domitian II: 35
Domitius Ahenobarbus, Lucius II: 139, 208, 214, 216
Domitius Calvinus, Gnaeus II: 216, 221
Doni, Anton Francesco II: 53
Doria Pamphilj, Palazzo I: 2
Draco I: 93
Drayton, Michael II: 11
Duff, Timothy I: 56-57, II: 2
Duris II: 91, 95

Earle, John I: 31
East and West I: 80, II: 2-3
Echepolus I: 317
education
    beating I: 156, 170, 171, 172
    grammar schools I: 19, 28, 29, 35-36, 39, 43, 44, 171-72, 212, 243, 246, II: 72
    royal I: 13-27, 38, 206, 207, 208, 209, 210, 215-16, 217-18
    universities I: 19, 28, 29, 38, 39, 43, 46, 50
        see also Cambridge, University of; Oxford, University of

women I: 46, 53, 81, 84-86, 92-94, 158, 170, 339
Edward VI, king of England I: 336, II: 15, 53
Edwards, Richard I: 61
eleutheria see liberty, political
Elizabeth I, queen of England I: 21, 25, 61-62, 91-92, 96, 111, 208-10, 213, 214, 215, 246, 247, II: 11–12, 53, 54-55, 159, 162, 245
Elyot, Margery I: 160-61, 174
Elyot, Sir Richard I: 158
Elyot, Thomas I: 119, 215, II: 10, 12
    life I: 21-22, 158-61
    works:
        The Banquet of Sapience I: 38
        The Book Named the Governor I: 21, 26, 39, 159, 166, 171, 187, 216
        Castle of Health I: 159
        The Defence of Good Women I: 160
        A Dialogue between Lucian and Diogenes I: 121
        Dictionary I: 22, 31, 159, 166, 200
        The Doctrinal of Princes I: 121, 159, 160
        The Education or Bringing Up of Children I: 9, 14, 21, 95, 103, 113, 118, 155-203, II: 243-44, 291
        The Image of Governance I: 161
        Of the Knowledge Which Maketh a Wise Man I: 160, 166, 167
        Pasquil the Playne I: 160
        A Preservative against Death I: 159
emotions I: 55-56, 108, 240, 241, 333, 334, II: 49, 50-52, 163, 167
Empedocles I: 141, 144, 276, 279
English Civil War I: 89-90
Epaminondas I: 133, 141, 190, 230, 290, 373, II: 91
Ephorus I: 373
Epicharmus I: 289, 363
Epictetus I: 122
Epicureanism and Epicureans I: 7, 109
Epicurus I: 129, 145, 242, 274, 327, 330, II: 235
epilepsy I: 69, 218, II: 173-74
Epimetheus I: 295
Episcopius, Eusebius I: 11-12, 247, 249
Erasmus, Desiderius I: 1, 34, 35, 49, 52, 170, 171, 209, 336
    Adagia I: 36-37, 42, 121
    Apophthegmata I: 16, 33, 37, 40, 42, 96, II: 71
    Ciceronianus I: 32, 37
    De civilitate morum I: 121, 170
    Colloquia I: 121
    De duplici copia verborum ac rerum I: 36, 43
    Editio princeps of Plutarch's *Moralia* I: 36-37
    Enchiridion I: 121
    Encomium matrimonii I: 39
    Institutio principis christiani I: 209, 215-16, 219
    Lingua I: 336-37, 339-40

INDEX 327

Panegyricus ad Philippum Austriae ducem II: 6-7
Parabolae I: 28, 29, 36, 42-43, 268
De pronuntiatione I: 170
De pueris instuendis I: 170
De ratione studii ac legendi interpretandique auctores I: 36
translations (Latin) of Plutarch's *Moralia* I: 9, 23-24, 29, 114
    'Advice on Health' I: 24, 95, 96
    'The Control of Anger' I: 24, 30-32, 45
    'Curiosity' I: 24, 30-32, 45, 96
    'Friends and Flatterers' I: 24, 95, 209
    'Harmful Scrupulousness' I: 24
    'How to Profit from your Enemies' I: 24, 31-32, 95, 96, 209, 212
    'Love of Money' I: 24
    'Philosophers and Princes' I: 24
    'The Uneducated Prince' I: 24, 96, 209-14, 219, 221-38 (commentary on Thomas Blundeville, *The Learned Prince*)
Eratosthenes II: 81, 102
Eros (friend of Plutarch) I: 127
errata I: 253, II: 248
essay genre I: 4, 43-52, 121, 123, 339
Essex, Robert Devereux, second earl of II: 53-54
Estienne, François I: 12, 248
Estienne, Henri II I: 11, 30, 247, 249, 250, 342, II: 60
Estienne, Paul I: 11, 247, 249, 250, 251
Eteocles I: 194, 281
Eumelus II: 8, 28
Eumenes of Cardia I: 251, 354
Euphorbus I: 363
Euphorion of Chalcis I: 141
Euphuism I: 41
Euripides I: 127, 130, 131, 139, 142, 144, 147, 149, 151, 176, 186, 194, 222, 226, 263, 266, 279, 281, 284, 286, 287, 292, 293, 294, 297, 298, 299, 305, 306, 311, 318, 319, 320, 321, 323, 328, 329, 338, 339, 344, 346, 354, 355, 372, II: 74, 79, 129
Eurydice of Illyria I: 170, 203
Euthycrates I: 363
Eutropion I: 196-98
Evander II: 33
exemplarity I: 5, 53-94, 158, 172, 266-67, II: 2-3, 12, 71-72, 162, 163-75
exile I: 54, II: 49, 50, 51-52

Fabius Maximus, Paullus I: 357
Fabius Maximus Aemilianus, Quintus II: 18 (n. 16), 27, 42
Fabius Maximus Verrucosus, Quintus II: 18
Fables of Bidpai II: 53
fall of princes I: 213, II: 3-4, 66, 160, 164
Favonius, Marcus II: 196
female gendering of talkativeness I: 338-41
Fenton, Geoffrey I: 18

Fidoe, John I: 219
Field, Richard I: 64, II: 258
Filelfo, Francesco I: 169, 170
Fleming, Rudd I: 2
Fletcher, John I: 61, II: 167-68
    Demetrius and Enanthe II: 167
    (with Philip Massinger) *The False One* I: 61, II: 166-68
    (with William Shakespeare) *The Two Noble Kinsmen* I: 61, II: 168
Florby, Gunilla I: 218
Florio, John I: 44, 123, II: 163
florilegia *see* commonplace-books and commonplacing
flower-gathering (image) I: 30-31, 32, 52-53
Ford, John I: 124
fortune I: 59, 102, 111-12, 121, 124, 170, 213, 217-18, II: 3-4, 12, 68, 166, 170
Forum Romanum II: 47, 58, 69, 123, 236
Francesco di Siena I: 2
Francis I, king of France I: 115, 335
Frellon, Paul I: 248
Froben, Johann I: 9, 114, 210
Fuller, Thomas I: 243
Fulvian basilica II: 203
Fulvius I: 357-58
Fundanus, Gaius Minicius I: 127

Gabinius, Aulus II: 131, 133
Galba, Publius Sulpicius II: 221
Galba, Servius Sulpicius II: 10, 39
Garnier, Robert I: 62, 94
Gaza, Theodore I: 1
Genthius I: 22, 25-26
gift presentations I: 9, 16, 21, 22, 103, 114, 211, 335, II: 54-55, 245, 255
    New Year I: 22-23, 31, 111, 118, 126, 209, 211, II: 5, 6
Giovio, Paolo II: 5
Giunta, Filippo I: 11
Giustian, Leonardo I: 9
Glaucus (Lycian commander in Trojan war) I: 315
Glaucus (sea-god) I: 28
Golding, Arthur I: 219
Gorgias (companion of Cicero's son) II: 126
Gorgias of Leontini I: 185, 273
Gorgon I: 268
Gosson, Stephen I: 263-65
Goulart, Simon I: 11, 12-13, 34, 169, 247-48, 254, 258, 335, II: 160, 239, 260
Grafton, Anthony I: 26
Grant, Edward I: 96, 169
Greene, Robert I: 41
Greenwich Palace II: 162
Griffin, Sarah II: 248

Grottaferrata, Abbey of I: 2
Grynaeus, Simon II: 8
Guarino, Battista I: 169
Guarino Guarini of Verona I: 8-9, 95, 96, 162-68, 176-203 (commentary on Thomas Elyot, *The Education or Bringing up of Children*)
Guevara, Antonio de I: 17-18, 20, 21, 26-27, 41, 121, II: 52-53
Guillard, Guillaume I: 9, 15
Gunpowder Plot I: 64, II: 165
Gyges I: 137
Gylippus I: 137

Haddon, Christopher I: 40
Haddon, Walter I: 56, 59-60
Hades II: 65
Hahn, Ulrich I: 9
Hales, John I: 14-15, 24-25, 96
Hall, John I: 262
Hellenism I: 3, 6, 31, 56-57, 70
Hampton, Timothy I: 57, 81-82
Hampton Court Palace II: 162
Hare, Robert II: 255
Harington, Sir John I: 263, 267-68
Harmodius I: 252, 352
Harpalus II: 60, 96-97, 153
Hartlib, Samuel I: 262
Hatfield, Arnold II: 248
Haudent, Guillaume I: 212
Hayne, William I: 172
Hector I: 91, 277, 283, 296-97, 309-11, 312, 324, 371
Hecuba I: 305
Helen I: 91, 282, 305
Henri II, king of France I: 19
Henri III, king of France I: 19, II: 53, 54
Henry, Prince I: 47, 48, 246
Henry VIII, king of England I: 21-22, 24, 25, 38, 58-59, 110-13, 115, 159, 160, 209, 211, 264, II: 3, 4-7, 14, 16, 255
Henryson, Edward I: 98
Heraclides I: 249, 272
Heraclitus I: 144, 306, 366
Hercules I: 74-77, 78, 138, II: 29, 31, 91
Hermes *see* Mercury
Hermippus of Smyrna II: 78, 83, 100, 101
Herodes II: 126
Hervet, Gentian I: 121
Hesiod I: 128, 142, 194, 229, 263, 293, 295, 296, 297, 298, 305, 321, 327
Heywood, Jasper I: 215, II: 52
Higgins, John II: 160, 200
Hippocrates I: 374

330   INDEX

Hippolytus I: 305
Hirtius, Aulus II: 43, 144
Hobbes, Thomas I: 90
Hoby, Sir Thomas I: 216
Holland, Abraham I: 243
Holland, Compton I: 243
Holland, Henry I: 243
Holland, John I: 243
Holland, Philemon:
    life I: 243-47
    translations:
        Ammianus Marcellinus's history of Rome I: 243, 246
        Camden's *Britannia* I: 243, 246
        Livy's *History of Rome from the Foundation of the City* I: 243, 244
        Pliny the Elder's *Natural History* I: 243, 244
        Plutarch's *Moralia* (*The Morals*) I: 11-12, 13, 22, 35, 50, 97, 102-03, 104, 117, 120, 121, 148, 167, 169, 213, 239-374, II: 248-54
        Regimen sanitatis Salerni I: 246
        Speed's *The Theatre of the Empire of Great Britain* I: 243, 246
        Suetonius's *Lives of the Caesars* I: 243, 247
        Xenophon's *Cyropaedia* I: 243, 246
Holtzman, Wilhelm *see* Xylander, Wilhelm
Homer I: 128, 140, 141, 143, 146, 149, 163-64, 182, 196, 240, 261, 263, 267, 277, 278, 282, 284, 285, 286, 291, 294, 298, 299, 302, 305, 308, 310, 314, 315, 319, 323, 324, 325, 349, 352, 355, 365, 371, II: 37, 41, 94, 189
    Iliad I: 129, 130, 139, 140, 143, 147, 172, 196, 217, 229, 230, 234, 251, 257, 273, 277, 279, 282, 283, 284, 285, 286, 287, 291, 292, 294, 295, 296, 297, 300, 301, 302, 305, 307, 308, 309, 310, 311, 312, 313, 314, 315, 316, 317, 318, 323, 324, 325, 327, 359, 360, 365, 371, II: 41, 84, 213
    Odyssey I: 146, 149, 227, 273, 274, 277, 278, 282, 283, 284, 285, 287, 291, 292, 296, 298, 300, 303, 304, 312, 313, 315, 347, 349, 350, 353, 365
honesty I: 65, 71, 91, II: 48, 51, 52
Horace I: 111, 123, 124, 275, 347
Hostilius Mancinus, Aulus I: 22
Howard, Katherine II: 5
Howe one may take profite of his enmies I: 95
Hume of Godscroft, David II: 165
Hurault, Jacques I: 219
Hyperides II: 47, 85, 86, 100
hypomnēmata I: 29, 35, 109-10, 127
Hyrde, Richard I: 92, 170

Ibycus I: 338, 362
Idomeneus (Cretan warrior) I: 325
Idomeneus of Lampsacus II: 88, 95
ille-ism I: 72, II: 171
indexes I: 11-12, 103, 105, 245, 248, 249, 251, II: 248, 260
Inimicus amicus: an excellent treatise, shewing, how a man may reape profit by his enemy I: 96

Inns of Court I: 158, 208, 215, II: 52-53
Ino I: 339, 354
Institutio Traiani I: 7, 13-27
Iole I: 76
Ion (officer of Perseus) II: 36
Ion of Chios I: 130, II: 75
Isaeus II: 77-78
Isauricus, Publius Servilius II: 210
Isauricus, Publius Servilius Vatia II: 182
Ismenias I: 141
Isocrates I: 121, 160, 169, II: 77-78, 152
Ixion I: 281, 284

James I, king of England (James VI of Scotland) I: 22, 64, 243, 245-47, 249, II: 12, 162, 165, 166
Jardine, Lisa I: 26, 48
Jeanes, Thomas I: 219
Jocasta I: 194, 280
John of Salisbury *see Institutio Traiani*
Jonson, Ben I: 51-52, 340-41
Josiah I: 219
Jove *see* Jupiter
Julia (Caesar's aunt) II: 180
Julia (Caesar's daughter) II: 188, 198, 225
Julius II, Pope I: 114, 115
Juno I: 75, 283, 284-85, 362
Junius, Hadrianus I: 95
Junta, Filippo *see* Giunta, Filippo
Jupiter I: 128, 130, 139, 141, 143, 183, 229, 251, 277, 284, 285, 294-97, 300, 301, 307, 312, 313, 314, 315, 317, 324, 327, 328, II: 11, 37, 99, 118, 126, 145, 230, 231

Kahn, Coppélia I: 57, 67, 77
kalon, to see honesty
Katherine of Aragon, queen of England I: 24, 92, 109, 110, 111-13, 118, 125-26, 160, 170, 264
Kempe, William I: 171-72
Kewes, Paulina II: 165
Kiernan, Michael I: 47, 49
King's Men I: 61, II: 167
Kyd, Thomas I: 62

Labienus, Titus II: 140, 192, 208
Lacritus II: 100
Laelius Balbus, Decimus II: 154
Laertes I: 128, 324, II: 141-42
Laimarie, Guillaume de I: 13
Lamprias, Catalogue of I: 7
Languet, Hubert I: 2
A Larum for London I: 60
Lathrop, H. B. I: 162, 166, 262

Laud, William II: 255
Leaena I: 252, 339, 352
Leicester, Robert Dudley, Earl of I: 56, 59-60, 208, II: 53, 55
Lentulus Crus, Lucius Cornelius II: 203, 205, 207
Lentulus Spinther, Lucius Cornelius II: 135, 139
Lentulus Spinther (son of previous) II: 237
Lentulus Sura, Publius Cornelius II: 64, 119-32, 182
Leosthenes II: 98, 153
Lepidus, Marcus Aemilius II: 50, 147, 233, 236
Le Preux, François II: 57
Le Preux, Jean I: 12, II: 57
liberty, political I: 67, II: 47-48, 49-50, 71, 157-58, 161, 164
Lichas I: 76
Licinius Crassus, Publius II: 22
Licinius Macer, Gaius II: 112
Lievsay, John L. I: 50-51
Ligarius, Quintus I: 69, II: 46, 140-41
Linacre, Thomas I: 158, 159
Ling, Nicholas I: 38
Livia Drusilla I: 358
Livy I: 2, 163, 243, 244, II: 11-12, 218, 228, 233
Lloyd, Lodowick I: 39-40, II: 162, 163
Lodge, Thomas I: 28-29, 61-62, 263
logos see reason
Longinus I: 240
Longueil, Christophe I: 211
Lorenzi, Giovanni I: 335
Lorich, Reinhard II: 72
Louis XII, king of France I: 115
Louvain, University of I: 336
Lucan I: 3, II: 161, 166
Lucian I: 121, 169, 336, II: 71
Lucilius I: 66-67
Lucius I: 69
Lucullus, Lucius Licinius I: 216, 237, II: 130, 133, 185, 189
Lucullus, Marcus Terentius Varro II: 179, 189
Lupercalia II: 172, 230, 231
Lycon I: 272
Lycosthenes, Konrad I: 28, 37
Lycurgus (Athenian orator) II: 95
Lycurgus (opponent of Dionysus) I: 274
Lycurgus (Spartan lawgiver) I: 93, 179-80, 364
Lydgate, John II: 3, 68, 161
Lyly, John I: 28, 41-42, 60, 95, 96, 169
Lysias I: 257, 349
Lysimachus I: 358
Lyttelton, Elizabeth I: 94

Macault, Antoine I: 37
Maecenas, Gaius Cilnius I: 77, II: 153
Magnani, Palazzo I: 2
Malory, Sir Thomas II: 61
Mamercus II: 16
Manutius, Aldus I: 8, 11, 36, 169, 192
Mapstone, Sally II: 164, 165
Marcellus, Gaius Claudius II: 145
Marcellus, Marcus Claudius II: 117, 203, 205
Marconville, Jean I: 337
marginalia I: 11-12, 103, 212, 245, 247, 248, II: 51, 57, 58-59, 60, 162-63, 166, 174, 259, 260
Margolin, J.-C. I: 28
Marion, Olga van I: 11
Marius, Gaius I: 61, 350, II: 177, 180-81, 189, 193
Marius, Gaius (son of the above) II: 177
Mark Antony *see* Antony, Mark
Marne, Claude de, heirs of I: 11
Mars I: 82, 129, 141, 251, 283, 284, 294
Mars, field of (Campus Martius) II: 117, 145, 198
Marston, John I: 124
Marsyas II: 90
Martial I: 265
martial valour I: 70, 74-76, 81-89, II: 171
Mary, queen of Scots I: 62, II: 159
Mary I, queen of England I: 243, 336, II: 5
masculinity I: 65, 69-70, 73, 74-76, 80, 83-89, 157-58, 339-40, II: 51-52, 70, 167, 172, 173, 174
Maso, Gaius Papirius II: 18
Massinger, Philip I: 61, 124, II: 167-68
    see also Fletcher, John, (with Philip Massinger) *The False One*
Master, William I: 97
Matthiessen, F. O. I: 168, II: 59-60, 61, 63-64
May, Steven W. II: 245
May, Thomas II: 166
Mazzocchi, Giacomo I: 114
McGrath, Elizabeth I: 2
McKerrow, R. B. I: 42-43
Medea I: 280
Medius I: 141
Megabyzus I: 140
Melanthius I: 285
Menander I: 114, 129, 139, 144, 146-47, 150, 263, 282, 288, 289, 298, 322, 371
Menedemus of Eretria I: 142
Menenius I: 78
Menippus of Caria II: 107
Mercury I: 141, 338, 345
Meres, Francis I: 38, 263, 268
Merops I: 127
Mery Tales, Wittie Questions, and Quicke Answeres I: 40

Metella Caecilia I: 351
Metellus, Lucius Caecilius II: 209
Metellus Celer, Quintus Caecilius II: 118, 130
Metellus Macedonicus, Quintus Caecilius I: 354
Metellus Nepos, Quintus Caecilius II: 125, 128
Metellus Pius, Quintus Caecilius II: 182
Metellus Scipio, Quintus Caecilius II: 117
Metrocles I: 133
Metzler, Johann I: 162
Miani, Pietro II: 7
Midias II: 84
military achievements I: 6, 55-56, 57, 58-59, 91, 92, II: 7, 46-49, 71, 156, 159, 162, 167
    see also martial valour
Milo (officer of Perseus) II: 28
Milo, Titus Annius II: 135, 136
Milton, John I: 172
Minerva I: 152, 302, 312, II: 98
Minturno, Antonio I: 263
Minutum I: 61
Mirabellius, Dominicus Nanus I: 38, 268
mirror (image) I: 5, 25, 40, 53-54, 58, 62, 63, 65, 67-68, 69, 70, 77-78, 92-93, II: 6, 14
Mirror for Magistrates II: 3, 12, 68, 160
mirror for princes (genre) I: 13, 17, 19, 23, 40, 209, 215-16, II: 6, 53
miscellaneity I: 5, 8, 45-47, 53
Mithridates VI Eupator I: 350, II: 133, 221
Moles, John I: 70, II: 110
Molin, Sébastien I: 247, 248
monarchy I: 27, 64, 78, 80, 89, 102, 206-08, 215-20, 247, II: 47-48, 50, 52, 157-61, 162, 165-66, 167, 168-69
    divine I: 72, 80, 206, 215, II: 171-72
    see also Caesar, Gaius Iulius, assassination; counsel; courts; education, royal; liberty, political; rebellion; tyranny
Montaigne, Michel de I: 1, 10, 29-30, 43-47, 48, 49-50, 51, 52, 123, II: 55, 63, 160, 163, 164
moral-historical compilations I: 39-40, 44, II: 11, 162
moralism, descriptive and protreptic II: 157, 163
More, Thomas I: 1, 158, 170
Morgan, Matthew I: 32, 261-62
Morley, Henry Parker, Baron:
    life I: 58-59, II: 4-7
    works:
        Exposition of Psalm 36 II: 5
        translations
            Boccaccio, *De claris mulieribus* II: 5
            Giovio, Paolo, *Commentari delle cose de' Turchi* II: 5
            Petrarch, *Trionfi* II: 5
            Plutarch, *Lives* (attributed) I: 9, 14, 22, 102, 166, 213, II: 60
                The Life of Theseus I: 58, 97, II: 5-6, 255
                The Liff of the Good King Agesilaius I: 58, 97, II: 5, 8

> *The Lives of Scipio and Haniball* I: 58, 60, 97, II: 5, 14
> *The Story of Paullus Aemilius* I: 25, 58-59, 97, 103, 104, II: 1-44, 255-57, 292

mosaic (image) I: 5, 29, 30, 31-32, 37, 214
Mossman, Judith II: 260
Munday, Anthony II: 53
Murena, Lucius Licinius II: 117, 136, 151
Muret, Marc-Antoine I: 156
Murfyn, Alice II: 52
Myron I: 227

names and naming I: 65-74, 78, 81-89, II: 157, 171
Naogeorgus, Thomas I: 124, 249, 250, 252, 257, 258, 261, 335, 336
Nashe, Thomas I: 41-43
Nasica *see* Scipio Nasica Corculum, Publius Cornelius
Nausicaa I: 303
Neill, Michael I: 79-80
Neon II: 33
Neoptolemus I: 354
Nepos, Cornelius I: 12
Neptune I: 257, 276, 292, 315, II: 100, 101, 154
Nero, emperor of Rome I: 351
Nessus I: 76
Nestor I: 91, 308, 348, 371
Newdigate, John I: 94
Newdigate, Sir John I: 26-27, 38, 39, 94
Nicander I: 254, 276
Nicias I: 361
North, Edward (son of Thomas) II: 53
North, Edward, first Baron North II: 52
North, Elizabeth II: 53
North, Roger II: 53, 54-55
North, Thomas:
    life II: 52-55
    works:
        The Dial of Princes I: 17, 26, II: 52-53, 59, 259
        The Lives of the Noble Grecians and Romans I: 1, 5, 11, 12-13, 15, 17, 20, 23, 26, 62, 64-65, 66, 74, 76, 78, 82-83, 84, 86, 87-88, 89, 92, 93-94, 98, 102, 103, 246, 253, 257, 258, 260, 261, II: 45-239, 258-71, 292-93
        The Moral Philosophy of Doni II: 53
        preface to English translation of Belleforest's *Tragicall Hystories* II: 54
Norton, Bonham II: 258
notebooks *see* commonplace-books and commonplacing; *hypomnēmata*
Numa Pompilius I: 26, 93, II: 16, 229

Octavian and Octavius (Caesar) *see* Augustus Caesar
Octavius (unidentified senator) II: 128
Octavius, Gaius II: 145
Octavius, Gnaeus II: 35, 36

Octavius Balbus, Gaius II: 237
Odysseus *see* Ulysses
Olympic Games I: 138, II: 74, 81
Omphale I: 75-76
Oppius, Gaius II: 191, 192
oratory I: 102, 167, II: 46-49, 56, 71-72
Orestes I: 280
Oromasdes I: 219, 226
Osório, Jerónimo I: 171
Ovid I: 28, 41, 265, 267, 268
Oxford, University of I: 2, 28, 61, 158, 264

Paccius I: 35, 109-10, 123, 127, 134
Pace, Richard I: 98, 335, 336
Pacini, Antonio I: 97
Painter, William I: 18, 40-41, 97
Panaetius I: 109, II: 51, 85
Pandarus I: 284, 315
Pansa Caetronianus, Gaius Vibius II: 43, 144, 146
Panthea I: 313
Papiria Masonis II: 18
Pappus II: 101
paratexts I: 11-13, 103, 118-19, 211, 245, 247-48, 249, 250, 253, 258, II: 53, 57, 58
    see also commentaries; dedications; errata; indexes; marginalia
Parinchef, John I: 37
Paris (mythic character) I: 282, 305, 323
Parker, Patricia I: 339
Parker, R. B. I: 83
Parmenides I: 276
Parmeno I: 280
Parrhasius I: 280
Parry, William II: 159
Paster, Gail Kern II: 172
Pataecion I: 290
patchwork (image) I: 30, 31, 32, 33, 37, 42-43, 44, 52-53
pathē see emotions
Patroclus I: 283, 325, II: 248
patronage I: 4, 9, 20, 22-23, 60, 62, 95, 111, 113, 126, 209, 211, 246, 336, II: 7, 55
    see also dedications; gift presentations
Paulus, Lucius Aemilius II: 147
Peacham, Henry I: 1, 171
pederasty I: 113, 156-57, 167, 197
Peleus I: 163-64, 182, 283, 324
Pelling, Christopher I: 79, II: 2, 157, 170, 173-74, 175, 222
Pelops of Byzantium II: 126
Pembroke, Mary Herbert, Countess of I: 62-63, 94
Penelope I: 167, 189, 254, 303, 353
Perdiccas II: 103

Pericles I: 90, 167, 186, 190, II: 79, 81, 86, 91, 140
Peripatetics I: 7
Perseus (king of Macedonia) I: 146, II: 2-3, 7, 12, 14, 20, 22-43
Perseus (mythical hero) I: 268
Petrarch (Francesco Petrarca) I: 109, 111-13, 118, 125, II: 4, 5
Pettie, George I: 41
Peyton, Anne I: 243
Phaedra I: 104, 305
Phaethon I: 131
Phanias I: 129
Pharnaces II, king of Bosporus II: 69, 221
Pharsalus, battle of I: 61, 89, II: 46, 140-41, 159, 166, 214-18, 222, 231
Phidias I: 227, II: 37
Philagrus I: 363
Philemon I: 326
Philip I, the Handsome, king of Castile II: 7
Philip II, king of Macedon II: 20-22, 25, 46, 48, 51, 52, 61, 71, 81-93, 126, 153
Philip II, king of Spain II: 71
Philippi, battle of I: 61, 64, 65, 71-72, 76, II: 158, 169, 238
Philippides I: 358
Philippus, Lucius Marcius II: 145
Philo of Larissa II: 106
Philocrates I: 363, II: 88
Philoctetes I: 280
Philopappus, Gaius Iulius Antiochus Epiphanes I: 24
philosopher-king, Platonic ideal of I: 206-08, 216, II: 49
philosophical eclecticism I: 3-4, 7, 109, 124, 156
philotimia see ambition
Philoxenus of Cythera I: 140, 272
Phiston, William I: 93
Phocylides I: 181
Phoenix I: 163, 172, 182, 302-03
Phylarchus II: 99
Piccolomini, Aeneas Silvius I: 169-70
Pindar I: 132, 141, 142, 151, 219, 225, 261, 263, 278, 287, 365
Pirckheimer, Willibald I: 335
Piso, Gaius Calpurnius II: 121, 182
Piso Caesoninus, Lucius Calpurnius II: 131, 133, 188, 210
Piso Frugi, Gaius Calpurnius II: 132, 143
Piso Frugi Calpurnianus, Marcus Pupius I: 366
Pittacus I: 139, 337, 353
plain style I: 113, 119-20, 121
Planches, Jérémie des I: 12
Plantin, Christophe I: 93
Planudes, Maximus I: 7-8
Plato I: 33, 34, 35, 79, 92, 109, 110, 127, 131, 132, 140, 141, 145, 148, 152, 160, 178, 181, 183, 189, 190, 191, 195, 206, 207, 213, 222, 226, 232, 241, 242, 263, 265, 274, 276, 279, 296, 301, 309, 327, 328, 329, 351, 364, 368, II: 49, 77, 78, 105, 126, 151, 153

338   INDEX

  see also Academy; philosopher-king, Platonic ideal of; Platonism and Platonists
Platonism and Platonists I: 6, 7, 78, 116, 156
Pliny the Elder I: 28, 243, 244
Pliny the Younger I: 21, 207
Plutarch:
  anecdotes, use of I: 3, 6, 7, 29, 38-40, 42, 43, 47, 50, 110, 156, 157, 207, 214, 216, 333, 335, 338, II: 53, 161
  connections between *Moralia* and *Lives* I: 4, 25, 35, 54, 92, 102, 207-08
  images, use of I: 1, 3, 27-29, 34, 36, 39, 41, 42-43, 108, 110, 120, 121, 156-58, 162, 172, 207, 210, 214, 216-18, 240, 241, 252, 265, 268, 333, 335, 338, 341
  life I: 5-6
    Trajan's tutor and counsellor (purportedly) I: 4, 7, 13-27, 38, 41
  quotations, use of I: 7, 31, 33, 34, 110, 116, 156, 207, 240, 242, 335
  works:
    Lives:
      Aemilius Paullus I: 9, 25, 58, 97, 102, II: 1-44, 157
      Alexander I: 6, 40, 60-61, 97, II: 156, 160
      Antony I: 9, 40, 54-55, 62-63, 64, 74-76, 77, 78, 79-80, 97, 98, II: 7, 161, 166
      Brutus I: 9, 64, 66, 69-71, 73-74, 161, II: 51, 232, 238
      Caesar I: 6, 9, 64, 102, II: 2, 14, 55-70 (passim), 129, 140, 156-239, 258-61, 267-71, 292-93
      Cato I: 89, II: 7, 61, 166
      Cicero I: 5, 6, 9, 102, II: 45-73, 104-50, 161, 184, 224
      Comparison of Demetrius and Antony I: 75-76
      Comparison of Demosthenes and Cicero I: 208, II: 47, 49, 50, 51, 66-67, 72, 151-54
      Comparison of Dion and Brutus I: 71, 78, 89, II: 158, 161
      Coriolanus I: 64-65, 70, 81-89, 156, 208, II: 51
      Demetrius I: 40, 54-55, 79, 95, 97, II: 167
      Demosthenes I: 5, 97, 102, II: 45-103, 151-54, 258-64, 267, 292
      Dion I: 9, 61, 94
      Fabius I: 54
      Flaminius II: 167
      Lycurgus I: 1, 93
      Numa I: 26, 61, 93
      Pericles I: 54, 90
      Phocion I: 9, II: 103
      Pompey I: 62, II: 160, 166
      Themistocles I: 9
      Theseus I: 58, 61, 97, 102, II: 5-6
      Timoleon I: 53, 54, II: 2, 6, 167, 168, 255
      see also Acciaiuoli, Donato
    Moralia:
      'Advice on Health' I: 14, 23, 24, 25, 96, 334
      'Advice on Marriage' I: 7, 24, 39, II: 18
      'Advice on Public Life' I: 7, 207
      'The Banquet of the Seven Sages' I: 98
      'Brave Deeds of Women' I: 40-41, 92-93, 97
      'Common Notions: Against the Stoic View' I: 98

'Comparison of Aristophanes and Menander' I: 248-49
'Consolation to My Wife' I: 6, 108, II: 248
'Contradictions of the Stoics' I: 7, 98
'The Control of Anger' I: 7, 24, 30, 108, 127, 195, 334
'Curiosity' I: 7, 23, 24, 30, 52, 96, 108, 215, 334, 358
'The Education of Children' I: 9, 16, 19, 21, 23, 39, 41, 95, 96, 113, 155-203, 270
'Exile' I: 108
'The Face in the Moon' I: 98
'Fortune and Virtue in Alexander the Great' I: 114, 207
'The Fortune of the Romans' I: 114, 248
'Friends and Flatterers' I: 114, 208, 248
'Harmful Scrupulousness' I: 24, 108, 334
De Homero (apocryphal) I: 267
'How to Profit from your Enemies' I: 7, 21, 23, 24, 31, 95, 96, 97, 98, 99, 114, 209, 211
'Ills of the Body and Ills of the Mind' I: 24, 97, 99
'The Intelligence of Animals' I: 28
'Is Vice a Sufficient Cause of Misery?' I: 248-49
'On Listening to Lectures' I: 19, 98
'Love of Money' I: 24, 98
'Love Stories' I: 23, 96
'Monarchy, Democracy, and Oligarchy' I: 207, 247, 248
'Music' I: 39
'Old Men in Politics' I: 42, 207
'Philosophers and Princes' I: 14, 20, 24, 27, 207, 216
'Quiet of Mind' I: 9, 15, 23, 24, 35, 52, 48, 54, 95, 96, 102, 107-53, 167, 186, 190, 210, 211, 214, 259
'On Reading the Poets' I: 19, 24, 33, 38, 102, 114, 239-330
'Roman Questions' II: 248
'Sayings of Kings and Commanders' I: 13, 16, 18, 20, 22, 23, 34, 37, 40, 48, 54, 96
'Self-Praise without Offence' I: 108, 334
'Socrates' Sign' I: 45
'Spartan Sayings' I: 24, 37, 40, 54, 96, 264
'Superstition' I: 98, 250
'Table Talk' I: 7, 95
'Talkativeness' I: 24, 27-29, 42, 54, 98, 102, 108, 156, 186, 196, 249-61, 331-74
'The Uneducated Prince' I: 23, 24, 25, 96, 102, 205-38, 246, 247, 248
'The Unnoticed Life' I: 24
see also Institutio Traiani
Polemon I: 226
Poliager I: 304
Poliziano, Angelo I: 23, 96
Pollio, Gaius Asinius II: 206, 218, 223
Polybius II: 2, 11, 27, 28, 31
Polyclitus I: 227
Polyphemus I: 167, 196, 197-98
Pompeia (wife of Caesar) II: 129-31, 180, 183-85
Pompeius Magnus, Gnaeus (elder son of Pompey) II: 140, 225-26

340   INDEX

Pompeius Magnus, Sextus (younger son of Pompey) II: 225-26
Pompey the Great (Gnaeus Pompeius Magnus) I: 61, 63, 230, II: 8, 12, 14, 50, 58, 111, 112, 113,
    114, 116, 120, 125, 128, 131-33, 135, 136, 138-40, 142, 145, 153, 157-58, 165-66, 180, 185, 187-89,
    194, 195-96, 198, 199, 201-25, 226, 231, 235, 236, 238, 258
Pope, Alexander I: 244
Popillius, Gaius II: 180
Popillius Laenas, Gaius II: 59, 149
popular politics I: 56-57, 85-86, 163, 187, II: 48-49, 62-63, 69, 157
    see also tribunes
Portia I: 69, 73, 340
Poseidon *see* Neptune
Posidonius (historian) II: 31, 32
Posidonius (philosopher) II: 107
Postumus, Marcus Vipsanius Agrippa I: 357
Pothinus II: 219-20
Poussin, Nicolas I: 2
Powell, Jason I: 103, 114, 118, 121, 132, 135, 137, 145, 150, II: 241
Poyntz, Sir Francis I: 121
Practica I: 96
Preston, Claire I: 52
Primaudaye, Pierre de la I: 26-27
Probus, Aemilius I: 12
Prometheus I: 295
Propertius I: 265
Proserpina I: 293
providence I: 80, 116, 246, II: 68, 164, 165
Pseudo-Lucian *see* Lucian
Pseudo-Plutarch *see* Plutarch, 'The Education of Children'; Plutarch, 'Love Stories'
psycho-therapy I: 109, 334, 338, 341
Ptolemy II Philadelphus I: 167, 196
Punic War, Second II: 2
Puttenham, George I: 160-61
Puttenham, Margery *see* Elyot, Margery
Pyanepsion II: 100, 102
Pydna, battle of II: 2-3, 28-33
Pynson, Richard II: 241
Pythagoras I: 178, 198-200, 327, II: 16
Pytheas II: 63, 80, 98-99, 151
Pythia *see* Delphic oracle (temple of Apollo)

Quellenforschung I: 3
Quintilian I: 31

Rainolds, John I: 21, 97, 99, 264-65
Ralegh, Sir Walter II: 11
readers
    model I: 53, 161, II: 6
    non-specialist I: 5, 23, 30, 33-35, 46-47, 49-51, 53, 109, 242, 334-35

    princes and nobles I: 20-21, 23-25, 49-50, 58-60, 210
    vernacular print I: 93-94, 103, 159-60, 161, 164-65, 209, 244-45, 249
    women I: 60, 65, 89-94, 161, 164
reason I: 27, 56, 70, 80, 85, 89, 108, 109, 112, 123, 156, 170, 206, 207, 216, 217-18, 219, 241, 333, 334, 335, 339, II: 48-49, 50-52, 172
rebellion II: 69, 174
Regnans in excelsis (Papal Bull) II: 159
religious controversy I: 68, 210, 323, 336, II: 5, 55, 66, 159, 172
Remedies against Discontentment I: 123
rhapsody (image) I: 37, 44, 53
Richard III, King I: 80
Romanness I: 56-57, 80, 81-89, 90, II: 172-74
Rostra II: 47, 125, 150
Roussard, Louis I: 335, 336
Rubens, Peter Paul I: 2
Rummel, Erika I: 211

S., T., *A Treatise of the Good and Evell Tounge* I: 337
Sadoleto, Jacopo I: 171
Sainte-Marthe, Scévole de I: 46
Sallust I: 2, II: 161
Salter, Thomas I: 92-93
Sanford, James I: 23, 96
Sant'Angelo, Castel I: 2
Santoro, Palazzo *see* Doria Pamphilj, Palazzo
Sappho I: 93
Satan II: 159
Saturn I: 314, II: 58, 209
Saturnalia I: 152, II: 120
Scaeva, Marcus Cassius II: 190
Scaliger, Julius Caesar I: 263
Scauri II: 104
Scilurus I: 366
Scipio Aemilianus Africanus (Numantinus), Publius Cornelius I: 216, 237; II: 10, 18, 32, 42, 43, 44, 222
Scipio Africanus (the elder), Publius Cornelius I: 59-60, II: 12, 14, 16, 18, 222
Scipio Nasica, Quintus Caecilius Metellus Pius II: 117, 190, 204, 205, 213, 214, 216, 222, 223, 224
Scipio Nasica Corculum, Publius Cornelius II: 27-30, 32, 36
Scipio Salvito II: 222
Scodel, Joshua I: 50
Scylla I: 28, 115, 197
Sedatus, Marcus I: 272
Seleucus I Nicator I: 40, II: 40-41
Seleucus II Callinicus I: 359, II: 40-41
self-control I: 76, 80, 148, 160, 241, 316, 333, 339, II: 52, 162, 166, 172-73, 174
Senant, Olivier I: 114
Seneca the Younger I: 3, 13, 17, 33, 46, 47, 51, 75, 80, 92, 108, 111, 122, 124, 207, 215, 242, 340, II: 53
Senecio, Quintus Sosius I: 6, 22, II: 74

Seres, William II: 245
sermons and theological writings I: 264, 337-38
Servilius Pulex Geminus, Marcus II: 39
Shackford, Martha Hale I: 2, 101
Shakespeare, William
    All's Well That Ends Well I: 40-41
    Antony and Cleopatra I: 1, 41, 64-65, 67, 74-81, II: 70–71, 167, 168, 220
    Coriolanus I: 1, 64-65, 78, 81-89, II: 70
    Julius Caesar I: 1, 57, 61, 64, 65-74, 340, II: 70, 161, 164, 168-75
    King Lear II: 174
    A Midsummer Night's Dream I: 64
    The Rape of Lucrece I: 64, 68
    Richard III I: 75, II: 174
    The Taming of the Shrew I: 340-41
    Timon of Athens I: 40, 64
    Titus Andronicus I: 340
    Venus and Adonis I: 64
    The Winter's Tale I: 340
    see also Fletcher, John, (with William Shakespeare) *The Two Noble Kinsmen*
Shawe, William I: 219
Shepherd, Geoffrey I: 266
Sidney, Sir Philip I: 1-2, 33, 34, 62, 263, 265-68
Silanion I: 280
Silanus, Decimus Iunius II: 117, 122, 123
Simonides I: 138, 273, 374
Sinorix I: 41
Sisyphus I: 280
Skinner, Quentin I: 20
slaves I: 63, 157-58, 167, 198, 339, II: 173
Sleidan, Johannes II: 161
Soclarus I: 272
Socrates I: 24, 49, 131, 138, 147-48, 170, 178, 183, 185, 195, 265, 276, 279, 289, 368, 369-70, 371
Solinus, Gaius Iulius I: 28
Solon I: 142, 333, 350
Sophocles I: 133, 263, 275, 278, 287-88, 290, 293, 294, 305, 319, 345, 348, 361, 367, II: 79, 101
Sorel, Charles I: 46
Southwell, Lady Anne I: 94
Speed, John I: 243, 246, II: 162
Spencer, T. J. B. II: 260
Spenser, Edmund I: 224, 333
Speusippus I: 195
Stapleton, Francellina I: 94
statues I: 28, 70, 72-73, 216, 217, II: 158, 168-69, 170, 171, 172
    see also Colossus of Rhodes
Stephanus *see* Estienne
Sthenelus I: 308
Stilpo I: 133, 147, 185
Stocker, Thomas I: 95, 97

INDEX

Stoicism and Stoics I: 7, 56, 109, 121-22, 124, 132, 141, 232, 242, 299, 373, II: 4, 107, 127, 151-52, 165
Strato I: 142
Sturm, Johannes I: 171
Suda I: 7, 15, 18, 22
Suetonius I: 243, 247, II: 161, 191, 222
suicide I: 67, 73, 89-90, 92, 116, 148, 339, II: 65
Sulla, Faustus Cornelius II: 129, 188
Sulla, Lucius Cornelius I: 61, 350-51, II: 65, 105-06, 107, 113, 114, 116, 119, 129, 177, 178, 180, 181, 188, 189, 210
synkrisis I: 6, 55-56, 58-60, 70-71, 86-87, 91-92, 102, II: 6-7, 8, 50, 72, 160-61

Tales, and Quicke Answeres, Very Mery, and Pleasant to Rede I: 40
Tanusius Geminus II: 197
Tarquinius Superbus, Lucius I: 68-70, II: 34-35
Taverner, Richard I: 37, 96
Taylor, Jeremy I: 337-38
Telemachus I: 292, 313
Terence I: 264
Tesmophoria II: 56, 102
Theaetetus I: 368
Themistocles I: 177, II: 154
Theocritus I: 196-98
Theodorus (actor) I: 280
Theodorus the Atheist of Cyrene I: 131
Theodotus II: 219
Theognis I: 276, 290
Theon of Samos I: 280
Theophrastus I: 332, II: 82, 89, 126
Theopompus (king of Sparta) I: 222, 223
Theopompus of Chios II: 51, 76, 85, 86, 90, 92, 97
Theopompus of Cnidus II: 219
Theramenes I: 140
Thersites I: 280, 307, 310, 325
Theseus I: 102, 305
Thespis I: 328
Thetis I: 276, 277, 317
Thomson, Patricia I: 118, 214, 259
Thucydides I: 92, 370, II: 78, 86
Thurzo, Alexius I: 24, 30, 45
Tibullus I: 265
Tillius Cimber, Lucius II: 235
Tilney, Edmund I: 39
Timocleia of Thebes I: 40
Timomachus I: 280
Timon of Athens I: 40
Timotheus (general) II: 59, 87
Timotheus (poet) I: 290, 316
Tissaphernes I: 370

Titus, emperor of Rome II: 6, 14
Titus Volturcius of Croton II: 120-21
Todd, Margo I: 38
Tomeo, Niccolò Leonico I: 336
tongue I: 27-29, 54, 90, 156, 333, 334, 336-41, II: 47
Tonkins, Thomas I: 340
Tottel's Miscellany I: 111
Tower of London I: 111
The Tragedy of Caesar and Pompey; or, Caesar's Revenge I: 61
Trajan, emperor of Rome I: 4, 6, 7, 13-27, 34, 38, 41, 48, 174, 207, II: 6, 14
translation
    cognates I: 166, 211, 250, II: 9, 61
    conversio ad sententiam I: 115, 163, II: 7-8
    diction I: 115-16, 119, 215, 247, 249-50, 255, 256-57, 258, II: 63-64
    domestication I: 116, 163, 164, 258, 261, II: 10, 56, 62, 65-70
    doublets I: 119, 163, 167-68, 211, 213, 258, 261, II: 10, 56, 63
    eloquence I: 116, 119, 163, 167-68, 212, 214, 247, 253, 259-62, II: 10, 65
    errors I: 113, 123, 162, 165, 211, 213-14, 250, 257, II: 9-11, 60, 61-62
    fidelity I: 103, 115, 165, 211, 213, II: 55-56
    glossing I: 115, 116, 118, 162, 163-64, 167, 211, 213, 247, 250-51, 254-55, 256, 258, 261, II: 56, 62, 66
    neologisms I: 119, 166, 167-68, 215, II: 64
    omissions I: 162, 164, 167, 213, II: 10, 62, 63
    paraphrase I: 103, 165-66, 211, 213, 258, II: 8, 10
    prose to verse I: 211, 212-15
    proverbs I: 115, 119, 260, II: 63
    rhetorical amplification I: 116, 118, 119-20, 163, 165, 167-68, 211, 213, 233, 260, II: 56
        see also translation, doublets
    syntax and word order I: 115-18, 166, 211, 213, 247, 251, 255-57, 258-60, II: 9, 10, 61-62, 64
    verse to prose I: 116, 213
    versification I: 211, 214-15, 261
    word for word I: 113, 116, 118, 258, II: 9, 61
tribunes I: 81, 83-84, II: 69, 172
triumphs I: 73, II: 3, 12, 168, 172
The Triumphs of King James the First II: 12
A true and plaine declaration of the horrible treasons, practised by William Parry the traitor, against the Queenes Majestie II: 159
Tubero, Quintus Aelius II: 18, 36, 38
Tunstall, Cuthbert I: 336
Turner, Paul II: 82, 122, 141, 202, 260
Tuvill, Daniel I: 50-51, 339
tyranny I: 22, 27, 54, 59, 63, 68, 69, 71, 72, 73, 80, 90, 102, 111, 160, 215, 216, II: 48, 50, 52, 157-58, 164-66
Tyrone, Hugh O'Neill, 3rd earl of II: 53

Udall, Nicholas I: 16, 37, 96, II: 20
Ulysses I: 91, 115, 146, 149, 167, 189, 196, 197-98, 251, 254, 256, 274, 280, 285, 292, 303-04, 308, 310, 312, 313, 322, 324, 325, 333, 352-53, II: 142

Valerius Leo II: 192
Valerius Maximus II: 11
Van Hoof, Lieve I: 22, 23-24, 54, 100, 339
Varro, Marcus Terentius II: 209
Vascosan, Michel de I: 12, II: 57
Vaughan, Henry I: 97, 262
Vautrollier, Thomas I: 39, II: 55, 258
Vegio, Maffeo I: 169, 170
Venus I: 59, 141, 251, 254, 273, 283-84, 317, 350, II: 214
Vergerio, Pier Paolo I: 169-70
Vesey, Judith II: 53
Vespasian, emperor of Rome II: 12
Virgil I: 3, 43, 80, II: 3
Virgilius, Gaius II: 134
Vitali, Bernardino I: 114
Vives, Juan Luis I: 92, 170, 171, 264-65
Volumnia I: 81, 82, 84-86, 88
Vulcan I: 293-94, 325

Walsingham, Sir Francis I: 25-26
Ward, Richard I: 338
The Wars of Cyrus, King of Persia I: 61
Wechel, Andreas I: 11
Whittington, Robert I: 121, II: 72
Wight, Thomas II: 258
Wilson (Volusenus), Florence I: 124
Wilson, Thomas I: 97-98, II: 71-72
Wolfe, Heather II: 245
Wolsey, Thomas I: 24, 31, 32, 209
Woodstock Palace II: 162
Worden, Blair I: 27
Worth, Valerie II: 64
Worthington, John I: 262
Wright, Herbert G. II: 255
Wyatt, Thomas the elder:
    life I: 110-13, 118
    works:
        Defence I: 121
        diplomatic letters I: 121
        epistolary satires I: 111, 121
            'Mine own John Poyntz' I: 111
            'My Mother's Maids' I: 122-23
        letters to his son I: 121
        Penitential Psalms I: 111
        Quiet of Mind I: 9, 22-23, 24, 95, 102, 103, 107-53, 166-67, 170, 211, 212, 259, 261, II: 241-42, 290
        'Stand whoso list upon the slipper top' I: 111
        'Whoso list to hunt' I: 111

Wyatt, Thomas the younger I: 110
Wyer, Robert I: 96
Wyndham, Francis I: 208
Wyndham, Sir George II: 61
Wyttenbach, Daniel I: 156

Xenagoras II: 8, 28
Xenocles of Adramyttium II: 107
Xenophanes I: 279
Xenophon I: 33, 58, 97, 121, 128, 191, 193, 243, 246, 313, 371, 372
Xerxes I I: 138
Xylander, Wilhelm I: 1, 8, 10-11, 15, 16, 34, 48, 52, 60, 63, 97, 120, 179, 219, 247, 249, 250-52, 254, 257, 258, 260, 261, 335, 338, II: 55, 59, 60, 138

Zeno of Citium I: 54, 132, 319, 348
Zeno of Elea I: 54, 352
Zenobia of Palmyra, Queen I: 160
Zeus *see* Jupiter
Zeuxis I: 59
Zuylen van Nyevelt, Adam van I: 11